The Impact of COVID on International Disputes

International and Comparative Business Law and Public Policy

VOLUME 2

The titles published in this series are listed at *brill.com/blpp*

The Impact of COVID on International Disputes

Edited by

Shaheeza Lalani and Steven G. Shapiro

BRILL
NIJHOFF

LEIDEN | BOSTON

The open access publication of this book has been published with the support of the Swiss National Science Foundation.

The Library of Congress Cataloging-in-Publication Data is available online at https://catalog.loc.gov
LC record available at https://lccn.loc.gov/2022017790

Typeface for the Latin, Greek, and Cyrillic scripts: "Brill". See and download: brill.com/brill-typeface.

ISSN 2667-3495
ISBN 978-90-04-51482-9 (hardback)
ISBN 978-90-04-51483-6 (e-book)

This book is printed on acid-free paper and produced in a sustainable manner.

This book is dedicated to the victims of the pandemic and their families, as well as to the first responders who stood their posts to heal and to protect

Contents

Preface

This book explores the idea that it is possible to make order in international arbitration out of the chaos of COVID-19. As a careful investigation of arbitration actors and actions during the sweep of the pandemic, this book assembles scholarly and pragmatic chapters to deliver content for readers to make strategic arbitration decisions, to gather best practices, and to otherwise learn from these experiences. The authors and editors are arbitrators, attorneys in private practice, arbitral institution executives, and academics writing based on their decisions, their experiences, and from their rigorous scholarly research.

With barest warning, COVID-19 quickly escalated into a generational crisis, leaving a devastating global health crisis and creating sustained havoc seen perhaps only in past cases of war, attack, and natural disasters. In the bedlam of the early months, health, science, political, and economic communities were hit with sudden force, required to quickly shift and rearrange the normal order of work. In arbitration, leaders took imperfect information to make dramatic decisions.

In process and procedure, arbitral institutions, arbitrators, legal counsel, and clients were swept into this turmoil. In some cases, bold initiatives, still in design and testing, were quickly put into service, upsetting norms and traditions and the very notions of traditional process. Yet, even in the deepest grip of the pandemic, arbitration continued, parties sought resolution of complex disputes and conflict, and decisions were rendered.

With room for some perspective, we organized a conference and sent a global call for papers with a stunningly enthusiastic response from arbitral institution executives, legal counsel, arbitrators, and academics from across cultures and continents. Receiving far more abstracts than expected, each topic was considered and evaluated by a group of peers and selected for merit and coverage of a range of topics. When assembled together, these points of view give voice to difficult decisions, agility to respond, and lessons learned.

As we send this book to publication, it is uncertain whether we are finally emerging from the pandemic or whether variants will continue to be a health crisis that disrupts international commerce. To our readers, we offer a sober analysis of what has worked and what may be later abandoned. Maybe most importantly, we offer chapters as guides to future decisions for arbitrators.

Over the course of paper submissions, commentary from experts, and a conference, we have developed some distinct tasks and themes in this book. Professor Mikkel Gudsøe, in his superb introduction, notes the extreme tension between in-person communication and the necessities that forced a move to embrace technology and remote arbitration. His comments get to the core of human instincts, beliefs, and desire for physical presence. These beliefs are intuitive and also expressed in constitutional laws.

Leaving the important ideas of physical arbitrations and access to justice, Professor Gudsøe rightly highlights our material that looks at the worries and risks of technology, including datasecurity, preservation of process protections, and matters of financial costs of arbitration.

A Note about the Authors and Commentators

With busy schedules and demanding commitments in place for their daily tasks, the authors delivered abstracts, revised versions of drafts, and finally delivered their papers, either in person in Lausanne, Switzerland, or by Zoom. Commentators offered wisdom and insights, plus edits and suggestions. In all cases, we asked for deep research, concise drafting, and reasoned judgment.

At every turn, authors delivered detailed analysis and commentators replied with candor and thoughtful edits and queries. In the end, the authors and commentators delivered the superb chapters that fill this book. Perhaps even better, we found a dialogue among authors and commentators that made this book so much more than a simple assembly of chapters.

A Note about My Co-Editor

Dr. Shaheeza Lalani, Executive Director of the LL.M. Programme in International Business Law at the University of Lausanne, imagined the conference and book, invited me to participate, then used her intellect, hard work, guile, and instincts to guide our many tasks. As expected, we faced mountains of tasks to coordinate material, important decisions, work to keep our authors on topic and on pace for our schedules, plus the inevitable surprise challenges. At all turns, she has been steady, adamant, and understands our collective and individual strengths and weaknesses. I'm fortunate that she invited me; I'm proud of our work together; and, I'm looking forward to next ideas.

Steven G. Shapiro

Acknowledgments

The editors would like to thank the contributors, as well as the following experts for sharing valuable insights and comments on the contributions in this book: Constance Bonzé (University of Lausanne and British Institute of International and Comparative Law), Benjamin Graham (Williams & Connolly LLP & Yale Law School), Vanessa Liborio Garrido de Sousa (Orrick, Herrington & Sutcliffe), Caroline Ming (Swiss Chambers' Arbitration Institution), Kevin Nash (Singapore International Arbitration Centre), Michael Nolan (Arbitration Chambers), Ana Reyes (Williams & Connolly LLP), Dr. Elza Reymond-Eniaeva (Sedlex Avocats), Dr. Katherine Simpson (Simpson Arbitration), Mladen Stojiljkovic (Vischer) and Hafez R. Virjee (Delos Dispute Resolution & Virjee Arbitration). We would also like to thank University of Lausanne LL.M. students, Derek Heath and Catherine Wagoko Mungai, for their assistance.

Figures and Tables

Figures

Tables

Notes on Contributors

Bamikole Martins Aduloju
is currently a doctoral researcher with the School of Law, Robert Gordon University, United Kingdom. Born in Nigeria, Bamikole was educated at the Obafemi Awolowo University, Nigeria, and graduated with a Bachelor of Law degree after which he was called to the Nigerian Bar in 2008. He is presently conducting his doctoral research on the jurisprudence of justice delivery through arbitration. He currently sits on the Board of the School of Law in the Robert Gordon University and he is a member of Association of Law Teachers, United Kingdom.

Edoardo Agamennone
has almost 20 years of experience in doing business with Asia, including seven years in private practice with leading law firms in Europe and Asia, more than six years as in-house counsel and five as entrepreneur and fund manager. *In 2020* Edoardo founded Levante Capital, the first investment fund focused on investing in Southern Europe's leading technology companies and assisting them in their development in Asia. Edoardo is a regular lecturer at, among others, the University of Turin, the Institut d'études politiques de Paris (SciencesPo), the University of Lausanne and several other universities in Europe and Asia. An author and researcher, his academic interests cover Europe-Asia trade and investment relation, data & intellectual property rights and strategies, as well as cross-cultural negotiations.

Aichell Alvarado
is a qualified attorney-at-law who trained in the United Kingdom, focusing in corporate and international commercial law. She has been involved in complex mergers and acquisitions transactions, including JCDecaux merger with Top Media, in Central America, Suzuki Motors acquisition by Inchcape PLC in Panama and Costa Rica, among others. Aichell holds an LL.M in International Commercial and Dispute Resolution Law from the University of Bedfordshire and an LL.B from the University of Panama. She is also a Fellow of the Global Institute of Law, an organization comprised of academics and practitioners aimed at improving legal education, research and training. Her research is focused primarily on international arbitration.

Bjorn Arp

is a Fellow and Adjunct Professor at American University Washington College of Law Center on International Commercial Arbitration. He co-teaches International Commercial Arbitration in the online Certificate Program on International Commercial Arbitration, as well as other courses. He is a partner at Aparicio, Arp & Associates LLC, in Washington, D.C., where he represents parties in international investment protection and human rights cases. Since 2017, he is on the list of FINRA (Financial Institutions National Regulatory Agency) arbitrators in the United States. Between 2016 and 2018, Björn Arp was part of the Roster of Experts of the Inter-American Development Bank's Independent Consultation and Investigation Mechanism. Björn holds a J.D. in Law from Alicante University, a Ph.D. in International Law from the University of Alcalá in Madrid, and an LL.M. in International Legal Studies from American University Washington College of Law.

Sean Croft

is an associate with DLA Piper, New York. His practice focuses on litigation and international arbitration. He has represented individuals, corporations, and sovereign states in the context of dispute resolution, investigations, and compliance. His sector experience extends to financial services, energy, and life sciences. Sean earned his B.S. and J.D. from Georgetown University.

James J. East Jr

is an associate at BakerHostetler in their international arbitration and litigation practice group in Washington, DC. Jim currently represents clients in investor-State disputes before the International Centre for the Settlement of Investment Disputes (ICSID) and the Permanent Court of Arbitration (PCA), as well as commercial disputes before the American Arbitration Association's International Centre for Dispute Resolution (ICDR). He is an alumnus of the University of Miami School of Law where he graduated with his J.D. and LL.M. in International Arbitration.

Helena Tavares Erickson

oversees the Dispute Resolution Services and Panels departments at the International Institute for Conflict Resolution & Prevention (CPR). In addition, Ms. Erickson serves as CPR's Corporate Secretary and CPR's Challenge Review Officer, is the liaison to the Arbitration and various Rules Revision Committees, and oversees CPR's Awards and Training Programs. Prior to joining CPR in 2004, Ms. Erickson practiced for over seventeen years with the litigation and arbitration groups of Dewey Ballantine and White & Case, including three years in White & Case's Paris office, where she was admitted to the Paris bar. Ms. Erickson is a native speaker of Portuguese and proficient in French and Spanish. She is a 2006 recipient of the NYSBA ADR Committee's award for contributions to the field of ADR and a 2017 *NLJ* ADR Champion.

Belen Olmos Giupponi
is a professor, researcher, and scholar with an expertise in EU law, international economic law, human rights law, and environmental law. She has extensive research experience and has published more than fifteen articles in leading journals. As a visiting fellow with the Brown International Advanced Research Institute (BIARI), she authored Inequality and Access to Water in Latin America: Implementing the Rights to Water in Argentina. She holds two Master's degrees in International Relations and Human Rights, a law degree, and a PhD in International Law.

Mikkel Gudsøe
is considered one of Denmark's leading experts in negotiation, ADR and nonverbal skills. Since 2008, he has created and taught the course Legal Negotiation at Aarhus University. He has served as Chief Attorney for almost a decade in the fashion and textile industries and as Executive Vice President in a large family-owned Danish corporation. Appointed Honorary Associate Professor in Negotiation at Aarhus University, he has taught and successfully coached internationally for more than a decade. He currently focuses on political negotiations and research on the role of media in conflict resolution and depolarization in society. He also serves as Senior Fellow at the Institute for Global Negotiation.

Bahar Hatami Alamdari
is an international arbitration law specialist. She holds a PhD in International Commercial Arbitration law from the Institute of Advanced Legal Studies (IALS) at University of London and an LL.M. in Commercial Law from Queen Mary University of London and an LL.B. from Tehran University. Dr. Hatami Alamdari has taught international commercial law and various LL.B. subjects in London; in addition, as a legal consultant, she provides expert legal opinions to clients on issues relating to investment law, legal contracts, oil and gas projects, International Comparative Law and Economic Sanctions Regulations in the Middle East. Currently, she teaches at St Mary's University as a senior lecturer.

Jennifer A. Ivers
is an associate in the Washington, DC office of White & Case, where she specialized in international arbitration and litigation. She has acted as counsel for arbitrations in various fora, and notably has been recognized as a Rising Star in the United States and in Commercial Arbitration by the International Financial Law Review. Jennifer is a graduate of the Georgetown University Law Center, where she was an Articles Editor on the Georgetown Law Journal and served as a Law Fellow for Legal Research and Writing.

Magdalena Łągiewska
is an Assistant Professor at the University of Gdańsk (Department of Public International Law), a Research Associate in the "China, Law and Development" project at the University of Oxford and a Director of the Confucius Institute at the University of Gdańsk. Professor Łągiewska received a Ph.D in Law from the University of Gdańsk in 2017 and a second Ph.D. in Law from the East China University of Political Science and Law in Shanghai in 2020 (her Ph.D. thesis is entitled "The Effectiveness of the Arbitration Agreement under Chinese and Polish Law: A Comparative Study" and is written in Chinese). In addition to her legal education, she completed a Master's degree in International Economic Relations with a specialization in International Finance and Banking (University of Gdańsk). She was granted a scholarship by the Shanghai Municipal People's Government to take part in the Shanghai Summer School 2015 (Belt and Road Countries Project) organized by the Shanghai International Studies University and other scholarships from the China Youth University for Political Sciences in Beijing. Professor Łągiewska has worked in international commercial arbitration with the Shanghai International Economic and Trade Arbitration Commission (SHIAC) and her research interests include Chinese arbitration, the protection of IP rights, and the legal dimensions of the" Belt and Road Initiative".

Shaheeza Lalani
holds a Bachelor of Arts Honours degree in History and French Studies from Queen's University (Canada), a Master of Science in Public Policy and Public Administration from the London School of Economics (United Kingdom), a Bachelor of Laws and Bachelor of Civil Law from McGill University (Canada), and a Ph.D. in Law from the University of Lausanne, where she won the Faculty Prize for her thesis. She is a barrister & solicitor, admitted to the Law Society of British Columbia and holds a British Columbia Ministry of Education Teaching Certificate. Dr. Lalani has taught courses at the Universities of Fribourg, Bern, Lausanne and Paris and was the Founding Director of two other postgraduate

programs in Switzerland. Previously Senior Legal Counsel with the Swiss Chambers' Arbitration Institution and Legal Counsel to the Swiss Institute of Comparative Law, Dr. Lalani has worked as an Assistant Legal Officer with The Hague Conference on Private International Law and has authored and edited several publications on international law and arbitration.

Michael A. Marra
is Vice President for the Construction Division and has served with the American Arbitration Association (AAA) for more than thirteen years. Mr. Marra was appointed District Vice President of the AAA Philadelphia Office in September 2001. He is currently responsible for expanding the use of AAA construction ADR services in the Mid-Atlantic and New England States and is a frequent presenter on the subject of Alternative Dispute Resolution. Mr. Marra is a graduate of Temple University with a B.A. in Marketing.

Luis M. Martinez
directs the International Centre for Dispute Resolution (ICDR) in the region including the East Coast of the United States, Central and South America, the Caribbean, and Spain and Portugal. Mr. Martinez recruits and maintains the highest qualified panel in those areas for the ICDR's International Panel of Arbitrators and Mediators. He is responsible for the ICDR's cross-border arbitration and mediation in the region, providing executive oversight of large cases. Luis received a J.D. degree from St. John's University School of Law.

Karthik Nagarajan
is Senior Counsel & Head of International Legal Affairs at RTI International. Karthik advises internal clients on legal and strategic matters and works closely with local counsel in several foreign jurisdictions to mitigate legal risk and resolve disputes. Prior to this role, Karthik was a Senior Associate at White & Case LLP, specializing in international arbitration, and represented sovereign and private sector clients in complex, high-stakes disputes under the ICSID, ICC, and Swiss Rules of Arbitration.

Edwin Nemesio
is an attorney admitted to practice in Mexico. He has a Law Degree from Universidad Nacional Autónoma de México, a Master of Laws in Human Rights and Constitutional Rights from Instituto Tecnológico Autónomo de México, both in Mexico City. He is currently an LL.M. Candidate in International Arbitration and Business Law at American University Washington College of Law.

Pratyush Panjwani
is an Associate with Hanotiau & van den Berg in Brussels. He focuses his practice on international commercial and investment arbitration, both ad hoc and under a wide variety of institutional rules, spanning various industry sectors. He also regularly acts as assistant to the tribunal in international arbitrations. He is a member of the Bar in New Delhi, India, obtained his LL.M. in International Dispute Settlement (MIDS) from the Graduate Institute of International and Development Studies and the University of Geneva and completed his Bachelors of Arts and of Laws at the National Law University, Delhi. He has published widely in the field of international commercial arbitration, speaks English and Hindi and is registered to practice in Brussels.

Elizabeth Roberts
is General Counsel at Arbitration Place. She advises on a full range of legal matters and provides legal and enterprise risk management expertise and strategic advice. Liz is a fellow of the Chartered Institute of Arbitrators, a contributing writer to Arbitration Matters Case Notes, a publication that provides updates of key arbitration decisions in Canada and guest lecturer at the Toronto Commercial Arbitration Society's Gold Standard Course. Prior to Arbitration Place, she worked as in-house counsel in the energy and utilities sector and at a boutique law firm in Toronto where Liz maintained a diverse commercial litigation practice, appearing as lead counsel at all levels of court in Ontario and in numerous arbitration hearings.

Ben Sanderson
is Of Counsel and the Practice Manager responsible for the global International Arbitration practice at DLA Piper. Ben also sits as an arbitrator and is a Fellow of the Chartered Institute of Arbitrators. He has extensive experience advising clients in international arbitration disputes across a range of sectors including energy, mining and technology. He has represented both States and commercial parties in investment treaty claims. He recently co-led a team which earned a decisive victory for the Republic of Kenya for which his team was nominated "International Arbitration Team of the Year" by Legal Business and the decision was shortlisted by Global Arbitration Review for the "Award of the Year".

Professor Amy J. Schmitz
is a professor at The Ohio State Moritz College of Law and Program on Dispute Resolution as the John Deaver Drinko-Baker & Hostetler Endowed Chair in Law. She is also affiliated with The Ohio State Program on Data Governance

and the Divided Community Project. Before teaching at Ohio State, Professor Schmitz taught at the University of Missouri School of Law and Center for Dispute Resolution as the Elwood L. Thomas Missouri Endowed Professor of Law, starting in 2016. Previously she was a Professor at the University of Colorado School of Law for over 16 years. Prior to teaching, Professor Schmitz practiced law with large law firms in Seattle and Minneapolis and served as a law clerk for the U. S. Court of Appeals for the 8th Circuit. Professor Schmitz also hosts The Arbitration Conversation, a highly regarded podcast that has reached over 100 episodes. She also is a researcher with the ACT Project exploring AI and dispute resolution at the Cyberjustice Lab in Montreal. She has published over 60 articles in law journals and books, is a co-author of the leading casebook, *Resolving Disputes: Theory, Practice and Law (Aspen/Wolters Kluwer 2021)*, the new book with Stipanowich, *Arbitration: Theory, Practice and Law (Forthcoming Aspen/Wolters Kluwer 2022)* and a book with C. Rule, *The New Handshake: Online Dispute Resolution and the Future of Consumer Protection.*

Katherine Schroeder
is a Law Clerk at White & Case in Washington, DC. Katherine received her Bachelor's degree from University of Washington and her Doctor of Law from the University of Pennsylvania Law School.

Maria Scott
is a Senior Associate with DLA Piper, London, specialising in International Arbitration. Her practice emphasizes disputes in the energy sector and she has extensive experience with disputes related to gas pricing, joint venture agreements concerning the production of commodities, and other commercial contracts. Maria has represented clients before leading arbitration institutions such as the London Court of International Arbitration, the International Chamber of Commerce, the Stockholm Chamber of Commerce and in proceedings before the High Court of England and Wales. Maria was part of the DLA Piper team which earned a decisive victory for the Republic of Kenya in a bilateral investment treaty claim, for which the team was nominated "International Arbitration Team of the Year" by Legal Business and the decision was shortlisted by Global Arbitration Review for the "Award of the Year" award. Maria is a member of the cross-firm working group on LegalTech Adoption in International Arbitration.

Steven G. Shapiro
teaches, writes, and speaks on topics in complex hospitality issues and construction law at the American University, Washington College of Law, blending

his career in law firm practice, construction engineering, and academics. Recognized for innovation in bringing the realities and economics of commercial practice into the classroom and in service to the law school, Steven imagined and proposed the idea of the Hospitality & Tourism Law program. In addition, Steven brings a distinct experience in the interplay of complex commercial transactions in law school courses in contract drafting, real estate and hotel development, construction law, and externship studies. Steven earned his undergraduate degree from Georgetown University in 1984, a law degree from the Georgetown University Law Center in 1987, and a Masters of Law degree from Georgetown Law Center in 1991. In 2001, Steven made a mid-career move from the practice of law to construction, and in 2004, he received a Masters of Engineering Degree from the University of Maryland.

Kristen M. Young
is a Partner at White & Case in Washington, DC, where her practice focuses on investment treaty arbitration. Kristen frequently represents multinational corporations and sovereign states in high-stakes international disputes, and has represented clients in arbitrations before all major arbitral forums, including the ICSID, the PCA, and the ICC, as well as in ad hoc arbitrations under UNCITRAL arbitration rules.

Introduction

Mikkel Gudsøe

This book touches upon important topics that may prove to be groundbreaking in international arbitration, mediation, negotiation and maybe even litigation. As human beings, we rely quite a lot on physical presence when communicating, observing and interpreting other human beings and creatures in general. It is inherent in our DNA and the construction of our brains to be focused primarily on the joy or danger currently "facing" us physically.

From the early development of smoke signals used in Ancient China, Sri Lanka and Greece, as well as among the North American Indigenous Peoples, humans have developed ways to communicate through forms and media when physical presence was impossible or distance hindered direct communication.

In the beginning, simple messages were limited and lacked precision. The development of various types of messaging and communication increased the possibilities of communicating more detailed and precise content and intentions. In just 200 years, we have gone from smoke signals to Morse code, telegraphs, landline telephones, fax machines, mobile phones, computers and the Internet. Now we have live images and sound feeds through the Internet and many of these technologies have been refined within the last 20 to 40 years.

Generally, our brains rely on verbal content, timing, intonation and body language for processing, interpreting and responding appropriately to any communication. Even though live images and sound feeds have been available and primarily commercialized since the 2013 development of Skype Free Video Messaging, the judicial system seems to have been reluctant to fully embrace this new technology.

Nevertheless, technology comes with significant cost savings in terms of minimizing travel and "out of office" time. In addition, sessions can sometimes be recorded for asymmetrical views across time zones such that it is unnecessary to have all people with an available spot in the calendar at the same dates. Finally, with technology, travel, and therefore, associated pollution, are reduced.

However, technology does not only offer opportunities. Cultural differences, particularly with respect to access, familiarity and trust in the use of technology are important considerations for the assessment of equality and the need to ensure a fair and/or optimal process. As explained in Chapter 1, cultural differences may also impact dispute resolution, as some cultures favor in-person face-to-face meetings and a building of trust through in-person talks, gestures and actions in order to make future deals. Other cultures can have a deeper – recognized or unrecognized – bias in favor of virtual meetings and Chapter 1 takes a social science approach to address these cultural issues.

As Chapters 2 through 11 demonstrate, technology holds a wealth of opportunity for the future of ADR, though challenges remain. For example, in virtual hearings, there could be issues of deep fake imaging or voice manipulation when it comes to witness examination; a witness or another person under pressure might deliberately "pull the cords" (lose the signal) to have more time to reply to a question convincingly. Chapters 4 to 6, with their focus on procedures, open the door to reflection on whether we can be sure that witnesses or others involved in virtual hearings are not being counselled "behind" the camera by sophisticated means. It is, thus, significant that this book includes contributions from arbitral institutions, including the American Arbitration Association, which anticipates these issues at section 4C of its AAA-ICDR® Model Order and Procedures for a Virtual Hearing via Videoconference: "At any time, the Chair may ask a witness to orient his or her webcam to provide a 360-degree view of the remote venue in order to confirm that no unauthorized persons are present; any authorized persons (counsel, etc.) in the room with the witness must be identified at the start of the witness' testimony".

The contributions from arbitral institutions in the final chapters of the book are also important in view of concerns that technology may somehow compromise the inherent confidentiality sought by most parties in an arbitration, mediation or negotiation process. The chapters before these final chapters raise important questions as to whether judges, arbitrators and mediators should be specifically trained in observing and interpreting behaviors displayed in virtual settings where a full picture (of hand movements and body language) is not available or anxiety and discomfort could be created due to the presence of a camera (especially in certain cultures). Questions remain regarding data protection, hacking, and the possibility that recordings (regarding business secrets or the dispute more generally) might fall into the "wrong hands".

The contributions made by the authors of this book are significant. They plant the seeds for future theoretical, empirical and cross-cultural research, as well as the continuous development of safe, reliable, stable, private and trustworthy technologies and procedures that can hopefully lead to universally accepted and recognized rules and best practices.

Chapter 1 demonstrates how cultural aspects can play an important role in the acceptance of virtual meetings when it comes to ADR and negotiation between what are called the West and the East cultures. Chapter 2 recognizes technology's potential to develop greener arbitrations and reasonable opportunities for parties to still present their cases without due process paranoia.

Chapter 3 examines these advantages in greater detail, shedding light on competing priorities that have arisen during the pandemic. Chapter 4 explains that new technologies had previously been used for some forms of ADR, and the Covid-19 pandemic sped up this development, leading to more electronic filings and virtual hearings, which could – in turn – start a trend toward more cases being filed and dealt with through such channels, and perhaps, a faster process, from filing to award time. The Chapter points to an ongoing need not only to address cyber-security risks, but also to address the loss of personal interactions.

Chapters 5 and 6 anticipate that virtual hearings are here to stay and the future will hold a range of possibilities from hybrid to in-person to remote hearings. Consequently, tribunals will have to consider a number of issues in order to guarantee due process and the enforceability of awards. Interestingly, chapter 7 distinguishes between cases that may be better suited to virtual hearings (dealing with technical or legal questions) and those that might be better suited for in-person hearings (dealing with evidentiary issues and cross-examination). Chapter 8 suggests that some parties will only accept virtual hearings due to pandemic restrictions. Surprisingly, some parties who seem to favor in-person hearings are the same parties that previously criticized the high cost of these hearings. Chapter 8 therefore points to the importance of a united stance from international arbitration centers on the issue virtual proceedings and due process concerns.

Chapter 9 highlights the potent opportunity that Online Arbitration (OArb) has to secure more equal access to justice. The author of Chapter 10 adopts the same perspective, highlighting the challenges of ODR, while exploring a more holistic approach. The author suggests that technology should be intrinsic to the dispute process and that all stakeholders should continue to learn in order to better mitigate the risks. Chapter 11 then demonstrates how the digitalization of courts and the experiments with technology can offer inspiration, solutions and guidance to the ADR community.

Chapters 12–14 offer interesting institutional views regarding equal access to justice and the use of technology since the beginning of the Covid-19 pandemic. The book ends with Chapter 15 suggesting that costs in international arbitration be reviewed in view of the savings made in arbitration since the beginning of the pandemic. It will be interesting to see if arbitration centers will take the policy recommendations of this chapter into account to lower arbitration costs in view of reduced travel costs and secretariat workload.

From my perspective, as a professional in negotiation and mediation, this book is a very much needed contribution to the literature on ADR. It is clear that virtual meetings are here to stay. For mediation services, virtual meetings will also create opportunities and challenges. Difficulties will certainly arise when it comes to communication among the mediator and the parties: interruptions, misunderstandings and tensions may arise more frequently in virtual settings, making it more difficult to know when to say or do something.

As an instructor on "Body Language in Negotiation", I am of the view that skills and signals need to be developed and taught to ensure best practices: delicate and sometimes fragile situations should not be made worse due to otherwise time and cost-efficient technologies. Best practices might include the following: a designated, controlled set-up or *ad hoc* setup with a supervisor on site to ensure that the quality and integrity of the hearing is ensured; rules on how much or how little the camera should capture (full body, face only, upper body only); and, proper training on biases. This is especially true when it comes to witness testimony, though it is also relevant in mediation and negotiation more generally. Whether consciously or subconsciously, we derive a huge part of our interpretation and assessment of other people from observation: a larger frame of reference may change ones perspective of the other entirely.

One thing is certain: we need better and fairer negotiations, more mediation earlier in the dispute process and faster and more cost-effective arbitration. Conflicts should create value and regain or strengthen relations where possible; conflicts should be viewed as opportunities to grow and learn. If negotiation and mediation skills could be taught in schools, this would ensure greater stability, unity and mutual acceptance among future generations: their skills in dispute resolution, and maybe even dispute avoidance, would certainly develop more rapidly than the development of live images and sound feeds from smoke signals.

CHAPTER 1

The Rise and Impact of the "Zoom Negotiation"

Cross-Cultural Variations in Virtual Negotiations and Lessons from the COVID-19 Pandemics

Edoardo Agamennone

1 Introduction

The COVID-19 pandemic has accelerated trends that were already in place before its eruption at the end of 2019. The most significant trend is the integral and almost overnight digitalization of workplace interactions, with conversations occurring almost exclusively through email, text chat, and video conference. Such rapid change affected personal and professional dynamics on many different levels: with individuals working mainly from home, work-life distinctions became blurred, sometimes beyond recognition; business travel disappeared; coordination within teams and departments became difficult; the time dedicated to negotiations and discussions expanded significantly, reducing in many circumstances productivity and the advancement of projects. Such adverse effects on firms and individuals were accompanied by others linked to the pandemic: companies saw their production output and turnover collapse or highly reduced almost overnight; boards of directors shifted their focus on survival rather than business development; and, uncertainty became the only certainty, both on a personal and professional level.

This paper will focus on a particular aspect of the revolution triggered by the outburst of the COVID-19 pandemic: the cultural determinants of the radical shift to virtual means to conduct business discussions, negotiations, and settlement of disputes. This "new normal" has been commonly defined as the "Zoom negotiation", in light of the market share that Zoom has acquired in the past months in the videoconferencing market (see Figure 1.1).

The global pandemic has represented a historical moment across countries and cultures. Individuals, organizations, and decision-makers in virtually every part of the globe found themselves in an unprecedented situation with significant challenges for which few of them were prepared; among them, the radical and rapid switch to virtual tools to conduct negotiations. What was one of the many options available to negotiators or parties to disputes became, in

DOI:10.1163/9789004514836_003

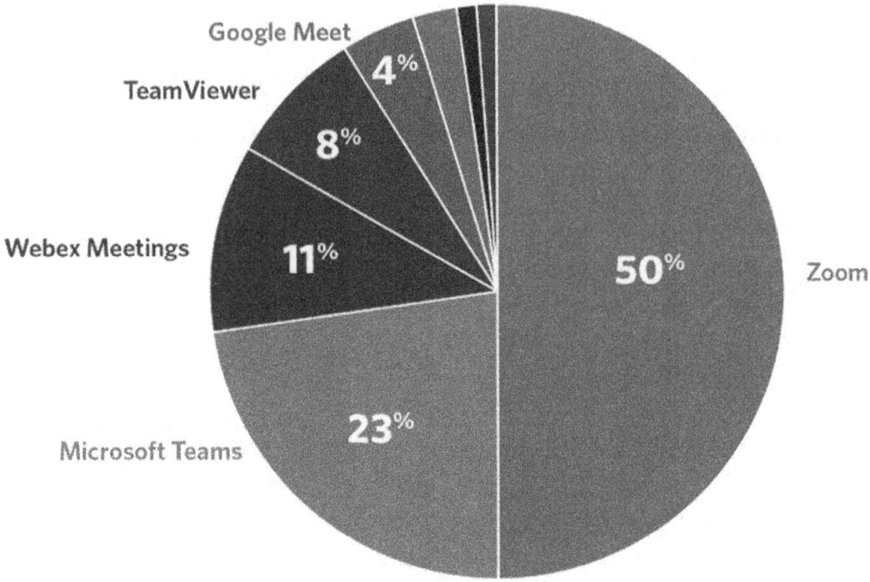

FIGURE 1.1 Market share of videoconferencing platforms
SOURCE: TRUSTRADIUS, HTTPS://WWW.TRUSTRADIUS.COM/VENDOR-BLOG/WEB-CONFERENCING-STATISTICS-TRENDS

a matter of days and weeks, the only option. The impact however has not been uniform across countries. Negotiators with certain cultural traits have been more significantly impacted by the switch from real to virtual. This paper in particular will test the following hypotheses:

- *Hypothesis 1*: the impact of COVID-19 has not been uniform across cultures, even controlling for the degree of strictness of the measures adopted by national and local governments to fight the pandemic.
- *Hypothesis 2*: the COVID-19 pandemic has affected those cultures in which the construction of trust relies on personal relations and in which face-to-face meetings have a more prominent role in negotiations and dispute resolution.
- *Hypothesis 3*: the degree to which countries will return to normality once the pandemic is over is unlikely to be consistent. Specifically, cultures which have been more deeply impacted by the switch to virtual meetings are more likely to return to pre-COVID-19 negotiation and dispute resolution practices compared to cultures in which the widespread use of online negotiation has shown clear benefits.

2 Methodology

This study aims to combine existing literature and evidence on two important research areas: intercultural and intracultural differences and their impact on the behavior of negotiators, on the one side; and the effects of the means used by negotiators to conduct discussions. To capture the complex interactions of cultural and technological aspects of negotiations, this study will concentrate on certain sub-areas of the two fields: in particular, the cultural analysis will focus on the so-called "East-West divide". For such purpose, with the term "West", reference is made to the Huntington's classification of civilizations including Western Europe and North America,[1] while with the term "East", reference is made to the definition by De Blij & Muller including China, Japan, and Korea in the East Asian macro-region.[2]

To support the main findings of the literary review, a survey was conducted among professionals with direct experience of and exposure to cross-cultural negotiations and dispute resolution processes. A target population of 150 qualified respondents was selected to conduct the survey, of which 104 completed the survey. Respondents were selected among consultants, executives, officials, and other professionals with significant experience (*i.e.*, >3 years) and exposure to cross-border and cross-cultural negotiations. Annex A contains an overview of the target audience. Respondents completed the survey on a strictly anonymous basis in the period between July 10 and August 28 2021.

The survey was designed to obtain both quantitative and qualitative responses. In addition to the first 12 questions used to profile the respondents and the final 4 covering the technical tools used to negotiate, the core questions (24) contained a mix of questions using a quasi-Likert scale (13), open questions in which respondents were invited to report their impressions using adjectives (3) and other multiple-choice questions (10). This was made in order to offset the problems in reliability of using Likert scales with Chinese/Asian respondents,[3]

1 Samuel P. Huntington, *The Clash of Civilizations and the Remaking of World Order* (New York: Simon and Schuster, 1996).

2 Harm J. de Blij, Peter O. Muller, *Geography: Regions and Concepts* (New York: Wiley, 1997).

3 Peter Newman, "Problems with Likert-type scales for measuring attitudes of Chinese people" (working paper presented at the Academy of Marketing Conference, Gloucester, July 2004), https://www.researchgate.net/publication/348806598_Problems_with_Likert-type_scales_for_measuring_attitudes_of_Chinese_people.

and more broadly the culture-specific challenges of using surveys with Chinese/Asian respondents.[4]

3 The Zoom Negotiation

Negotiations and the resolution of disputes have historically been associated with discussions conducted in person. Over time it has become possible to conduct part of the negotiation process remotely, by correspondence, and via telegraph. It has only been since the early 2000s – due to factors such as globalisation, the accessibility of videoconferencing tools and the appearance of the internet – that notable attention has been given to the impact, on negotiations and dispute resolution, of the means of communication used to conduct the discussions. The term "e-negotiation" has been widely used[5] to designate any form of negotiation/discussion conducted through electronic means. An important portion of this early literature focused on the use of email to conduct negotiation.[6] Emails however are a peculiar type of virtual negotiation in part because they only allow an asynchronous interaction among negotiators. With the widespread use of teleconferencing and videoconferencing, the gap between virtual and in-person negotiations has significantly narrowed, making analyses more meaningful.

A literature review[7] suggests that vocal cues, visual cues, and synchronicity – all elements partially made available by videoconferencing tools – all promote more efficient outcomes by facilitating information sharing and the use of complex strategies, such as making multiple equivalent simultaneous offers. It is curious to note, however, that apparently imperceptible differences, such as a slight asynchronicity, can have an impact on the process and results of a negotiation. It has been found for example that positive answers to questions, even the simplest ones (*e.g.* "can you give me a ride?") are rated as less

4 Melanie Manion, "Survey Research in the Study of Contemporary China: Learning from Local Samples," *The China Quarterly* 139 (September 1994): 741–765.

5 Janice Nadler and Donna Shestowsky, "Negotiation, Information Technology, and the Problem of the Faceless Other," in *Negotiation Theory and Research*, ed. Leigh L. Thompson (New York: Psychosocial Press, 2006), 145–172. See also Gerardine De Sanctis and Peter Monge, "Communication Processes for Virtual Organizations," *Organization Science* 10, no. 6 (1999): 693–703.

6 Noam Ebner, "Negotiation Via Email," in *The Negotiator's Desk Reference*, eds. Chris Honeyman and Andrea Kupfer (St Paul: DRI Press, 2017).

7 Victoria Medvedec and Adam Galinsky, "Putting More on the Table: How Making Multiple Offers Can Increase the Final Value of the Deal," *HBS Negotiation Newsletter* 8 (2005): 4–6.

genuine if the respondent took more than 700 milliseconds to reply, something that in an online negotiation is almost inevitable.[8]

Empirical evidence suggests it is better to communicate in person. This assumption is confirmed by the results of the survey (cfr. Section 5), and plenty of corresponding evidence. A significant part of such evidence focuses on the cornerstone of any negotiation or conflict resolution process: trust. Trust is key to enabling cooperation,[9] achieving integrative solutions[10] and resolving disputes.[11] Virtually any commercial interaction has within itself an element of trust.[12] Ebner illustrates how virtual negotiations present several obstacles in the construction of trust.[13] The absence of a physical interaction between negotiators hinders the research of mutually beneficial solutions by depriving negotiators of contextual cues, amplifying the attribution effect,[14] in generating within negotiators' low expectations, presenting the counterpart as a "faceless other", making it difficult for negotiators to dissociate physical distance from interpersonal distance, creating a sub-optimal form of empathy (e-empathy), and hindering the creation of the momentum necessary to finalize the discussions.

Such challenges and barriers are not only generated by psychological effects but also by "physical" ones. A simple gesture such as a handshake – something that often occurs at the outset of social interactions – influences deal-making

8 Felicia Roberts, Alexander L. Francis, and Melanie Morgan, "The interaction of inter-turn silence with prosodic cues in listener perceptions of 'trouble' in conversation," *Speech Communications* 48 (2006): 1079–1093, https://web.ics.purdue.edu/~francisa/Articles/Roberts-etal_SpeechCom06.pdf.

9 Morton Deutsch, "Cooperation and trust: Some theoretical notes," in *Nebraska Symposium on Motivation*, ed. M.R. Jones (Lincoln: University of Nebraska Press, 1962), 275–318.

10 David A. Lax and James K. Sebenius, *The Manager as Negotiator: Bargaining for Cooperation and Competitive Gain* (New York: Free Press, 1986).

11 Christopher Moore, *The Mediation Process* (San Francisco: Jossey Bass, 2003).

12 Kenneth J. Arrow, "Gifts and Exchanges," *Philosophy & Public Affairs* 1, no. 4 (1972): 343–62, http://www.jstor.org/stable/2265097.

13 Noam Ebner, "Trust-Building in E-Negotiation," in *Computer-Mediated Relationships and Trust: Managerial and Organizational Effects*, eds. L. Brennan and V. Johnson (Hershey, PA: Information Science Publishing, 2007).

14 The attribution effect (also known as correspondence bias) is a cognitive bias, codified by Lee Ross, "The Intuitive Psychologist And His Shortcomings: Distortions in the Attribution Process," in *Advances in Experimental Social Psychology*, vol. 4, ed. Leonard Berkowitz (New York: Academic Press, 1977), 173–220, explaining the general tendency by people to under-emphasize situational and environmental explanations for a certain observed behavior in the other party while over-emphasizing personality-based explanations for their own behavior.

by signaling cooperative intent, increasing people's cooperative behavior and affecting deal-making outcomes.[15]

A meta-analysis of research comparing decision making in face-to-face vs computer-mediated communication[16] further supported the hypothesis that computer-mediated communication leads to decreases in group effectiveness, increases in the time required to complete tasks, and decreases in member satisfaction compared to face-to-face groups. In this regard, the use of a Zoom negotiation rather than an in-person meeting seems to negatively impact all three key objectives of any negotiation or dispute resolution process, and all the activities constituting each of such three categories, as outlined below.

While some advantages certainly exist, they seem to be outnumbered by the disadvantages. It is therefore not surprising that Zoom negotiations or other forms of virtual settings are less effective than face-to-face meetings in reaching the objective of finding a mutually accepted agreement and/or resolving disputes. Maruca found that negotiations conducted via email have a risk of up to 50% ending in an impasse, versus only 19% in face-to-face negotiations.[17]

4 Multiculturalism and Virtual Negotiations

Cultural traits deeply affect negotiation and dispute resolution dynamics at various levels. The definition of culture, starting from one of its oldest forms with Cicero[18] to today has attracted strong interest, with philosophers, anthropologists, sociologists, and representatives of other academic fields giving an extremely wide variety of interpretations.

One of the most cited and complete definitions is the one provided by Blumenthal, according to which culture is a:

> complex (necessarily a complicated one) (1) in which a group (usually a large one) of human beings give expression to their major cultural

15 Juliana Schroeder, Jane L. Risen, Francesca Gino, and Michael I. Norton, "Handshaking Promotes Deal-Making by Signaling Cooperative Intent," *Journal of Personality and Social Psychology* 116, no. 5 (May 2019): 743–768.

16 Boris B. Baltes et al., "Computer-Mediated Communication and Group Decision Making: A Meta-Analysis," *Organizational Behavior and Human Decision Processes* 87, no. 1 (January 2002): 156–179.

17 Regina F. Maruca, "The Electronic Negotiator," *Harvard Business Review* 78, no. 1 (2000): 16–17.

18 In the *Tusculanae Disputationes*, Cicero provided one of the first definitions of culture as "*cultura animi*" using an agricultural metaphor for the development of a philosophical soul, understood teleologically as the highest possible ideal for human development.

TABLE 1.1 Negotiation objectives and COVID-19 impact

Macro-objective	Activities of negotiators	Negative impact of virtual setting	Positive impact of virtual setting
I. INFORMATION GATHERING	– Pre-negotiation assessment; – Preparation of information to be obtained; – Analysis of information/data provided by the counterpart; – Fixation of bottom lines; – Determination of the negotiation strategy; – Conduct of the preliminary discussions.	– Impossibility to conduct onsite visits and physical due diligence investigations; – Comparatively lower trust starting levels on both sides; – Absence of "side meetings/discussions" to gather insightful information.	– Possibility to involve a wider range of participants; – Possibility to organize a higher number of meetings.
II. BEHAVIOUR INFLUENCING	– Execution of the negotiation strategy; – Persuasion of the counterpart; – Submission of offers and counter-offers.	– Persuasion negatively affected by emotional and physical barriers; – Difficulties in reading the other party's language and body language; – Absence of "side meetings/discussions" to gather insightful information.	– Persuasion can be reinforced by repeated meetings.

TABLE 1.1 Negotiation objectives and COVID-19 impact (*cont.*)

Macro-objective	Activities of negotiators	Negative impact of virtual setting	Positive impact of virtual setting
III. SITUATION CRYSTALLIZATION	– Conclusion of the final agreement; – Enforcement of contractual arrangements; – Renegotiations/amendment to original agreements.	– Low trust final levels on both sides; – Difficulties in applying pressure to ensure contracts are complied with; – Physical and emotional distance creating incentives for non-compliant behavior; – Obstacles to judicial and other forms of enforcement.	– Possibility to organize meetings to verify the progress/execution of the agreement.

> activities, (2) that usually is quite different from any other body of functionally inter-related culture traits in which a group of human individuals give expression to most of their cultural activities, (3) that usually has a geographical area on which it predominates and (4) that is usually largely functionally independent of other similar complexes.[19]

Despite its age, this definition remains appropriate.

Unlike other popular definitions, such as that of Fukuyama who conceives it as an "inherited ethical habit",[20] according to Blumenthal, culture is not a static and exclusive concept but rather a dynamic, complex and constantly changing one. From this definition and other important studies, several conclusions relevant to the topic of this paper can be drawn: cultures can be divided in macro-groups based on their general affinities and common origins;[21] affiliation to a cultural group is not exclusive, with the same individual being capable of presenting behavioral patterns belonging to more than one cultural group (such individuals identifying themselves with and showing traits of more than one culture being identifiable as multicultural); among such groups, a hierarchy is possible, with "primary groups" (*i.e.*, extensions of the family structure) and secondary belonging groups;[22] although the country and culture of origin are important factors, they only contribute for a fraction of the cultural background of an individual: by way of example, country of origin explains on average only 2–12% of inter-individual variance in value hierarchies;[23] and, multiculturalism tends to be self-reinforcing: persons who have significant exposure to multicultural situations are likely to develop multiple and flexible identities, are less ethnocentric and more open to effective intercultural communication.[24]

---

19 Albert Blumenthal, "A New Definition of Culture," *American Anthropologist Part I* 42, no. 4 (October – December, 1940): 571–586.

20 Francis Fukuyama, *Trust: The Social Virtues and the Creation of Prosperity* (New York: Free Press, 1995), 34.

21 For an overview, see Jiri Anděl, Ivin Bičík, and Jan D. Bláha, "Concepts and Delimitation of the World's Macro-Regions," *Miscellanea Geographica - Sciendo* 22, no. 1 (March 2018): 16–21.

22 Jean Claude Rouchy, "Cultural Identity and Groups of Belonging," *Group* 26, no. 3 (September 2002): 205–217.

23 Ronald Fischer and Shalom Schwartz, "Whence Differences in Value Priorities? Individual, Cultural, or Artifactual Sources," *Journal of Cross-Cultural Psychology* 42, no. 7 (September 2010): 1127–1144.

24 Lily A. Arasaratnam, "A Review of Articles on Multiculturalism in 35 Years of IJIR," *International Journal of Intercultural Relations* 37, no. 6 (November 2013): 676–685.

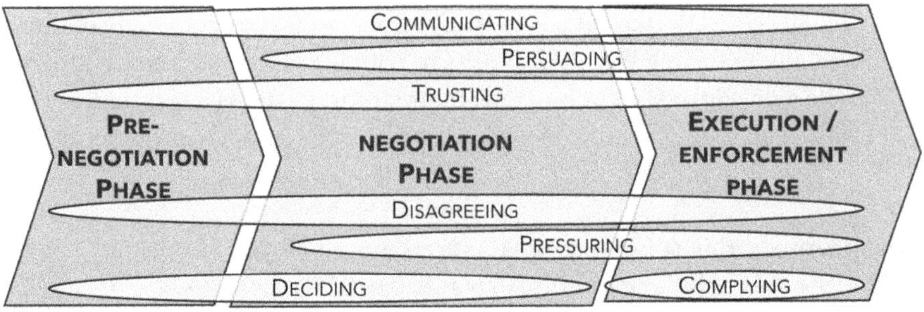

FIGURE 1.2 Negotiation activities on which culture has a direct impact

Note, however, that the relevance of between-country cultural differences has been challenged by a part of the literature. For example, in a study conducted by Hanel *et al.*, within-country variability in values outweighed between-country differences, even though many of such differences could be linked to contextual factors.[25] Regarding the last point, Figure 1.2 summarizes the main activities of negotiators. Such activities share an important point relevant to the topic of this paper: their degree and exercise depends on the negotiation forum (*i.e.*, in person, video, phone, email) and – more importantly – they are all deeply influenced by cultural factors.

Not only do cultural differences affect the behavior of negotiators *ex ante* but these differences also impact the way negotiators communicate *in itinere.* Intracultural and intercultural dyads affect, although not always in clear and distinguishable patterns, dynamic tactical exchange in negotiation processes across all different negotiation phases.[26] Most research on country effects on trust is based on comparing results obtained from each country separately. A limited portion of literature examines the role of trust in inter-country interactions.[27]

25 Paul Hanel et al., "Cross-Cultural Differences and Similarities in Human Value Instantiation," *Frontiers in Psychology* 9 (May 2018).

26 Anne L. Lytle and Harold W. Willaby, "Intracultural and Intercultural Negotiations," in *IACM 2006 Meetings Paper*, accessed August 10, 2021, http://dx.doi.org/10.2139/ssrn.905462.

27 See Toshio Yamagishi et al., "Comparisons of Australians and Japanese on group-based cooperation," *Asian Journal of Social Psychology* 8, no. 2 (July 2005): 173–190; see also Ko Kuwabara et al., "Culture, Identity, and Structure in Social Exchange: A Web-Based Trust Experiment in the United States and Japan," *Social Psychology Quarterly* 70, no. 4 (December 2007): 461–479.

Some of these studies reveal interesting results on how the background of each culture interplays: a study of the behavior of Chinese and American cross-country supply chain, for example, reveals that (i) Chinese individuals exhibit higher spontaneous trust toward U.S. partners than Chinese ones, and (ii) Chinese supply chain enjoys a larger efficiency gain from repeated interactions than a U.S. one does, as the prospect of building a long-term relationship successfully sustains trust and trustworthiness by Chinese partners.[28] This may appear in contrast with the idea of Chinese as a low-trust society. In reality, however, it is not how trust is spread within a society that matters but also the behavior and trust level that individuals expect from their counterparts. In this case, the findings are motivated by the fact that Chinese perceive that individuals from the U.S. are more trusting and trustworthy in general. This positive perception toward U.S. people is indeed consistent with the U.S. participants' behavior in forecast sharing. The difference between "Eastern" and "Western" negotiators has attracted a strong interest not only because of the economic importance of the exchanges between the two areas of the world but also for the depth and significance of differences between these two macro-cultures.

Starting from the outset of negotiations, with the establishment and build-up of trust, Eastern and Western negotiators differ significantly: Meyer includes the former in the definition of "coconut cultures", with low initial levels of trust but a gradual opening up until soft and warm relations are established with close ties.[29] Most western cultures on the other side fall in the category of "peach cultures" with an initially friendly interaction followed by a strengthening of the relationship until reaching a hard shell of the pit protecting the real self. Huang *et al.* point out the challenges created by this different trust paradigm: not only is earning trust in China and Eastern cultures essential to success and complicated, due to the "coconut skin", but the process of trust construction also requires entirely different psychological patterns compared to the Western culture.[30]

Another defining element of the divide between East and West is the juxtaposition between low context vs high context cultures. This classification was introduced by Hall to distinguish between cultures in which messages are

---

28 Özalp Özer, Yanchong Zheng and Yufei Ren, "Trust, Trustworthiness, and Information Sharing in Supply Chains Bridging China and the U.S.," *Management Science* 60, no. 10 (2014): 2435–2460.

29 Erin Meyer, *The Culture Map* (New York: Public Affairs, 2016).

30 Lihua Huang, Sulin Ba, and Xianghua Lu, "Building Online Trust in a Culture of Confucianism: The Impact of Process Flexibility and Perceived Control," *ACM Transactions on Management Information Systems* 5, no. 1 (2014): 1–23.

expected to be explicit, direct, and clear so as not to require knowledge of the counterpart's background (*i.e.*, low context) and cultures in which the context of the message is important to interpret the message (*i.e.*, high context).[31] Although the robustness of Hall's classification does not seem to be supported by a strong, consistent and unequivocal literature,[32] the classification of culture is relevant to the topic of this paper, as efficient communication in high context culture requires high levels of prior knowledge and long-standing relationships between speakers, unlike in low context cultures.

The number and complexity of the other cultural differences would go beyond the scope of this paper but below is a high-level overview of the main cultural traits of each culture group with respect to each of the main activities of negotiators described in Figure 1.2.

The symbols close to the activities listed above indicate how, based on the advantages and disadvantages outlined in Table 1.1, each of the activities is positively (↑) or negatively (↓) impacted[33] by the use of Zoom negotiation and more broadly by the effects of COVID-19 described below.

5 The Impact of Covid

How has this pre-existing picture been impacted by the COVID-19 global pandemics since the first quarter of 2020? The most significant impact has been that Zoom negotiation is no longer just one of the different options to conduct negotiation and settle disputes, but has instead become the predominant, if not the only way to negotiate, mediate and arbitrate. Starting with China in January 2020, most countries worldwide adopted measures to ban or restrict regional, national and international travel. Such measures forced individuals to switch to virtual means of running businesses, conducting negotiations, and resolving disputes. The extent of such measures has varied significantly, both over time, from country to country and within countries. Throughout 2021 for example, China and most Asian countries maintained tight restrictions to both inbound and outbound international travel, while domestic travel and movement remained almost unaffected. Europe and the United States, on the contrary, took the decision to keep their borders comparatively more open, while enacting restrictions to domestic travel. During the 18 months between

31 Edward Hall, *The Silent Language* (Greenwhich: Fawcett Publications, 1959).

32 Peter W. Cardon, "A Critique of Hall's Contexting Model: A Meta-Analysis of Literature on Intercultural Business and Technical Communication," *Journal of Business and Technical Communication* 22, no. 4 (October 2008): 399–428.

33 × in case of no/low impact.

TABLE 1.2 Main cultural traits and virtual negotiations

	West		East	
COMMUNICATING	Direct style of communication	↑↓	Indirect style of communication	↓
			Prominent role of the concept of "face"	↓
	Positive and negative comments provided in clear and straightforward wording	↑	■	■
			Use of downsizing formulas	×
			Unclear wording;	↓
	Inclusiveness	↑	■	■
PERSUADING	Deductive reasoning as default methodology	×	– Inductive and deductive reasoning	×
			– Logic playing a limited role	×
	Logic as key element to persuade and be persuaded	×	– Context playing a key role in defining the dispute/matter and, as a result, to persuade and be persuaded	↓
TRUSTING	Higher starting level of trust between the parties	↑	– Lower starting level of trust between the parties	↓
			– Affective type of trust, mainly based on subjective elements (prior knowledge of the counterpart, affinities, relationships, *etc.*)	↓
	Cognitive type of trust, mainly based on objective elements (experience, context, *etc.*)	↑	■	■

TABLE 1.2 Main cultural traits and virtual negotiations (*cont.*)

	West		East	
DISAGREEING	Confrontation and disagreement considered as constructive elements of a negotiation	↑	– Disagreement and debate considered as negative	↓
	■	■	Diverging views often communicated with delay or in a fragmented, indirect way	↓
	Divergences of views communicated promptly and unambiguously	↑	■	■
PRESSURING	Leverage as main tool to exercise pressure on the counterpart	↓	Implicit and explicit threats used	↓
	■	■	Time and time pressure considered as a key form of leverage	↓
	Undue pressure and threats considered as a lack of respect	×		
DECIDING	Higher incidence of perception biases	↓	Lower incidence of perception biases	↑
	■		Hierarchical decision making	↓
	■		Top-down (Japan as exception being consensual BUT hierarchical)	↓
	Comparatively more egalitarian power structures	↑		
	Comparatively more consensual power structures	↑		

TABLE 1.2 Main cultural traits and virtual negotiations (*cont.*)

	West		East	
COMPLYING	Expectation of parties complying with the principle of *pacta sunt servanda*	×	Compliance depending on circumstances	→
	Adversarial approach in enforcing contracts	×	Non-adversarial approach in enforcing contracts	→
	■		Lower level of litigiousness	→
	High litigiousness	→	■	■

the eruption of the COVID-19 pandemics and the finalization of this paper, the Asia-Pacific region had the highest share of destinations with a complete border closure (~70%) and Europe, on the other extreme, had the most open borders (with closures for only ~13% of destinations).[34] Individuals, firms, organizations, and other key business stakeholders, therefore, turned to virtual meetings to unprecedented and largely unforeseeable levels.

Such an exceptional situation has made it possible to test the limits of virtual negotiations. The terms "Zoom fatigue" or "Zoom exhaustion" have been coined to refer to the effects of excessively using videoconferencing as a tool for negotiation and dispute resolution. It has been observed for example that the frequency, duration, and intensity of Zoom meetings are associated with a higher level of fatigue, and that fatigue has been linked to negative attitudes toward the Zoom meetings and the negotiations conducted using this platform.[35] Bailenson identifies four main causes for such negative effects: (i) an excessive amount of close-up eye contact, (ii) the distraction caused by the fact that negotiators constantly see themselves in real time during video chats, (iii) the extensive reduction in mobility in videoconferences, and (iv) the significantly higher cognitive load in this form of discussions.[36]

The radical shift of personal and professional balances towards remote work, virtual meetings and deals closed, or disputes settled directly from people's living rooms or home offices would have been *per se* an unprecedented moment in the history of the world economy and human behavior.[37] However, the COVID-19 pandemics also had major secondary effects, deeply affecting individuals' daily lives and organizations during the past 18 months. Table 1.2 provides a high-level summary of the main such effects.

Such effects have been produced in all negotiations – domestic and cross-border, bilateral and multilateral, monocultural or multicultural. Craft *et al.* provide a comprehensive analysis of the impact of global pandemics on multilateral negotiations.[38] Many of the problems outlined by their research

---

34 Sustainable Development of Tourism Department, "Covid-19 Related Travel Restrictions - A Global Review for Tourism," United Nations World Tourist Organization, accessed August 15, 2021, https://webunwto.s3.eu-west-1.amazonaws.com/s3fs-public/2021-07/210705-travel-restrictions.pdf.

35 Geraldine Fauville et al., "Zoom Exhaustion & Fatigue Scale," *Computers in Human Behavior Reports* 4, no. 100119 (August–December 2021).

36 Jeremy N. Bailenson, "Nonverbal Overload: A Theoretical Argument for the Causes of Zoom Fatigue," *Technology, Mind, and Behavior* 2, no. 1 (February 2021).

37 Kevin M. Kniffin et al., "COVID-19 and the workplace: Implications, issues, and insights for future research and action," *The American Psychologist* 76, no. 1 (January 2021): 63–77.

38 Brianna Craft et al., *The impacts of COVID-19 on climate diplomacy: Perspectives from the Least Developed Countries* (London: casa and iied, 2021).

TABLE 1.3 COVID-19 impact on organizations, individuals and negotiations

	Effects on organizations	Effects on individuals	Effects on negotiations/Disputes
HIGH IMPACT	– Disruption of supply chains; – Reduction in/zeroing of companies' turnover in many industries; – Impossibility to deliver goods/services due to border closures and other governmental measures; – Uncertainty becoming the only certainty and companies moving in "visual navigation" mode.	– Anxiety; – Workplace becoming virtual; – Restrictions to movements and other personal freedoms; – Unemployment/low employment; – Financial pressure.	– Restrictions on domestic and international travel; – Virtual workplace making planning and preparation of due diligence investigations difficult; – Disruption in the activities of judicial systems and other administrative services.
MODERATE IMPACT	– Pressure to reduce risk exposure and change business models; – Border closures; – Changes in consumer behavior.	– Loneliness; – Reduced access to healthcare system; – Rising inequality.	– Renegotiations of existing agreements prioritized over negotiations of new agreements/projects; – Uncertainty over the enforcement/implementation of agreements; – Higher anxiety of negotiators.
LOW IMPACT	– Changed people's lifestyles.	– Disruption in education and effects on personal/family lives.	– Companies' budgeting and planning reducing resources for disputes/negotiations.

apply also to other forms of negotiations and dispute resolution processes. The distribution of such effects has not been homogeneous across cultures and organizations. The impact of the pandemic on individuals has varied according to such factors as gender, age, nationality, occupation, economic status, and cultural background. Focusing on the last point, the most prominent division is among collectivist and individualist cultures.[39] Collectivist cultures – prioritizing social order, efficiency, and directive leadership – tend to be more adaptive during a crisis, more willing to accept restrictions on individual freedoms and rights,[40] and more maladaptive as recovery becomes timely, and looseness and its associated creativity are needed.[41] Historically, nations with more infectious disease threats are culturally tighter and, as a result, less innovative.

It is hardly possible to isolate the effects caused by the switch to online negotiations from the other negative effects, listed above, of the COVID-19 pandemics. While, in designing the survey, efforts were made to focus the respondents' attention to the topic of this paper, it is undeniable that cross-contamination of effects has taken place.

6 Findings

The main questions addressed in this paper are: how has COVID-19 impacted the Zoom negotiation and what are the cultural variants of such impact? Based on the elements discussed in the previous sections and the answers provided by the respondents to the 40-question survey, the following considerations can be made with respect to each of the three hypotheses made.

6.1 *Hypothesis 1: "The effects of COVID-19 have not been uniform across cultures."*

As discussed in Section 4, the extent to which negotiators have been forced to rely on Zoom negotiations has not been uniform across countries and it has been largely dependent on the form of travel and movement restrictions

39 Geert Hofstede, *Culture's Consequences: International Differences in Work-Related Values* (New York: sage, 1984).

40 Brian Y. An and Shui-Yan Tang, "Lessons From COVID-19 Responses in East Asia: Institutional Infrastructure and Enduring Policy Instruments," *The American Review of Public Admininistration* 50, no. 6–7 (July 2020): 790–800.

41 Michele Gelfand, *Rule Makers, Rule Breakers: Tight and Loose Cultures and the Secret Signals That Direct Our Lives* (New York: Scribner, 2019).

FIGURE 1.3 Wordcloud of responses to the question "describe in three adjectives the effects that COVID-19 and travel restrictions had on your negotiations/disputes"

adopted by different governments. Overall respondents from the Western countries sample have been subjected to more significant restrictions on local travel while Eastern Asian countries isolated themselves, closing international borders and leaving local movement and internal travel possible.

Eastern respondents showed a pre-existing aversion to Zoom negotiations, indicating (Q13) that prior to the pandemic they relied on in-person meetings to a larger extent than Western negotiators (68%, vs 60%) and (Q14) that they considered virtual negotiations as "significantly less effective" in a larger number than Western respondents (28% vs 21%). These findings are consistent with the idea of Eastern cultures relying more significantly on in-person meetings.

6.2 *Hypothesis 2: "Cultures in which trust relies on personal relations and in which face-to-face meetings have a more prominent role in negotiations have been more heavily affected by the COVID-19 pandemic."*

Trust and trust-building are core elements of any negotiation and the way in which such trust is built affects the degree to which COVID-19 has impacted negotiators across cultures. As discussed in Section 3, Chinese and Eastern cultures, in general, tend to rely more significantly on affective trust as a means to create and develop business relations. This element is supported by the indications of the single main negative effect on businesses (Q30), with Eastern respondents selecting "the impossibility/difficulty in developing new business relations" as the main cause even more firmly than Westerners (56% vs 42%). Such conclusions are further supported by the subjective answers to the question (Q22) on how the pandemic has impacted ongoing disputes and negotiations. The results are illustrated in Figure 1.3.

Trust and trust-building are core elements of any negotiation and the way in which such trust is built affects the degree.

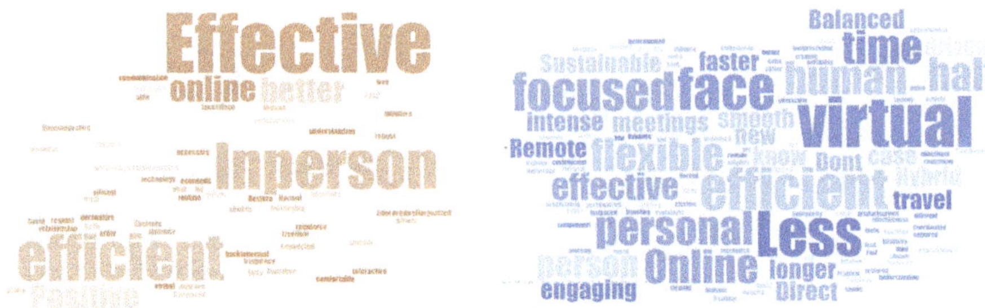

FIGURE 1.4 Wordcloud of responses to the question "Describe in 3 adjectives how you envisage your post-pandemic negotiation/dispute resolution normality"

6.3 *Hypothesis 3 "The degree to which countries will return to normality once the pandemic is over is unlikely to be even."*

The third hypothesis can be viewed as the most complex to test, also considering the difficulty in defining the term "normality" (*e.g.*, in Asia as of April/May 2020, companies recalled all employees to work at the office and domestic travel became possible). The term is here intended as the return to pre-COVID-19 settings, with negotiators free to decide whether to conduct both domestic and international negotiations in person or via virtual means. Eastern respondents showed (Q32) a stronger desire to return to pre-pandemic negotiation and dispute resolution routine compared to Western ones (28% vs 8%), with, in the same question, Western respondents also showing more willingness to "significantly adapt" their routine to the conditions experienced during the pandemic (27% vs 12% of Eastern respondents). When asked about the reason for returning to business travel and in-person meetings rather than relying on Zoom negotiations (Q34), the "strengthening of the relations with counterparts" is unsurprisingly quoted as the main driver (52% for Eastern respondents and 54% for Western ones). Interestingly, "time effectiveness" is the third main reason chosen by Eastern respondents (12%) and least quoted by Western ones (1%). This is consistent with the idea that the Zoom negotiation is widely considered efficient by Europeans and Americans (*i.e.*, lower costs, faster process, more free time in the agendas) while in Eastern and more in general high context/affective-trust cultures, it takes significantly more time to achieve the same results via virtual means as opposed to in-person meetings. Such desire to return to pre-pandemic routines without excessive adaptation is further supported by the adjectives described by Eastern respondents when requested (Q33) to indicate how they envisage the return to normality.

The two main considerations that can be made are (i) a higher concentration of negative adjectives among the answers provided by Eastern respondents and (ii) a broader focus on subject-related and object-related adjectives among Western respondents, unlike representatives of Eastern cultures who concentrated their responses on the personal elements of the post-pandemic normality. This is consistent with the view of Asian countries as "tight cultures" and less adaptive to radical social changes.[42]

While this study focuses on the cultural variants in negotiations, the survey shows interesting results in terms of other variables, such as gender or level of experience. With regard to gender, for example, female respondents showed a higher preference for in-person meetings (Q13) – indicating loneliness as a key downside of Zoom negotiations during the pandemic (Q30) – and are more keen to a return to in-person meetings (Q32), even though pre-COVID-19 they were more open to the idea of negotiating virtually (Q14).

7 Conclusions

This study has explored in particular how the COVID-19 pandemic has impacted ongoing and new negotiations and dispute resolution processes, and how such impact has varied based on cultural factors. The purpose of this study was to test how the impact of COVID-19 on ongoing and new negotiations has greatly depended on the cultural traits of the participants in such negotiations. Taking Chinese and European negotiations as examples of culturally distant groups, this paper has analyzed the pre-COVID-19 attitude and attitude towards a radical switch to Zoom negotiations, the way such switch was integrated in the negotiation routine of such groups throughout the pandemic and how they envisage the post-pandemic normality. The findings of this study are relevant as a first indicator of what the post-pandemic negotiation and dispute resolution practices will look like.

About a third of business travelers plan to reduce their business travel post-pandemic because teleconferencing and remote working arrangements were as effective as being in the office and traveling.[43] The extent of such reductions however is unlikely to be even between East and West. This is supported by anecdotal evidence: surveys among companies' top executives in the West

42 *Id.*

43 Jessica Stansbury, et al., "Anticipating the Travel Recovery: Travel Sentiment Survey Edition 2," OliverWyman, accessed August 14, 2021, https://www.oliverwyman.com/our-expertise/insights/2020/oct/anticipating-the-travel-recovery.html?utm_source=pr&utm_medium=referral&utm_campaign=global-traveler-sentiment-survey&utm_content=2020-nov&utm_id=cmp-10500-w7w3l6.

confirm a significant reduction in business travels[44] while in countries such as China, the recovery of business travelers has been more robust.[45] This is also linked to factors other than the attitudes toward virtual meetings and negotiations even though the role of such attitudes seems significant. Overall, the findings can be summarized as follows.

Over the next months, with the reopening of borders – in the West first and gradually in Asia as well – it will be possible to observe the evolution of the situation and how the Zoom negotiation will be integrated in the negotiation and dispute resolution routine across cultures.

Annex A

Survey Population

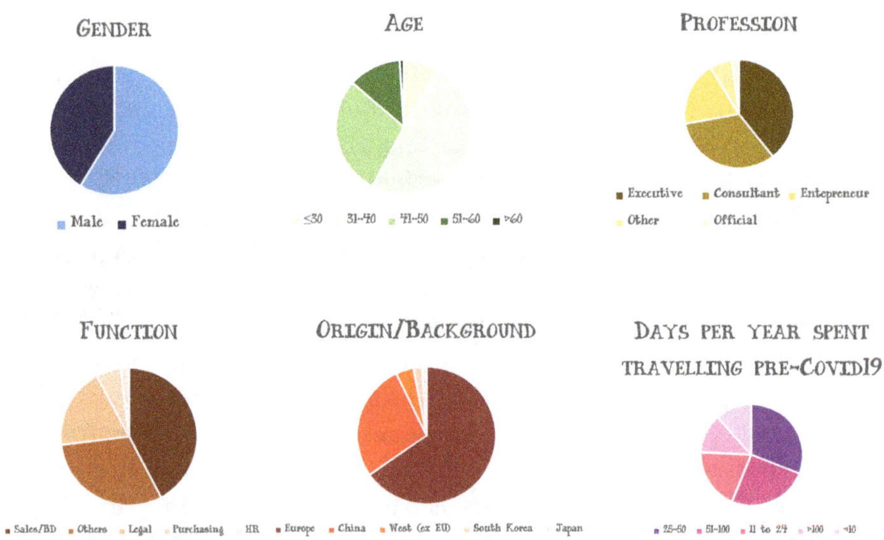

44 Alexander Michael Pearson, Tara Patel, and William Wilkes, "'Forever Changed': CEOs Are Dooming Business Travel – Maybe for Good," Bloomberg, August 31, 2021, https://www.bloomberg.com/news/features/2021-08-31/will-business-travel-come-back-data-show-air-hotel-travel-forever-changed.

45 Guang Chen et al., "China's travel sector is undergoing a nonlinear recovery: What should companies do?," McKinsey & Company, March 26, 2021, https://www.mckinsey.com/industries/travel-logistics-and-infrastructure/our-insights/chinas-travel-sector-is-undergoing-a-nonlinear-recovery-what-should-companies-do.

TABLE 1.4 Findings

	West	East
PRE-EXISTING ATTITUDE TOWARDS THE ZOOM NEGOTIATION	– Limited use; – Gradual integration into negotiation/dispute resolution routines, mainly for reasons relating to cost control and efficiency; – Move toward Zoom negotiations considered as inevitable.	– Very limited use, mainly for international negotiations; – Marginal integration into negotiation/dispute resolution routines, with confidentiality as the main obstacle; – Move towards Zoom negotiations considered with caution, particularly with respect to the maximum portion of the virtual part.
IMPACT OF COVID	– Limitations to domestic travel pushing companies toward a wider use of the Zoom negotiation; – Strong adaptability to the Zoom negotiation; – Long effects and high business stress levels pushing companies toward adaptation.	– Limits to international travel and rapid internal recovery limiting the use of the Zoom negotiation to international negotiations/disputes; – Cultural traits making adaptability to the Zoom negotiation difficult for structural reasons; – Trust creation and business development as the main reason for resuming in-person meetings.
POST-COVID NORMALITY	– Hybrid system widely considered as certain; – Changes to companies' travel policies already being implemented; – In-person meetings to be considered as residual.	– In-person meetings to remain as the main form of negotiation; – Gradual adaptation to hybrid systems.

CHAPTER 2

The Impact of the COVID-19 Pandemic on International Arbitration Practices

Greener Arbitrations with Reduced Due Process Paranoia?

Pratyush Panjwani

1 Introduction

Humanity has not faced a catastrophe of the magnitude of the COVID-19 pandemic in several years.[1] Not only has the pandemic consumed human lives in the millions,[2] but it has also had a severe socio-economic impact, impeding the prosperity of several industries while possibly permanently damaging others. Accordingly, in order to survive the distorted realities of the times, industries – much like the rest of humanity – have had to adapt their conduct drastically.[3] Probably the most significant adaptation is represented by the complete transformation of inter-personal communication, which has shifted, with exponential acclivity,[4] to the digital space.[5]

Unsurprisingly, this holds true for the legal services industry as well, since inter-personal communication constitutes a vital foundation of the industry,

1 For a visual comparator of the impact caused by pandemics across ages, see Nicholas LePan, "Visualizing the History of Pandemics," Visual Capitalist, March 14, 2020, https://www.visualcapitalist.com/history-of-pandemics-deadliest/. Notably, catastrophes, natural or manmade, have in the past opened the door to several institutional changes at a societal and economic level, including, most relevantly, the incorporation of the International Chamber of Commerce after the First World War in 1919 and the incorporation of the United Nations and its sister organizations after the Second World War in 1945 (see Ema Vidak-Gojkovic and Michael McIlwrath, "The COVID-19 Revolution: The Future of *International Arbitration Is Not Over Yet,*" in *International Arbitration and the COVID-19 Revolution*, eds. Maxi Scherer et al. (Kluwer Law International, 2020), 192).

2 While this paper is being published, data suggests that the COVID-19 pandemic has resulted in more than 6 million deaths.

3 See Max McKeown, *Adaptability: The Art of Winning in an Age of Uncertainty* (Kogan Page, 2012).

4 Regarding the rise in digital adoption in the European Union, see Jan Maarten de Vet et al., "Impacts of the COVID-19 pandemic on EU industries," European Parliament (March 2021), 32–33.

5 Regarding the rise of Zoom, see Pilita Clark, "Year in a word: Zoom," Financial Times, December 21, 2020, https://www.ft.com/content/170649d0-4cdf-454b-a4ec-e28d130974cd.

 | DOI:10.1163/9789004514836_004

especially in the sector of dispute resolution. With the evolution of communication from inter-personal to inter-screen, legal communication needed to organically metamorphosize so as to ensure continued effectiveness.

Insofar as the sector of dispute resolution is concerned, particularly international arbitration, there are two significant developments that have occurred in the realm of legal communication. First, the phenomenon of "virtual hearings",[6] *i.e.*, hearings conducted through videoconferencing platforms,[7] has become relatively commonplace.[8] Second, there has been a growing discourse about paper-less or "green" arbitrations, *i.e.*, arbitration proceedings wherein all (or most) correspondence and submissions are exchanged over the internet without the use of hard-copies.[9]

This chapter examines these two developments, with the objective of assessing whether they constitute temporary shifts to keep pace with the pandemic or permanent changes that are here to stay. This examination is conducted not only in respect of the theoretical and practical viability of virtual hearings and green arbitrations, but also their environmental sustainability.

In particular, the theoretical and practical viability of these two developments is measured against their implications on the parties' due process rights. Undoubtedly, the dispute resolution front of the legal services industry is predicated, amongst other tenets of natural justice, on the guarantee that every disputing party has the right to a fair audience before a court or tribunal (as the case may be).[10] The moment the concerned court or tribunal falls afoul of this guaranteed right to be heard, due process is compromised. This chapter analyzes whether the phenomena of virtual hearings and green arbitrations

---

6 It is notable that some practitioners refer to such hearings as "*remote hearings*" as opposed to "*virtual hearings*," in order to avoid any misconceptions about the physical reality of such hearings, since the term "*virtual*" could carry the connotation that it is "*not physically present as such but made by software to appear to be so from the point of view of a program or user*" (see Maxi Scherer, "Remote Hearings in International Arbitration: An Analytical Framework," *Journal of International Arbitration* 37, no. 4 (2020): 410–411). To the author, this appears to be a (semantic) distinction without a (practical) difference. The term used throughout this article is "*virtual hearing*," since the author believes that this term accurately represents hearings conducted through videoconferencing platforms.

7 E.g., Zoom, Cisco Webex, and Microsoft Teams.

8 Gary Born et al., "Empirical Study of Experiences with Remote Hearings: A Survey of Users' Views," in *International Arbitration and the COVID-19 Revolution*, ed. Maxi Scherer et al. (Kluwer Law International, 2020), 137–150.

9 See "Campaign for Greener Arbitrations: Driving sustainable change," Campaign for Greener Arbitrations, accessed December 6, 2021, https://www.greenerarbitrations.com/.

10 This is based on the fundamental Latin maxim "*audi alteram partem*," which translates to "listen to the other side" or "let the other side be heard as well."

sufficiently protect a disputing party's right to be heard. Section 2 examines the propriety of virtual hearings from this perspective, examining whether and how the right to be heard differs from the right to a hearing. Then, Section 3 examines the propriety of green arbitrations from a similar lens and against the backdrop of the environmental impact of international arbitrations. The chapter makes a case for a third tenet of efficiency to the two oft-cited boons of arbitration, *i.e.*, time-efficiency and cost-efficiency. This third tenet is defined as "environmental efficiency".

As a matter of context, it is important to bear in mind that the legal services industry is a tertiary industry that, in turn, serves several other industries, including dispute resolution through arbitration. Thus, the propriety of virtual hearings and green arbitrations cannot be assessed in a vacuum, since – like many other questions of law (and/or fact) – the answer may vary from case to case.

2 Virtual Hearings

Before discussing the recent phenomenon of virtual hearings, it is important, as a preliminary matter, to understand what the meaning of a "hearing" is and whether virtual hearings fall within that understanding. The National Report of Switzerland in response to the questionnaire distributed by the International Council for Commercial Arbitration ("ICCA") as part of its project entitled 'Does a Right to a Physical Hearing Exist in International Arbitration?' ("ICCA Hearing Project") offers a succinct definition of a hearing as "a judicial session held with a view to deciding issues of fact, procedure or law, including hearing witnesses and oral pleadings".[11] While informative, this definition of a "hearing", which aligns with the Black's Law Dictionary definition,[12] does not specifically address whether a hearing needs to be convened in person.

The National Reports of various jurisdictions, including Switzerland, have responded to this precise query as part of the ICCA Hearing Project. Most of them have reported, based on a review of their respective national laws on arbitration and civil procedure, that a hearing is not likely to entail, directly or by inference, a "physical hearing".[13] While some, such as the Australian

11 Paolo Marzolini and Daniel Durante, "Switzerland: Does a Right to a Physical Hearing Exist in International Arbitration?," ICCA Projects, accessed December 1, 2021, 2, https://cdn.arbitration-icca.org/s3fs-public/document/media_document/Switzerland-Right-To-A-Physical-Hearing-Report.pdf.

12 Bryan A. Garner, *Black's Law Dictionary*, 9th ed. (West, 2009), 788.

13 For instance, see James Hosking, Yasmine Lahlou, and Marcel Engholm Cardoso, "United States of America: Does a Right to a Physical Hearing Exist in International Arbitration?,"

National Report,[14] have gone on to say that an interpretation of the procedural rules in their jurisdictions would "potentially exclude" the right to a physical hearing, others, such as the Dutch[15] and Norwegian National Reports,[16] have considered the issue to be "unsettled". This is on grounds that arbitration is viewed as an extension of litigation, and thus the rights that are afforded to litigants in courts should also be made available to disputants in arbitration, especially in light of Article 6 of the European Convention on Human Rights.[17] The Zimbabwean National Report has exceptionally reported that a right to a hearing can be considered to entail a right to a physical hearing pursuant to its procedural rules.[18]

It is also relevant to examine how arbitration institutions have dealt with this issue. In this regard, the Guidance Note on Possible Measures Aimed at Mitigating the Effects of the COVID-19 Pandemic ("ICC Guidance Note"), issued by the International Court of Arbitration of the International Chamber of Commerce ("ICC") on 9 April 2020, serves as an interesting case study. Notably, while Article 25(2) of the ICC's Rules of Arbitration 2017 ("ICC Rules 2017") required a tribunal to *"hear the parties together in person"*, the ICC Guidance Note interpreted this phrase with abandon in the below passage:

ICCA Projects, accessed December 1, 2021, 2, https://cdn.arbitration-icca.org/s3fs-public/document/media_document/USA-Right-to-a-Physical-Hearing-Report.pdf; Valentine Chessa, Nataliya Barysheva, and Arianna Camillacci, "France: Does a Right to a Physical Hearing Exist in International Arbitration?," ICCA Projects, accessed December 1, 2021, 2–3, https://cdn.arbitration-icca.org/s3fs-public/document/media_document/France-Right-to-a-Physical-Hearing-Report_0.pdf; Kingshuk Banerjee and Ritvik Kulkarni, "India: Does a Right to a Physical Hearing Exist in International Arbitration?," ICCA Projects, accessed December 1, 2021, 2–3, https://cdn.arbitration-icca.org/s3fs-public/document/media_document/India-Right-to-a-Physical-Hearing-Report.pdf.

14 See Lucy Martinez and Jay Tseng, "Australia: Does a Right to a Physical Hearing Exist in International Arbitration?," ICCA Projects, accessed December 1, 2021, 5, https://cdn.arbitration-icca.org/s3fs-public/document/media_document/Australia-Right-to-a-Physical-Hearing-Report_0.pdf.

15 See Bas van Zelst, "The Netherlands: Does a Right to a Physical Hearing Exist in International Arbitration?," ICCA Projects, accessed December 1, 2021, 2, https://cdn.arbitration-icca.org/s3fs-public/document/media_document/Netherlands-Right-To-A-Physical-Hearing-Report.pdf.

16 See Ola Ø. Nisja and Per Aleksander Tønnessen, "Norway: Does a Right to a Physical Hearing Exist in International Arbitration?," ICCA Projects, accessed December 1, 2021, 2-3, https://cdn.arbitration-icca.org/s3fs-public/document/media_document/Norway-Right-to-a-Physical-Hearing-Report.pdf.

17 Notably, this is despite the fact that Article 1072b(4) of the Dutch Code of Civil Procedure specifically envisages the possibility of a virtual hearing.

18 See Davison Kanokanga and Tafadzwa Pasipanodya, "Zimbabwe: Does a Right to a Physical Hearing Exist in International Arbitration?," ICCA Projects, accessed December 1, 2021, 3, https://cdn.arbitration-icca.org/s3fs-public/document/media_document/Zimbabwe-Right-to-a-Physical-Hearing-Report.pdf.

> While Article 25(2) of the Rules provides that after studying the written submissions of the parties and all documents relied upon, the tribunal 'shall hear the parties together in person if any of them so requests,' *this language can be construed as referring to the parties having an opportunity for a live, adversarial exchange and not to preclude a hearing taking place 'in person' by virtual means if the circumstances so warrant* .... The French version of Article 25(2) reflects this meaning, providing: '*Après examen des écritures des parties et de toutes pièces versées par elles aux débats, le tribunal arbitral entend contradictoirement les parties si l'une d'elles en fait la demande; à défaut, il peut décider d'office de leur audition*'. Hence ... whether the arbitral tribunal construes Article 25(2) as requiring a face-to-face hearing, or whether the use of video or teleconferencing suffices, will depend on the circumstances of the case.[19] [emphasis added]

It is clear that the above passage of the ICC Guidance Note advanced an expansive interpretation of Article 25(2) of the ICC Rules 2017. It can even be argued that this interpretation went beyond, and effectively novated the terms of the said provision. Although this anomalous situation has now been rectified in the ICC's revised Rules of Arbitration 2021 ("ICC Rules 2021"), which now specify that a hearing may be conducted "by physical attendance or remotely by videoconference, telephone or other appropriate means of communication",[20] the above passage of the ICC Guidance Note nonetheless offers important insight regarding the term "hearing": it includes a "live, adversarial exchange" that does not necessarily need to be "in person".

Further insight is offered by a minor, but significant, qualification of verbiage used in the Rules of Procedure for Arbitration Proceedings associated with the International Centre for Settlement of Investment Disputes ("ICSID Arbitration Rules"). Unlike many other institutional rules, the ICSID Arbitration Rules, in Rule 32, describe a hearing as a constituent part of what is referred to generally as the "oral procedure". The interpretative relevance of this unique language has not been the subject of extensive commentary in case law or legal scholarship. However, for the purposes of this chapter, it does help to obtain a simplified – or perhaps oversimplified – understanding of a hearing, which, after all, is nothing more than an "oral procedure", which does not require a physical meeting of all participants.

---

19 "ICC Guidance Note on Possible Measures Aimed at Mitigating the Effects of the COVID-19 Pandemic," International Chamber of Commerce, April 9, 2020, para. 23–24 ("ICC Guidance Note").

20 "2021 Arbitration Rules," International Chamber of Commerce, in effect as of January 1, 2021, Article 26(1) ("ICC Rules 2021").

In light of this basic understanding of a "hearing", it can comfortably be stated that in most situations, it is not mandatory for the arbitral tribunal and the parties to meet in person for a "live, adversarial exchange" or an "oral procedure" to qualify as a proper "hearing". Thus, as described by the ICC Guidance Note, a "virtual hearing" also constitutes a hearing, but one that is conducted "by audioconference, videoconference, or other similar means of communication".[21] However, this proposition is, of course, subject to important exceptions that could emanate from either the national law of the seat of the arbitration or the parties' agreement to the contrary based on due process. For instance, if all parties to an arbitration agree to conduct the hearing in person, the tribunal will not be able to exercise its discretion to impose a virtual hearing. Similarly, if one of the parties before the tribunal objects to the conduct of the hearing virtually, the tribunal's discretion to impose a virtual hearing will need to be examined carefully, bearing in mind the implications on due process.

In the forthcoming subsections, we explore (i) how the move from in-person hearings to virtual hearings has been integrated in institutional rules and guidelines; (ii) whether virtual hearings raise any due process concerns that compromise a party's right to be heard; and (iii) whether virtual hearings are the future in international arbitration practice.

2.1 *The Move to Virtual Hearings Resulting from the COVID-19 Pandemic*

The COVID-19 pandemic may have made the phenomenon of virtual hearings more commonplace, but it is certainly not the harbinger of this phenomenon. Even prior to the pandemic, several arbitral institutions did already specifically envisage the possibility of virtual hearings. For instance, the 2014 version of the Arbitration Rules ("LCIA Arbitration Rules 2014") of the London Court of International Arbitration ("LCIA") explicitly stipulated that "[a]s to form, a hearing may take place by video or telephone conference or in person (or a combination of all three)".[22] Similarly, the Swiss Chambers' Arbitration Institution Rules in effect as of 2012 also specifically stated that "[t]he arbitral tribunal may direct that witnesses or expert witnesses be examined through means that do not require their physical presence at the hearing (including by videoconference)".[23] While the ICC Rules 2017, already discussed above, did not expressly envisage the possibility of virtual hearings, Appendix VI thereof, pertaining to expedited arbitrations, did mention that "[w]hen a hearing is to

21 ICC Guidance Note, para. 2.

22 "LCIA Arbitration Rules (2014)," London Court of International Arbitration, in effect as of October 1, 2014, Article 19.2 ("LCIA Arbitration Rules 2014").

23 Swiss Chambers' Arbitration Institution Rules, in effect as of 2012, Article 25(4).

be held, the arbitral tribunal may conduct it by videoconference, telephone or similar means of communication".[24]

This was followed by the development of the Seoul Protocol on Video Conferencing in International Arbitration in March 2020 ("Seoul Protocol"), the publication of which coincided with the onset of the pandemic.[25] The Seoul Protocol was far-sighted in its prescription of guidelines for conducting virtual hearings. It described a "Hearing Venue" to mean "the site of the hearing, being the site of the requesting authority, typically where the majority of the participants are located", and, in turn, also described a "Remote Venue" to mean "the site where the remote Witness is located to provide his/her evidence (*i.e.* not the Hearing Venue), typically where a minority of the participants are located". The term "Venue" was, in turn, defined to mean "a video conferencing location, including the Hearing Venue and the Remote Venue(s)".[26]

Accordingly, virtual hearings were already being explored by the international arbitration community before the COVID-19 pandemic struck. In fact, ICSID reported that already in 2019, *i.e.*, before the pandemic struck, "60 per cent of the 200 hearings and sessions organized by ICSID were held by video-conference."[27]

That is not to say, of course, that things did not change dramatically afterwards and as a result of the pandemic. In the past year, several arbitral institutions have either updated their institutional rules to now specifically envisage (or further enhance) the possibility of virtual hearings,[28] or prepared guidance notes and checklists to encourage and assist disputing parties and arbitral tribunals to conduct hearings virtually so as to avoid inordinate delays

---

24 "2017 Arbitration Rules," International Chamber of Commerce, adopted March 1, 2017, Appendix VI, Article 3(5) ("ICC Rules 2017").

25 See "Seoul Protocol on Video Conferencing in International Arbitration," KCAB International, March 18, 2020, http://www.kcabinternational.or.kr/user/Board/comm_notice_view.do?BBS_NO=548&BD_NO=169&CURRENT_MENU_CODE=MENU0025&TOP_MENU_CODE=MENU0024.

26 *Id.* at Definitions.

27 See "A Brief Guide to Online Hearings at ICSID," ICSID, March 24, 2020, https://icsid.worldbank.org/news-and-events/news-releases/brief-guide-online-hearings-icsid.

28 For instance, see Article 26(1) of the ICC Rules 2021, which now envisages the possibility of virtual hearings even in usual (i.e., non-expedited) arbitration proceedings ("A hearing shall be held if any of the parties so requests or, failing such a request, if the arbitral tribunal on its own motion decides to hear the parties. When a hearing is to be held, the arbitral tribunal, giving reasonable notice, shall summon the parties to appear before it on the day and at the place fixed by it. The arbitral tribunal may decide, after consulting the parties, and on the basis of the relevant facts and circumstances of the case, that any hearing will be conducted by physical attendance or remotely by videoconference, telephone or other appropriate means of communication.").

at the behest of the pandemic.[29] In fact, in April 2020, many arbitral institutions issued a joint statement pledging to take steps to "ensur[e] that pending cases may continue and that parties may have their cases heard without undue delay."[30] Further, a plethora of service providers have gained prominence recently as specialists in organizing virtual hearings, with services ranging from (i) information technology assistance for preparing the hearing participants before and during the virtual hearing; (ii) remote display of documentary evidence available for the duration of the virtual hearing; (iii) tailored video conferencing platforms for virtual hearings in arbitration proceedings; and (iv) preparation of electronic bundles for use before and during the virtual hearing.[31] Correspondingly, court reporters and interpreters have also adjusted their services to now include the provision of transcription and interpretation services virtually.

Therefore, while the phenomenon of virtual hearings had already entered the discourse prior to the pandemic, its scope and range have extensively been explored and put into practice after the pandemic. Indeed, the international arbitration community has made rapid advancements to facilitate arbitrations during these dire times. As described in the LCIA's Annual Casework Report 2020 ("LCIA 2020 Report"), the COVID-19 pandemic has resulted in a "*new normal*", with which arbitration users and service providers have had to keep pace.[32] The LCIA 2020 Report interestingly recounts, based on the LCIA's interactions and

---

29 For example, see "HKIAC Guidelines for Virtual Hearings," HKIAC, May 15, 2020; "Checklist on Holding Arbitration and Mediation Hearings in Times of COVID-19," Delos, March 2020; ICC Guidance Note; "AAA-ICDR Virtual Hearing Guide for Arbitrators and Parties," American Arbitration Association-International Centre for Dispute Resolution, April 2020 ("AAA-ICDR Virtual Hearing Guide"); "Guidance Note on Remote Dispute Resolution Proceedings," The Chartered Institute of Arbitrators, April 8, 2020; "ICODR Video Arbitration Guidelines," The International Council for Online Dispute Resolution, April 1, 2020 ("ICODR Video Arbitration Guidelines").

30 These arbitral institutions include "Arbitration and COVID-19," the ICC, the ICSID, the Cairo Regional Centre for International Commercial Arbitration, the German Arbitration Institute, the International Centre for Dispute Resolution, the Korean Commercial Arbitration Board, the London Court of International Arbitration, the Milan Chamber of Commerce, the Hong Kong International Arbitration Centre, the Stockholm Chamber of Commerce, the Singapore International Arbitration Centre, the Vienna International Arbitration Centre and the Institute of Chartered Financial Analysts of India, accessed September 8, 2021, https://iccwbo.org/content/uploads/sites/3/2020/04/covid19-joint-statement.pdf; see also Angeline Welsh, "Arbitration Not Locked Down: Has the Covid-19 Pandemic Accelerated Inevitable Change?," Essex Court Chambers, May 13, 2020.

31 Examples of such virtual hearing service providers are mentioned in Section 3.1 below.

32 "LCIA Annual Casework Report 2020 and changes to the LCIA Court and European Users' Council," LCIA, May 17, 2021, 6, https://www.lcia.org/News/lcia-news-annual-casework-report-2020-and-changes-to-the-lcia-c.aspx.

experiences during the pandemic, that although "at first, there was reluctance to embrace virtual hearings, particularly those involving the hearing of witnesses", over the past year, the increased embrace of virtual hearings "[p]aradoxically . . . allowed some cases to proceed where in the past this would not have been possible".[33] Similarly, the 2021 International Arbitration Survey conducted by the School of International Arbitration, Queen Mary University of London in association with White & Case ("QMUL-W&C 2021 Survey") reports that "[t]he increase in the use of virtual hearing rooms appears to be the result of how the practice of arbitration has adapted in response to the COVID-19 pandemic".[34] In fact, the results of the interviews supporting the QMUL-W&C 2021 Survey showed that the comfort of international arbitration users with virtual hearings has increased to such as an extent that "[i]f a hearing could no longer be held in person, 79% of respondents would choose to 'proceed at the scheduled time as a virtual hearing'. Only 16% would 'postpone the hearing until it could be held in person', while 4% would proceed with a documents-only award."[35]

In light of the above, it is unsurprising that the COVID-19 pandemic has been referenced as having triggered a "revolution" of arbitration practice.[36]

2.2 *Virtual Hearings and Due Process Concerns*

The onset of virtual hearings has, however, not been met with unanimous optimism. Cases wherein all disputing parties have agreed that the hearing should be conducted virtually are largely uncontroversial as they do not come with any concerns of due process. However, as mentioned above, such concerns assume relevance when any (or all) of the disputing parties object to the conduct of the hearing virtually and insist that the hearing should be convened in person. These concerns create an apparent conflict between the arbitral tribunal's discretion to organize the arbitration procedure, on the one hand, and the objecting parties' due process rights (to be heard in a fair trial), on the other. This conflict was best articulated by the representative of the Republic of Turkey during the discussions relating to the currently ongoing amendment procedure for the ICSID Rules, wherein Turkey objected to the vesting of discretion on the arbitral tribunal to decide the form or method of conducting the hearing in the following terms:

---

33 *Id.*

34 White & Case, "2021 International Arbitration Survey conducted by the School of International Arbitration," Queen Mary University of London, accessed September 10, 2021, 20, http://www.arbitration.qmul.ac.uk/media/arbitration/docs/LON0320037-QMUL-International-Arbitration-Survey-2021_19_WEB.pdf.

35 *Id.* See also, for a similar survey results, Gary Born et al., "Empirical Study," 137–150.

36 Maxi Scherer et al., "Preface," in *International Arbitration and the COVID-19 Revolution*, eds. Maxi Scherer et al. (Kluwer Law International, 2020), xxix.

> [T]he form of hearings should be decided on the consent of the parties. In other words, if one party does not consent on the method proposed by the other party or the tribunal, the proposed method should not have an effect. This position is more appropriate than delegating the power to a tribunal taking the right of fair trial and due process right of parties into account.
>
> [T]he prevalent practice is in-person hearing ... Other methods of hearing (remote-online-virtual hearings) are envisaged to provide flexibility for the participation of an expert, witness, or Tribunal Member via video conferencing in exceptional cases. Therefore, Turkey suggests adding a default rule to Article 32, which requires that the hearings shall be held in-person unless otherwise agreed by the parties, with reserve to exceptional circumstances.[37]

The ICSID's Working Paper # 5 relating to the proposed amendments to the ICSID Rules rejected Turkey's objection on grounds that "there may be circumstances where Tribunal discretion is useful to determine whether to proceed with a hearing remotely."[38]

This subsection discusses how this apparent conflict between the disputing parties' due process rights and the arbitral tribunal's discretion to organize the arbitration procedure has been addressed in the rules of various arbitral institutions, and has manifested and been dealt with in legal proceedings either emanating from a challenge to an award rendered after a virtual hearing or, more commonly, from a challenge to the arbitral tribunal's independence and impartiality based on its decision to convene a hearing virtually despite a disputing party's insistence to the contrary. First, however, this subsection addresses a more foundational theoretical question, *i.e.*, whether the parties' right to be heard includes the right to a hearing at all, in person or virtual.

---

37 "Compendium of Comments for Working Paper # 4 relating to Proposed Amendments to the ICSID Arbitration Rules," ICSID, March 23 2021, 31, https://icsid.worldbank.org/sites/default/files/amendments/Compendium%20of%20State%20Comments%20on%20Proposed%20Amendments%20to%20the%20ICSID%20Rules%20-WP%20%23%204%20-%20As%20of%202021.03.23.pdf.

38 "Proposals for Amendment to ICSID Rules – Working Paper # 5," ICSID, June 15, 2021, para. 62, https://icsid.worldbank.org/sites/default/files/publications/WP%205-Volume1-ENG-FINAL.pdf.

2.2.1 The Right to Be Heard Versus the Right to a Hearing

The guarantee of due process has been said to date back several centuries.[39] Nevertheless, it has been difficult to identify the precise contours of what due process entails. It has been said that the concept of due process "has roots that to some degree parallel the origins of [the principles of] natural justice".[40] The principles of natural justice consist of two related rights, *i.e.*, the right to be heard and the right to an unbiased tribunal.[41] The Singapore Court of Appeal has described these as the "two pillars" of natural justice,[42] while relying on the seminal 1978 decision of the Supreme Court of Victoria in *Gas & Fuel Corporation v. Wood Hall Ltd.*, which had helpfully pointed to "sub-branches or amplifications" of the two constituent rights of natural justice. In particular, the Supreme Court of Victoria had noted that one important sub-branch of the right to be heard was that "each party must be given a fair hearing and a fair opportunity to present its case."[43]

Against this backdrop, it is interesting to examine how case law and scholarly writing has interpreted this entitlement to a "fair hearing" or the so-called "fair hearing rule" and the "opportunity to present [one's] case", especially in the context of arbitration.

The Singapore Court of Appeal has understood the "fair hearing rule" as "only encompass[ing] a reasonable opportunity to present one's case".[44] Similarly, the High Court of Australia has found that "procedural fairness requires only that a party be given 'a reasonable opportunity to present his case' and not that the tribunal ensure 'that a party takes the best advantage of the opportunity to which he is entitled'."[45] This aligns with the position in literature, which is best represented by the words of Prof. Lucy Reed in her 2016 Queen Mary School of International Arbitration-Freshfields Lecture titled 'Ab(use) of due process: sword vs shield', wherein she candidly warned her colleagues to:

39 Franco Ferrari et al., "Chapter 1: General Report," in *Due Process as a Limit to Discretion in International Commercial Arbitration*, eds. Franco Ferrari et al. (Kluwer Law International, 2020), 1.

40 Frederick F. Shauer, "English Natural Justice and American Due Process: An Analytical Comparison," *William and Mary Law Review* 18, no. 1 (October 1976): 51.

41 *Id.* at 48.

42 *Soh Beng Tee & Co Pte Ltd v. Fairmount Development Pte Ltd.*, [2007] SGCA 28, para. 43.

43 *Gas & Fuel Corporation of Victoria v. Wood Hall Ltd & Leonard Pipeline Contractors Ltd*, [1978] VR 385, 396.

44 *Triulzi Cesare SRL v. Xinyi Group (Glass) Co Ltd*, [2014] SGHC 220, para. 131.

45 *Re Association of Architects ex parte Municipal Officers Association*, [1989] HCA 13, para. 19; see also *Sullivan v Department of Transport*, (1978) 20 ALR 323, 343.

> [N]ot promise the parties a 'full' opportunity to present their cases, and thereby invite due-process labelled complaints that a hearing was one day too short or that a cross-examination went one hour too long. Look instead at what is a 'reasonable' opportunity at an 'appropriate' stage of the proceedings, not at 'any' stage.[46]

Accordingly, it can be asserted, with sufficient certainty, that the "fair hearing rule" entails – or at least should entail – not an unlimited, but a reasonable opportunity, to present one's case. In this regard, a recent decision of the Singapore Court of Appeal is particularly relevant. In that February 2020 case, *China Machine v Jaguar*, the Court made the following relevant findings on the scope and extent of parties' right to be heard:

> [I]t has been suggested – rightly, in our view – that the parties' right to be heard is impliedly limited by considerations of reasonableness and fairness. This has especial relevance in cases such as the present one, where the complaint is that the failure to grant some sort of procedural accommodation to a party adversely impacted that party's due process rights . . .
>
> [W]hile the parties have, in general, a right to be heard effectively on every relevant issue, the 'overriding concern ... is fairness', and the 'best rule of thumb to adopt is to treat the parties equally and allow them reasonable opportunities to present their cases as well as to respond'.[47]

Taking into account the above understanding of the right to be heard and, in turn, to a fair hearing, the obvious question that follows is whether the right to be heard necessarily includes the right to a hearing in the sense of a "*live, adversarial exchange*" in the words of the ICC Guidance Note. Two remarks can be made in response to this question.

First, it is important to bear in mind that there cannot be one ubiquitous answer to this question. This is because the precise scope of the right to be heard and, in turn, to a fair hearing is not set in stone and is malleable. As noted by the Singapore Court of Appeal in *Triulzi Cesare SRL v. Xinyi Group (Glass) Co Ltd*, "the content of the fair hearing rule can vary greatly from case to

46 Lucy F. Reed, "Ab(use) of due process: sword vs shield," *Arbitration International* 33, no. 3 (2017): 370.

47 *China Machine New Energy Corporation v. Jaguar Energy Guatemala LLC and AEI Guatemala Jaguar Ltd*, [2020] SGCA 12, para. 97.

case depending on the circumstances of each case since what may be a breach in one context may not be a breach in another."[48]

Second, the search for the answer to this question should start with the national law of the seat of the arbitration. For instance, interestingly, while the UNCITRAL Model Law on International Commercial Arbitration 1985 (with amendments as adopted in 2006) ("UNCITRAL Model Law") guarantees to each of the parties "a full opportunity of presenting his case",[49] it does not guarantee an automatically available right to a hearing. Article 24(1) of the UNCITRAL Model Law regulates the right to a hearing in the following manner:

> Subject to any contrary agreement by the parties, the arbitral tribunal shall decide whether to hold oral hearings for the presentation of evidence or for oral argument, or whether the proceedings shall be conducted on the basis of documents and other materials. However, unless the parties have agreed that no hearings shall be held, the arbitral tribunal shall hold such hearings at an appropriate stage of the proceedings, if so requested by a party.[50]

From the above provision, it is evident that the determination of whether to hold an oral hearing or not falls within the tribunal's discretion by default. The parties are entitled to either jointly agree to have an oral hearing convened, or to individually request the tribunal to convene such a hearing. In either scenario, the tribunal is duty-bound to convene an oral hearing. However, absent such a request by one of the parties or an agreement between all of the parties, the tribunal is not duty-bound to convene, nor are the parties entitled to present their cases at an oral hearing. This is how courts in jurisdictions that have adopted the UNCITRAL Model Law appear to have understood this regime.

In Germany, it is recognized that the right to a full opportunity to present one's case "does not necessarily require an oral hearing if none of the parties requests a hearing",[51] since tribunals enjoy discretion in their decisions to schedule hearings, which discretion could be validly exercised by granting parties the opportunity to comment only in writing.[52] The same legal position is

48 *Triulzi Cesare SRL v. Xinyi Group (Glass) Co Ltd*, [2014] SGHC 220, para. 125.

49 UNCITRAL Model Law on International Commercial Arbitration (1985), Article 18 ("UNCITRAL Model Law").

50 *Id.* at Article 24(1).

51 Friedrich Jakob Rosenfeld, "Chapter 8: Country Report: Germany," in *Due Process as a Limit to Discretion in International Commercial Arbitration*, eds. Franco Ferrari et al. (Kluwer Law International, 2020), 181.

52 Court of Appeals Frankfurt, decision of 16 January 2014, case reference 26 Sch 2/13; Court of Appeals Naumburg, decision of 21 February 2002, case reference 10 Sch 08/01.

taken in several other jurisdictions that have adopted the UNCITRAL Model Law, such as Spain,[53] Belgium,[54] India,[55] and Singapore.[56] The laws of several other countries, which have not adopted the UNCITRAL Model Law, such as the United States[57] and Switzerland[58] also reflect this position.

Of course, the relevance of the above demarcation between a right to be heard and a right to a hearing, while important in theory, is relatively limited in practice, since parties generally request or agree to a hearing. Indeed, tribunals will run the risk of having their awards set aside if they have not given the parties an opportunity to present their cases at a hearing, when faced with such a request or agreement.[59] Accordingly, tribunals should usually tread with care before proceeding with a case without convening a hearing, since, as appositely pointed out by the High Court of Australia, even though a right to a hearing may not be automatically available to the parties as part of their opportunity to present their case, absent a specific request or agreement, "the fact that a hearing has taken place may have particular significance in determining whether or not the opportunity was given."[60]

With the above context in mind, the next subsection will examine how institutional rules and case law have dealt with the question of whether, in a situation where all parties wish to have a hearing, an arbitral tribunal can impose a virtual hearing, even if one of the parties objects to the hearing being conducted virtually.

53 Belgian Judicial Code, Article 1705(1).

54 Spanish Arbitration Act 2011, Article 30(1).

55 *Sukhbir Singh v. Hindustan Petroleum Corp*, 2020 SCCOnLine Del 228.

56 *Gov't of the Repub. of the Philippines v. Philippine Int'l Air Terminals Co., Inc.*, [2006] SGHC 206; *PT Asuransi Jasa Indonesia (Persero) v. Dexia Bank SA*, [2006] SGCA 41.

57 Hosking, *supra* note 13, at 2; *ST Shipping & Transp. PTE, Ltd. v. Agathonissos Special Mar. Enter.*, 2016 wl 5475987, at 4 (S.D.N.Y. June 6, 2016) ("*there is no brightline rule requiring arbitrators to conduct oral hearings. ... "[t]he key issue is whether the arbitral panel 'allow[ed] each party an adequate opportunity to present its evidence and argument*").

58 *X. et al. v. Z. GmbH*, decision of the Federal Supreme Court, para. 4.1.1 published in BGE/ATF 142 III 360, 26 April 2016; *U. v. Spouses G.*, decision of the Federal Supreme Court, para. 1.b.aa published in BGE/ATF 117 II 346, 1 July 1991; *X. v. Fédération Internationale de Football Association* (*FIFA*), decision of the Federal Supreme Court No. 4A_260/2017, para. 4.1 (not published in BGE/ATF 144 III 120), 20 February 2018.

59 For instance, see Judgment of 1 July 1999, 1999 Rev. arb. 834 (*Paris Cour d'appel*); Judgment of 19 January 1990, *Immoplan v. Mercure*, 1991 Rev. arb. 125 (*Paris Cour d'appel*).

60 *Re Association of Architects; ex parte Municipal Officers Association*, [1989] HCA 13, para. 19; see also *Sullivan v Department of Transport*, (1978) 20 ALR 323, 343.

2.2.2 Imposition of Virtual Hearings Absent Parties' Consent

As mentioned above, in the context of the ICCA Hearing Project, national laws rarely require that a hearing be conducted physically or in person. Be that as it may, when a party specifically requests that a hearing be conducted in person, an arbitral tribunal cannot indiscriminately impose a virtual hearing upon such a party without examining whether it may have any negative implications on that party's right to be heard.[61] In this situation, the fact that the national law of the seat envisages the possibility of a virtual hearing cannot automatically come to the tribunal's rescue since the national law may also inevitably subject the tribunal's discretion to convene a hearing to the parties' agreement or request to the contrary. Accordingly, this situation creates a quintessential conflict between the tribunal's procedural discretion to organize the proceedings or its case management powers, on the one hand, and the parties' due process rights, on the other. In this context, the Singapore Court of Appeal has laid out the playing field for this conflict eloquently in the *Triulzi Cesare SRL v. Xinyi Group (Glass) Co Ltd* case:

> [T]he arbitral tribunal's case management powers are not without limits. The exercise of case management powers is subject to the rules of natural justice which includes the right to be heard. However, this right only encompasses a reasonable opportunity to present one's case, the fair hearing rule, which must be considered in light of other competing factors. For instance, the Tribunal is also obligated … to [*sic*] make every effort to conduct the arbitration in an expeditious and cost-effective manner, having regard to the complexity and value of the dispute. Weight must be accorded to 'the practical realities of the arbitral ecosystem such as promptness and price'…
>
> In this regard, an arbitral tribunal exercising case management powers will take into consideration a myriad of factors, including the arbitral tribunal's obligation to conduct the arbitration fairly and expeditiously.[62]

It is interesting to note that there is no unanimous resolution to a conflict between the arbitral tribunal's procedural discretion and disputing parties' due process rights emerging from the institutional rules of the various arbitral institutions. On one end of the spectrum lie institutions that prioritize the

61 Of course, in a situation where all parties to an arbitration object to a virtual hearing, the arbitral tribunal's discretion to impose a virtual hearing is practically non-existent, as mentioned above.

62 *Triulzi Cesare SRL v. Xinyi Group (Glass) Co Ltd*, [2014] SGHC 220, paras. 131–132.

arbitral tribunal's procedural discretion over the parties' due process rights in rather express terms. On the other end are institutions that treat the issue of whether or not a virtual hearing is appropriate as one to be determined by agreement between the disputing parties and the arbitral tribunal.

For instance, the ICC Arbitration Rules 2021, which were prepared in view of the influence of the pandemic on arbitration practice, lie at the former end of the spectrum. In other words, these Rules appear to give the arbitral tribunal discretionary power to determine whether and when a virtual hearing is appropriate. In this regard, they stipulate, in Article 26(1), that "[t]he arbitral tribunal may decide, after consulting the parties, and on the basis of the relevant facts and circumstances of the case, that any hearing will be conducted by physical attendance or remotely by videoconference, telephone or other appropriate means of communication."[63] It is clear from this provision that the arbitral tribunal is only required to consult the disputing parties before determining the appropriateness of a virtual hearing. In other words, the disputing parties' consent is not a precondition to conducting a hearing virtually.

Similarly, the LCIA Arbitration Rules 2014 and the updated version that came into effect in 2020 ("LCIA Arbitration Rules 2020") both provide that while the arbitral tribunal should "organise the conduct of any hearing in advance, in consultation with the parties", it has "the *fullest authority* . . . to establish the conduct of a hearing, including its . . . *form*" [emphasis added], *i.e.*, whether it should be conducted virtually or in person.[64] Similarly, it appears from the discussions that are currently underway regarding the modifications to the ICSID Arbitration Rules, discussed above, that they also prefer the decision regarding the form or method of conducting a hearing to be one that falls squarely within an arbitral tribunal's discretion.

On the other hand, certain arbitral institutions, such as the Hong Kong International Arbitration Centre ("*HKIAC*"), provide in their guidelines associated with virtual hearings that "[w]hether or not a virtual hearing, in part or in full, is suitable for a particular matter remains a matter for the parties and the arbitral tribunal", and not just the arbitral tribunal.[65] Similarly, the American

---

63 This aligns with the language used in Article 22(2) of the ICC Arbitration Rules 2021, which prescribes that "[*i*]*n order to ensure effective case management, after consulting the parties, the arbitral tribunal shall adopt such procedural measures as it considers appropriate, provided that they are not contrary to any agreement of the parties.*"

64 LCIA Arbitration Rules 2014, Article 19.2; LCIA Arbitration Rules (2020), London Court of International Arbitration, in effect as of October 1, 2020, Article 19.2 ("LCIA Arbitration Rules 2020").

65 HKIAC Guidelines for Virtual Hearings, Introduction. This aligns with the provision concerning the general conduct of the arbitration contained in Article 13.1 of the HKIAC

Arbitration Association and the International Centre for Dispute Resolution ("AAA-ICDR"), in their Model Order and Procedures for a Virtual Hearing via Videoconference, treat the suitability of a virtual hearing as a matter on which the arbitral tribunal and the disputing parties have to agree.[66]

Accordingly, it is evident that the question of the extent to which an arbitral tribunal is authorized to impose a virtual hearing on disputing parties in the absence of any one of their consent is a matter that may receive different responses from different arbitral institutions. In fact, even the ICC, which appears to lie at the discretionary end of the spectrum, has warned arbitral tribunals against quick decisions to conduct virtual hearings without considering all the appropriate factual and legal implications of these decisions. In this regard, the ICC Guidance Note states the following:

> If a tribunal determines to proceed with a virtual hearing *without party agreement, or over party objection, it should carefully* consider the relevant circumstances, including those mentioned in paragraph 18 above, *assess whether the award will be enforceable at law*, as provided by Article 42 of the [ICC Arbitration Rules 207], and *provide reasons for that determination*. In making such a determination, tribunals may wish to take account of their broad procedural authority under Article 22(2) of the [ICC Arbitration Rules 207], to, after consulting the parties, 'adopt such procedural measures as [the tribunal] considers appropriate, provided that they are not contrary to any agreement of the parties'. [emphasis added]

From the above-quoted passage, it becomes evident that while the ICC assures arbitral tribunals of their broad discretion to organize procedural matters, it also advises them to take a decision to conduct a hearing virtually in the absence of the parties' consent after assessing whether that decision could put the award at risk of non-enforcement and after providing appropriate reasons for that decision. Similarly, the reference to paragraph 18, in turn, requires the arbitral tribunal to keep an eye on, *inter alia,* "the complexity of the case and number of participants, whether there are particular reasons to proceed without delay, whether rescheduling the hearing would entail unwarranted or

---

Administered Arbitration Rules 2018 ("*Subject to these Rules, the arbitral tribunal shall adopt suitable procedures for the conduct of the arbitration in order to avoid unnecessary delay or expense, having regard to the complexity of the issues, the amount in dispute and the effective use of technology, and provided that such procedures ensure equal treatment of the parties and afford the parties a reasonable opportunity to present their case.*").

66 AAA-ICDR Model Order and Procedures for a Virtual Hearing via Videoconference, Article 1a.

excessive delays".[67] Thus, arbitral tribunals resolving a dispute being administered by the ICC would be well-advised to decide on the appropriateness of virtual hearings on a case-by-case basis, after taking into account not only the contextual factors specific to a case, but also the future enforceability of their award.

While the former aspect involves considerations such as complexity and timing, the latter assessment entails examining whether the national law of the seat and any other laws of potential enforcement jurisdictions could threaten an award if the hearing is conducted in a manner that the parties did not consent to.

At this stage, there is limited clarity on how different jurisdictions perceive virtual hearings since the issue has not yet come up for consideration before many courts. However, some court decisions do exist on the issue of virtual hearings in arbitration proceedings as well as in court proceedings.

For instance, the Austrian *Oberste Gerichtshof* (Supreme Court) rendered a decision in July 2020 in the context of a party's challenge to the arbitral tribunal on grounds that it had decided to conduct the hearing virtually.[68] The arbitral tribunal in that case had refused to postpone the hearing to accommodate the COVID-19 pandemic and had, instead, ordered a virtual hearing despite the party's objection. The party challenging the arbitral tribunal argued that this order resulted in the said party having lesser preparation time for the hearing, and, in turn, violated the said party's right to equal treatment as well its right to a full opportunity to present its case, especially since the party's counsel was located in a different time zone. The Supreme Court rejected each

67 ICC Guidance Note, para. 18 provides as follows: "In deciding on the appropriate procedural measures to proceed with the arbitration in an expeditious and cost-effective manner, a tribunal should take account of all the circumstances, including those that are the consequence of the COVID-19 pandemic, the nature and length of the conference or hearing, the complexity of the case and number of participants, whether there are particular reasons to proceed without delay, whether rescheduling the hearing would entail unwarranted or excessive delays, and as the case may be the need for the parties to properly prepare for the hearing."

68 OGH 18 ONc 3/20s, July 23, 2020, https://www.ris.bka.gv.at/Dokumente/Justiz/JJT_20200723_OGH0002_018ONC00003_20S0000_000/JJT_20200723_OGH0002_018ONC00003_20S0000_000.pdf; see also Maxi Scherer et al., "In a 'First' Worldwide, Austrian Supreme Court Confirms Arbitral Tribunal's Power to Hold Remote Hearings Over One Party's Objection and Rejects Due Process Concerns," Kluwer Arbitration Blog, October 24, 2020, http://arbitrationblog.kluwerarbitration.com/2020/10/24/in-a-first-worldwide-austrian-supreme-court-confirms-arbitral-tribunals-power-to-hold-remote-hearings-over-one-partys-objection-and-rejects-due-process-concerns/.

of the above arguments, finding that none of them gave rise to any justifiable doubts as to the independence or impartiality of the arbitral tribunal. The Supreme Court also endorsed the arbitral tribunal's decision to conduct the hearing virtually to avoid delay and considered such an order to be fair and in alignment with the parties' due process rights in the facts and circumstances of the case.[69]

Unlike the Austrian Supreme Court, the Swiss Federal Tribunal, around the same time, upheld an appeal against a lower court's order to conduct the hearing virtually in the absence of the disputing parties' consent, on the ground that such an order violated the Swiss Code of Civil Procedure. The Swiss Federal Tribunal's considerations were premised on the fact that the Swiss Code of Civil Procedure envisaged specific instances where electronic means could be used by courts, but virtual hearings was not one of them. Due to this distinguishing feature in Swiss procedural law, it has been suggested that this decision of the Swiss Federal Tribunal may not be extended to implicate orders of arbitral tribunals directing a hearing to be conducted virtually, keeping in mind also that the Swiss Private International Law Act endows arbitral tribunals with broad discretion to organize arbitral procedure.[70]

Jurisdictions outside continental Europe have also either authorized arbitral tribunals to conduct virtual hearings in their arbitration laws (for instance, the United Arab Emirates)[71] or have seen courts render decisions, such as the ones from Singapore and Australia, discussed above, that implicitly suggest that they do not consider the parties' due process rights to be unlimited and, in this regard, accord a significant "margin of deference to the tribunal in its exercise of procedural discretion".[72] This recognition of a "margin of deference" also aligns with scholarly opinion. Authors have sought to draw a distinction between "due process" and "ordinary process", stating that "'[o]rdinary process' is ... the decisions that arbitrators take in 'their discretion and judgment' to protect due process which, in turn, constitutes the 'fundamental fairness' of

69 OGH, *supra* note 68, at secs. 7–8, 10.2.1, and 11.2.4; see also Scherer et al., *supra* note 68.

70 DFT 146 III 194, July 6, 2020, http://relevancy.bger.ch/php/clir/http/index.php?highlight_docid=atf%3A%2F%2F146-III-194%3Ade&lang=de&type=show_document; Niklaus Zaugg, "Imposing Virtual Hearings in Times of Covid-19: The Swiss Perspective," Kluwer Arbitration Blog, January 14, 2021, http://arbitrationblog.kluwerarbitration.com/2021/01/14/imposing-virtual-arbitration-hearings-in-times-of-covid-19-the-swiss-perspective/.

71 See Federal Arbitration Law No. 6 of 2018, Articles 28(2)(b) and 33(3).

72 *China Machine New Energy Corporation v. Jaguar Energy Guatemala LLC and AEI Guatemala Jaguar Ltd*, [2020] SGCA 12, para. 103.

the procedure".[73] On this basis, they consider that an arbitral tribunal's decision to conduct a hearing virtually, despite a party's objection, falls within its broad procedural discretion and is a matter of "ordinary process" that "will not likely provide a basis to challenge a remote award", *i.e.*, an award rendered in a case where the hearing took place virtually. However, these considerations, of course, do not apply when all disputing parties agree that a hearing should only be conducted in person and not virtually.[74]

The above scholarly view is also reflected in the recent practice in ICSID arbitrations, where two respondent States have challenged arbitral tribunals alleging that their decision to conduct a hearing virtually despite the State's objections to this course of action, exceeded their procedural powers under the ICSID Arbitration Rules and thereby reflected bias. However, all of such challenges launched to date have been rejected.[75] The reasoning contained in the ICSID Secretary General's Recommendation issued in May 2020 in the *Vattenfall v. Germany* case is interesting in this regard:

> With respect to the Tribunal's powers under the ICSID Rules to conduct videoconference hearings, I consider this to be a matter that falls to the Tribunal itself to decide as a matter of *kompetenz-kompetenz*. While I take no position on the proper interpretation of this aspect of the ICSID Rules, I do not see that even an erroneous interpretation of the Rules would – without more – support an inference that the ruling was the product of a lack of independence or impartiality.
>
> Turning to the appropriateness of a videoconference hearing in the present matter, I note that any arbitral tribunal is called on to balance considerations of efficiency and avoiding delay with ensuring that the parties are properly heard. It will frequently be the case that one party will be more concerned with speed and see less need to delve deeply

73 Erica Stein, "Challenges to Remote Arbitration Awards in Setting Aside and Enforcement Proceedings," in *International Arbitration and the COVID-19 Revolution*, ed. Maxi Scherer et al. (Kluwer Law International, 2020), 170.

74 *Id.* at 172.

75 Sebastian Perry, "Spain fails to unseat ICSID panel over refusal to travel," Global Arbitration Review, December 16, 2020, https://globalarbitrationreview.com/spain-fails-unseat-icsid-panel-over-refusal-travel; Cosmo Sanderson, "Germany fails second challenge to Vattefall panel," Global Arbitration Review, July 9, 2020, https://globalarbitrationreview.com/arbitrator-challenges/germany-fails-in-second-challenge-vattenfall-panel.

> into issues it considers straightforward, while the other may be less concerned regarding delay and prefer a more extensive exploration of the matter. Indeed, the recent record of the present proceedings, set out in detail above, shows stark differences between the Parties concerning the time required for the final procedural steps. *Due process may be infringed if a party's opportunity to present its case is unduly curtailed; but due process may also be infringed if proceedings are so delayed as to impair the relief envisaged by the Treaty. The Tribunal itself is best placed to balance these considerations* and I do not see that a procedural disagreement – or the fact that the Tribunal's decision was supported by the Claimants and opposed by the Respondent – reasonably provides a basis for an inference of bias. Accordingly, I do not consider that the Tribunal's decision to proceed with a hearing by videoconference can reasonably be considered to support an inference that the Tribunal manifestly cannot be "relied upon to exercise independent judgment."[76] [emphasis added]

From the above discussion, it is evident that the balance of views tilts in favor of arbitral tribunals' discretion to impose a virtual hearing on the disputing parties even in a situation where one of them objects to it. This is because, as rightly pointed out by the ICSID Secretary General's Recommendation in *Vattenfall v. Germany,* due process may be infringed not only when a party's right to present its case is unduly curtailed but also when arbitration proceedings are unnecessarily delayed.

Arbitral tribunals are, indeed, best placed to be mindful of all considerations regarding not only the parties' right to be heard but also of time and cost efficiency and determine, as part of their discretion to organize "ordinary process", whether a virtual hearing is appropriate in the facts and circumstances of a case. The facts and circumstances to be taken into account include (i) the complexity of the case; (ii) the number of participants; (iii) the amount in dispute; (iv) the possibility of effectively using technology; and (v) whether there are particular reasons to proceed without delay.[77]

76 *Vattenfall AB et. al. v. Federal Republic of Germany*, ICSID Case No. ARB/12/12, Recommendation Pursuant to the Request by ICSID dated 8 May 2020 on the Respondent's Proposal to Disqualify all Members of the Arbitral Tribunal dated 16 April 2020, paras. 138–139.

77 ICC Guidance Note, para. 18.

2.3 *Conclusion: Are Virtual Hearings the Future?*

It is evident that, at this stage, virtual hearings do not appear to be a mere transitional coping mechanism that will fade away with the COVID-19 pandemic. What the future holds may not be predictable with sufficient certainty, but what is certain is that dispute resolution practice today is at an interesting crossroads. It has been suggested that in the coming years advocacy, in terms of making submissions as well as preparing and presenting witness testimony, may undergo a significant transformation, for instance, to make way for part *"asynchronous hearings"* that see opening statements recorded prior in time to the actual hearing.[78] Whether and to what extent such innovative recommendations will be applicable in practice will have to be measured against the traditional understanding of a hearing. Similarly, the viability of virtual hearings in complex cases will have to be measured against the onset of *"Zoom fatigue"*, which has been said to inhibit how the viewer "process[es] information over video" since on videoconferences, the viewer is only "paying attention . . . to look at the camera", but, in interpersonal interactions the viewer is "able to use . . . peripheral vision" too, which may enhance concentration.[79] Interestingly, the QMUL-W&C 2021 Survey reported, based on its empirical studies that:

> Going forward, respondents would prefer a 'mix of in-person and virtual' formats for almost all types of interactions, including meetings and conferences. Wholly virtual formats are narrowly preferred for procedural hearings, but respondents would keep the option of in-person hearings open for substantive hearings rather than purely remote participation.[80]

Considerations of the future aside, for the moment, it is possible to conclude, based on how various arbitral institutions and courts across jurisdictions have dealt with the phenomenon of virtual hearings, that arbitral tribunals may order virtual hearings even when one of the parties objects to this course of action during the arbitral proceedings. In other words, there is no need for

78 Wendy Miles, "Remote Advocacy, Witness Preparation & Cross-Examination: Practical Tips & Challenges," in *International Arbitration and the COVID-19 Revolution*, ed. Maxi Scherer et al. (Kluwer Law International, 2020).

79 Liz Fosslien et al., "How to Combat Zoom Fatigue," Harvard Business Review, April 29, 2020, https://hbr.org/2020/04/how-to-combat-zoom-fatigue; see also Manyu Jiang, "The reason Zoom calls drain your energy," BBC, April 22, 2020, https://www.bbc.com/worklife/article/20200421-why-zoom-video-chats-are-so-exhausting.

80 White & Case, *supra* note 34.

arbitral tribunals to succumb to "due process paranoia" while determining the suitability of virtual hearings. "Due process paranoia" has been described as "a perceived reluctance by [arbitral] tribunals to act decisively in certain situations for fear of the award being challenged on the basis of a party not having had the chance to present its case fully".[81] Arbitral institutions vest a broad procedural discretion on arbitral tribunals to determine the need and appropriateness of virtual hearings, while balancing considerations of time and cost efficiency and the parties' right to be heard in light of various case-specific and industry-specific factors.[82] Similarly, from a preliminary review of the limited case law on this issue, courts across jurisdictions may also endorse the conduct of hearings virtually, so long as the parties have not previously agreed to conduct the hearing only in person and the contextual setting of a case does not militate against the conduct of virtual hearings to protect the parties' right to be heard and to present their case.

3 Green Arbitrations

Another impact that the COVID-19 pandemic has had is the increase in the overall human consciousness about the relationship with the natural environment. Indeed, there is a growing realization about how the exponential rise in infectious diseases over the past several decades, including the COVID-19 pandemic, is, at least in part, attributable to the excessive and disproportionate (mis)utilization of the environment by humans.[83] The international arbitration community is no exception to this realization, as is evidenced by the rise

81 See Remy Gerbay, "Due Process Paranoia," Kluwer Arbitration Blog, June 6, 2016, http://arbitrationblog.kluwerarbitration.com/2016/06/06/due-process-paranoia/; Michael Polkinghorne and B.A. Gill, "Due Process Paranoia: Need We Be Cruel to Be Kind," *Journal of International Arbitration* 34, no. 6 (February 2018): 935.

82 See Franco Ferrari et al., "Chapter 1: General Report," in *Due Process as a Limit to Discretion in International Commercial Arbitration*, eds. Franco Ferrari et al. (Kluwer Law International, 2020), 38–39 ("Due process paranoia is unwarranted. This is not only due to the limited scope of review at the post-award stage and the high level of deference that courts generally pay to arbitral tribunals in exercising their review. Arbitral tribunals also have various case management tools at their disposal – be it cutoff dates, directions to specifically reference relevant passages in voluminous documents, limitations of page numbers or other measures to enhance the efficiency of the proceedings – that may assist them in completing their mission.").

83 See Ferris Jabr, "How Humanity Unleashed a Flood of New Diseases," New York Times, June 25, 2020, https://www.nytimes.com/2020/06/17/magazine/animal-disease-covid.html.

in initiatives that promote environmentally sustainable arbitration proceedings, referred to as "green arbitrations".

Green arbitrations are understood to encompass several practices that could contribute in reducing carbon emissions associated with the conduct of arbitrations, such as reducing long-haul travel by flight or otherwise, eliminating the use of disposables such as coffee cups and eliminating hard copy filings and exchanges altogether.[84] While each of these objectives is laudable, this Section focuses primarily on the latter objective of eliminating hard copies. Of course, the first objective of reducing travel has already, to some extent, been covered by the discussion on virtual hearings in Section 2 of this Chapter.

In the forthcoming subsections, we explore (i) how the conversation about green paperless arbitrations has evolved in the past few years and has recently been integrated in institutional rules and protocols; (ii) whether moving towards greener arbitrations is necessary and appropriate; and (iii) whether greener arbitrations are the future in international arbitration practice.

3.1 *The Conversation about Greener Arbitrations Resulting from the COVID-19 Pandemic*

Much like for virtual hearings, the discourse about making arbitrations greener and paperless dates back to before the COVID-19 pandemic. The ICC's Commission on Arbitration and Alternative Dispute Resolution had set up a Task Force on the Use of Information Technology ("*ICC IT Task Force*") in the early 2000s. The ICC IT Task Force came out with its first report in 2004 on the 'Operating Standards for Using IT in International Arbitration', which report included a section dedicated to "paperless arbitrations" that called upon each participant in the arbitration to "convert all documents that it normally would submit only in hard copy form (*e.g.* submissions, letters, witness statements, transcripts) into the machine-readable and processable file format(s)" and to attempt submitting documents in such electronic file format(s) as opposed to in physical hard-copy form.[85] Immediately thereafter, in 2005, the ICC set up its case management product called NetCase, through which the tribunals,

84 "A Significant Impact," Campaign For Greener Arbitrations, accessed September 10, 2021, https://www.greenerarbitrations.com/impact.

85 ICC Commission on Arbitration and Alternative Dispute Resolution, Task Force on the Use of Information Technology, "Operating Standards for Using IT in International Arbitration," in *Special Supplement 2004: Using Technology to Resolve Business Disputes*, ICC's Digital Library, sec. 2, P.3.

parties and the institution could access all pleadings, correspondence and other submissions electronically and in real time.[86]

Moreover, there were sporadic pleas advanced by arbitration practitioners to make arbitrations greener by reducing the amount of paper used in international arbitrations.[87] Simultaneously, court litigations also sought to transform to the paperless model. A major impetus on that front came in the high-profile litigation between the two Russian oligarchs, Boris Berezovsky and Roman Abramovich, which was tried before Mrs. Justice Gloster of the United Kingdom's High Court of Justice. During that trial, the High Court decided to use, for the first time, a product launched by Opus2 International, *i.e.*, Magnum-Cloud, which was "a secure, cloud-based interface for accessing, annotating, tagging and managing transcripts and other electronic documents and files".[88] That litigation was widely reported, as were the costs implications of using Opus2 International's Magnum-Cloud. The use of this product resulted in saving GBP 30,000 for each trial bundle that might have been produced physically, since the case involved over 15,000 documents and 200,000 pages in pre-trial paperwork alone.[89]

Indeed, Opus2 International has been, and continues to remain, one of the leading service providers that makes paperless arbitrations more accessible and efficient. In the wake of the COVID-19 pandemic, it provided several novel services that integrated its electronic bundle solutions, which entailed creating hyperlinked electronic bundles stored on a cloud, with the organization of virtual hearings, which entailed services pertaining to document management and evidence presentation during the virtual hearings.[90] It has also branched out into virtual workspaces for disputes teams, which law firms can

86 "Information Technology in International Arbitration - Report of the ICC Commission on Arbitration and ADR", ICC, accessed September 1, 2021, https://iccwbo.org/publication/information-technology-international-arbitration-report-icc-commission-arbitration-adr/.

87 Gillian Carmichael Lemaire, "Paperless Arbitrations – Where Do We Stand?," Kluwer Arbitration Blog, February 19, 2014, http://arbitrationblog.kluwerarbitration.com/2014/02/19/paperless-arbitrations-where-do-we-stand/; Leon Kopecký, "A Case for Paperless Arbitration," Kluwer Arbitration Blog, February 5, 2017, http://arbitrationblog.kluwerarbitration.com/2017/02/05/a-case-for-paperless-arbitration/.

88 "The paperless trial," Fenwick Elliott, October 9, 2013, https://www.fenwickelliott.com/research-insight/annual-review/2013/paperless-trial.

89 "End of paper trial: technology saves 5m pages in court case," Evening Standard, March 19, 2012, https://www.standard.co.uk/news/uk/end-of-paper-trial-technology-saves-5m-pages-in-court-case-7577254.html.

90 See "Virtual Hearings," Opus2, accessed September 28, 2021, https://www.opus2.com/virtual-hearings.

use from the outset of a case.[91] Similarly, other similar service providers, such as Epiq,[92] TrialView,[93] and FTI's TrialConsultants,[94] and Law In Order,[95] have also become commonplace names when it comes to end-to-end services relating to e-discovery, document management and evidence presentation during and prior to virtual hearings.[96]

Arbitral institutions have also recently taken up the objective of paperless arbitrations in a more mainstream manner. Until the ICC Rules 2017, the preliminary submissions in arbitrations administered by the ICC (*i.e.*, the Request for Arbitration and the Answer thereto) were required to be filed in sufficient "number of copies" for each party, each arbitrator, and the ICC's Secretariat.[97] The ICC IT Task Force in its 2017 report on "Information Technology and International Arbitration" had referenced paperless arbitrations incidentally, observing that despite electronic submissions becoming commonplace "some arbitrators may prefer not to work in a completely paperless environment". However, the ICC Rules 2021 have unambiguously opted for paperless arbitrations, providing that the preliminary submissions are required to be filed only electronically by default, unless the party filing the submission wishes transmission thereof by courier in hard copy.[98] A similar change, applicable not only to the preliminary submissions but to all communications between the tribunal and the parties, has also been introduced into the LCIA Arbitration Rules 2020,[99] and the Belgian Centre for Arbitration and Mediation Arbitration Rules in force as from 1 January 2020 ("CEPANI Rules 2020").[100] In fact, the LCIA

---

91 See "Opus 2 Case Preparation" Opus2, accessed September 28, 2021, https://www.opus2.com/virtual-workspace.

92 See "The Epiq Difference," Epiq, accessed September 28, 2021, https://www.epiqglobal.com/en-us.

93 See "The Complete Solution for Dispute Resolution," TrialView, accessed September 28, 2021, https://www.trialview.com/.

94 See "Better govern, secure, find, analyze and rapidly understand data," FTI TrialConsultants, accessed September 28, 2021, https://www.ftitechnology.com/.

95 See Law In Order, accessed September 28, 2021, https://www.lawinorder.com.au/.

96 In addition to these service providers, other service providers that arrange for virtual data rooms, including services ranging from e-discovery, document management and evidence presentation, are FirmRoom (see https://firmroom.com/), Knovos (see https://www.knovos.com/) and Dealroom (see https://dealroom.co/).

97 ICC Rules 2017, Articles 3(1), 4(4), and 5(3).

98 ICC Rules 2021, Articles 3(1), 4(4), and 5(3).

99 Compare LCIA Rules 2020, Articles 4.1 and 4.3 to LCIA Arbitration Rules, Articles 4.1 and 4.3.

100 "Rules of CEPANI," The Belgian Centre for Arbitration and Mediation, in effect as of January 1, 2020, Article 8(2) ("CEPANI Rules 2020").

Arbitration Rules 2020 also envisage awards being "signed electronically and/or in counterparts and assembled into a single instrument".[101]

Other arbitration institutions, while not (yet) having altered their institutional rules in the above manner, have expressed a preference for and, in turn, sought to ease electronic communications in other ways. For instance, the Stockholm Chamber of Commerce ("SCC") has launched the SCC Platform, which is "a secure digital platform for communication and file sharing between the SCC, the parties and the tribunal", and has also extended the use of the Platform for *ad hoc* cases.[102] Similarly, in the wake of the pandemic, the Singapore International Arbitration Centre ("SIAC") also "encourage[d] tribunals in existing SIAC cases to discuss ... with the relevant SIAC Case Counsel" whether the awards can be issued electronically in the jurisdictions where the concerned arbitrations are seated.[103] The ICSID Rules, which are in the process of being amended, may also undergo a change from requiring the Request for Arbitration as well as other communications and submissions filed before the tribunal to "be accompanied ... additional ... copies"[104] to requiring them to be "filed electronically".[105]

The above evolution in practice reflects a collective realization in the international arbitration community of making arbitration proceedings environmentally sustainable. One of the most evident indicators of this realization is the Campaign for Greener Arbitration ("CGA") launched in 2019, which has taken the initiative to "raise awareness of the significant carbon footprint of the arbitration community" and, to that end, has advanced important objectives and pragmatic solutions to achieve a sustainable change in which arbitrations are conducted. The CGA's recent work includes designing a so-called "Green Pledge" that aims to create sustainable work spaces less reliant on hard copies and more reliant on electronic communications,[106] as well as preparing

101 LCIA Rules 2020, Article 26.2.

102 See "SCC Platform," SCC, accessed September 1, 2021, https://sccinstitute.com/case-management/.

103 See "COVID-19 Frequently Asked Questions," SIAC, accessed September 1, 2021, https://www.siac.org.sg/faqs/siac-covid-19-faqs.

104 ICSID's Institutional Rules (currently in force), Rule 4; ICSID Arbitration Rules (currently in force), Rule 23.

105 See ICSID, *supra* note 38; ICSID's Institutional Rules (proposed amendment), Rule 4; ICSID's Arbitration Rules (proposed amendment), Rule 4.

106 See "The Green Pledge," Campaign For Greener Arbitrations, accessed September 10, 2021, https://www.greenerarbitrations.com/greenpledge.

draft "Green Protocols" and a "Model Green Procedural Order".[107] The Green Protocols, which are a set of six protocols, are directed towards minimizing the environmental impact and carbon emissions of (i) arbitral proceedings; (ii) law firms, chambers and legal service providers; (iii) arbitrators; (iv) arbitration conferences; (v) arbitration hearing venues; and (vi) arbitration institutions.[108] In general, the objective is to achieve a set of "sustainability measures" that focus on three priority areas, *i.e.*, "the use of clean energy, the avoidance or reduction of travel and the avoidance or reduction of waste".[109]

The Green Protocol for Arbitral Proceedings ("CGA Green Protocol for Arbitral Proceedings") provides solutions such as (i) requiring all correspondence and submissions to be filed electronically by default; (ii) considering, at the outset of a case, whether shared technology platforms or case management systems can be used for the receipt and organization of correspondence and submissions; (iii) asking parties and tribunals to "carefully consider" the need for printing documents and to endeavor to "only print what is deemed strictly necessary"; and (iv) asking parties and tribunals to dispose "all printed documents in an environmentally friendly way".[110] More specific solutions along these lines are contained in the Model Procedural Order designed by the CGA ("CGA Model Procedural Order"). In light of the above, there can be no doubt that the international arbitration community has taken concrete steps towards making arbitrations greener.

3.2 *Greener Arbitrations and Their Necessity and Appropriateness*

To ask whether making arbitrations greener is necessary is akin to asking whether the Earth's climate is changing. While the United Nations' Intergovernmental Panel on Climate Change ("IPCC") Working Group I Report, released in August 2021 to much attention, has been described by its Co-Chair as a "reality check",[111] this Report was preceded by several such studies conducted

---

107 See "Green Protocols," Campaign For Greener Arbitrations, accessed September 10, 2021, https://www.greenerarbitrations.com/green-protocols.

108 "Framework for Adoption of the Green Protocols," Campaign for Greener Arbitrations, accessed September 10, 2021, 1–4, https://www.greenerarbitrations.com/green-protocols.

109 *Id.* at 3.

110 "Green Protocol for Arbitral Proceedings," Campaign for Greener Arbitrations, accessed September 10, 2021, sec. II, https://www.greenerarbitrations.com/green-protocols.

111 See "Climate change widespread, rapid, and intensifying," IPCC, August 9, 2021, https://www.ipcc.ch/2021/08/09/ar6-wg1-20210809-pr/; see, for the report, Masson-Delmotte et al., *Climate Change 2021: The Physical Science Basis. Contribution of Working Group I to the Sixth Assessment Report of the Intergovernmental Panel on Climate Change* (Cambridge University Press, 2021).

by the four Working Groups of the IPCC in the past. One such industry-specific study from 2014 had described the pulp and paper industry as an "emission-intensive" industry, while identifying a significant increase in the demand for paper worldwide.[112] The pulp and paper industry has been widely criticized for its high energy and water consumption, the use of toxic chemicals in the manufacturing process as well as the excessive wastage resulting in landfills and methane gas.[113]

Moreover, studies estimate somewhere around 42% of the wood harvested for industrial usage,[114] accounting for somewhere between 10%[115] to 14% of global deforestation,[116] is aimed at manufacturing paper. Even the more conservative estimates amount to no less than 4.1 million hectares of forest land being used annually for manufacturing paper.

There can be no doubt that the legal services industry is amongst the largest consumers of paper. Although the international arbitration community constitutes only a small part of the legal services industry, that does not imply that it bears any lesser responsibility to reduce paper consumption. In fact, according to some studies, the international arbitration community is responsible for enough of this deforestation to take steps toward changing course. For instance, an initial study conducted by the CGA estimated that a total of approximately 20,000 trees would be required to offset the total carbon emissions resulting from a medium to large scale arbitration in today's times.[117]

---

112 Joyashree Roy et. al., "Industry," in *Climate Change 2014: Mitigation of Climate Change, Contribution of Working Group III to the Fifth Assessment Report of the Intergovernmental Panel on Climate Change*, eds. Ottmar Edenhofer et al. (Cambridge University Press, 2014), 746, 760.

113 Eugene Xiong, "The Sustainable Impact Of A Paperless Office," Forbes, May 11, 2021, https://www.forbes.com/sites/forbestechcouncil/2021/05/11/the-sustainable-impact-of-a-paperless-office/?sh=5f1d045c1095; M. Suraj and Akram Khan, "Environmental Impact of Paper Industry: Review Paper on Part of Each Country in this Impact," *International Journal of Engineering Research & Technology* 3, no. 20 (2015).

114 *Id*; "The State of the Paper Industry: Monitoring the Indicators of Environmental Performance," Steering Committee of the Environmental Paper Network, accessed September 12, 2021, https://environmentalpaper.org/wp-content/uploads/2017/09/state-of-the-paper-industry-2007-executive.pdf.

115 Daniel Matthews, "Sustainability Challenges in the Paper Industry," AIChE, October 12, 2016, https://www.aiche.org/chenected/2016/10/sustainability-challenges-paper-industry.

116 See "What is the environmental impact of deforestation for paper production?," paper / on the rocks, accessed September 13, 2021, https://paperontherocks.com/2018/11/28/environmental-impact-of-deforestation/.

117 See "A Significant Impact," Campaign for Greener Arbitrations, accessed September 10, 2021, https://www.greenerarbitrations.com/impact.

While the carbon footprint, as per this study, was measured by accounting not only for the use of paper, but also other carbon-producing components, such as air, rail and car journeys, hotel stays *etc.*, there is no doubt that a significant amount of forest land is wasted in supporting only the paper-related needs of international arbitration.

Going paperless is, in fact, not only environmentally sustainable, but is also financially viable. For instance, in the trial before the UK High Court between Boris Berezovsky and Roman Abramovich, discussed above, it was estimated that using Opus2 International's Magnum-Cloud saved approximately GBP 30,000 per trial bundle that may have been produced in hard-copy.[118] Similarly, one arbitration practitioner estimated that, in a construction arbitration, only by avoiding printing (and/or photocopying) chronological hearing bundles of more than 200,000 documents thrice-over, an estimated GBP 65,000 (plus related administration costs) were saved.[119]

In general, it is estimated that the United States spends around USD 8 billion per year only on managing paper, and, in turn, ends up wasting approximately 1 billion trees' worth of paper per year.[120] These figures clearly show that working in a paperless environment is not only necessary for ensuring less interference with the environment, but it is also financially beneficial. This also holds true in international arbitration.

Moreover, unlike virtual hearings that, in certain situations, may give rise to justifiable due process concerns, paperless arbitrations face no such hindrance. In today's times, correspondence and submissions can be filed electronically regardless of the size or type of files in question. This is true ubiquitously for all industries that use arbitration as a dispute resolution mechanism.

So long as the disputing parties participate in the proceedings and they share with the members of the arbitral tribunal the vision and the technological know-how to conduct arbitrations in a paperless manner, there are several service providers in today's times (enlisted in subsection 3.1 above) that can, either independently or in conjunction with arbitration institutions, assist in making paperless filings efficient in all kinds of arbitrations. To this end, it is recommended that the disputing parties and the members of the arbitral tribunal consult each other, at the outset of the proceedings, to create a document in the nature of the CGA Model Procedural Order, which can serve as

118 Evening Standard, *supra* note 89.

119 Fenwick Elliott, *supra* note 88.

120 Eugene Xiong, *supra* note 113.

the basis for paperless filings in the course of the proceedings. The said Model Procedural Order contains some useful insights into the steps that can be taken in this regard, such as (i) agreeing to use "shared electronic technology platforms or case management systems . . . for the receipt and organisation of all documentation and correspondence"; (ii) agreeing to use "electronic platforms, tools and / or devices to annotate documents"; and (iii) agreeing on the format (for example, word-searchable PDF) and structure (for example, a separate PDF per document) at the outset, "so as to ensure consistency, ease of use and compatibility across the different systems".[121] Similarly, in order to make hard copy filings as environmentally sustainable as possible, the Model Procedural Order as well the various CGA Protocols include the following pragmatic advice for situations when the disputing parties and the members of the arbitral tribunal wish to exchange hard copies: (i) "[u]sing less paper (e.g. A5 size), grayscale, double-sided and / or reduced margin format where appropriate"; (ii) "[u]sing environmentally friendly toner and ink" and "recycled and recyclable, chlorine-free and / or tree-free paper"; and (iii) "[d]isposing of printed documents and associated materials (*e.g.* toner bottles) in an environmentally friendly way (*i.e.* by recycling shredded documents)".[122]

If the above measures are put in place, arbitration proceedings can suitably be made paperless and more environmentally sustainable.

3.3 *Conclusion: Are Greener Arbitrations the Future?*

The future of greener arbitrations seems more secure than that of virtual hearings. Although the phenomenon of virtual hearings has received some pushback, primarily on the ground of due process concerns arising out of the imposition of virtual hearings on the parties in complex cases when they have not agreed to the same, there is little to no opposition to the ongoing shift to paperless arbitrations. The international arbitration community is unanimously applauding the initiatives taken to make arbitrations greener. For instance, the CGA received the Global Arbitration Review's Award for Best Development of 2020.[123] Starting 2021 onwards, the Global Arbitration Review has included a category of awards titled the "Campaign for Greener

121 "Model Procedural Order," Campaign for Greener Arbitrations, accessed September 10, 2021, secs. II, IV, https://www.greenerarbitrations.com/green-protocols.

122 *Id.* at sec. II(b).

123 See "Campaign for Greener Arbitrations Wins GAR Award for Best Development," Campaign For Greener Arbitrations, accessed September 10, 2021, https://www.greenerarbitrations.com/news/campaign-for-greener-arbitrations-wins-gar-award-for-best-development.

Arbitration Award for sustainable behaviour", which was awarded to an initiative by Freshfields Bruckhaus Deringer that entailed establishing a Green Arbitration Task Force to further reduce the carbon footprint of its international arbitration practice through the implementation of the CGA's Green Pledge and launching the firm's five-year environment strategy, which includes a carbon offsetting program supporting the livelihoods of 9,000 farmers in Kenya and Uganda.[124]

Several other organizations and law firms have dedicated their energies towards similarly green programs, such as launching a carbon footprint application (CMS),[125] organization of collaborative drafting events to create new, practical contract clauses that deliver climate solutions (the Chancery Lane Project),[126] and creating net-zero carbon emission targets (Herbert Smith Freehills).[127] With arbitration institutions insisting on making electronic filings the default rule, arbitrators would also be more reluctant to overreach this default rule and request hard-copy filings. Accordingly, the international arbitration community has already taken assertive steps towards making arbitrations greener; steps that are likely to outlast the COVID-19 pandemic.

4 Conclusion: A Case for Environmental Efficiency

There is often a clash between two equally desirable objectives in international arbitration procedure: on the one hand, efficiency in terms of time and cost, and on the other hand, due process considerations stemming from the parties' right to present their case. This clash has affected several facets of the arbitration procedure, and in most situations, the latter considerations (of due process) have emerged victorious. Arbitral tribunals today exercise significant

124 See "Freshfields wins inaugural Green Arbitration Award," Campaign For Greener Arbitrations, accessed September 10, 2021, https://www.greenerarbitrations.com/news/freshfields-wins-inaugural-green-arbitration-award.

125 See "CMS Launches Carbon Footprint App To Encourage Behavioural Change," CMS, February 28, 2020, https://cms.law/en/gbr/news-information/cms-launches-carbon-footprint-app-to-encourage-behavioural-change.

126 See "About the Chancery Lane Project," The Chancery Lane Project, accessed September 14, 2021, https://chancerylaneproject.org/about/.

127 See "Herbert Smith Freehills Commits To Net-Zero Carbon Emissions By 2030," Herbert Smith Freehills, December 2, 2020, https://www.herbertsmithfreehills.com/latest-thinking/herbert-smith-freehills-commits-to-net-zero-carbon-emissions-by-2030.

restraint while resorting to their broad procedural discretion that allows them to fix concrete procedural mandates. For instance, tribunals, especially in high-profile arbitrations, are increasingly amenable to setting overly relaxed procedural timetables at the behest of the parties or to grant leave to the parties to file submissions or produce documentary (or other) evidence at a very late stage of the proceedings. Such conduct is the consequence of what has been referred to above as "due process paranoia". The reason that arbitral tribunals often fall prey to this paranoia is that most arbitration laws across jurisdictions allow State courts to set aside awards on grounds that the parties were "unable to present" their case. Article 34(2)(a)(ii) of the UNCITRAL Model Law stipulates these grounds for setting aside awards, as does Article V(1)(b) of the Convention on the Recognition and Enforcement of Foreign Arbitral Awards 1958 for refusal of enforcement of awards.[128]

When it comes to their discretion to conduct hearings virtually, arbitral tribunals may, in the coming times, be faced with situations that lie at the crossroads between time and cost efficiency and due process considerations. In other words, conducting a virtual hearing, in a given situation, may be the more efficient solution, but may nonetheless be painted by the parties as a violation of their right to present their case. In this regard, as discussed in the preceding Section 2, arbitral tribunals should, while taking the more efficient route, derive comfort from the broad discretion afforded to them by institutional rules to organize arbitral procedure in the manner deemed appropriate. Such discretion has also been upheld in recent case law that has rejected challenges to arbitral tribunals' independence and impartiality implicating their decision to conduct hearings virtually. Further, as also discussed in the preceding Section 3, although such due process considerations may not inhibit the conduct of arbitrations in a paperless manner, except when one of the disputing parties is defaulting, it is still incumbent upon arbitral tribunals to start walking the more efficient path and setting out greener procedural mandates for exchange of correspondences and submissions.

Other than the factors discussed in the preceding Sections, there is one additional factor that arbitral tribunals should bear in mind while prioritizing an efficient conduct of arbitration proceedings over their due process paranoia.

When it comes to procedural efficiency, time and cost have long been the only parameters against which such efficiency is measured. While there is no doubt that time and cost efficiency are important objectives that international

---

128 See Franco Ferrari et al., "Chapter 1: General Report," in *Due Process as a Limit to Discretion in International Commercial Arbitration*, eds. Franco Ferrari et al. (Kluwer Law International, 2020).

arbitration procedure should strive to achieve, the time is ripe to add a third tenet to this understanding of efficiency, namely "environmental efficiency". Ensuring that the arbitral process is organized keeping in mind environmental sustainability is an important objective that is not only necessary to pursue but is also relatively achievable in the context of international arbitration. After all, international arbitration is lauded for its procedural flexibility, which is indeed one of its biggest strengths, allowing it to seamlessly adapt to changing realities. The absence of rigid procedural mandates should accentuate the re-orientation of arbitral procedure in order for it to become more environmentally friendly. To that end, adding the tenet of environmental efficiency as a complementary factor to the objectives of time and cost efficiency can provide a pragmatic legal basis to support the viability of environmentally friendly measures, such as virtual hearings.

For instance, undertaking long-distance flight travels to convene in-person hearings that could just as easily have been conducted virtually may be justified on grounds of preserving due process if the only countering force to these due process concerns are considerations of efficiency relating to time and cost. However, if the countering force to frivolous allegations of due process violations includes not only time and cost but also environmental efficiency, arbitral tribunals may feel more comfortable rejecting such allegations and using their discretion more freely. Of course, if the due process concerns raised by parties are legitimate in the facts and circumstances of a case, no considerations of efficiency – be it time, cost or environment – can or should be able to offset the same. However, in situations where due process-related allegations are intended more to incite due process paranoia in tribunals as opposed to drawing their attention to a genuine due process concern, it is recommended that the objective of efficiency be broadened from time and cost efficiency to also include the notion of environmental efficiency.

Indeed, making environmental efficiency a mainstream objective that the international arbitration community sets out to pursue collectively is the only way to ensure that the phenomena of virtual hearings and greener arbitrations outlive the COVID-19 pandemic, without falling prey to due process paranoia, which is often all-consuming but seldom reasonable.

CHAPTER 3

"Virtual" Dispute Resolution in International Arbitration

Mapping Its Advantages and Main Caveats in the Face of COVID-19

Belen Olmos Giupponi

1 Introduction[1]

Before the COVID-19 pandemic, international arbitration embarked on the reform of the rules dealing with remote arbitration prompting a new wave of procedural regulations on the use of telematic means for the conduct of hearings and taking of evidence. As part of this trend, for instance, the German Arbitration Institute (DIS) and the Arbitration Institute of the Stockholm Chamber of Commerce (SCC) revised their respective rules. The COVID-19 pandemic acted as a major disruptor by bringing in significant effects on online dispute resolution. The impact of the pandemic has been significant on both substantial and procedural rules leading to adjustments. The panoply of rules emerging in the various arbitral setting poses several important questions.

The paper aims at throwing light on COVID-19-related effects on international arbitration rules by examining the delicate balance between competing priorities and the observance of legal principles (both of substantive and procedural nature). Even though e-arbitration is a major component of online dispute resolution ('ODR'), there are other processes in which parties can solve any dispute arising out of their contractual relationship online. Before the COVID-19 pandemic, e-arbitration was mainly used for the resolution of Business to Business ('B2B') cross-border e-commerce disputes, and only partly relied upon for the settlement of traditional cross-border commercial disputes.

The analysis proceeds in four parts. Firstly, it addresses the question of legitimacy and authority of norms providing for online arbitration. Although many arbitration rules already referred to virtual hearings, some of the more recent

1 This project was funded through an SNF Grant aimed at studying the impacts of COVID-19 on dispute resolution and international trade law. Previous versions of this paper were presented at the 7th Kuwait Law School Conference, "Digital revolution and its impact on investment dispute settlement" in 2020 and at the University of Lausanne in October 2021.

provisions were adopted as "technical notes" or "protocols" as emergency solutions. Their continuity in time might be subject to confirmation once the pandemic effects will be lessened. Secondly, the article turns the attention to the nature of the process and the different roles played by the parties and potential stakeholders. For those cases in which the arbitral agreement stipulated a specific "place of arbitration", the shift to a virtual environment could be considered detrimental for the parties' rights. This entails looking at these provisions through the lens of the due process of law principle and further examining the scope of the arbitrators' mandate. Thirdly, the article considers online dispute resolution's main advantages and drawbacks. Whereas online arbitration presents advantages in terms of cost efficiency, it may hinder transparency and the enjoyment of third party's rights, a rather recent achievement in international arbitration. This requires gearing new ways in which transparency could be articulated in a virtual environment. Fourthly, confidentiality and security concerns are examined. Although cyber security protocols and procedural orders dealing with the organization of virtual hearings attempt to avoid this, it might be difficult to rule out all risks in a real context. Finally, the paper advocates for a holistic approach to "virtual" dispute resolution, acknowledging the various interests at stake.

2 Legitimacy and Authority of the Emerging Online Arbitration Provisions: Is There a Right to Physical Hearings?

As the global pandemic unfolded, unprecedented measures adopted by governments across the globe to control the spread of the pandemic caused by novel coronavirus disease (COVID-19) led to an increase in the use of online technologies to manage both judicial and arbitral proceedings. This "new normal" pervaded different areas of the legal profession and ADR proceedings were no exception. The pandemic caused first disruption and then, adaptation to disruption. Even though the use of online dispute resolution (ODR) methods was widespread before the beginning of the COVID-19 pandemic, the restrictions imposed accelerated the digitalization of arbitral proceedings.

Portrayed as a "turning point", the COVID-19 pandemic prompted contrasting and conflicting views on the use of virtual means for international dispute settlement, particularly concerning arbitration.

At first glance, international arbitration might appear as a sector which would have been at the forefront of the use of new technologies. Parties tend to be located in different countries around the world and there was a somehow widespread use of the video-technology for some parts of the arbitral proceedings. Beyond the Case Management Conferences, however, the use of technology was less common for hearings. The prevailing tradition of in-person hearings, coupled with the notion of a right to a physical hearing, was regarded as a core element of "due process of law" or right to a fair trial.

Different concerns were raised as the COVID-19 pandemic was unfolding. At the beginning, videoconference hearings were introduced as emergency measures across different arbitral venues. Issues such as cybersecurity, effective conduct of virtual cross-examination, confidentiality, and potential breaches of due process were common in different jurisdictions. In an effort to efficiently face the challenge, arbitral institutions updated their rules while publishing guidelines and guidance to deal with these concerns.

2.1 *The Legal Nature of the Norms Regulating "Online Arbitration"*

Clearly, there is no "one-size-fits all" stance when it comes to online arbitration, as the approaches taken to deal with the disruption caused by the COVID-19 pandemic vary across arbitral institutions and in national settings. In terms of legitimacy and authority of these provisions, while many arbitration rules already referred to virtual hearings, some of the more recent provisions were adopted in the shape of "technical notes" or "protocols" more as emergency solutions rather than as new rules. Some of these protocols address practical problems faced at remote hearings and built-in safeguards for the appropriate conduct of the hearings (See Table 3.1). Thus, in the former case, the continuity of the rules in time might be subject to confirmation once the pandemic effects will be lessened.

One of the central questions posed is what type of proceedings can be considered as online or "e-arbitration". *Strictu sensu*, in e-arbitration the arbitration agreement is concluded, and the entire arbitral process is conducted online. Many computer software programs had already enabled multiple parties to participate in arbitral proceedings before the COVID-19 pandemic started. The question posed by the pandemic was whether the entire arbitral process could be held online.

Based on the existing rules, a safe assumption one can make is that the different stages of the arbitral proceedings may take place remotely if needed or decided by the parties or the arbitral tribunal. The controversial question arises when it comes to the main hearing. Hence, the crucial issue in this regard is what constitutes a "hearing"? UNCITRAL rule 17(3) states if any party request to hearing, there will be a hearing.

Clearly, wherever both parties to the arbitration consent to remote arbitration no legal question is posed. In the opposite scenario, however, if the arbitral tribunal would like to proceed with the virtual hearing it should adequately balance the rights of the parties.

2.2 *The "Right" to a Physical Hearing*

Another issue that was at the center of the debates was the existence of a right to a physical hearing as such and if, in the event of an online arbitration, that right was at risk. While the pandemic emphasized the need for a more widespread use of new technologies in arbitration, it brought questions about the legitimacy of the remote procedures and online proceedings.

The right to a hearing in international arbitration has been extensively analyzed in the literature by scholars such as Scherer[2] and Born.[3] The so-called right to a physical hearing is rooted in the right to be heard and coupled with equal treatment, which is, in turn, rooted in the human right to a fair trial.

In response to the increasing controversy generated by the remote arbitration procedures that were conducted during the COVID-19 pandemic, the International Council for Commercial Arbitration (ICCA) launched a project comprising a multitude of jurisdictions around the globe.[4] This project unveiled some differences between Civil and Common Law jurisdictions in terms of written and oral proceedings, without clearly identifying a divide between the different systems. The practice of international arbitration tends to focus on the physical hearing rather than on-screen proceedings. The opportunity for the parties to examine the evidence and cross-examine the witnesses by the other party is the core of adversarial proceedings.

Other issues raised during the pandemic are more related to the questions of oral advocacy and the right to directly address the witnesses. This correlates to the right to be heard and the right to receive proper notice. In turn, the right to be heard orally could be differentiated from the right to be heard in

2 Maxi Scherer, Dharshini Prasad, and Dina Prokic, "The Principle of Equal Treatment in International Arbitration," in *Cambridge Compendium of International Commercial and Investment Arbitration*, eds. Andrea Bjorklund, Franco Ferrari & Stefan Kröll (Cambridge University Press, 2020). Velislava Hristova and Malcolm Robach, "Legal and Practical Aspects of Virtual Hearings During (and After?) the Pandemic: Takeaway From the SCC Online Seminar Series," Kluwer Arbitration Blog, May 16, 2020, http://arbitrationblog.kluwerarbitration.com/2020/05/16/legal-and-practical-aspects-of-virtual-hearings-during-and-after-the-pandemic-takeaway-from-the-scc-online-seminar-series/.

3 Alvaro Galindo, "Arbitration Unplugged Series – Virtual hearing: Present or Future?," May 23, 2020, http://arbitrationblog.kluwerarbitration.com/2020/05/23/arbitration-unplugged-series-virtual-hearing-present-or-future/.

4 "Does a Right to a Physical Hearing Exist in International Arbitration?," ICCA, accessed December 20, 2021, https://www.arbitration-icca.org/right-to-a-physical-hearing-international-arbitration, ("ICCA Report on Right to Hearings" or "ICCA Report").

writing, which is a common procedural principle. It stems from the right to receive equal treatment, which is a widespread right across different jurisdictions. Online arbitration may raise concerns about anything that can limit the parties' freedom to design their own arbitration procedure.

The right to a hearing or to a fair trial is also related to the recognition and enforcement of arbitral awards. The New York Convention on the Recognition and Enforcement of Foreign Arbitral Awards of 1958 ("The New York Convention") stipulates the non recognition of an award if the party facing recognition of the award "was not given proper notice of the appointment of the arbitrator or the arbitration proceedings or was otherwise unable to present his case".[5]

In terms of the UNCITRAL Model Law, articles 18 and 24 refer to equal treatment and the conduct of hearings during the arbitral procedure. Article 18 deals with the equal treatment of parties.[6] The parties shall be treated with equality and each party shall be given a full opportunity of presenting his case. Though, in the 2010 amended version, this was narrowed to state that each party should be given reasonable opportunity to present its case at an appropriate stage of the proceeding. Despite apparent differences, the divide between Civil Law and Common Law traditions dissipates when it comes to online arbitration.[7]

The determination of whether a hearing could take place through virtual means entails a case-by-case analysis. Article 24 states that "(1) Subject to any contrary agreement by the parties, the arbitral tribunal shall decide whether to hold oral hearings for the presentation of evidence or for oral argument, or whether the proceedings shall be conducted on the basis of documents and other materials. However, unless the parties have agreed that no hearings shall be held, the arbitral tribunal shall hold such hearings at an appropriate stage of the proceedings, if so requested by a party. (2) The parties shall be given sufficient advance notice of any hearing and of any meeting of the arbitral tribunal for the purposes of inspection of goods, other property or documents. (3) All statements, documents or other information supplied to the arbitral tribunal by one party shall be communicated to the other party. Also, any expert report

5 United Nations Convention on the Recognition and Enforcement of Foreign Arbitral Awards (New York, June 10, 1958), Art. V.1.b.

6 UNCITRAL Model Law on International Commercial Arbitration, Chapter V. Conduct of Arbitral Proceedings, Art. 18. Equal treatment of parties.

7 Ihab Amro, "Online Arbitration in Theory and in Practice: A Comparative Study in Common Law and Civil Law Countries," Kluwer Arbitration Blog, April 11, 2019, http://arbitrationblog.kluwerarbitration.com/2019/04/11/online-arbitration-in-theory-and-in-practice-a-comparative-study-in-common-law-and-civil-law-countries/.

or evidentiary document on which the arbitral tribunal may rely in making its decision shall be communicated to the parties".[8]

Even before the pandemic started, the Prague rules[9] and the LCIA rules provided guidance for online hearings.[10] The Prague rules contemplate the resolution of the dispute on a documents only basis, if it is appropriate, and to promote cost-efficiency.[11] The rules also provide for online arbitration, in the following terms: "[i]f one of the parties requests a hearing or the arbitral tribunal itself finds it appropriate, the parties and the arbitral tribunal shall seek to organize the hearing in the most cost-efficient manner possible, including by limiting the duration of the hearing and using video, electronic or telephone communication to avoid unnecessary travel costs for arbitrators, parties and other participants".[12]

The controversy arises when holding a virtual hearing even against the objection of a party. It should be noted that there is consensus about the legal power of arbitrators under their mandate to order a virtual hearing, as there are no national laws or institutional rules which either prohibit or impose the use of virtual hearings. In the face of silence of the norms, arbitral tribunals would follow some general principles. Ultimately, the arbitral tribunal may decide to have an oral hearing or to have proceedings on the documents only.

3 Nature of the Online Dispute Resolution Processes, Parties' Roles, and Applicable Principles

Turning now the attention to the nature of the process and the different roles performed by the parties to the arbitration proceedings, in online arbitration the parties display similar roles as in traditional arbitration. The arbitrator's mandate includes the power to organise the hearing and decide on the manner

8 UNCITRAL Model Law on International Commercial Arbitration, *supra* note 6, at Art. 24. Hearings and written proceedings.

9 "Rules on the Efficient Conduct of Proceedings in International Arbitration," accessed December 11, 2021, https://praguerules.com/upload/medialibrary/9dc/9dc31ba7799e26473d92961d926948c9.pdf ("Prague Rules").

10 The "Prague Rules" were adopted on December 14, 2018, and are available for parties to adopt in their arbitration proceedings. The Rules were drafted by a Working Group formed of representatives from mostly civil law based jurisdictions. The rules may be used alongside any institutional or ad hoc rules that might apply.

11 Prague Rules, Art. 8. Hearings, Art. 8.1.

12 *Id.* at Art. 8.2.

in which the arbitral proceedings will be conducted. In the face of the COVID-19 pandemic, many courts suspended court proceedings. Due to court closures and proceeding postponements, online arbitration was the preferred method. Key issues and considerations regarding virtual arbitration are mainly related to the fairness of arbitral proceedings so conducted.

The form applicable to online arbitral proceedings is not as strict when compared to traditional arbitration.[13] In an arbitration held completely online, as seen before, different stages and elements of the arbitral proceedings take place online. Some commentators argue that, in some cases, such as in e-commerce the form is even less relevant. Hence, if the electronic document is sufficiently precise, setting up clear elements that may infer online dispute resolution, this can be used in the future to hold a remote arbitration.

Various Civil Law jurisdictions, such as Germany, France, Austria, Slovenia, Greece, The Netherlands, Ukraine, and Switzerland have expanded the form requirement as regulated by the New York Convention to also include electronic communications such as e-mail notifications. This broad consideration of "form" has led to case law about the interpretation of "any other means of communication" as in *Compagnie de Navigation et Transports SA v. MSC Mediterranean Shipping Company SA*, decided by the Swiss Supreme Court.[14] In that case, Article II (2) of the New York Convention was interpreted broadly, to also comprise within its wording the "exchange of letters or telegrams".[15] In addition, the Court found that the form requirement was also met, as this was equivalent to the form stipulated by Article 178(1) of the Swiss Code on Private International Law.[16]

Emphasis has been placed on the arbitrators' mandate; commentators agree on the arbitral tribunal's power to decide whether a procedure should take place remotely or on documents if they deem it appropriate. This decision ought to be made as a balancing exercise weighing, on one hand, the duty (and the correlative power) to conduct the proceedings efficiently and, on the other hand, the parties' right to be heard and to equality. When properly dealt with and the rights are respected in a virtual hearing, all parties would have been heard online.

13 Amro, *supra* note 7.

14 "Switzerland," New York Convention Data Base, January 16, 1995, https://newyorkconvention1958.org/index.php?lvl=notice_display&id=564.

15 *Id.*

16 *Id.*

In certain jurisdictions, applicable national laws grant parties a right to a hearing, as the Swedish Arbitration Act (SAA), however, this does not translate, *strictu sensu,* into a right to a physical hearing.

With regard to the question of location (place and venue to conduct the hearing), the law of the arbitral seat and the institutional procedural rules applicable to arbitration may refer to the right to a hearing in a less stringent fashion. A common rule found across institutional arbitration rules stipulates that if any party to an arbitration requests a hearing, the arbitral tribunal should hold a hearing. For those cases in which the arbitral agreement stipulated a specific "place of arbitration" the shift to a virtual environment could be considered detrimental for the parties' rights. This entails looking at these provisions through the lens of the due process of law principle and further examining the scope of the arbitrators' mandate.

Before the pandemic, it was usual for hearings to be held remotely by tele-conferencing. As the adaption to disruption became the new normal, arbitrators would include the virtual setting to conduct international arbitrations. Arbitrators' powers depend on the various stages of the arbitral proceedings.

Exploring more closely the advantages and paradoxes of online international arbitration, one should examine the arbitrator's power vis-à-vis the parties' rights. From a certain viewpoint, it seems as if the question at issue would be whether the arbitrator's powers might be in contradiction with the parties' rights to fairly conducted arbitral proceedings.

What transpires when examining the different rules is that there is no one-size-fits-all approach in terms of ODR. Different levels of automation are observed across the board. Contrary to the impression that ODR may offer the possibility of an easy "click and settle", there are several layers of complexity. There is a wide range of possibilities according to different types of norms on online arbitration.

Clauses may stipulate the number of arbitrators required to decide a case. The legacy of emerging rules and protocols during the pandemic also relates to properly identifying the applicable international procedural or evidence principles.

Going forward, what is interesting is the contribution to more substantive principles about international online dispute settlement or resolution (IODR). IODR has a broader scope, as it encompasses, negotiation and mediation as well. It has grown exponentially during the pandemic. If it is possible to draw a comparison between arbitration and mediation, in the case of mediation the disruption caused by the pandemic has had a bigger impact because of the nature of the method. Space precludes a more detailed analysis.

Distinctive features of the rules present different nuances. The design of effective mechanisms to regulate the resolution of disputes online should take into consideration these differences. Positive externalities as incentives to broaden the use of online international arbitration include cutting down the greenhouse gas emissions. These positive environmental externalities are highlighted by the different protocols on greener arbitrations.[17]

Overall, the advantages offset the downsides of online international arbitration. There are questions like data protection and cyber-security that may pose a challenge to the confidentiality of the proceedings, the privacy of the parties and the protection of industrial secrets. The leeway different rules allow to the parties in order to choose the type of dispute resolution rules varies, an example of this is the 2021 Arbitration Rules of the Danish Institute for Arbitration.[18]

Confidentiality concerns have been at the heart of the debates, as new technologies also raise the question of cyber security breaches. Some ODR protocols provide for solutions to minimize the risks of cybersecurity breaches. Others provide a range of cyber-arbitration options along with other dispute resolution methods, including negotiation and mediation.

There has been an exponential increase in the number of ODR platforms in recent years. The variety of available platforms reveals different levels of sophistication. These platforms give technological leverage to handle uploads and downloads, granting a certain level of protection in the face of cyber threats. Different platforms align with rules and international standards to ensure cybersecurity, such as the 2020 Cybersecurity Protocol for International Arbitration.[19] Platforms embody stricter measures to ensure cybersecurity in line with international standards (ISO).

Given the relevance of the principle of confidentiality in international arbitration, measures like multi-factor authentication to accessing sensitive information have become crucial. The 2020 Protocol in Principles 7 (b) and (c) refer to security measures in international arbitration that should contemplate

17 "Introduction to the Green Protocols," Campaign For Greener Arbitration, accessed December 20, 2021, https://www.greenerarbitrations.com/global-session-invitation.

18 "The 2021 Arbitration Rules," The Danish Institute of Arbitration, entered into force April 13, 2021, https://voldgiftsinstituttet.dk/en/arbitration/rules-arbitration/.

19 "Protocol on Cybersecurity in International Arbitration (2020 Edition)," ICCA-NYC Bar-CPR, accessed December 20, 2021, https://cdn.arbitration-icca.org/s3fs-public/document/media_document/icca-nyc_bar-cpr_cybersecurity_protocol_for_international_arbitration_-_print_version.pdf.

"asset management", "access controls", "encryption of data", and "information security incident management".[20]

As with traditional international arbitration, the question of fairness remained central in the debates about the convenience of online arbitration. Generally, online arbitration offers greater flexibility vis-à-vis traditional international arbitration. To ensure that arbitration takes place in an appropriate setting that offers the guarantees of stability, transparency, and communication, parties should follow the protocols and the applicable norms.

Other issues raised with regard to IODR, concern how to catch up with the ever-evolving technology and adjust the arbitral procedure to the virtual/online environment. In the post-pandemic context, for some cases, face-to-face arbitration should be seen still as a priority. Online arbitration, would offer the benefits of more agile and flexible methods, which represents an advantage when dealing with international and very complex cases.

4 Exploring Advantages and Disadvantages of Virtual Arbitration beyond the Pandemic

In view of the rules adopted during the pandemic, the question is how such rules will evolve in a post-pandemic context.[21] At the same time, different logistics must be in place to guarantee an efficient conduct of the arbitration that respects the parties' rights. In terms of cost efficiency, online dispute resolution presents its clear advantages over traditional arbitration as it entails cost-efficiency in terms of travel and organization. The ability to proceed remotely to hold arbitration hearings has been made clear during the COVID-19 pandemic. Arbitral procedures could be efficiently managed in a virtual environment through the various available online dispute resolution platforms.[22] As a general matter, remote arbitration could take place through different paths. Parties and their legal teams can be located in the same venue

20 *Id.*

21 Namrata Mayur Shah, "Think Arbi: Has Technology Worsened the Conduct of Arbitrations?," Lexology, December 23, 2021, https://www.lexology.com/library/detail.aspx?g=6b27e7da-d318-4017-8e42-2faebe402e05.

22 Wendy Gonzales and Naimeh Masumy, "Online Dispute Resolution Platforms: Cybersecurity Champions in the COVID-19 Era? Time for Arbitral Institutions to Embrace ODRs," Kluwer Arbitration Blog, September 25, 2020, http://arbitrationblog.kluwerarbitration.com/2020/09/25/online-dispute-resolution-platforms-cybersecurity-champions-in-the-covid-19-era-time-for-arbitral-institutions-to-embrace-odrs/.

and then communicate remotely with the other party and the respective legal team.

However, online arbitration may hinder transparency and the enjoyment of the so-called third party's rights, a rather recent achievement in international arbitration. Prior to the COVID-19 pandemic, many arbitral institutions modified their rules to allow for more transparency by allowing third parties to make submissions, to access the documents and to attend the hearings in some cases. Remote arbitration would require creating new ways in which transparency could be articulated in a virtual environment. Another potential downside of remote arbitration relates to the issue of confidentiality, as several security concerns were voiced particularly regarding issues such as electronic data breaches, or cyberattacks that could affect the security and privacy of the parties, industrial secrets, and case information. There are some precedents already available before the pandemic whereas others were adopted during the COVID-19 pandemic, like the Cybersecurity Protocol for International Arbitration (2020).[23]

Setting the scene for a new era in international arbitration, this pandemic reinforced the idea of cutting costs, increasing the efficiency of the arbitral proceedings, and, also, promoting environmental considerations. The Protocols for Greener Arbitrations, include the guidance on hearing venues: "provides arbitration facilities and hearing centers and individuals therein with concrete steps to minimize their environmental impact as regards their daily operating procedures or as related to a particular matter".[24]

To illustrate the impact of rules adopted during the COVID-19 pandemic, three different sets of rules are examined: *the ICC Guidance Note on Possible Measures Aimed at Mitigating the Effects of the COVID-19 Pandemic* (adopted on 19 April 2020) (hereinafter referred to as "ICC Guidance Note"), *HKIAC Guidelines for Virtual Hearings* (issued on 14 May 2020) (hereinafter referred to as "HKIAC Guidelines") and *Seoul Protocol on Video Conference in International Arbitration* (released on 18 March 2020)[25] (hereinafter referred to as "Seoul Protocol") were drafted to assist tribunals (See Table 3.1).[26]

---

23 The Protocol was developed jointly by representatives of the International Council for Commercial Arbitration, the New York City Bar Association and Alternatives' publisher and the International Institute for Conflict Prevention & Resolution.

24 "Green Protocols," Campaign For Greener Arbitrations, accessed December 20, 2021, https://www.greenerarbitrations.com/green-protocols.

25 Tariq Mahmood, "The Seoul Protocol on Video Conferencing in light of Covid-19," 33 Bedford Row, April 11, 2020, https://www.33bedfordrow.co.uk/insights/articles/the-seoul-protocol-on-video-conferencing-in-light-of-covid-19.

26 The Seoul Protocol is a joint-project by the Korea Commercial Arbitration Board ("KCAB") and the Seoul International Dispute Resolution Center ("Seoul IDRC").

TABLE 3.1 Comparison between some of the rules adopted during the COVID-19 pandemic

Rules	ICC Guidance Note	HKIAC Guidelines	Seoul Protocol
Guidance for virtual hearings	Basic rules	Very detailed rules	Guidelines for best practice
Efficiency	Parties to consider certain measures that promote efficiency during arbitral proceedings.	Parties should promote efficiency during arbitral proceedings, but encourages parties to use available resources of the institution.	There is no specific provision on efficiency. Parties should test all video conferencing equipment and that adequate backup equipment is available for use.
Submissions	Rather than submitting hard copies, for instance, the ICC Guidance Note recommends that tribunals encourage parties to communicate electronically to the fullest extent possible.	The HKIAC Guidelines aim at promoting efficiency during arbitral proceedings, encouraging parties to use available resources of the institution. Some services (i.e., video conferencing, interpretation, electronic bundling and presentation of evidence, etc.) are considered essential when organizing a virtual hearing. The HKIAC offers resources such as IP-based encrypted and cloud-based video conferencing.	The Seoul Protocol offers guidance concerning the logistical challenges presented by remote arbitration hearings. The focus is placed on default standards applicable to streamline video-conference proceedings. There are some basic rules to avoid disruption, like, for instance, testing of all video conferencing equipment and backup equipment (i.e., cable back-ups, teleconferencing, etc.).

TABLE 3.1 Comparison between some of the rules adopted during the COVID-19 pandemic (*cont.*)

Rules	ICC Guidance Note	HKIAC Guidelines	Seoul Protocol
Logistics and venue	The ICC Guidance Note provides no guidance regarding venue.	HKIAC Guidelines do not comprise any rules about logistics and venue.	The Seoul Protocol contains very detailed rules, covering minimum standards for venues where the video conference take place, referring to on-call IT technicians, safeguarded cross-border connections to prevent unlawful interception by third parties and security of video conference participants. Art. 5.1 to 5.6, address various points from audio output device to communication lines and screen width.
Hearings Examination of Witnesses and Experts	The Guidance Note includes the use of multi-screens, and synchronous communications between witnesses and parties are permissible in chat rooms or through concealed channels of communication. As an innovative feature, the Guidance includes provisions on connection, time and duration of availability.	The HKIAC Guidelines briefly mention remote witness and expert hearings. The guidelines include arranging a hearing invigilator to attend at the same place as the witness. As another special feature, the guidelines provide for a 360-degree viewing of the room by video at the beginning of each session of the virtual hearing.	The Seoul Protocol addresses witness examination hearings in Art. 1. Under the Protocol the tribunal holds considerable discretion to decide to terminate the witness examination via video conferencing, in cases when it deems the video conference unsatisfactory making it unfair for either party to continue.

TABLE 3.1 Comparison between some of the rules adopted during the COVID-19 pandemic (*cont.*)

Rules	ICC Guidance Note	HKIAC Guidelines	Seoul Protocol
		Security is paramount and an update on how security can be maintained throughout the entire hearing is required.	Witness statements should be given, including "a reasonable part of the interior of the room in which the Witness is located be shown on screen, while retaining sufficient proximity to clearly depict the Witness".

SOURCE: AUTHOR'S OWN ELABORATION BASED ON RULE AND KLUWER INTERNATIONAL ARBITRATION

Drivers or factors for online case management in arbitration are, amongst others, cost reduction, increase of the efficiency, and speedy solutions. Each factor should be properly assessed to determine relevance, depending on the circumstances of the particular case. The relevance and weight of these factors vary across jurisdictions, depending on the approach taken by the respective procedural law applicable to the case. It is crucial for arbitral participants to adopt adequate online case management tools for processing of data during the proceedings.

Efficiency and effectiveness are considered key factors when assessing the convenience of the virtual setting and tools in international arbitration. Before the pandemic, there were already efforts to shift towards the use of digital tools in international arbitration to increase efficiency and effectiveness of the arbitral proceedings. Platforms can help to facilitate collaboration by sharing documents in a secure manner. In the report compiled by the aforementioned task force, it is also noted that platforms could significantly reduce the number of asynchronous communications (such as email or other data storage facilities) over the course of the proceedings.[27]

With regard to the convenience of having an online repository of case data in the handling of proceedings, this is seen as a way of avoiding duplication of tasks and enhancing consistency across the board. More advanced platforms include other possibilities which enable arbitration stakeholders to add up other tasks going beyond upload, download, and the storage of documents.

A particular question concerning the use of platforms is with respect to other functionalities offered by them, such as quality, control, and appropriate referencing. These new platforms could assist parties, tribunals, and institutions in establishing efficient workflows, providing better communication channels, running analytics over case data, identifying and handling particular types of data (e.g. personal data) and managing pleadings, evidence, hearing bundles, and awards. In this manner, parties may be in a better position to present their respective cases, particularly, in complex disputes that involve high volumes of documentary evidence.[28]

In other arbitral venues, such as the ICSID, arbitral institutions provide general guidance on services and technology. Although there are no specific rules, there is some general guidance about the proceedings and the benefits of using virtual hearings in ICSID administered arbitrations, conciliations, mediations,

27 ICCA Report, *supra* note 4, at point 20.

28 *Id.* at point 21.

and fact-finding proceedings.[29] These virtual solutions involve first-class security by using end-to-end encryption, following the World Bank Group's security and risk requirements. As an example of best practice, within the ICSID, there is a service for court reporting and interpretation: a virtual court stenographer provides a real-time transcript of the proceeding, visible to all participants on the video-conference and simultaneous interpretation in multiple languages.

At the heart of all these initiatives, the controversial question that is posed is whether a right to a physical hearing exists. Seemingly, there is not such an established right that is universally recognized across all jurisdictions.[30] Some studies have unveiled how legal issues arose in different jurisdictions due to the increased use of remote arbitral hearings triggered by the COVID-19 pandemic.[31] The project conducted in the framework of the ICCA and the resulting report concluded that, in the majority of jurisdictions, there is no such right.

According to the reports, the right to a physical hearing does not seem to be included in jurisdictions' arbitration laws. The study demonstrated that many provisions give arbitral tribunals broad procedural discretion to decide how hearings are conducted and provisions in the arbitration rules of the most relevant institutions in those jurisdictions expressly allowing remote hearings. Based on this analysis, most legislations foresee the possibility for tribunals to order virtual hearings, documents-only arbitration being quite exceptional.

Disadvantages may depend on advocacy style and the adaptation of cross-examination to the new virtual arbitral environment. Another drawback relates to risks of technological failures and cybersecurity issues. Closely related to this there is the question of confidentiality of the arbitral proceedings, which covers and protects the hearings themselves, related-events, and access to any data (documents, videos, and transcripts). Protocols guarantee that data can be properly secured and safeguarded. Nevertheless, some procedural fairness implications remain, such as when a party opposes a virtual hearing.

Whether this can be implied from the *lex arbitri*, clear separation of the rules of legal procedure which may entail such a right to a physical hearing. There is almost a universal recognition that a party, who alleges it has a right

29 "Virtual Hearings," ICSID, accessed October 1, 2021, https://icsid.worldbank.org/services/hearing-facilities/virtual-hearings#:~:text=ICSID%20provides%20comprehensive%20services%20and,of%20rules%20at%20competitive%20rates.

30 In September 2020, Giacomo Rojas Elgueta, James Hosking, and Yasmine Lahlou, in collaboration with ICCA, launched the research project "Does a Right to a Physical Hearing Exist in International Arbitration?," *supra* note 4.

31 See the reports per jurisdiction in "Does a Right to a Physical Hearing Exist in International Arbitration?," *supra* note 4.

to a physical hearing must object during the proceedings to its violation or be deemed to have waived that right to seek the setting-aside or non-recognition of the award. As to the question of whether a right to a physical hearing is expressly recognized or, if it can be inferred from the *lex arbitri* (or other rules), the vast majority of the reports from different jurisdictions did not find that such a right exists. The surveys did not yield an express provision prohibiting the conduct of remote hearings, subject to the fulfillment of certain fundamental procedural guarantees.

Some jurisdictions recognize the right of the party to request an oral hearing, but whether such oral hearing translates to the right to a physical hearing is excluded in many Model Law jurisdictions, like Argentina, Croatia, Iran, Ireland, and Jamaica.[32] In a minority of jurisdictions, of which Zimbabwe is an example, the right to an oral hearing may arguably lead to a right to a physical hearing.[33]

Ultimately, it is the arbitrator's power to decide on the hearing and the proceedings in the way he or she deems appropriate, so long as the parties are allowed to present their case. From the arbitrator's perspective, there are two balancing considerations: one is due process which requires a case-by-case and fact-specific logistical inquiry of the party's ability to attend a hearing remotely and effectively present its case.

There are also considerations to be made about access to justice and the duty to decide the disputes within a reasonable time as set out in Article 6 of the European Convention of Human Rights. Whenever the parties have agreed to a remote hearing, can the arbitral tribunal ignore or override that agreement if they had agreed before the pandemic started? In some cases this may lead to the setting aside of the award like in Bangladesh, Benin, Dominican Republic and Finland. The requirement for the setting aside is qualified as it requires that the violation of the parties' agreement has had a material impact on the outcome of the case or caused substantial injustice.

Another controversial issue is whether the parties' agreement can be superseded. In many jurisdictions, the parties' agreement can be superseded on the grounds of fairness or efficiency, if holding a physical hearing would no longer be possible due to COVID-19 pandemic restrictions, as in Bulgaria, Bolivia, Hong Kong or Mauritius. Or, for example, if respecting the parties' agreement would delay the conclusion of the arbitration beyond the statutory limit, as in the UAE or violate the arbitrator's duty to conduct the proceedings without any

32 ICCA Report, *supra* note 4.

33 *Id.*

delays. This seems to be the general trend based on the results of the survey reports about the right to a physical hearing.

As an emerging trend, after the pandemic restrictions have been lifted, potentially, States and governments may attempt to further define a physical hearing is. In terms of governments legislating on the basis of this trend and States' behavior while considering how to amend legislation in this regard, most governments have been dealing with this pandemic and no attention has been paid to either amending the *lex arbitri* or the rules of civil procedure.

While during the pandemic, some emergency orders have been put in place to deal with the access to justice issues in certain jurisdictions; those orders were adopted in relation to cases that involved the violation of human rights, such as gender-based violence; in other words, in cases in which it was necessary to grant access to justice as a matter of human rights. With regard to commercial disputes in the context of international commercial arbitration, there is no similar urgency related to arbitral proceedings and the right to a fair trial is not intended to be taken literally. In the vein of the right to physical hearings, when the public health emergency will be lessened, it is foreseeable that there will be an amendment to the rules to confirm that there is no violation of the right when hearings are held remotely. Logistically, there have been cases in which the hardware has been provided to counteract the illegitimate or unwise protest by some parties to a remote hearing.

Clearly, there are technological constraints determined by the specific circumstances of the countries, such as the lack of reliable internet connections. Access to a stable connection and frequent power outages may affect the right to a fair trial. Internet access varies considerably amongst countries and regions. According to the World Bank data (2019), internet accessibility and speed varies across regions and countries, whilst 80% of the population has access to the internet in the Americas and 88% in Europe, the percentages are less in Asia (48.8%) and Africa (28%).[34]

5 An Emerging New Paradigm or Returning to Business as Usual?

Even before the pandemic, case management hearings could be held online with less resistance from the parties. Evidence-taking hearings were far more

34 "Individuals using the Internet (% of population)," The World Bank, accessed December 20, 2021, https://data.worldbank.org/indicator/IT.NET.USER.ZS.

controversial, particularly, in complex cases involving expensive disputes. The COVID-19 pandemic has emphasized the need for more detailed rules on virtual hearings. However, the question consists of whether in a post-pandemic context we will witness a new paradigm or be returning to a business as usual situation. Claims such as those concerning the need for a "greening" of international arbitration (both commercial and investment) are raising awareness and building on pressure to use more sustainable methods and tools in dispute resolution.

In the current scenario, if the arbitral tribunal so wishes, the hearings may proceed remotely. Practical and logistical issues may arise as discussed in the previous sections. Lack of consensus may happen if any of the parties does not want to conduct the hearings in person. Valid arguments can be posed by the claimant (e.g. need to present the case with in-person examination of evidence) or by the respondent (similarly, when the party objects to virtual hearings as an impairment to their right of defense). Those cases may be tackled and solved by setting a hybrid type of proceeding combining both methods. More complicated are those disputes in which both parties oppose the tribunal's decision or invitation for virtual proceedings. In these controversial cases, if the arbitral tribunal decides to go ahead, this can lead to recognition or setting aside proceedings against the award.

Although cyber security protocols and procedural orders dealing with the organization of virtual hearings attempt to avoid and minimize risks, it might be difficult to rule them out. From a more holistic approach to "virtual" dispute resolution as a whole, the various interests at stake should be taken into consideration. As discussed previously, different positions concerning online hearings have demonstrated the need for a more consistent approach to virtual proceedings in a post-pandemic context. It became apparent that a virtual hearing does not necessarily mean that the hearing meets all the requirements under article 18 of the Model Law and Article 5.1 (b) and (d) of the New York Convention, in the sense of equal treatment and full opportunity of presenting the case as well as the right to be heard.

This entails unpacking the right to willingly participate in a virtual hearing and separating it from the right to be heard and equally treated. Insofar as virtual hearings are concerned, the acceptance to conduct the hearing through remote means does not imply the exercise of the right to be heard. The latter can nevertheless be infringed, like in the case of unequal access to the use of technology and accessibility that can have practical implications. In any event, the new "business as usual" scenario with regard to international arbitration may incorporate some elements of remote arbitration and virtual proceedings.

Summing up the arguments, in a non-exhaustive way, in terms of advantages and drawbacks of remote arbitration, several features can be noted.

5.1 *Remote Arbitration, Efficiency, Time and Cost Management*

One of the key questions in international arbitration is how to effectively manage time and costs; e-arbitration offers these benefits, as a clear comparative advantage. In line with green arbitration protocol claims, remote arbitration eliminates the need for the parties to move between countries, hence, reducing travelling and costs. Overall, e-arbitration improves time and costs, offering solutions when it is not possible to convene the parties in one place or the same venue.

5.2 *Flexibility of the Arbitration Rules*

During the COVID-19 pandemic, arbitration proceedings became more flexible and the various arbitral rules adjusted, responding to the challenges posed by the several restrictions imposed by governments. In comparison with rigid court procedures or, even, with traditional arbitration, remote arbitration encourages a more agile resolution of disputes in a less formal manner.

5.3 *Confidentiality and Access to Justice*

In a broad sense, access to justice is facilitated due to the removal of geographical barriers, however, potential obstacles arise from unequal access to connectivity and familiarity with the virtual environment. E-arbitration may bring challenges to the confidentiality due to potential breaches of cybersecurity attacks.

5.4 *Asynchronous Procedures and Streamlined Communication*

Unlike face-to-face discussions, when asynchronous proceedings take place, they offer an opportunity to cool off and revisit the claims and arguments presenting an opportunity to amicably resolve the dispute. Equally, when effectively managed, communication can be facilitated and the overall speed of the proceedings improved.

Remote arbitration still faces various obstacles on different fronts, the lack of face-to-face contact may create difficult communication. Similarly, access to resources and tools as well as access to appropriate literacy, coupled with insufficient confidentiality and secrecy of proceedings, and other barriers may be considered as some of the main critical problems.

5.5 *Consent*

This is a central challenge with respect to remote arbitration. As discussed, although, the arbitral tribunal can exercise its power and decide to conduct the proceedings online, it can meet the resistance of one or both parties. During the COVID-19 pandemic, there were fewer options available but in a relatively normal context opposition can happen and curtail the possibilities of an e-procedure. Amendments to the arbitration rules could pre-empt these problems from happening.

5.6 *Place of Arbitration*

The choice of the place of arbitration has legal implications and ramifications. The geographical location of the proceedings cannot be determined when they are held completely electronically with the parties in different locations. In principle, it seems difficult to pinpoint the place of the arbitral proceedings unless there is clear agreement between the parties about this.

5.7 *Access to Justice and Transparency Issues*

In accordance with the arbitral tribunal's powers and the requirements of the parties based on their own convenience, remote arbitration can be accessed anywhere at any time where an internet connexion is available. However, this does not translate into immediate and equal access to a connection. One of the most important drawbacks of video conferencing is the lack of a stable connection. In terms of transparency, third parties with a legitimate interest may see their rights curtailed.

5.8 *Data Storage and Data Protection*

These are two sensitive areas in e-arbitration which are intertwined with the question of confidentiality. Filing problems are also considered when discussing the advantages and disadvantages of remote arbitration. Cyber-attacks are exposing the weaknesses of the e-arbitration system. Some practical solutions exist, such as agreeing on a single IT provider or using a specifically-designed platform such as the ones used for institutional arbitrations (such as those administered by the ICC).[35]

6 Concluding Remarks

Before and after COVID-19, transnational contracts and investment projects with parties located in different countries prompted the remote resolution of disputes. The dynamics of transnational contracts resulting from COVID-19-related developments are posing new challenges to the international

35 International Chamber of Commerce (ICC), "ICC Virtual Hearings," International Chamber of Commerce (ICC), accessed December 20, 2021, https://iccwbo.org/dispute-resolution-services/hearing-centre/icc-virtual-hearings/.

arbitration system. Cases of force majeure and breach of specific contracts clauses across different areas are emerging, including commercial law and investment law disputes, drawing on relevant case law.

During the COVID-19 pandemic, major international arbitration institutions already began accepting the necessity of virtual hearings in certain situations. Guidelines for virtual hearings were officially announced with the escalation of the COVID-19 pandemic.

In a post-pandemic scenario, it will be quintessential for the correct management of virtual arbitral proceedings that new rules and norms concerning virtual hearings will be adopted. The neutrality of the international arbitral procedures and settings have been put in the spotlight during the COVID-19 pandemic.

Best practice models are looking at ways to effectively conduct arbitral proceedings. Inequality in access to connectivity and tools was heightened during the pandemic. Moving forward, a more streamlined view of international arbitration, that envisions minimizing travel costs and cutting emissions is sorely needed.

The various responses in international arbitration to deal with the disruptions caused by the pandemic have not been uniform. Some sets of rules already existing were fit to address the situation. Rules set up in some institutional frameworks have spelled out criteria in rules and protocols.

For the future of remote arbitration, the focus will be placed on dispute resolution of emerging controversies in light of the obligation to negotiate in good faith, which implies an analysis of the different possible legal avenues to settle the disputes through remote arbitration.

Hybrid or semi-remotely held hearings are less controversial and will take place without much difficulty. The law of the seat will still be relevant to determine the applicable principles to govern the hearing. Applicable arbitral rules would determine if the hearing can be conducted remotely.

Measures to adapt to COVID-19 represented a shift in the conduct of the arbitration. Guidelines, rules and protocols to expedite online procedures are in order. In the context of the pandemic, with all the measures on border closure, essential travel regulations, entry and exit bans, the decisions to conduct the arbitral proceedings online was justified. Ultimately, the arbitral tribunal must conduct a balancing exercise. Debates about what constitutes a virtual hearing have underlined the relevance of clearly defining concepts and terms in light of technology and progress in communications. Once the restrictions are lifted, the legacy of these challenging times will stay. Virtual hearing guidelines, rules and protocols have consolidated good practice across different arbitral venues.

CHAPTER 4

The Impact of COVID-19 on International Arbitration Procedure

Kristen M. Young, Jennifer A. Ivers and Katherine Schroeder

1 Introduction[1]

In this Chapter, we highlight two of the most significant changes in international arbitration procedure as a result of the COVID-19 pandemic: (1) the transition to electronic-only submissions, and (2) the increased use of virtual or remote hearings. We note some of the benefits and limitations of these changes, and consider how these procedural issues may continue to evolve in the future, as pandemic-related restrictions are eased and lifted.

As is now familiar history, instances of the COVID-19 virus first were reported in Wuhan, China, in December 2019.[2] The virus thereafter quickly spread throughout China and the greater Asia-Pacific region and, on January 30, 2020, the World Health Organization ("WHO") declared a Public Health Emergency of International Concern.[3] By the end of February 2020, at least 38 countries

1 This Chapter was prepared for the University of Lausanne ("UNIL") Conference on the Impact of COVID on Dispute Resolution in October 2021. Any views expressed in this publication are strictly those of the authors and should not be attributed in any way to White & Case LLP. White & Case means the international legal practice comprising White & Case LLP, a New York State registered limited liability partnership, White & Case LLP, a limited liability partnership incorporated under English law and all other affiliated partnerships, companies and entities. This chapter is prepared for the general information of interested persons. It is not, and does not attempt to be, comprehensive in nature. Due to the general nature of its content, it should not be regarded as legal advice. The Authors thank Meenu Mathews and Robin Liu for their research assistance in preparing this Article, and UNIL for the opportunity to present it.

2 Scott LaFee, "Novel Coronavirus Circulated Undetected Months before First COVID-19 Cases in Wuhan, China," Newsroom, last modified March 18, 2021, https://health.ucsd.edu/news/releases/Pages/2021-03-18-novel-coronavirus-circulated-undetected-months-before-first-covid-19-cases-in-wuhan-china.aspx.

3 "Statement on the second meeting of the International Health Regulations (2005) Emergency Committee regarding the outbreak of novel coronavirus (2019-nCoV)," WHO, last modified January 30, 2020, https://www.who.int/news/item/30-01-2020-statement-on-the-second-meeting-of-the-international-health-regulations-(2005)-emergency-committee-regarding-the-outbreak-of-novel-coronavirus-(2019-ncov).

had imposed health measures and restrictions that significantly limited international travel to and from China, among other countries, including by denying entry to certain passengers, restricting the issuance of visas, and/or imposing mandatory quarantine for returning travelers.[4]

Notwithstanding these measures, the virus continued to spread across the globe, with over 118,000 cases reported across 114 countries as of March 11, 2020.[5] In mid-March 2020, the WHO declared that the COVID-19 virus had reached the status of a pandemic.[6] By the end of March 2020, the United States had declared a state of national emergency,[7] over 250 million people were quarantined throughout Europe,[8] and more than 100 countries had issued lockdown orders.[9] In a survey conducted by the Global Business Travel Association from March 18–21, 2021, over 95 percent of survey respondents reported that their companies had canceled or suspended all or most business trips to China, other Asia-Pacific countries, Europe, the Middle East, and Africa, while 86 percent of respondents reported that their companies had instituted work-from-home policies.[10] With billions of people subject to quarantine orders and

4 "Updated WHO Recommendations for International Traffic in Relation to COVID-19 Outbreak," who, last modified February 28, 2020, https://www.who.int/news-room/articles-detail/updated-who-recommendations-for-international-traffic-in-relation-to-covid-19-outbreak/.

5 "WHO Director-General's opening remarks at the media briefing on COVID-19," who, last modified March 11, 2020, https://www.who.int/director-general/speeches/detail/who-director-general-s-opening-remarks-at-the-media-briefing-on-covid-19---11-march-2020.

6 *Id.*

7 U.S. President, Proclamation, "Declaring a National Emergency Concerning the Novel Coronavirus Disease (COVID-19) Outbreak, Proclamation 9994 of March 13, 2020," *Federal Register* 85, no. 53 (March 18, 2020): 15337, https://www.federalregister.gov/documents/2020/03/18/2020-05794/declaring-a-national-emergency-concerning-the-novel-coronavirus-disease-covid-19-outbreak.

8 Jon Henley and Philip Oltermann, "Italy records its deadliest day of coronavirus outbreak with 475 deaths," The Guardian, last modified March 18, 2020, https://www.theguardian.com/world/2020/mar/18/coronavirus-lockdown-eu-belgium-germany-adopt-measures.

9 "Coronavirus: The world in lockdown in maps and charts," BBC, last modified April 7, 2020, https://www.bbc.com/news/world-52103747.

10 "Coronavirus Is Decimating Entire Global Travel Industry; Travel Comes to a Halt Across the Globe," Global Business Travel Association, last modified March 24, 2020, https://www.gbta.org/blog/coronavirus-is-decimating-entire-global-travel-industry-travel-comes-to-a-halt-across-the-globe/; "Coronavirus Poll Results," Global Business Travel Association, last modified March 23, 2020, https://www.gbta.org/Portals/0/Documents/GBTA_Coronavirus-key-findings032320.pdf.

travel restrictions,[11] international business operations were forced to change overnight.

International arbitration, by definition, involves parties – as well as arbitrators, counsel, and other participants – based in multiple jurisdictions. Those in the international arbitration community immediately felt the impact of quarantine orders and restrictions on international travel. Many no longer could travel abroad for hearings or meetings, nor could they access their offices, limiting the ability to work with pleadings and other documents in hard copy.

Without knowing when the pandemic would end or when quarantine orders and restrictions would be lifted, the international arbitration community was required to adapt swiftly to this evolving situation and to implement measures that would allow proceedings to continue in a timely fashion, while preserving the due process rights of all parties.

2 The Transition to Electronic-Only Submissions

One of the primary effects of the COVID-19 pandemic on international arbitration procedure has been the adoption of electronic-only submissions. As detailed below, while electronic submissions and electronic case management systems have been used by many arbitral institutions for years,[12] the pandemic has accelerated the move away from hard-copy submissions.

The submission of pleadings and other documents in international arbitration is governed by rules that differ based on the stage of the proceeding: the submission of the request for arbitration and corresponding notification to the respondent(s) prior to the constitution of the tribunal generally is governed by the applicable arbitration rules and/or the applicable treaty or agreement, while the submission of pleadings and other documents following the constitution of the tribunal generally is governed by the procedural rules set by the tribunal and/or agreed between the parties.

11 "Coronavirus: The world in lockdown in maps and charts," BBC, last modified April 7, 2020, https://www.bbc.com/news/world-52103747.

12 See, e.g., "Information Technology in International Arbitration- Report of the ICC Commission on Arbitration and ADR," ICC, accessed October 23, 2021, https://iccwbo.org/publication/information-technology-international-arbitration-report-icc-commission-arbitration-adr/; *see also* Kevin Ongenae and Maud Piers, "Procedural Formalities in Arbitration: Towards a Technologically Neutral Legal Framework," *Journal of International Arbitration* 38, no. 1 (2021): 27.

With respect to the request for arbitration, before the COVID-19 pandemic, most arbitration rules required that the request for arbitration be sent in hard copy to the respondent(s) and to the relevant arbitral institution.[13] Article 23 of the International Centre for Settlement of Investment Disputes (ICSID) Arbitration Rules, for example, states that, except as otherwise provided, "every request … shall be filed in the form of a signed original accompanied by the following number of additional copies: (a) before the number of members of the Tribunal has been determined: five; (b) after the number of members of the Tribunal has been determined: two more than the number of its members."[14] The International Chamber of Commerce (ICC) likewise required a claimant to "submit [hard] copies" to initiate an arbitration.[15]

Other institutions, such as the Hong Kong International Arbitration Centre ("HKIAC"), the London Court of International Arbitration ("LCIA"), the Singapore International Arbitration Centre ("SIAC"), the German Arbitration Institute ("DIS"), and the World Intellectual Property Organization ("WIPO"), allow the request for arbitration to be submitted in electronic and/or hard-copy form in rules published before the onset of the pandemic.[16]

---

13 Kevin Ongenae and Maud Piers, "Procedural Formalities in Arbitration: Towards a Technologically Neutral Legal Framework," *Journal of International Arbitration* 38, no. 1 (2021): 33.

14 ICSID Arbitration Rules, Rule 23; *see also* ICSID (Additional Facility) Arbitration Rules, Article 3(3) ("The request shall be accompanied by five additional signed copies. . ."). Similarly, Article 3.1 of the Swiss Chambers' Arbitration Institution Arbitration Rules "SCAI" (now known as the Swiss Arbitration Centre Ltd., https://www.swissarbitration.org/swiss-arbitration/history/) provides that the claimant "shall submit a Notice of Arbitration to the Secretariat at any of the addresses listed in Appendix A." *See* SCAI Arbitration Rules 2012, Art. 3.1 (citing Appendix A) (listing the addresses of the Secretariat of the Arbitration Court).

15 ICC Arbitration Rules 2017, Article 4.4.

16 HKIAC Administered Arbitration Rules 2018, Arts. 3.1, 4.1 ("Any written communication pursuant to these Rules shall be deemed to be received by a party, arbitrator, emergency arbitrator or HKIAC if … communicated to the address, facsimile number and/or email address communicated by the addressee."); LCIA Arbitration Rules 2014, Art. 1.3 ("The Claimant may use, but is not required to do so, the standard electronic form available on-line from the LCIA's website for LCIA Requests."); SIAC Arbitration Rules 2016, Art. 2.1 ("Any such notice, communication or proposal may be delivered by hand, registered post or courier service, or transmitted by any form of electronic communication (including electronic mail and facsimile), or delivered by any other appropriate means that provides a record of its delivery."); DIS Arbitration Rules 2018, Arts. 4.1, 4.2, 4.3 ("Requests for Arbitration pursuant to Article 5 and Article 19 shall be sent to the DIS in paper form as well as in electronic form."); WIPO Arbitration Rules 2002, Art. 4(a) ("Any notice or other communication that may or is required to be given under these Rules shall be in writing and shall be delivered by expedited postal or courier service, or transmitted by telefax, e-mail or other means of telecommunication that provide a record thereof.").

With respect to pleadings and other documents submitted after the constitution of the tribunal, electronic submissions were common before the COVID-19 pandemic, but arbitration rules generally did not articulate a preference for electronic over hard-copy submissions.[17] Article 4.1 of the 2014 LCIA Arbitration Rules, for example, provided that written communications may be "delivered personally or by registered postal or courier service or (subject to Article 4.3)[18] by facsimile, e-mail or any other electronic means of telecommunication that provides a record of its transmission, or in any other manner ordered by the Arbitral Tribunal."[19] The HKIAC Administered Arbitration Rules, the SIAC Arbitration Rules, the DIS Arbitration Rules, and the WIPO Arbitration Rules provide similarly.[20]

In some instances, a party would request, and the tribunal would order, the production of documents in hard copy. In *Gami Investments v. Mexico*, for example, the tribunal ruled that the parties must provide hard copies of each

---

17 Prior to the pandemic, some arbitral institutions already had adopted electronic-only submissions as their preferred transmission method. *See, e.g.*, Netherlands Arbitration Institute ("NAI") Arbitration Rules 2015, Art. 3.2 (providing that "[u]nless the sender is unable to do so, all requests, communications and other documents to the administrator, the Committee, the third person as referred to in Article 39 and/or the NAI shall only be sent electronically by e-mail. . ."). Other institutions had developed online filing systems to facilitate electronic submissions before the pandemic. *See, e.g.*, "Ad Hoc Platform – Powered By the SCC," SCC, accessed July 16, 2021, https://sccinstitute.com/case-management/ad-hoc-platform/#:%7E:text=Any%20ad%20hoc%20arbitration%20registered,the%20use%20of%20the%20platform ("The Ad Hoc Platform provides participants with a secure and efficient way of communicating and filing case materials in the arbitration, such as procedural orders, submissions and exhibits.").

18 LCIA Arbitration Rules 2014, Art. 4.3 ("Delivery by electronic means (including e-mail and facsimile) may only be effected to an address agreed or designated by the receiving party for that purpose or ordered by the Arbitral Tribunal.").

19 LCIA Arbitration Rules 2014, Art. 4.1.

20 See, e.g., HKIAC Administered Arbitration Rules 2018, Arts. 3.1, 4.1 ("Any written communication pursuant to these Rules shall be deemed to be received by a party, arbitrator, emergency arbitrator or HKIAC if ... communicated to the address, facsimile number and/or email address communicated by the addressee."); SIAC Arbitration Rules 2016, Art. 2.1 ("Any such notice, communication or proposal may be delivered by hand, registered post or courier service, or transmitted by any form of electronic communication ..."); DIS Arbitration Rules 2018, Art. 4.1 ("[A]ll Submissions of the parties and the arbitral tribunal to the DIS shall be sent electronically, by email, or on a portable storage device, or by any other means of electronic transmission that has been authorized by the DIS."); WIPO Arbitration Rules 2002, Art. 4(a) ("Any notice or other communication that may or is required to be given under these Rules shall be in writing and shall be delivered by expedited postal or courier service, or transmitted by telefax, e-mail or other means of telecommunication that provide a record thereof.").

fact exhibit.[21] The tribunal in *Mobil v. Canada* similarly ordered that the parties file hard copies of pleadings, witness statements, expert reports, and other documents.[22]

In early March 2020, arbitral institutions quickly recognized the impact of quarantine and lockdown orders on hard-copy filing requirements. On March 13, 2020, ICSID announced that it was "taking further steps to reduce reliance on paper-filings in its cases" and that it would require "only an electronic copy of a request for arbitration . . . and any accompanying documents."[23] ICSID also "encourage[d] parties to submit all written submissions . . . electronically," with arbitrators "also encouraged to use electronic copies of case-related documents."[24] As ICSID Secretary-General Meg Kinnear commented at the time, "[g]iven the state of information technology – and the ease with which participants in ICSID cases have adapted to online file sharing in recent years – it made sense to make electronic filing the norm."[25]

Shortly thereafter, the ICC issued a similar "urgent communication" to "strongly advise" that all communications with the ICC Secretariat be conducted by email, and that all requests for arbitration also be filed with the Secretariat by email.[26] In July 2020, DIS likewise announced that electronic submissions were the preferred method for all filings, observing that it "already foresees transmission to the DIS electronically as the standard procedure."[27]

In October 2020, the LCIA adopted new Arbitration Rules that also reflect a shifting approach to hard-copy submissions. While the 2014 LCIA Arbitration

21 See *Gami Investments Inc v. The Government the United Mexican State*, Procedural Order No. 1, last modified January 30, 2003, https://www.italaw.com/sites/default/files/case-documents/italaw11253_1.pdf.

22 See *Mobil Investments Canada Inc. v. Canada* (ICSID Case No. ARB/15/6), Procedural Order No. 1, last modified November 24, 2015, http://icsidfiles.worldbank.org/icsid/ICSIDBLOBS/OnlineAwards/C4205/DC7592_En.pdf.

23 "ICSID Makes Electronic Filing its Default Procedure," ICSID, last modified March 16, 2020, https://icsid.worldbank.org/news-and-events/news-releases/icsid-makes-electronic-filing-its-default-procedure.

24 *Id.*

25 *Id.*

26 "Urgent COVID-19 Message to DRS Community," ICC, last modified March 17, 2020, https://iccwbo.org/media-wall/news-speeches/covid-19-urgent-communication-to-drs-users-arbitrators-and-other-neutrals/.

27 "Announcement of Particular Procedural Features for the Administration of Arbitrations in View of the Covid-19 Pandemic," DIS, last modified July 1, 2020, https://www.disarb.org/en/about-us/update-covid-19.

Rules made hard-copy submissions optional,[28] the 2020 LCIA Arbitration Rules omit all references to hard copies and require "the Request [for Arbitration] (including all accompanying documents) [to] be submitted to the Registrar in electronic form..."[29]

The transition to electronic-only submissions brings substantial efficiencies to the arbitral process, reducing the time and expense previously required to prepare and ship hard copies to the relevant parties, including the arbitrators, opposing counsel, and the administering arbitral institution.[30] As Ms. Kinnear observed when ICSID moved to electronic-only submissions, "[t]he result will be cost and time-savings to parties."[31] Furthermore, smaller arbitral institutions may be able to rely on the investments that larger organizations have made with respect to electronic-filing software, further reducing overall costs.[32]

Eliminating hard-copy submissions also reduces the volume of paper in an arbitration, resulting in a more environmentally sustainable practice.[33]

---

28 "LCIA Arbitration Rules (2014)," LCIA, last modified October 1, 2014, https://www.lcia.org/Dispute_Resolution_Services/lcia-arbitration-rules-2014.aspx.

29 LCIA Arbitration Rules 2020, Art. 1.3. ICSID also currently is in the process of conducting an extensive review to amend its rules and regulations, with the fifth and most recent Working Paper on the amendments providing that the request for arbitration "shall be filed electronically." See "Working Paper #5," ICSID, accessed June 15, 2021, https://icsid.worldbank.org/sites/default/files/documents/WP 5-Volume1-ENG-FINAL.pdf.

30 See, e.g., Patricia Shaughnessy, "Initiating and Administering Arbitration Remotely," in *International Arbitration and the COVID-19 Revolution* (Wolters Kluwer, 2020), 37; "Working Group on LegalTech Adoption in International Arbitration," in *Protocol for Online Case Management in International Arbitration* (2020), 3, https://www.lw.com/thoughtLeadership/protocol-online-case-management-international-arbitration; "5 Benefits of E-Filing Legal documents," Nationwide Legal, last modified March 18, 2020, https://nationwidelegal.com/1285/.

31 "ICSID Makes Electronic Filing its Default Procedure," ICSID, last modified March 16, 2020, https://icsid.worldbank.org/news-and-events/news-releases/icsid-makes-electronic-filing-its-default-procedure.

32 Patricia Shaughnessy, "Initiating and Administering Arbitration Remotely," in *International Arbitration and the COVID-19 Revolution* (Wolters Kluwer, 2020), 39 ("Institutions that are connected to a larger organization, such as a Chamber of Commerce, may be able to benefit from the larger organization's investment into digitalization and it use development and support. In the context of the pandemic, some such 'integrated' institutions received support from the larger organization in moving to remote service.").

33 See Mohit Mahla and Kabir A.N. Duggal, "When the Answer is Becoming the Question: Impact of Arbitrations on the Environment," Kluwer Arbitration Blog, last modified November 29, 2020, http://arbitrationblog.kluwerarbitration.com/2020/11/29/when-the-answer-is-becoming-the-question-impact-of-arbitrations-on-the-environment/.

This transition aligns with the increased interest in paperless arbitration,[34] as well as the recent Campaign for Greener Arbitrations Pledge, which, among other things, encourages the elimination of hard copies in favor of electronic submissions.[35]

Electronic submissions, however, are not without potential issues. One potential issue is whether the electronic submission of a request for arbitration provides adequate and sufficient notice of the dispute to the respondent. Unlike paper copies, the delivery of which can be confirmed by a courier or other package service, it may be difficult to ascertain whether the respondent, in fact, has received notice of a request for arbitration.[36]

In addition, the increased use of electronic submissions and online data storage has given rise to heightened concerns about cybersecurity and data protection in arbitration proceedings. In a 2019 survey, 90 percent of survey respondents agreed that cybersecurity was an "important issue" for international arbitration, with 11 percent indicating that they had experienced a cybersecurity breach in an arbitration.[37]

Given the high-stakes nature of many international arbitration disputes and the exchange of often highly confidential commercial information between the

34 See Gillian Carmichael Lemaire, "Paperless Arbitrations – Where Do We Stand?," Kluwer Arbitration Blog, last modified February 19, 2014, http://arbitrationblog.kluwerarbitration.com/2014/02/19/paperless-arbitrations-where-do-we-stand/; Karen Mills, "Lists, Checklists, Guidelines, Principles, Techniques, Protocols, Best Practices: Are They Useful?," Kluwer Arbitration Blog, last modified January 16, 2014, http://arbitrationblog.kluwerarbitration.com/2014/01/16/lists-checklists-guidelines-principles-techniques-protocols-best-practices-are-they-useful/?print=print; Leon Kopecky, "A Case for Paperless Arbitration," Kluwer Arbitration Blog, last modified February 5, 2017, http://arbitrationblog.kluwerarbitration.com/2017/02/05/a-case-for-paperless-arbitration/.

35 "The Green Pledge Guiding Principles," Campaign for Greener Arbitrations, accessed June 24, 2021, https://www.greenerarbitrations.com/greenpledge; "Individual Signatories," Campaign for Greener Arbitrations, accessed June 24, 2021, https://www.greenerarbitrations.com/signatories; "Institutional Supporters," Campaign for Greener Arbitrations, accessed June 24, 2021, https://www.greenerarbitrations.com/institutional-supporters; *see also* Lucy Greenwood and Kabir A.N. Duggal, "The Green Pledge: No Talk, More Action," Kluwer Arbitration Blog, last modified March 20, 2020, http://arbitrationblog.kluwerarbitration.com/2020/03/20/the-green-pledge-no-talk-more-action/.

36 See, e.g., *Communs. Network Int'l, Ltd. v. MCI WorldCom Communs., Inc.*, 708 F.3d 327, 331 (2d Cir. 2013) (providing an example of a defendant failing to receive notice because said notice was sent to defendant's former email address).

37 "International Arbitration Survey: Cybersecurity in International Arbitration," Bryan Cave, accessed July 16, 2021, https://www.bclplaw.com/images/content/1/6/v2/160089/Bryan-Cave-Leighton-Paisner-Arbitration-Survey-Report-2018.pdf.

parties, the International Council for Commercial Arbitration, the New York City Bar, and the International Institute for Conflict Prevention and Resolution issued in November 2019 a Protocol on Cybersecurity in International Arbitration, which is designed to increase awareness of information security in arbitration.[38] The Protocol addresses the importance of maintaining cybersecurity order to maintain user confidence in the arbitral system, and sets out a framework for determining reasonable information security measures for arbitration proceedings.[39] Other organizations, including the International Bar Association, have issued similar guidance on security in international dispute resolution.[40]

Despite these concerns, the move towards electronic-only submissions likely will continue, given the efficiencies in time and expense, as well as the environmental benefits.

3 The Increased Use of Virtual Hearings

Before the COVID-19 pandemic, the vast majority of arbitral hearings were held in person.[41] The imposition of travel restrictions and quarantine requirements

38 "Working Group Releases Cybersecurity Protocol for International Arbitration," ICCA, last modified November 21, 2019, https://www.cpradr.org/news-publications/press-releases/2019-11-21-working-group-releases-cybersecurity-protocol-for-international-arbitration-2020.

39 "ICCA-NYC Bar-CPR Protocol on Cybersecurity in International Arbitration (2020 Edition)," ICCA, accessed July 16, 2021, https://cdn.arbitration-icca.org/s3fs-public/document/media_document/icca-nyc_bar-cpr_cybersecurity_protocol_for_international_arbitration_-_electronic_version.pdf.

40 "Cybersecurity Guidelines," IBA's Presidential Task Force on Cybersecurity, last modified October 2018, https://www.ibanet.org/MediaHandler?id=2F9FA5D6-6E9D-413C-AF80-681BAFD300B0; *see also* "The ICCA Reports No. 6: ICCA-NYC Bar-CPR Protocol on Cybersecurity in International Arbitration," ICCA, accessed July 16, 2021, https://www.arbitration-icca.org/icca-reports-no-6-icca-nyc-bar-cpr-protocol-cybersecurity-international-arbitration.

41 "How Will the Coronavirus Impact International Arbitration?," Kluwer Arbitration Blog, last modified March 13, 2020, http://arbitrationblog.kluwerarbitration.com/2020/03/13/how-will-the-coronavirus-impact-international-arbitration/; "SCC Virtual Hearing Survey," SCC, accessed July 15, 2021, https://sccinstitute.com/media/1773182/scc-rapport_virtual_hearing-2.pdf (noting that only eight percent of participants from a 2018 survey had used a virtual hearing room in an international arbitration).

by many countries by mid-March 2020, however, made such in-person hearings impossible.[42]

At the outset of the pandemic, given the uncertainty surrounding the duration of the pandemic and related travel restrictions, several arbitral hearings were simply postponed.[43] It soon became clear, however, that the pandemic would continue for the foreseeable future and that arbitration would need to adapt, so that hearings and resulting awards would not be delayed indefinitely.[44]

On March 16, 2020, several of the largest arbitral institutions, including the ICC, ICSID, the LCIA, and the Vienna International Arbitral Centre, issued a joint statement, emphasizing their focus on "international arbitration's ability to contribute to stability and foreseeability in a highly unstable environment, including by ensuring that pending cases may continue and that parties may have their cases heard without undue delay."[45] The institutions encouraged parties and tribunals to "mitigate the effects of any impediments to the largest extent possible while ensuring the fairness and efficiency of arbitral proceedings."[46]

In addition, several arbitral institutions issued individual guidance specific to their proceedings. In an ICSID press release issued on March 24, 2020 in light of the "unprecedented disruptions to travel" that had "spurred further interest in online hearings," ICSID noted that it already had measures in place

42 "Coronavirus: The world in lockdown in maps and charts," BBC, last modified April 7, 2020, https://www.bbc.com/news/world-52103747.

43 See, e.g., "Urgent COVID-19 message to the DRS community," ICC, last modified March 17, 2020, https://iccwbo.org/media-wall/news-speeches/covid-19-urgent-communication-to-drs-users-arbitrators-and-other-neutrals/.

44 Patricia Shaughnessy, "Initiating and Administering Arbitration Remotely," in *International Arbitration and the COVID-19 Revolution* (Wolters Kluwer, 2020), 28 ("Out of necessity, the arbitration community is forging new approaches to arbitration that employ existing and new procedures, tools, and technology.").

45 "Arbitration and COVID-19," ICC, accessed October 23, 2021, https://iccwbo.org/content/uploads/sites/3/2020/04/covid19-joint-statement.pdf.

46 "Arbitration and COVID-19," ICC, accessed October 23, 2021, https://iccwbo.org/content/uploads/sites/3/2020/04/covid19-joint-statement.pdf. Arbitral institutions have allowed flexibility in view of difficulties posed by the pandemic as well. In July 2020, for example, the DIS encouraged tribunals to permit extensions to deadlines where needed, stating that the tribunal in a particular case may "provide for an automatic extension of such time limit[s] in those cases in which a request for an extension is made expressly based upon the COVID-19 pandemic and such request is sent to all participants in the proceedings." See "Announcement of Particular Procedural Features for the Administration of Arbitrations in View of the Covid-19 Pandemic," DIS, last modified July 1, 2020, https://www.disarb.org/en/about-us/update-covid-19.

for virtual hearings and that there had been a "steady uptick in its number of online hearings," with approximately 60 percent of the 200 hearings and sessions organized by ICSID in 2019 held by video-conference.[47] SIAC similarly issued guidance directing users to Maxwell Chambers, which supports virtual hearings and other meetings through an online portal.[48]

The ICC likewise encouraged the use of virtual hearings where possible, noting that steps should be taken to guarantee "that parties are treated with equality and each party is given a full and fair opportunity to present its case during a virtual hearing,"[49] while the HKIAC noted that "whether or not a virtual hearing, in part or in full, is suitable for a particular matter remains a matter for the parties and the arbitral tribunal."[50]

In addition, some arbitral institutions have issued new arbitration rules, which include a virtual option for hearings. In August 2020, the LCIA issued guidance encouraging virtual hearings, noting that Article 19 of the amended LCIA Arbitration Rules, effective in October 2020, would provide that hearings may take place "in person, or virtually by conference or videoconference or using other communications technology."[51]

In October 2020, the ICC also released new arbitration rules, effective in January 2021, which permit the arbitral tribunal to hold virtual hearings, after consultation with the parties.[52] Similarly, in December 2020, the IBA released

47 "A Brief Guide to Online Hearings at ICSID," ICSID, last modified March 24, 2020, https://icsid.worldbank.org/news-and-events/news-releases/brief-guide-online-hearings-icsid?CID=362.

48 "About Maxwell Chambers," Maxwell Chambers, accessed July 19, 2021, https://www.maxwellchambers.com/about-maxwell-chambers/; "COVID-19 Information for SIAC Users," SIAC, last modified March 16, 2020, https://www.siac.org.sg/images/stories/press_release/2020/%5bANNOUNCEMENT%5d%20COVID-19%20Information%20for%20SIAC%20Users.pdf.

49 "ICC Guidance Note on Possible Measures Aimed at Mitigating the Effects of the COVID-19 Pandemic," ICC, last modified April 9, 2020, https://iccwbo.org/content/uploads/sites/3/2020/04/guidance-note-possible-measures-mitigating-effects-covid-19-english.pdf.

50 "HKIAC Guidelines for Virtual Hearings," HKIAC, last modified May 15, 2020, https://www.google.com/search?q=HKIAC+GUIDELINES+FOR+VIRTUAL+HEARINGS&rlz=1C1GCEA_en__954__954&oq=HKIAC+GUIDELINES+FOR+VIRTUAL+HEARINGS&aqs=chrome..69i57j69i60.295j0j7&sourceid=chrome&ie=UTF-8.

51 LCIA Arbitration Rules 2014. This was a notable change from the previous 2014 version of the LCIA rules, which contained no reference to virtual hearings. See also "Notable amendments in the 2020 Rules," White & Case LLP, last modified August 13, 2020, https://www.whitecase.com/publications/alert/lcia-introduces-new-arbitration-rules-new-era.

52 "Note to Parties and Arbitral Tribunals on the Conduct of the Arbitration Under the ICC Rules of Arbitration," ICC, last modified January 1, 2021, https://iccwbo.org/content/uploads/sites/3/2020/12/icc-note-to-parties-and-arbitral-tribunals-on-the-conduct-of-arbitration-english-2021.pdf.

modified Rules on the Taking of Evidence in International Arbitration, which provide that a tribunal, either on its own or via a party motion, may decide to hold a remote hearing.[53] The modified rules specify that the protocol for a remote hearing may include time zone information, advanced technology testing, and standards for oral testimony.[54]

As a result of the COVID-19 pandemic and the encouragement of arbitral institutions, the number of virtual hearings in international arbitration has greatly increased. In a 2018 survey, 64 percent of survey respondents reported that they had "never" used virtual hearings in international arbitration; by contrast, in a similar survey conducted in May 2021, 72 percent of respondents reported having used virtual hearings at least "sometimes."[55]

Virtual hearings, however, present unique challenges and may not be suitable in all arbitration disputes, particularly where holding a hearing virtually may affect a party's right to present its case or violate the principle of equal treatment of the parties.[56] One party and its witnesses and experts, for example, may be located in a country with limited technological capabilities or internet connectivity, making it more difficult for that party to prepare for and participate in the hearing.[57]

Time zone differences also may be problematic.[58] In a Survey conducted by White & Case and Queen Mary's University of London and published in May

53 IBA Rules on the Taking of Evidence in International Arbitration 2020.

54 IBA Rules on the Taking of Evidence in International Arbitration 2020.

55 White & Case LLP, "2021 International Arbitration Survey: Adapting arbitration to a changing world," Queen Mary University of London, last modified May 24, 2021, http://www.arbitration.qmul.ac.uk/media/arbitration/docs/LON0320037-QMUL-International-Arbitration-Survey-2021_19_WEB.pdf.

56 See, e.g., Alan Redfern, et al., *Redfern And Hunter On International Arbitration*, 5th ed. (Oxford University Press, 2009), § 10.47 (providing that fundamental principles of due process require arbitral tribunals "to ensure that the parties [have] . . . a full and proper opportunity to present their respective cases"); Jeffrey Waincymer, "Reconciling Conflicting Rights in International Arbitration: The Right to Choice of Counsel and the Right to an Independent and Impartial Tribunal," *Arbitration International* 26, no. 1 (2010): 597–598 ("Perhaps the most central procedural rights of a party are the right to equal treatment and the right to an adequate opportunity to present its case").

57 Vinson & Elkins llp and Elena Guillet, "Challenges and Opportunities of Virtual Hearings in International Arbitration," JD Supra, last modified October 19, 2020, https://www.jdsupra.com/legalnews/challenges-and-opportunities-of-virtual-55893/; Saniya Mirani, "Due Process Concerns in Virtual Witness Testimonies: An Indian Perspective," Kluwer Arbitration Blog, last modified November 17, 2020, http://arbitrationblog.kluwerarbitration.com/2020/11/17/due-process-concerns-in-virtual-witness-testimonies-an-indian-perspective/.

58 "The risk and rewards of arbitration's digital frontier," Global Arbitration Review, last modified August 10, 2020, https://globalarbitrationreview.com/the-risk-and-rewards-of-arbitrations-digital-frontier.

2021, 40 percent of respondents reported that difficulty accommodating multiple or disparate time zones was a key disadvantage of virtual hearings.[59] As a result of time zone differences, fact and expert witnesses may be compelled to testify early in the morning or late at night, which may impact the quality of their testimony. The Survey also emphasizes that it may be "harder for counsel teams and clients to confer during hearing sessions," as separate video feeds need to be arranged between counsel and clients who are physically located in separate locations in order to ensure their confidentiality.[60]

Virtual hearings also may limit the ability of the arbitrators to assess the credibility of fact and expert witnesses.[61] At an in-person hearing, the arbitrators – as well as the counsel conducting the examination – are able to see the witness directly in front of them and assess not only the substance of his or her responses, but also his or her body language. Virtual hearings also prevent participants from assessing the reaction of other hearing participants on a real-time, in-person basis – which is particularly problematic given that a reported 55 percent of all communication is nonverbal.[62] In light of these intangible aspects of in-person hearings, some commentators have questioned whether virtual hearings or trials conducted solely by video may constitute a due process violation in U.S. criminal cases.[63]

"Zoom fatigue" also is a legitimate concern, as video-conferencing requires increased energy to process facial emotions and body language.[64] Particularly

59 White & Case LLP, *supra* note 55.

60 *Id.*

61 *Id.*

62 "Criminal Court Reopening and Public Health in the COVID-19 Era," NACDL Executive Committee, last modified June 2, 2020, https://nacdl.org/getattachment/56802001-1bb9-4edd-814d-c8d5c41346f3/criminal-court-reopening-and-public-health-in-the-covid-19-era.pdf.

63 *Id.*

64 Manyu Jiang, "The reason Zoom calls drain your energy," last modified April 22, 2020, https://www.bbc.com/worklife/article/20200421-why-zoom-video-chats-are-so-exhausting; Vignesh Ramachandran "Stanford researchers identify four cases for "Zoom fatigue" and their simple fixes," last modified February 3, 2021, https://news.stanford.edu/2021/02/23/four-causes-zoom-fatigue-solutions/;HannahRoberts,"ZoomandGloom: Lawyers Getting Fatigue from Endless Video Calls," Law.com, last modified July 22, 2020, https://www.law.com/legaltechnews/2020/07/22/zoom-and-gloom-lawyers-are-growing-tired-of-endless-video-calls-397-36539/?slreturn=20210616142809; Cristina Ryan, "Lessons Learned from Running a Virtual Arbitration: A First-Person Account," American Arbitration Association, last modified December 1, 2020, https://www.adr.org/Lessons-Learned-from-Running-a-Virtual-Arbitration-A-First-Person-Account; NACDL Executive Committee, *supra* note 62.

when virtual hearings are held for eight or more hours per day, participants may easily lose focus. This may make it more difficult for arbitrators to analyze witness and expert testimony, as well as to control the witness examinations, a trend that could open the door for procedural abuse.[65] In addition, even slight delays in a video connection may give the impression that witnesses are less focused than they would appear in an in-person setting,[66] which may influence the tribunal's assessment of the witness's credibility.

As detailed above, the use of technology also increases the potential for cybersecurity breaches, including in virtual hearings. While numerous institutions have taken measures to ensure the use of high-security platforms for virtual hearings,[67] there remains the potential for security breaches. In 2015, for example, hackers launched a cyber-attack on the Permanent Court of Arbitration ("PCA"), the Ministry of Justice of the Philippines, and counsel to the Philippines in the midst of a highly-sensitive dispute between the Philippines and China regarding the South China Sea.[68]

While virtual hearings may continue to be used for procedural conferences and smaller hearings with no or few witnesses and experts, there are indications of a return to in-person hearings in at least some disputes. The HKIAC, for example, resumed in-person hearings in March 2021, where "all parties have remained in Hong Kong continuously for the 14-day period prior to admittance, submit to temperature checks, and otherwise comply with its COVID-19

65 "The Psychological Impact of Remote Hearings," BRG, accessed September 8, 2021, https://media.thinkbrg.com/wp-content/uploads/2021/08/05105717/BRG-Remote-Hearing-Impact-2021-Final.pdf.

66 Jiang, *supra* note 64.

67 See, e.g., "A Brief Guide to Online Hearings at ICSID," International Centre for Settlement of Investment Disputes, last modified March 24, 2020, https://icsid.worldbank.org/news-and-events/news-releases/brief-guide-online-hearings-icsid?CID=362.

68 Jason Healey and Anni Piiparinen, "Did China Just Hack the International Court Adjudicating Its South China Sea Territorial Claims?," The Diplomat, last modified October 27, 2015, https://thediplomat.com/2015/10/did-china-just-hack-the-international-court-adjudicating-its-south-china-sea-territorial-claims/; "'Chinese Cyberspies' Hack International Court's Website to Fish for Enemies in South China Sea Dispute," South China Morning Post, Bloomberg, last modified October 16, 2015, https://www.scmp.com/news/china/policies-politics/article/1868395/chinese-cyberspies-hack-international-courts-website; David Turner and Gulshan Gill, "Addressing Emerging Cyber Risks: Reflections on the ICCA Cybersecurity Protocol for International Arbitration," Practical Law, last modified May 17, 2019, http://arbitrationblog.practicallaw.com/addressing-emerging-cyber-risks-reflections-on-the-icca-cybersecurity-protocol-for-international-arbitration/.

protocols."[69] In June 2020, the ICC similarly began to permit a hybrid format for hearings, with some participants attending via video and some attending in-person.[70]

4 Conclusion

Just as every other field has been forced to adapt in view of the COVID-19 pandemic, so too has international arbitration. While many of the procedural changes seen since the outset of the pandemic were not entirely new to international arbitration, the pandemic has served to spur the transition towards electronic-only filings and virtual hearings, allowing cases to be heard and proceedings to continue. Perhaps due in part to their swift response to the challenges posed by the pandemic, the majority of major arbitral institutions experienced increased caseloads in 2020.[71] SIAC more than doubled its caseload from 479 cases in 2019 to 1,000 cases in 2020, while the ICC and the LCIA also saw an increase in the number of cases registered in that same time period.[72]

While the transition towards electronic-only filings and virtual hearings have brought about efficiencies in both time and cost, as well as environmental

69 Neil A.F. Popović and James V. Fazio, "Insisting on Live, In-Person Arbitration Hearings During the Pandemic," National Law Review, accessed March 9, 2021, https://www.natlawreview.com/article/insisting-live-person-arbitration-hearings-during-pandemic.

70 "ICC Hearing Centre reopens doors for physical presence dispute resolution hearings," ICC, last modified July 1, 2020, https://iccwbo.org/media-wall/news-speeches/icc-hearing-centre-reopens-doors-for-physical-presence-dispute-resolution-hearings/.

71 Simon Chapman and Jacob Sin, "Rise in arbitration cases in 2020 despite reduced volume of in person hearings due to coronavirus pandemic," Lexology, last modified March 3, 2021, https://www.lexology.com/library/detail.aspx?g=caa661ab-434a-4856-8783-84f349e06036.

72 *Id.*; "Annual Casework Report 2019 – The LCIA Records its Highest Number of Cases," last modified May 19, 2020, https://www.lcia.org/News/annual-casework-report-2019-the-lcia-records-its-highest-numbe.aspx; Wei Ming Tan, Zachary Song, and Lakshanthi Fernando, "The SIAC Annual Report 2019: Findings and Takeaways in the light of COVID-19," last modified April 15, 2020, https://www.lexology.com/library/detail.aspx?g=e0204c24-535a-40b6-9b7c-ab54390309ed; "ICC Arbitration Case Statistics Show Positive Trends in Global Reach, Diversity and Efficiency," last modified July 22, 2020, https://www.velaw.com/insights/icc-arbitration-case-statistics-show-positive-trends-in-global-reach-diversity-and-efficiency/.

benefits, they also have introduced increased cybersecurity risks and the loss of in-person interactions at hearings. Arbitral institutions will need to be vigilant in addressing these challenges, as they continue to promote the use of electronic-only filings and virtual hearings, where appropriate.

CHAPTER 5

Salient Considerations for Remote International Arbitration Hearings

Karthik Nagarajan and James J. East, Jr.

1 Introduction*

In 2020, in response to the unprecedented disruptions caused by the COVID-19 pandemic, the international arbitration community including institutions, practitioners, arbitrators, and disputants—pivoted admirably to conducting arbitrations remotely. This response was consistent with arbitration's reputation as a flexible and dynamic form of dispute resolution.[1]

Pre-pandemic, remote technologies were often utilized for procedural conferences and, less frequently, during a jurisdictional or merits hearing for select witness or expert examinations. Today, fully remote hearings[2] are increasingly utilized for full hearings on jurisdictional and merits issues. Since March 2020, several arbitral institutions have adopted new rules[3] and published model procedural orders or other practical guidance[4] to facilitate remote hearings.

* The authors wish to thank Jillian Timko, Summer Associate at BakerHostetler, for her invaluable research in preparing this chapter.

1 See, e.g., Gary Born, *International Commercial Arbitration*, 3rd ed. (Kluwer, 2021), 19 ("[A]rbitral procedures have varied substantially, both over time and in different geographic and political settings. At least in part, that reflects the inherent flexibility of the arbitral process, which leaves the parties (and arbitrators) free to devise procedures tailored to a particular dispute and legal or cultural setting.").

2 For the purposes of this chapter, "remote hearing" means "a hearing conducted, for the entire hearing or parts thereof, or only with respect to certain participants, using teleconference, videoconference or other communication technology by which persons in more than one location simultaneously participate." See IBA Rules on the Taking of Evidence in International Arbitration (2020), 8.

3 See, e.g., International Centre for Dispute Resolution Arbitration Rules (2021) ("ICDR Rules"); International Chamber of Commerce Arbitration Rules (2021) ("ICC Rules").

4 Given the absence of express provisions addressing remote hearings in most arbitral rules or national arbitration legislation at the start of the pandemic, many arbitral institutions promptly released guidance to assist arbitration users. See, e.g., "COVID-19: Information and Guidance in SCC Arbitrations," SCC, March 27, 2020, https://sccinstitute.com/about-the-scc/news/2020/covid-19-information-and-guidance-in-scc-arbitrations/; "ICC Guidance Note on Possible Measures Aimed at Mitigating the Effects of the COVID-19 Pandemic," ICC, April

While a substantial segment of the arbitral community utilized the option of fully remote hearings post March 2020, it remains to be seen whether this specific response to the unique challenges posed by the pandemic will become a permanent feature of international arbitration practice and whether such a transition is desirable.

This chapter analyzes salient issues that are implicated in a decision to conduct a remote hearing, including: (1) select procedural and policy considerations of conducting an arbitration that utilizes only remote hearing platforms (Section 2); (2) the due process implications of this transition to remote hearings (Section 3); and (3) sector-specific considerations for parties in the tourism and hospitality industry (Section 4).

As elaborated below, the framework and technology for conducting remote hearings were largely established and available prior to March 2020, but the pandemic has accelerated the utilization of remote hearings. As a general matter, the increased use of remote hearings is a welcome development. Benefits likely include time and cost efficiencies, enhanced diversity, a reduced carbon footprint, and increased technological innovation that will improve outcomes for clients. Indeed, prior to the pandemic, stakeholders in international arbitration[5] had indicated that further use of videoconferencing would result in a more efficient process.[6] Today, a consensus appears to be emerging that remote hearings, subject to some qualifications, will likely continue to be an enduring feature of international arbitration and improve the overall process.[7]

9, 2020, https://iccwbo.org/publication/icc-guidance-note-on-possible-measures-aimed-at-mitigating-the-effects-of-the-covid-19-pandemic/; "HKIAC Guidelines for Virtual Hearings," HKIAC, May 14, 2020, https://www.hkiac.org/news/hkiac-guidelines-virtual-hearings.

5 See White & Case LLP, "2021 International Arbitration Survey: Adapting arbitration to a changing world," Queen Mary University of London, May 7, 2021, 1, https://arbitration.qmul.ac.uk/media/arbitration/docs/LON0320037-QMUL-International-Arbitration-Survey-2021_19_WEB.pdf ("QM Survey") (Stakeholders interviewed for the qm Survey included "in-house counsel from both public and private sectors, arbitrators, private practitioners, representatives of arbitral institutions and trade associations, academics, experts and third-party funders").

6 See White & Case LLP, "2018 International Arbitration Survey: The Evolution of International Arbitration," Queen Mary University of London, May 9, 2018, 32, https://arbitration.qmul.ac.uk/media/arbitration/docs/2018-International-Arbitration-Survey---The-Evolution-of-International-Arbitration-(2).PDF (89% of respondents indicated that videoconferencing should be more widely used in international arbitration).

7 See, e.g., QM Survey, *supra* note 5, ("The arbitration community had to adapt quickly [to the pandemic], and some of these changes will remain after the pandemic recedes. Virtual hearings and increased reliance on technology are clear examples of changes that will persist"); "The Psychological Impact of Remote Hearings," Berkeley Research Group, August 18, 2021, 10, https://media.thinkbrg.com/wp-content/uploads/2021/08/05105717/BRG-Remote-Hearing-Impact-2021-Final.pdf ("[I]t is widely accepted that virtual hearings and tribunals are here to stay in some form. The degree to which varies considerably, depending on one's

Moreover, if the arbitral community continues to embrace remote hearing platforms, there is a likelihood that—over the long-term—advanced technologies will be developed and used to lessen or perhaps, even eliminate, some drawbacks[8] arising from remote hearings as they exist today.

With regard to the due process implications of remote hearings, our research does not, to date, reveal a single instance where a tribunal or enforcing court has found that a party's due process rights were infringed due to a decision to hold a remote hearing or the manner in which a remote hearing was conducted. Notwithstanding this, it is incumbent upon arbitrators to ensure that due process challenges relating to remote hearings are taken seriously, while at the same time guarding against "due process paranoia." Tribunals must be prepared to deal with unique challenges relating to remote hearings, which may include allegations of unfair treatment arising from differences in time zones for participation, technological arrangements, interpretation issues, and witness or expert coaching, amongst other issues. Thus, tribunals will be expected to continue to conduct proceedings in an efficient manner, while not compromising the rights of a party such that a remote hearing leads to unequal treatment.

Furthermore, the hospitality and tourism industry may be uniquely positioned to benefit from the increased utilization of remote hearings. The efficiency and accessibility of remote hearings may allow for the smooth resolution of disputes relating to ongoing hotel projects and enable parties under an active management contract to continue their contractual relationship and not endanger business goodwill.

On balance, all indications suggest that remote hearings will likely endure as a permanent and increasingly common feature of conducting international arbitrations, even if used in combination with in-person hearings throughout the case. At a minimum, remote hearings will continue to be considered as an

---

own personal circumstances and factors such as geographical location"); Patricia Louise Shaughnessy, "Chapter 2: Initiating and Administering Arbitration Remotely," in *International Arbitration and the COVID-19 Revolution*, eds. Maxi Scherer et al. (Kluwer Law International, 2020), 28–29 ("As arbitral institutions enjoy positions of influence and control in developing arbitration procedures and practices, they can and will significantly shape the post-COVID-19 future of arbitration. This future will reflect innovations wrought out of the crisis and developed into hybrid, technologically enhanced procedures that will facilitate fair, efficient, and effective dispute resolution"); Richard Laudy and Thethe Mokele, "The strong case for virtual hearings in Africa," Pinsent Masons, September 30, 2021, https://www.pinsentmasons.com/out-law/analysis/the-strong-case-for-virtual-hearings-in-africa# ("There is now a willingness to consider modern arbitral procedures and the expectation that the hearing will be conducted virtually is universal").

8 See Section 2, *infra*. Drawbacks of remote hearings, as noted briefly herein, include scheduling around multiple time zones, potential lack of access to adequate technology, inability to view the body language of a witness or expert under cross-examination, so-called "Zoom fatigue," stunting the visibility of aspiring practitioners, and a lack of in-person communication amongst hearing participants.

option for the conduct of hearings, particularly as the pandemic continues. Notwithstanding this, and for the reasons discussed below, there will remain a substantial demand for fully in-person merit hearings as the default procedure into the future, particularly with regard to complex, high-stakes disputes wherein numerous witnesses and technical experts are called to testify.

2 Procedural and Policy Considerations for Conducting Remote Hearings

The COVID-19 pandemic catalyzed a fundamental behavioral shift toward the adoption of remote hearing platforms, including for merits hearings. That shift has created, in many instances, substantial and tangible benefits for arbitration users and stakeholders. As elaborated below, key benefits include proceedings that are more time and cost effective, enhanced diversity and improved access to justice for end users, the facilitation of environmentally sustainable proceedings, and an opportunity for the arbitral community to be at the forefront of adopting innovative technologies that ultimately can enable the arbitral community to gain a competitive advantage over other forms of dispute resolution.

It is worth noting, as an initial matter, that the rules and guidance issued by leading arbitral institutions[9] issued following the onset of the pandemic supports the option for parties to continue utilizing remote hearing platforms.[10]

9 Arbitral institutions were quick to produce meaningful guidance on remote hearings at the onset of the pandemic. See, e.g.,: (1) the ICDR published its Model Order and Procedures for a Virtual Hearing via Videoconference that serves as a template for disputants' remote hearing procedural order and a veritable checklist of best practices for conducting virtual hearings; (2) the ICC issued a Guidance Note on Possible Measures Aimed at Mitigating the Effects of the COVID-19 Pandemic, followed by a comprehensive virtual hearing checklist, suggested remote hearing clauses, and model procedural order; (3) ICSID published its guide to online hearings in which encouraged parties to continue leveraging its bespoke hearing platform in light of the pandemic; and (4) siac published a guide for conducting remote hearings. "AAA-ICDR Model Order and Procedures for a Virtual Hearing via Videoconference," AAA-ICDR, May 9, 2020, https://go.adr.org/rs/294-SFS-516/images/AAA270_AAA-ICDR%20Model%20Order%20and%20Procedures%20for%20a%20Virtual%20Hearing%20via%20Videoconference.pdf; "ICC Guidance Note on Possible Measures Aimed at Mitigating the Effects of the covid-19 Pandemic," ICC, April 9, 2020, https://iccwbo.org/content/uploads/sites/3/2020/04/guidance-note-possible-measures-mitigating-effects-covid-19-english.pdf; "A Brief Guide to Online Hearings at ICSID," ICSID, March 24, 2020, https://icsid.worldbank.org/news-and-events/news-releases/brief-guide-online-hearings-icsid; "SIAC Guide: Taking Your Arbitration Remote," SIAC, August 31, 2020, https://www.siac.org.sg/69-siac-news/672-release-of-the-siac-guides-taking-your-arbitration-remote.

10 It is also worth noting that there has recently been a significant increase in non-institutional guidance in this area. See, e.g., "[Press Release] Seoul Protocol on Video

2.1 *Arbitral Institutional Framework for Remote Hearings*

For the purposes of this article, we have surveyed the following arbitral institutions to cover diverse geographic regions and commercial and investor-State rules: International Centre for the Settlement of Investment Disputes ("ICSID"), American Arbitration Association's International Centre for Dispute Resolution ("ICDR"), International Chamber of Commerce ("ICC"), United Nations Commission On International Trade Law ("UNCITRAL"), and Singapore International Arbitration Centre ("SIAC"). As elaborated below, the ICC and ICDR Rules, which were updated in 2021, expressly provide for the use of remote hearings. By contrast, the ICSID, SIAC, and UNCITRAL Rules are silent with respect to the use of remote hearings but do not prohibit them. Accordingly, parties in arbitral proceedings under the ICSID, SIAC, and UNCITRAL Rules have the flexibility to agree to conduct a remote hearing. It remains to be seen whether these institutions follow the ICC and ICDR's lead by providing express provisions for remote hearings.

- *ICDR:* The AAA's ICDR Rules (2021) provide that a "hearing or a portion of a hearing may be held by video, audio, or other electronic means" when either the parties agree or the tribunal decides, "after allowing the parties to comment," that a remote hearing is "appropriate and would not compromise the rights of any party to a fair process."[11] Furthermore, under Article 22(1), the Tribunal "may conduct the arbitration in whatever manner it considers appropriate, provided the parties are treated with equality and that each party has the right to be heard and is given a fair opportunity to present its case."[12] Notably, Article 22(2) requires that the Tribunal "shall conduct the proceedings with a view to expediting the resolution of the dispute" and in this context, states that the "tribunal and the parties may consider how technology, including video, audio, and other electronic means, might expedite the proceedings or decrease costs."[13] Further Article 22(3) requires the tribunal to discuss with the parties on steps to be implemented that ensure that the adequate cybersecurity, privacy,

Conferencing in International Arbitration," KCAB International, March 18, 2020, http://www.kcabinternational.or.kr/user/Board/comm_notice_view.do?BBS_NO=548&BD_NO=169&CURRENT_MENU_CODE=MENU0025&TOP_MENU_CODE=MENU0024; "Protocol on Virtual Hearings in Africa," Africa Arbitration Academy, August 2020, https://www.africaarbitrationacademy.org/protocol-virtual-hearings/.

11 ICDR Rules, *supra* note 3, at Art. 26(2).

12 *Id.* at Art. 22(1).

13 *Id.* at Art. 22(2).

and data protection measures are established for the conduct of the proceedings.[14]

- *ICC:* The ICC Rules (2021) expressly permit the arbitral tribunal to decide "after consulting the parties, and on the basis of the relevant facts and circumstances of the case, that any hearing will be conducted by physical attendance or remotely by videoconference, telephone or other appropriate means of communication."[15] The arbitrator is thus explicitly given the discretion, after consulting with the parties, to hold a hearing remotely by videoconference, telephone or other appropriate means. Article 22(4) states that the arbitral tribunal must act fairly and impartially and ensure that each party has a reasonable opportunity to present their case.[16]
- *ICSID:* The ICSID Arbitration Rules (2006) do not expressly reference but do not prohibit remote hearings. In its March 2020 publication, ICSID in fact noted that the popularity of remote hearings was steadily increasing prior to the pandemic.[17] Notably, however, the ICSID Convention Article 44 provides the tribunal broad discretion to decide "any question of procedure" that is not covered by the Convention or the applicable arbitral rules.[18] Furthermore, ICSID Arbitration Rule 20 calls for "the views of the parties on questions of procedure" during the preliminary procedural conference, and, in particular, the parties' views on "dispensing with the written and oral procedure."[19] At that time, the parties may offer their views on whether remote hearings will be appropriate under the circumstances.
- *SIAC:* The SIAC Rules (2016) also provide flexibility to the parties and the arbitrators to decide whether a remote hearing is appropriate for the case.[20] Article 19 of the SIAC Rules requires the Tribunal to ensure

14 *Id.* at Art. 22(3).

15 ICC Rules, *supra* note 3, at Art. 26(1).

16 *Id.* at Art. 22(4).

17 ICSID, "A Brief Guide to Online Hearing at ICSID," *supra* note 9 (reporting that 60% of cases before the Centre at that time were conducted remotely).

18 ICSID Convention (1966), Article 44.

19 ICSID Arbitration Rules (2006), Rules 20(1), 20(1)(e).

20 See, e.g., SIAC Arbitration Rules (2016), Arts. 19.1 ("The Tribunal shall conduct the arbitration in such manner as it considers appropriate, after consulting with the parties, to ensure the fair, expeditious, economical and final resolution of the dispute."), 19.3 ("As soon as practicable after the constitution of the Tribunal, the Tribunal shall conduct a preliminary meeting with the parties, in person or by any other means, to discuss the procedures that will be most appropriate and efficient for the case."), 19.7 ("The President may, at any stage of the proceedings, request the parties and the Tribunal to convene a

that the arbitration is conducted fairly, expeditiously, and economically, with the goal of arriving at a final resolution of the dispute.[21] Although remote hearings are not expressly referenced, a decision to hold such a hearing, if appropriate under the circumstances, would adhere to the principles set forth in Article 19.

- *UNCITRAL:* Article 15 of the UNCITRAL Arbitration Rules (2020) gives the tribunal wide discretion to conduct the arbitration in a manner suitable to the parties and the circumstances of the case, which logically extends to the option for holding remote hearings.[22] Article 15 also requires the tribunal to treat the parties "with equality" and provide each party a full opportunity to present its case. Similar to the ICSID and SIAC frameworks, the UNCITRAL Arbitration Rules rely on party autonomy and arbitrator discretion for deciding whether to hold a remote hearing.

Assessing whether the relevant arbitral rules expressly or implicitly permit a remote hearing, however, is only one piece of the calculus as to whether a remote hearing is appropriate and required. As briefly noted in Section 3, *infra*, parties considering whether to utilize a remote hearing, especially one involving dispositive issues of jurisdiction or the merits, must *inter alia* consider potentially relevant national laws on remote hearings for the purposes of enforcement after an award is rendered.

2.2 *Time and Cost Efficiencies*

Notwithstanding its historical reputation as a more efficient and economical alternative to national court litigation, international arbitration has recently been criticized as slow and costly.[23] The arbitral community's widespread adoption of remote hearings has the potential to significantly increase efficiency and reduce costs in an enduring fashion, which can help address this criticism.[24]

---

meeting to discuss the procedures that will be most appropriate and efficient for the case. Such meeting may be conducted in person or by any other means.").

21 *Id.* at Art. 19.1.

22 See, e.g., UNCITRAL Arbitration Rules (2020), Art. 15.1 ("Subject to these Rules, the arbitral tribunal may conduct the arbitration in such manner as it considers appropriate, provided that the parties are treated with equality and that at any stage of the proceedings each party is given a full opportunity of presenting his case."); see also UNCITRAL Arbitration Rules (2020), Art. 25.

23 See QM Survey, *supra* note 5, at 13 ("Time and cost are perennially acknowledged as the biggest concerns for arbitration users.").

24 See Jennifer Kirby, "Efficiency in Arbitration: Whose Duty Is It?," *Journal of International Arbitration* 32, no. 6 (2015): 689–695 (The former Deputy Secretary General of the ICC,

At a traditional in-person evidentiary hearing, the parties' representatives, counsel, arbitrators, witnesses, and experts would meet at a pre-determined physical location—typically at an arbitral institution's facilities or conference center—to convene the hearing. The costs for such a hearing are substantial for the parties concerned and typically include expenses for *inter alia* travel, lodging and hospitality, hearing room rental fees, transcription fees, and audio-visual equipment rental fees.[25] It has been estimated that travel and subsistence alone account for approximately one quarter of the costs to hold an in-person hearing.[26]

Remote hearings can significantly reduce these costs. In a survey of nineteen arbitral institutions, Patricia Shaughnessy noted that "the institutions have found the procedures for facilitating remote arbitration have worked well and meet the needs of clients for fair, efficient, and cost-effective arbitration."[27] The prevalence and familiarity of remote hearing platforms sparked by the pandemic has led many arbitral users to experience significant efficiency gains without compromising the quality of the arbitral process. Further, in the White & Case and Queen Mary School of International Arbitration Survey for 2021 ("QM Survey"), 25% of the respondents surveyed noted that they would be prepared to forgo in-person hearings altogether.[28] That one-quarter of respondents would be willing to forgo the all-important merits hearing in a physical setting is striking, but, as the QM Survey points out, this statistic seems to reflect the newfound level of comfort with remote hearing platforms amongst stakeholders.[29] Moreover, the QM Survey found that "[i]f a hearing could no longer be held in person, 79% of respondents would choose to 'proceed at the scheduled time as a virtual hearing'. Only 16% would 'postpone the hearing

Jennifer Kirby, posits that efficiency in arbitration involves the relationship between time, cost, and quality).

25 See Nigel Blackaby et al., *Redfern and Hunter on International Arbitration*, 6th ed. (Oxford University Press, 2015), para. 6.160 ("The task of organising hearings in a major international commercial arbitration should not be underestimated nor should the cost. A suitable hearing room must be provided, with ancillary breakout rooms and facilities for the parties and the arbitral tribunal. Access to printing facilities, and a Wi-Fi connection, is invariably essential. A live transcript and verbatim record of the proceedings is often considered essential. Accommodation is also required for witnesses, experts, and the parties' legal teams").

26 See Laudy and Mokele, *supra* note 7.

27 Shaughnessy, *supra* note 7, at 46.

28 See QM Survey, *supra* note 5, at 14.

29 *Id.* at 14 ("This seems to reflect, to some extent, the increased level of comfort users have acquired with remote hearings in recent times, and particularly as a result of logistical difficulties for in-person hearings resulting from the COVID-19 pandemic.").

until it could be held in person', while 4% would proceed with a documents-only award."[30]

The QM Survey also revealed that the following features would make certain institutions or arbitral rules more attractive: administrative/logistical support for remote hearings (38%); and provision for arbitrators to order both remote and in-person hearings (23%).[31] One could reasonably surmise that the higher costs associated with in-person merits hearings played a role in motivating these responses. In-person hearings typically involve numerous parties travelling internationally to either an arbitral institution or an *ad hoc* venue of the parties' choice. No matter which venue is chosen, the parties shoulder significant expenses for transportation, lodging, catering, equipment rentals and so on. Remote hearings, if appropriate under the circumstances of the case, could be the answer for reducing these significant hearing costs and achieving a resolution in an expeditious fashion. Given that remote hearings are typically held only for four or five hours a day, as opposed to eight hours a day for an in-person hearing, users are also incentivized to more efficiently use the available hearing time. In this context, practitioners must more succinctly identify the key arguments for presentations and examinations. Remote hearings thus can impose self-discipline to focus on the issues that are most material to the dispute, which can result in greater efficiencies.

Notwithstanding these time and costs savings, high-stakes, technically complex merits hearings involving multiple witnesses, experts, and time zones are likely better suited to a traditional in-person hearing—or at a minimum a hybrid hearing—instead of a remote hearing.[32]

First, it may not be logistically feasible to find a mutually agreeable time slot for all parties involved.[33] Given the various international time zones that may be implicated in a particular case, parties, counsel, and arbitrators may only have a narrow time slot to conduct the hearing each day. In such a case, parties or counsel may be at a serious disadvantage because that limited time range could fall during an inconvenient time, such as early morning or late at night. After considering all relevant circumstances, if time zone conflicts

30 *Id.* at 20.

31 *Id.* at 12, Chart 8.

32 See *id.* at 20 ("Going forward, respondents would prefer a 'mix of in-person and virtual' formats for almost all types of interactions, including meetings and conferences. Wholly virtual formats are narrowly preferred for procedural hearings, but respondents would keep the option of in-person hearings open for substantive hearings, rather than purely remote participation").

33 *Id.* at 24 (40% of respondents cited difficulties in accommodating time zones as a drawback of remote hearings).

substantially impede the efficient conduct of a hearing, an in-person hearing would likely be warranted.

Second, the arbitrators, counsel, and, if applicable, the arbitral institution should ensure that all participants are equipped with adequate and reliable technology. If one party or counsel has drastically asymmetrical technological resources or is disadvantaged due to unreliable internet services, the quality of the process would be in peril.

Third, it may be difficult to control cross-examinations and assess the witnesses' credibility,[34] particularly in a case with many witnesses. If a proper remote hearing protocol is not concluded, witnesses may appear with inadequate camera angles or poor lighting that renders it difficult to assess the witness' demeanor and body language.[35]

Fourth, notwithstanding the efficiency of remote hearings, participants in such hearings can experience significant mental and physical toll.[36] Mental and physical symptoms can include screen fatigue, physical exhaustion, mental health deterioration, and a waning ability to focus.[37] The impact of screen fatigue is amplified in the context of longer hearings and may jeopardize the quality of the process. As such, a tribunal must consider these negative side effects when deciding whether to hold a remote hearing.

Fifth, when a case requires several days of taking evidence and oral argument, counsel may prefer to confer internally and with witnesses and experts in-person.[38] For example, a recent study by Berkeley Research Group found that a lack of in-person preparation amongst counsel and experts diminishes

---

34 *Id.* (38% of respondents determined that remote hearings make it "more difficult to control witnesses and assess their credibility").

35 See, e.g., ICDR, "Model Order and Procedures for a Virtual Hearing via Videoconference," *supra* note 9.

36 See Berkeley Research Group, *supra* note 7, at 8 ("[S]taring at a screen for long periods of time, often in an observational capacity, is considerably less engaging than if the proceedings are taking place within the atmosphere of a physical courtroom"); Sophie Nappert and Mihaela Apostol, "Healthy Virtual Hearings," Kluwer Arbitration Blog, July 17, 2020, http://arbitrationblog.kluwerarbitration.com/2020/07/17/healthy-virtual-hearings/ ("[R]esearchers at Keio University (Tokyo), 35% of online workers reported that their mental health had deteriorated as a result of working remotely amidst the COVID-19 lockdown. Amongst the factors that were found to lead to health deterioration were the lack of transition between work and personal lives, as well as reduced physical activity and difficulty in communicating with co-workers").

37 See generally Nappert and Apostol, *supra* note 36.

38 See QM Survey, *supra* note 5, at 24 (40% of respondents said that a pitfall of remote hearings is difficulty in conferring during the hearing session outside of breaks).

the quality of mental preparedness.[39] Taking into account the relevant circumstances of the case, it thus may be more efficient to hold in-person hearings, or at a minimum, hold in-person preparatory meetings, even if the hearing is conducted remotely.

Thus, a tribunal may consider the above five points when determining if an in-person hearing or remote hearing is warranted. At the same time, it should also consider the significant cost and time efficiencies of holding a remote hearing, as discussed above, as well as the due process related implications noted in Section 3, *infra*.

2.3 *Enhancing Diversity in International Arbitration*

Continued use of remote hearings will likely help achieve greater diversity in international arbitration. As Dr. Shaughnessy posits, "[t]here is a great need for greater diversity and more inclusiveness in arbitration" as it "will improve arbitration performance and legitimacy."[40] Diversity may take many forms and encompasses differing racial, gender, cultural, socio-economic, sexual orientation, geographical, or disability-related backgrounds. While a comprehensive and sustained approach is required to improve diversity, the utilization of remote hearings presents one tangible way forward to make international arbitration more inclusive. Remote hearings could lower the barriers to entry in arbitration, which will permit arbitrators, parties, and counsel with diverse backgrounds more opportunities to achieve more visibility and garner first rate experience.[41]

First, increased reliance on remote hearings could provide counsel from underrepresented groups and geographic regions with more exposure to international arbitration, which in turn would provide them with expertise to serve as arbitrators in due course.[42] Reducing the time and costs associated with travel may also result in more frequent appointments of qualified counsel from

---

39 See Berkeley Research Group, *supra* note 7, at 6 ("The lack of in-person preparation before entering proceedings was cited by many as a major drawback of remote hearings, and seen by some to have a negative impact on the performance of both the expert witness and wider legal team."); see also Nappert and Apostol, *supra* note 36 ("Coordination with team members/co-arbitrators presents its own challenges. Often this is done in parallel with the main hearing, with Post-it notes being replaced by instant messaging chat rooms. This adds to the dissonance, or gap, referred to above: these platforms are usually social, not professional, outlets").

40 Shaughnessy, *supra* note 7, at 47.

41 *Id.*

42 See, e.g., QM Survey, *supra* note 5, at 19; Shaughnessy, *supra* note 7, at 47.

underrepresented regions.[43] For instance, in a recent conference on remote hearings and arbitration in Africa, there was a consensus among participants that remote hearings present a unique opportunity for Africa to "position itself as a leading dispute resolution hub."[44] Striving for that outcome would thus "promote the expansion of arbitration practices, resulting in the transmission of arbitration expertise to African practitioners and the eventual development of African arbitrators."[45] Improving access through remote technologies will give the next generation of African arbitrators the opportunity to garner experience, seek appointments inside and outside Africa, and likewise improve African arbitral institutions. As Kenfack Douajni has previously observed, international arbitration will only become "truly international" when Africans can participate as arbitrators in cases that do not have a nexus with Africa.[46] The continued use of remote hearings, whenever appropriate, can play a role in creating a more inclusive environment and encouraging progress in this direction.

Second, counsel with diverse backgrounds may enjoy newfound opportunities to attract potential clients and contribute to arbitral discourse. In contrast to travel schedules associated with physical presence, remote settings permit more flexible schedules. A more flexible environment may improve the representation of minorities and women and men with young families for whom physical attendance and long travel schedules may prove challenging. For example, as noted in the International Council for Commercial Arbitration's report on gender diversity, a general lack of flexible work schedules particularly affects women in law firms.[47] But this new remote paradigm could result in more flexible arrangements for women with families and may diminish the difficulties of conducting one's professional duties solely in an in-person setting.

---

43 See Laudy and Mokele, *supra* note 7 ("The shift to virtual hearings offers an opportunity to African practitioners who have not previously been involved in international arbitrations as party representatives. It relieves African parties of the requirement to designate legal representation in one of Europe's legal centres, allowing them to participate in arbitration proceedings at a lower cost").

44 *Id.*

45 *Id.*

46 Cosmo Sanderson, "Don't condescend to African arbitrators," Global Arbitration Review, September 8, 2021, https://globalarbitrationreview.com/dont-condescend-african-arbitrators.

47 "Report of the Cross-Institutional Task Force on Gender Diversity in Arbitral Appointments and Proceedings," International Council for Commercial Arbitration, July 29, 2020, 47, https://www.arbitration-icca.org/icca-reports-no-8-report-cross-institutional-task-force-gender-diversity-arbitral-appointments-and.

Moreover, a remote setting allows those with physical disabilities to remain in a location that is best for their health. Remote platforms allow greater flexibility for those with physical disabilities to contribute and play critical roles in the arbitral process despite an inability or unwillingness to participate in a physical setting.

Third, remote hearings may enable greater access to justice. For instance, remote arbitrations could reduce legal costs for claimants such as individuals or small businesses. Conversely, remote arbitrations may allow a financially disadvantaged respondent, including a fiscally strained sovereign State or State-owned enterprise, to defend itself without expending significant resources for an in-person hearing. Removing the costs associated with an in-person hearing may allow a disputing party to fully litigate its case rather than, for instance, seeking settlement early in the proceedings.[48]

There may, however, be certain circumstances under which remote hearings could have the collateral impact of impeding diversity initiatives.[49] For instance, arbitral users may be averse to appointing counsel or arbitrators whom they have not had the opportunity to meet in-person, whether in a professional or social setting. The current remote work paradigm could limit aspiring practitioners' ability to interact with clients and senior colleagues. There is thus a risk that arbitral users may continue to rely upon the more experienced counsel and arbitrators.

Furthermore, in the context of access to justice, it is critical to ensure that financially disadvantaged parties have access to adequate and reliable technology.[50] If a party lacks access to reliable technology, such as high-speed internet access required for remote hearings, the arbitrators must carefully consider those circumstances before determining whether a remote hearing is warranted.

48 See Laudy and Mokele, *supra* note 7 ("These additional costs [for an in-person hearing] have commonly influenced the approach taken by African parties in international arbitration, with many seeking to settle rather than incur the cost associated with international arbitration hosted in one of the European centres").

49 See, e.g., QM Survey, *supra* note 5, at 2 ("The general consensus amongst respondents is that caution should be exercised when exploring whether adaptations in arbitral practice experienced during the COVID-19 pandemic may have an impact on promotion of diversity objectives, as it can go both ways. Virtual events, meetings and hearings may facilitate participation by more diverse contributors, but this may be hindered by unequal access to technology and the challenges of building relationships remotely").

50 See QM Survey, *supra* note 5, at 19 ("Unequal access to reliable and affordable technology required for remote participation in hearings, meetings and community events was also flagged by many as a challenge").

Notwithstanding these potential drawbacks, if the arbitral community leverages the available technological capabilities for conducting remote hearings effectively, it may promote greater access to the international arbitration and allow fresh, diverse perspectives.

2.4 *Advancement of Environmental Initiatives*

Climate change is at the forefront of the challenges facing the global community. The past five years have been the warmest on record, a trend that the United Nations Secretary General, António Guterres, stated could put the world on "the verge of the abyss."[51] As noted previously, in-person hearings tend to imply long-distance travel for numerous individuals.

The arbitral community has increasingly become aware of its substantial carbon footprint and has taken strides to reduce its negative effects on the environment through efforts such as "The Green Pledge" by the Campaign for Greener Arbitrations, which has now been signed by over 600 individuals and organizations.[52] Initiatives have also emerged with creative contract drafting solutions for reducing the legal industry's carbon footprint, such as the Chancery Lane Project.[53] One of the dispute resolution model clauses developed in the Chancery Lane Project calls for the parties to disclose their projected carbon footprint throughout the proceedings and develop an environmental impact plan for reducing carbon emissions.[54] Notably, that same clause calls for all hearings to be conducted remotely but preserves arbitrator discretion on that point. Guidance like the Chancery Lane Project may become more common in the years ahead because, while not a carbon-neutral proposition, remote meetings and hearings can help reduce international arbitration's carbon footprint.

At the time of this article, there are discernible signs of a shift from an industrial era to a low carbon era. In 2015, 196 States adopted the Paris Agreement with the goal of achieving a climate neutral world by the mid-century mark.[55] Recently, some governments and business executives alike have taken a more aggressive approach with the "Race to Zero" campaign ahead of the COP26 in

51 "World on the verge of climate 'abyss', as temperature rise continues: UN chief," UN News, April 19, 2021, https://news.un.org/en/story/2021/04/1090072.

52 See "The Green Pledge," Campaign for Greener Arbitrations, accessed April 22, 2022, https://www.greenerarbitrations.com/news/freshfields-wins-inaugural-green-arbitration-award.

53 See "Low Carbon Arbitration Hearings: Mia's Clause," Chancery Project, last modified September 27, 2021, https://chancerylaneproject.org/climate-clauses/low-carbon-arbitration-hearings/.

54 See, e.g., Shaughnessy, *supra* note 7, at 47.

55 See "The Paris Agreement," United Nations Climate Change, accessed on April 22, 2022, https://unfccc.int/process-and-meetings/the-paris-agreement/the-paris-agreement.

Glasgow, where global leaders strengthened their contributions to the Paris Agreement. As of March 2021, it was reported that at least one fifth of the world's 2,000 largest public corporations have committed to meet net zero targets.[56] Repeat users of international arbitrations have committed to these objectives. For instance, in November 2021 the International Federation of Consulting Engineers, or FIDIC, launched a Climate Change Charter, which calls upon its nearly one million engineering professionals and 40,000 engineering firms to develop corporate policies in line with the COP26 objectives.[57] In light of COP26, many sovereign States will likewise likely continue their efforts to enact climate-friendly policies.[58] As such, it is probable that future corporate policies or government procurement guidelines may require the use of remote litigation technologies whenever possible in order to keep potential disputes in line with their net zero ambitions.

To align itself with those potential disputants' environmental values, the arbitral community ought to proactively consider the use of remote hearings as frequently as possible in order to combat climate change. While the energy use required for remote hearings is not carbon neutral, the adoption of fully remote or hybrid hearings is a step in the right direction from an environmental standpoint. Furthermore, the decreased carbon footprint of a remote hearing could make carbon offset programs for hearings a more feasible and more affordable proposition that could be explored by future disputants.

In summary, international arbitration must continue to adapt to global environmental initiatives to remain an attractive method for resolving disputes—both from the perspective of sovereign and corporate clients. Remote hearings may be one of the keys for achieving that end.

2.5 *Adoption of Remote Technology as a Means of Invigorating Further Technological Advances*

As noted above, the pandemic has accelerated the arbitration community's embrace of remote hearing technologies. In September 2019, Paul Cohen and

56 See Disha Shetty, "A Fifth of the World's Largest Companies Committed to Net Zero Target," Forbes, March 24, 2021, https://www.forbes.com/sites/dishashetty/2021/03/24/a-fifth-of-worlds-largest-companies-committed-to-net-zero-target/?sh=18f96cea662f.

57 "Transformative climate change charter launched for global infrastructure sector," FIDIC, November 10, 2021, https://fidic.org/node/34378.

58 For instance, the United Kingdom has pledged to derive all of its electricity from renewable sources by 2035, and the United States announced its goal to halve its emissions by 2030 (compared to 2005 levels). See "Climate change: Australia pledges net zero emissions by 2050," BBC News, October 26, 2021, https://www.bbc.com/news/world-australia-59046032.

Sophie Nappert observed that disruptive technological innovation "comes slowly from apparently afar, and before we know it, it's upon us."[59] Remote litigation platforms were at our fingertips but used most commonly for minor procedural hearings and sparingly used for hybridized evidentiary hearings. Then, suddenly, the age of fully remote hearings was suddenly upon us.

While many national courts also utilize remote hearings, the international arbitration community has the opportunity to be at the forefront in promoting and advance remote hearing capabilities. International arbitration must remain an attractive business proposition for its potential disputants—constantly leveraging efficiencies, including cutting-edge litigation technology. If reliance on remote hearing technologies does continue, the sustained demand for these platforms will likely lead to more advanced and higher quality remote hearing technologies.

This demand could result in the elimination of certain drawbacks associated with remote hearings. For example, a common criticism of remote hearings is that the tribunal or counsel is unable to physically view and assess the demeanor and body language of a witness while conducting a cross-examination. However, simple videoconferencing, which has been the default remote hearing medium, is still rather primitive and more advanced technologies are already available. Improved camera angles with 360-degree views of the witness are available and further advanced technologies, such as augmented reality ("AR") are in the prototype stages of development. Some commentators have suggested that AR could drastically improve the quality of remote hearings.[60] Participants could remain in separate physical locations but, with the use of additional hardware, view a full-body hologram of the party speaking in real-time. Having a more interactive experience through AR may also mitigate screen fatigue, as users may feel more physically present. Thus, technologies such as AR may reduce the common criticisms associated with today's most common remote hearing platforms.

The international arbitration community may find that continued reliance on technology could catalyze new innovation beyond remote hearing

---

59 Paul Cohen and Sophie Nappert, "Robots redux: blockchain, augmented reality, quantum computing and the future of arbitration," Global Arbitration Review, September 3, 2019, https://globalarbitrationreview.com/robots-redux-blockchain-augmented-reality-quantum-computing-and-the-future-of-arbitration.

60 See, e.g., Lucas Bento, "Arbitration Tech Toolbox: Toward Pandemic-Proof Arbitrations: The Augmented View," Kluwer Arbitration Blog, July 8, 2021, http://arbitrationblog.kluwerarbitration.com/2021/07/08/arbitration-tech-toolbox-toward-pandemic-proof-arbitrations-the-augmented-view/.

platforms. AR, artificial intelligence, and blockchain are all in the nascent stages of being applied to dispute resolution. Even so, some national courts, for example in the Peoples' Republic of China, have already piloted these technologies in the adjudicative context.[61] While it remains to be seen how and if this new wave of technology will be embraced by the larger arbitral community, it is inevitable that they will—to a certain extent—play a role in dispute resolution. It is incumbent upon all stakeholders in arbitration to stay ahead of the technological curve such that arbitral mechanisms and institutions are able to provide users a wide selection of the most advanced remote hearing technologies. As these technologies become more reliable and user-friendly, they may offer opportunities to improve the quality of the process, whether in a remote or hybrid hearing context. Thus, there could be an opportunity for international arbitration to set itself apart from national courts as a truly cutting-edge and dynamic model of dispute resolution and thereby improve its attractiveness to a wider range of users.

3 Due Process Implications of Remote Hearings

As Julian Lew has observed, "the ultimate purpose of an arbitral tribunal is to render an enforceable award."[62] As part of this "ultimate purpose," tribunals must ensure that the proceedings are held in accordance with general principles of due process or otherwise risk exposing the award to set-aside or enforcement related challenges. Due process, which is the minimum level of procedural fairness required in the arbitral process,[63] includes the following four elements: (i) a party must be given notice of the case against it; (ii) so the party has an opportunity to present its case and respond to the case put against it; (iii) before an impartial and independent tribunal; (iv) that treats all parties with equality.[64]

---

61 See Kun Fan, "The Impact of COVID-19 on the Administration of Justice," Kluwer Arbitration Blog, July 10, 2020, http://arbitrationblog.kluwerarbitration.com/2020/07/10/the-impact-of-covid-19-on-the-administration-of-justice/ (explaining that in the People's Republic of China, internet courts are utilizing decision-makers with artificial intelligence to undertake routine functions).

62 Julian D.M. Lew, "The Law Applicable to the Form and Substance of the Arbitration Clause," in *Improving the Efficiency of Arbitration Agreements and Awards: 40 Years of Application of the New York Convention*, ed. Albert Jan van den Berg (Kluwer Law International, 1999), 114–145.

63 Born, *supra* note 1, at 3828.

64 Lucy Reed, "Ab(use) of due process: sword vs shield," *Arbitration International* 33, no. 3 (September 2017): 6.

While there is a widespread recognition that due process is a key foundation that underpins the legitimacy of the international arbitration system,[65] there is also a consensus that arbitrators have a duty to efficiently manage the dispute resolution process.[66] Furthermore, arbitrators must guard against "due process paranoia,"[67] which Justice Sundaresh Menon has described as posing as a "real threat" to the arbitration process.[68] Thus, tribunals must remain vigilant to ensure that remote proceedings are conducted in accordance with due process, while also guarding against "due process paranoia" and upholding the principles of efficiency. In the context of remote hearings, the above-identified second and fourth elements of due process are particularly relevant.

To date, the authors have not identified a case from a major arbitration *situs* that has been set-aside or refused recognition or enforcement on the grounds that the hearings were conducted remotely or that the remote hearing procedures violated due process. Notwithstanding this, it is important for tribunals,

---

65 *Id.*; Born, *supra* note 1, at 1734–1735; see also UNCITRAL Rules, Art. 17(1) (conferring the power of the tribunal to "conduct the arbitration in such manner as it considers appropriate, provided that the parties are treated with equality and that at an appropriate stage of the proceedings, each party is given a reasonable opportunity of presenting its case").

66 See Born, *supra* note 1, at 2139, 2175, 2191–2192; ICC Rules, Art. 22(1) ("The arbitral tribunal and the parties shall make every effort to conduct the arbitration in an expeditious and cost-effective manner, having regard to the complexity and value of the dispute"); ICDR Rules, Art. 20(2) ("The tribunal shall conduct the proceedings with a view to expediting the resolution of the dispute"); SIAC Rules, Art. 19 (requiring the tribunal to ensure that the arbitration is conducted fairly, expeditiously, and economically, with the goal of arriving at a final resolution of the dispute).

67 White & Case LLP, "2015 International Arbitration Survey: Improvements and Innovations in International Arbitration," Queen Mary University of London, October 7, 2015, https://arbitration.qmul.ac.uk/media/arbitration/docs/2015_International_Arbitration_Survey.pdf (explaining that "due process paranoia" is a "perceived reluctance by tribunals to act decisively in certain situations for fear of the award being challenged on the basis that a party not having had the chance to present its case fully"); see also Reed, *supra* note 64.

68 Sundaresh Menon, "Dispelling Due Process Paranoia: Fairness, Efficiency and the Rule of Law," *Asia International Arbitration Journal* 17, no. 1 (2021): 1-27; see also, e.g., *The Estate of Julio Miguel Orlandini-Agreda and Compañía Minera Orlandini Ltda. v. The Plurinational State of Bolivia*, PCA Case No. 2018–39, Procedural Order No. 7, Apr. 10, 2020, para. 40 (In March 2020, Respondent had requested a suspension of its deadline to submit its Statement of Defense citing recent government lockdowns, which caused disruptions to travel and thus prevented counsel and government officials from meeting with witnesses and conferring with experts. The tribunal, however, denied Bolivia's request, explaining that "the proceeding can move forward, albeit with some delay, in a socially responsible manner by adapting to the new reality of communicating remotely—a practice that, as noted earlier, has already been established in other proceedings").

users, and other stakeholders to consider the following points as remote hearings are increasingly utilized in the coming years.

A court faced with a set-aside or enforcement challenge arguing that the tribunal violated due process by conducting part or all of the hearing remotely, or otherwise did not comply with due process standards as part of its remote hearing procedures, would inquire if the parties had an agreement that expressly excluded remote hearings. In such an instance, a tribunal's decision to hold a remote hearing may lead to a conclusion that the arbitral procedure violated the agreement of the parties or violated a fundamental rule of procedure.[69]

In the absence of party agreement, the court would assess whether the tribunal was empowered by the relevant rules to conduct a remote hearing. As noted above, institutions such as the ICDR and the ICC are at the forefront of adopting rules that expressly permit arbitrators to conduct remote hearings, while other institutions have also embraced flexibility in permitting arbitrators to exercise discretion to conduct remote hearings, albeit in a less emphatic manner than the ICDR or ICC. Additionally, a court would examine whether the tribunal conducted the remote hearings in harmony with the guidance issued by the relevant institution. In this context, the court would *inter alia* inquire as to whether the parties were given a sufficient opportunity to explain their respective positions on the viability of remote hearings and the procedures for different aspects of such a hearing, the tribunal's efforts to balance the parties' due process rights *vis-à-vis* its obligations to conduct proceedings efficiently, and whether the challenged aspects of the tribunal's decisions materially impacted the outcome of the case.

Most importantly, a court would examine whether a right to a physical hearing exists under the relevant *lex arbitri*[70] or if remote hearings are expressly prohibited. In 2021, the International Center for Commercial Arbitration ("ICCA"), surveyed 77 national jurisdictions and concluded that not a single jurisdiction granted an express right to a physical hearing.[71] Given that several national

69 Erica Stein, "Chapter 9: Challenges to Remote Arbitration Awards in Setting Aside and Enforcement Proceedings," in *International Arbitration and the COVID-19 Revolution*, eds. Maxi Scherer et al. (Kluwar Law International, 2020), 172.

70 As a general matter, the following legal regimens would govern whether an award can be successfully challenged on the basis of a remote hearing: (i) the UNCITRAL Model Law may govern set-aside proceedings in a national jurisdiction; (ii) the New York Convention would govern recognition and enforcement challenges to an award in a jurisdiction outside the seat of the arbitration; (iii) the ICSID Convention would apply to challenges awards issued under the ICSID Convention.

71 "Right to a Physical Hearing Project: Newly Released Reports Confirm Core Trends and Divergences," ICCA, last modified May 26, 2021, https://www.arbitration-icca.org/right-physical-hearing-project-newly-released-reports-confirm-core-trends-and-divergences.

courts[72] themselves have adopted remote hearings, it is highly unlikely that a tribunal's holding of a remote hearing itself would result in a successful challenge;[73] and indeed this is confirmed by recent rulings from courts in Austria,[74] Egypt,[75] and, in the context of a Financial Industry Regulatory Authority ("FINRA") arbitration, the United States.[76]

While the threshold for setting aside or refusing enforcement of an award is high and due process-related challenges are rarely successful, remote hearings could pose a unique set of issues for arbitrators and courts to tackle. For example, as Erica Stein has observed arbitrators will have to ensure that time zone differences, screen fatigue, access to reliable technology, simultaneous

---

According to the ICCA survey, the domestic laws of major arbitral seats, including *inter alia* the United States, United Kingdom, France, Singapore, and Switzerland, do not recognize a right to a physical hearing. Of the 77 countries surveyed, only 6 jurisdictions (Bahamas, Ecuador, Sweden, Tunisia, Vietnam, and Zimbabwe) may have a right to a physical hearing that may arguably be inferred from the relevant domestic laws, but those jurisdictions are not major arbitral seats. Moreover, it was revealed that the United Arab Emirates expressly permits the use of remote hearings in arbitration.

72 See "Videoconferencing, Courts and COVID-19: Recommendations Based on International Standards," International Commission of Jurists, November 2020, 4, https://www.unodc.org/res/ji/import/guide/icj_videoconferencing/icj_videoconferencing.pdf ("[I]n response to the COVID-19 outbreak, many judiciaries are making available an option, or imposing a requirement, that individuals and their lawyers appear at such hearings only by video-conferencing or similar substitutes for physical presence"); Mohamed Hafez, "Remote Hearings and the Use of Technology in Arbitration," Global Arbitration Review, May 26, 2021, https://globalarbitrationreview.com/review/the-middle-eastern-and-african-arbitration-review/2021/article/remote-hearings-and-the-use-of-technology-in-arbitration (finding that Australian and English courts have resorted to remote hearings).

73 Born, *supra* note 1, at 3451 (Born generally mentions that virtually all courts refuse to annul awards because hearings were conducted remotely and acknowledges that this trend will likely continue).

74 Maxi Scherer, "In a 'First' Worldwide, Austrian Supreme Court Confirms Arbitral Tribunal's Power to Hold Remote Hearings Over One Party's Objection and Rejects Due Process Concerns," Kluwer Arbitration Blog, October 24, 2020, http://arbitrationblog.kluwerarbitration.com/2020/10/24/in-a-first-worldwide-austrian-supreme-court-confirms-arbitral-tribunals-power-to-hold-remote-hearings-over-one-partys-objection-and-rejects-due-process-concerns (explaining that the Austrian Supreme Court (OGH) rejected respondents' challenge that a remote hearing before a Vienna International Arbitration Centre panel violated its due process rights).

75 Hafez, *supra* note 72 (explaining that the Egyptian Court of Cassation refused to set aside a Cairo Regional Centre for International Commercial Arbitration award rendered after a remote hearing because such hearings are consistent with Egyptian law).

76 *Slaney v. The Int'l Amateur Athletic Fed'n*, 244 F.3d 580, 592–93 (7th Cir. 2001) (Illinois district court denying a preliminary injunction seeking to prevent a FINRA arbitration and finding that the decision to hold a remote hearing was for the FINRA arbitral institution to decide, not the courts).

translations, and other safeguards (such as preventing witness coaching and maintaining cybersecurity) are accommodated.[77] While it remains to be seen whether these issues may lead to substantive due process violations such that an award could be set aside, such circumstances have yet to materialize. Accordingly, the arbitrator(s) and the parties must consider those issues when deciding whether to hold a remote hearing, as it will preserve the integrity of the process.

4 Potential Impact on Arbitration in the Tourism and Hospitality Industry

Taking into account the considerations of remote hearings highlighted in this Chapter, it is likely the case that the tourism and hospitality industry is uniquely positioned to benefit from the time and cost efficiencies of remote hearings.[78]

In the context of major hotel construction projects, the employer, contractor, and sub-contractors frequently encounter disputes during the construction phase. One method for resolving these mid-project disputes is through a Dispute Adjudication Board, which is a form of alternative dispute resolution, or through institutional arbitration, such as the ICC. Expeditiously resolving disputes related to an ongoing project are critical for keeping the project on track with contractual milestones. In addition, swift resolution of disputes during a project preserves the parties' contractual relationship under, for example, hotel management agreements, customer-supplier contracts, and construction contracts.

Remote hearings may be particularly advantageous for such disputes because they represent significant cost savings and could prove to be more expeditious. Frequently, these disputes are decided by an engineer or adjudicator with particularized experience in the subject matter without taking oral testimony from witnesses. Holding such proceedings in person may lead to undue delay and jeopardize the contractual relationship, especially if multiple disputes must be resolved.

---

77 See Stein, *supra* note 69, at 174–176.

78 See, e.g., Arif Ali et al., "Litigation Alternatives For COVID-19 Hospitality Disputes," Law360, May 11, 2020, https://www.law360.com/articles/1271694/litigation-alternatives-for-covid-19-hospitality-disputes (noting that "while virtual hearings may be the only option for the near future given travel restrictions, they may still be used in the long term in order to reduce time and costs" in hospitality and tourism arbitrations).

Indeed, the policy considerations identified above would likewise play a role for hospitality and tourism dispute resolution. Resorting to remote arbitrations presents a higher likelihood that the disputants would have access to a larger pool of more specialized adjudicators, counsel, and experts. Furthermore, based on the targets set forth in the Paris Agreement, the International Tourism Partnership set a goal for reducing carbon emissions by 66 percent by 2030 and 90 percent by 2050.[79] As part of reducing its carbon footprint, the hospitality and tourism industry could opt for green arbitrations that incorporate remote hearing capabilities, in addition to other features, such as paperless submissions and carbon offset programs.

As such, should these disputes arise during a major resort construction or renovation project, the use of remote hearings may increase the prospect of preserving the parties' relationship and viability of the project while simultaneously achieving certain policy objectives.

5 Conclusion

With indications that COVID-19 may become endemic in the near future, it remains to be seen whether the era of fully remote merit hearings were an aberration or will become an enduring feature of international arbitration. For the reasons discussed above, in-person hearings will likely continue as a desirable format for hearings, especially in the context of complex, multi-week merits hearings. Yet, at the same time, given the success with remote hearings, tribunals and parties should not rely on in-person hearings as a default matter. Rather, they must consider whether a remote hearing or a hybrid hearing would be more beneficial from a procedural and policy perspective, even in a post-pandemic world.

While the foregoing procedural and policy considerations are not intended to be exhaustive, the ultimate decision on which hearing format is appropriate should take into account these considerations, as well as the unique circumstances of each case. Ultimately, the tribunal serves as the gatekeeper of the process. It should thus endeavor to hear each party's views on the type of hearing that is preferable, seek to ensure an efficient and expeditious resolution of the dispute that complies with principles of due process and results in an enforceable award.

---

79 "UN Works with Global Hotel Industry to Reduce Emissions," United Nations Climate Change, January 31, 2018, https://unfccc.int/news/un-works-with-global-hotel-industry-to-reduce-emissions.

CHAPTER 6

Hearings in International Arbitration

What Has the Pandemic Taught Us about Virtual Hearings and What They Can Offer in the Future?

Ben Sanderson, Maria Scott and Sean Croft

1 Introduction

Parties to legal disputes often prefer international arbitration due to its procedural flexibility. This extends to the format of hearings. Telephone or video hearings have been a common feature of international arbitration long before the COVID-19 pandemic, particularly for procedural hearings.[1] Indeed, many practitioners predicted the inevitable migration towards virtual hearings, despite the traditional assumption that evidentiary hearings should take place face-to-face.[2]

Notwithstanding some initial reluctance,[3] that assumption was reversed during the period of lockdowns and travel restrictions caused by the pandemic, which accelerated the widespread adoption of virtual hearings. The normalization of virtual hearings has seen rapid developments in software and technology, and a marked strengthening of the arbitration community's familiarity with these services.

Beyond a pandemic necessity, virtual hearings have become a genuine alternative to traditional in-person hearings and no longer need to be viewed only as a second choice. Clients and their lawyers must now weigh the benefits of each alternative and decide what format is most suitable for their case. Below we discuss the potential efficiencies offered by virtual hearings, and the extent to which perceived difficulties associated with them have been overcome.

1 See, e.g., Derric Yeoh, "Is Online Dispute Resolution The Future of Alternative Dispute Resolution?," Kluwer Arbitration Blog, March 29, 2018, http://arbitrationblog.kluwerarbitration.com/2018/03/29/online-dispute-resolution-future-alternative-dispute-resolution/.

2 André de Luizi Correia, Leticia Barbosa e Silva Abdalla, and Rebeca Franzoni Mateus, "Virtual hearings on the merits of the arbitration: a step too far or the only path to follow?," The Legal 500, accessed July 14, 2021, https://www.legal500.com/guides/hot-topic/virtual-hearings-on-the-merits-of-the-arbitration-a-step-too-far-or-the-only-path-to-follow/.

3 Amy J. Schmitz, "Arbitration in the Age of Covid: Examining Arbitration's Move Online," *Cardozo Journal of Conflict Resolution* 22 (Winter 2021): 249.

 | DOI:10.1163/9789004514836_008

Ultimately, the inherently singular nature of each arbitration dispute means that no hearing format can offer a one-size-fits-all solution. To the contrary, with virtual hearings having proven their viability, the range of options available to clients and practitioners is wider than ever.

2 Virtual Hearings: Opportunities and Efficiencies

Virtual hearings offer several distinct opportunities and efficiencies in terms of cost and time, access to justice, client experience, and environmental benefits. Parties should weigh these potential benefits against any potential drawbacks in their particular case. We examine each of these aspects in further detail below.

2.1 *Cost/Time Efficiencies*

A major benefit of virtual hearings (and perhaps the benefit that is most cited) is that they are typically cheaper and require a shorter time commitment than in-person hearings.

Travel and accommodation costs, for example, may be entirely eliminated. Of course, any resulting cost reduction will be partly offset by the cost of the technology solutions required to carry out a virtual hearing.[4] The decrease in hearing costs may also be less noticeable for domestic arbitrations where an in-person hearing would normally be held in the country or even city where both parties and their legal teams are based.

The real source of cost savings, in fact, may arise from the move towards shorter hearings prompted by virtual hearings.[5] In a survey of arbitrators conducted by the Arbitration Institute of the Stockholm Chamber of Commerce (“*SCC*”), practitioners cited time, cost, convenience and environmental impact as the primary benefits of virtual hearings, with 75% of arbitrators highlighting time-saving in particular.[6] As the SCC noted in its report following this survey:

> *Because a virtual hearing does not require time-consuming travel, it can be scheduled for every other day or for shorter days, meaning that*

4 Jean-Pierre Douglas-Henry and Ben Sanderson, “Virtual hearings report: Virtual hearings,” DLA Piper, May 14, 2020, 13, https://www.dlapiper.com/en/uk/insights/publications/2020/05/virtual-hearings-report/ (“dla May 2020 Report”).

5 *Id.*

6 “SCC Virtual Hearing Survey,” Arbitration Institute of the Stockholm Chamber of Commerce, October 2020, 6–7, https://sccinstitute.com/media/1773182/scc-rapport_virtual_hearing-2.pdf.

> *participants do not need to put all other work on hold during the hearing. According to the arbitrators surveyed, this makes it easier to find suitable hearing dates within a reasonable time frame, and awards can be rendered faster.*[7]

Survey respondents also pointed out that virtual hearings may be more efficient, as a result of being shorter and therefore more focused.[8] They may be logistically easier to arrange, with cancellations found to be less likely.[9] One respondent to a survey carried out by DLA Piper in 2021 reported:

> *The preparation for the virtual hearing seemed effortless. The virtual hearing was conducted seamlessly* [...] *the cross examination was clear, the recording/transcript was real time, the camera monitoring was completely captive. One wonders why we should ever have a physical hearing flying numerous parties across the world when technology can facilitate a hearing that is real time, face-to-face, much like the physical hearing in every sense that matters in an arbitration case.*[10]

The 2021 International Arbitration Survey, conducted by the School of International Arbitration at Queen Mary University of London ("*Queen Mary Survey*"), yielded similar feedback: respondents reported that the use of technology as part of virtual hearings resulted in greater efficiency.[11]

In this way, virtual hearing technology helps to close the resource gap by allowing parties to minimize time and costs incurred.[12] This may present a significant benefit for increasingly cost-conscious and time-poor clients.

---

7 *Id.* at 7.

8 *Id.*

9 Schmitz, *supra* note 3, at 272.

10 Jean-Pierre Douglas-Henry et al., "Virtual Hearings 2021: Virtual hearings," DLA Piper, September 21, 2021, 8, https://www.dlapiper.com/en/uk/insights/publications/2021/07/virtual-hearings-2021/ ("DLA September 2021 Report").

11 White & Case LLP, "2021 International Arbitration Survey: Adapting arbitration to a changing world," Queen Mary University of London, May 7, 2021, 5, http://www.arbitration.qmul.ac.uk/media/arbitration/docs/LON0320037-QMUL-International-Arbitration-Survey-2021_19_WEB.pdf.

12 Allison Goh, "Digital Readiness Index for Arbitration Institutions: Challenges and Implications for Dispute Resolution Under the Belt and Road Initiative," *Journal of International Arbitration* 38, no. 2 (2021): 253–290.

2.2 *Access to Justice*

In a lecture in 2020, Chief Justice of the Supreme Court of Singapore, Sundaresh Menon, noted that "*technology has the potential to help close—and not merely bridge*" all dimensions of the "*justice gap*", i.e., "*the disparity between the legal needs of low-income persons and the resources available to meet those needs.*"[13] For example, technology can "[remove] *the need for convergence, both physically and temporally.*"[14]

While the access to justice argument arises most acutely in the context of low-value litigation, it is also relevant to arbitration. Virtual hearings have the potential to allow parties, witnesses, and experts to attend or participate in hearings that, for a range of reasons, they may otherwise have been unable to. Where, for example, it is the cost of travel to a hearing venue, particularly one that is overseas, which proves to be prohibitive, virtual hearings offer an accessible alternative. Easier access may prove a significant benefit for, by way of example, public interest groups who wish to intervene in investment disputes by way of "*amicus curiae*" submissions.

To some extent, virtual hearings may thus permit international arbitration to become more inclusive by facilitating voices that might not otherwise be heard. This could include not only the voices of parties who might otherwise be bound by certain geographical, medical, financial, or legal constraints preventing their physical attendance at a hearing, but also witnesses and experts, potentially even extending to counsel and arbitrators. In sum, virtual hearings may offer a more level playing field in international dispute resolution. Of course, virtual hearings are not a cure-all in respect to other inequalities present in the international legal system, such as a lack of access to legal education or adequate legal representation.

2.3 *The Client Experience*

While "*aspects of the hearing room drama might be lost,*"[15] virtual hearings may offer clients a preferable hearing experience, at least in some respects.[16] In an in-person hearing, a client's ability to communicate with her/his legal team and/or to assess the arbitrator(s)' reaction instantaneously, may be curtailed

---

13 Sundaresh Menon, "Technology and the Changing Face of Justice," Negotiation and Conflict Management Group (NCMG), November 14, 2019, ADR Conference 2019, 10 (original emphasis).

14 *Id.* at 11.

15 DLA May 2020 Report, *supra* note 4, at 14.

16 *Id.*

by room layout/configuration, and clients (often sat behind counsel) can feel disconnected from the proceedings, particularly if they do not have a clear view of all the advocates or the tribunal.[17]

In virtual hearings, the experience of the hearing room is the same for all.[18] Anecdotally, many clients appear to view this positively: they have the same visibility over the proceedings as all other participants,[19] leading them to feel "*much more connected with the proceedings*."[20]

As for other participants, analysis of the United Kingdom published by the Standing International Forum of Commercial Courts suggests that, in the eyes of judges and arbitrators, oral submissions and arguments are no less effective when delivered via video than they would be in person, as the insight and assistance provided to the judge is not hindered.[21]

An improved client (and/or arbitrator) experience at hearings is perhaps a more unexpected benefit of virtual hearings. However, this may not be appreciated by all. The general consensus seems to be that the experience is more practical and accessible in terms of viewing and following the hearing, but it seems likely that some will miss the feel of "*real life*", particularly after living with the pandemic for so long.

2.4 *Environmental Benefits*

Choosing a virtual hearing makes it easier for parties and their law firms to achieve increasingly ambitious sustainability targets. Virtual hearings reduce travel,[22] and accordingly, associated carbon emissions. They reduce paper waste by encouraging the electronic submission and presentation of documents,[23] particularly when combined with other software such as online case management platforms[24] which provide electronic management of the case file throughout the life of a case.[25] A significant portion of respondents to the

17 *Id.*

18 *Id.*

19 *Id.*

20 *Id.*

21 "Second SIFoCC COVID-19 memorandum," Standing International Forum of Commercial Courts, March 2021, 8, https://s3-eu-west-2.amazonaws.com/sifocc-prod-storage-7f6qtyoj7wir/uploads/2021/03/6.7119_JO_Second_SIFoCC_COVID-19_memorandum_WEB.pdf.

22 See *supra* section 2.2.

23 DLA September 2021 Report, *supra* note 10, at 13.

24 "Protocol for Online Case Management in International Arbitration," The Working Group on LegalTech Adoption in International Arbitration, November 2020, https://protocol.techinarbitration.com/p/1.

25 DLA September 2021 Report, *supra* note 10, at 11.

Queen Mary Survey[26] cited the low environmental impact of virtual hearings as a plus.

Amongst the arbitration community itself, in 2019, a group of practitioners launched the Campaign for Greener Arbitrations ("Greener Arbitrations Campaign"),[27] with the aim of reducing international arbitration's carbon footprint. What started as "*a promise by an international arbitrator to manage her arbitrations in an environmentally friendly manner*"[28] evolved into an international campaign including a "Green Pledge"[29] and, most recently, a series of "Green Protocols" to "*promote better environmental behavior through a series of action items*".[30]

As is to be expected, the Green Protocols encourage the use of electronic correspondence and electronic documents/bundles, avoiding printing, and reduction of travel.[31] Arguably, holding a virtual hearing will allow parties to fulfil, at least partially, many of these aims. As highlighted by the Greener Arbitrations Campaign, just under 20,000 trees could be required to offset the total carbon emissions resulting from just one major international arbitration.[32] Flights alone can contribute to over three quarters of these total carbon emissions.[33] Practitioners can substantially reduce such emissions by taking just three measures, all of which might be achieved through the choice of a virtual hearing: reducing long-haul travel by one return flight at each stage of the arbitration; eliminating hard copy filings; and eliminating the use of disposable coffee cups.[34]

In this regard, "[e]*ncouraging the use of videoconferencing facilities as an alternative to travel* (*including for the purposes of conducting fact finding or interviews with witnesses*)" is one of the Green Pledge's guiding principles.[35]

---

26 White & Case LLP, *supra* note 11, at 28.

27 "About Us," Campaign for Greener Arbitrations, accessed April 22, 2022, https://www.greenerarbitrations.com/about.

28 *Id.*

29 "The Green Pledge: Guiding principles," Campaign for Greener Arbitrations, accessed April 22, 2022, https://www.greenerarbitrations.com/greenpledge.

30 "Green Protocols," Campaign for Greener Arbitrations, accessed April 22, 2022, https://www.greenerarbitrations.com/green-protocols.

31 "The Green Pledge: Guiding principles," Campaign for Greener Arbitrations, accessed April 22, 2022, https://www.greenerarbitrations.com/greenpledge.

32 "A significant impact," Campaign for Greener Arbitrations, accessed April 22, 2022, https://www.greenerarbitrations.com/impact.

33 *Id.*

34 *Id.*

35 "The Green Pledge: Guiding principles," Campaign for Greener Arbitrations, accessed April 22, 2022, https://www.greenerarbitrations.com/greenpledge.

The more recent Green Protocols go one step further, recommending that all hearings should be conducted remotely, including by virtual hearing,[36] thereby flipping on its head the assumption that in-person hearings are the default.[37]

While pre-pandemic sustainability targets might have seemed difficult to fulfil, whether out of inertia, a resistance to change or some other reason, COVID-19 has essentially forced the arbitration community, over the months in which relevant restrictions have been in place, to reduce its carbon footprint. Given the pandemic's duration, it seems likely that at least one effect will be to alter deep-seated assumptions as to the conduct of arbitration proceedings. The positive environmental impact of the increase in virtual hearings, which, setting aside other issues, seems to be indisputable, is likely to last.

That being said, the increase in virtual hearings is not a complete answer to environmental concerns in international arbitration. Since "*transitioning to increased virtual proceedings naturally requires greater energy usage*", it has been suggested that practitioners review the energy sources being used to power their workspaces and home offices, to "*ensure that it is clean and that the tools they are using are energy efficient*".[38] This is of particular importance since, as a study conducted by Herbert Smith Freehills identified, carbon emissions from non-clean energy sources are the largest contributor of emissions in proceedings.[39]

3 Concerns Regarding Virtual Hearings Have Largely Been Dispelled

The conventional preference for in-person hearings has, at least in part, been sustained by a number of perceived limitations traditionally held against virtual hearings. We address certain of these below and consider the extent to which they have, in practice, been overcome.

---

36 See e.g. "Green Protocol for Arbitration Proceedings," Campaign for Greener Arbitrations, accessed April 22, 2022, para. VI.A., https://www.greenerarbitrations.com/green-protocols/arbitral-proceedings.

37 See also the example set out in the DLA September 2021 Report, *supra* note 10, at 13.

38 Maguelonne de Bruglere and Cherine Foty, "Sustainability and Diversity in the Newly Virtual World of International Arbitration," Kluwer Arbitration Blog, December 9, 2020, http://arbitrationblog.kluwerarbitration.com/2020/12/09/sustainability-and-diversity-in-the-newly-virtual-world-of-international-arbitration/.

39 Herbert Smith Freehills, "Inside Arbitration: Perspectives On Cross-Border Disputes," *Inside Arbitration*, no. 10 (August 2020): 30, https://www.herbertsmithfreehills.com/latest-thinking/inside-arbitration-issue-10; see also Bruglere and Foty, *supra* note 38.

3.1 *Practical Concerns*

There are several practical concerns often cited against virtual hearings. Here, we focus on those relating to witness testimony and technology and connectivity, before discussing confidentiality and cybersecurity, and the risk of legal challenges to the conduct of the proceedings.

3.1.1 Witnesses

A recurring concern regarding virtual hearings centers around witness evidence, particularly in common law systems in which credibility issues can often only be fully explored during cross-examination, and in which witness evidence can make or break a party's case. This is arguably becoming more relevant as the numbers of witnesses called to give evidence appears to be increasing: one study found that, from March 2020, the average number of persons called for examination in a given hearing rose by 62%, from 3.7 to 6.0.[40]

Possible concerns include that a virtual hearing may allow witnesses to benefit from clandestine assistance throughout their testimony,[41] or that video causes difficulties in reading body language or "*soft*" signals, thereby hindering effective communication and/or the creation of an accurate impression of a witness's credibility. Advocates may also worry that the conduct of a hearing via video may make it more difficult for a cross-examiner to interrogate a witness in the manner to which they are accustomed.[42]

However, in reality, such matters can be adequately resolved as part of the logistical arrangements for a hearing, and published guidelines such as the Seoul Protocol provide a useful starting point.[43] For example, there are multiple options available to parties concerned about witness interference, whether it be additional technology such as the use of a second or roving camera, or the agreed presence of a neutral lawyer in the witness's room. Parties may also

---

40 Gary Born, Anneliese Day, and Hafez Virjee, "Remote Hearings (2020 Survey): A Spectrum of Preferences," *Journal of International Arbitration* 38, no. 3 (2021): 2.

41 Schmitz, *supra* note 3, at 289–90.

42 Jean-Pierre Douglas-Henry, "Online Arbitration Hearings: A review of key developments in response to COVID-19," DLA Piper, September 28, 2020, 8, https://www.dlapiper.com/en/us/insights/publications/2020/09/virtual-hearings-report/ ("DLA Piper September 2020 Review").

43 "[Press Release] Seoul Protocol on Video Conference in International Arbitration is Released," KCAB International, March 18, 2020, http://www.kcabinternational.or.kr/user/Board/comm_notice_view.do?BBS_NO=548&BD_NO=169&CURRENT_MENU_CODE=MENU0025&TOP_MENU_CODE=MENU0024.

request that the arbitrator or tribunal issue a reminder to each witness of their duty to provide honest testimony. In many instances this will be in addition to the oaths already provided for under some arbitral rules.[44]

As for issues regarding body language, arbitrators have indicated that, in practice, there is no real difference in examining witnesses in person as opposed to over video conference, particularly as advances in technology and appropriate preparation can make it easier to see witnesses.[45] In fact, at least one practitioner observed that "*the process* [of presentation of witness evidence in a virtual hearing] *was to an extent enhanced by the online circumstances*".[46]

For those with experience of virtual hearings, that concerns of this nature are still levied against them may be surprising. As explained above, the options available for assuaging any such concerns are plentiful and are bolstered by professional and ethical rules which prohibit lawyers from interfering (directly or indirectly) with witness testimony. Indeed, concerns regarding the credibility and honesty of witness evidence exist regardless of the chosen hearing format. Whilst there will inevitably be individual cases in which the specific circumstances dictate that an in-person hearing is the only (or manifestly the better) way to reduce the risk of witness interference, such instances may in practice be rare.

3.1.2 Technology and Connectivity

The obvious difference between virtual hearings and in-person hearings is the need, in a virtual hearing, for sophisticated audio-video software allowing submission and presentation of documents alongside live witness and/or expert testimony. The need for such services, whichever is ultimately chosen, brings with it certain concerns: the potential for technological limitations or interruptions, a lack of sufficient screen space to share documents, and/or poor audio-video quality, to name a few. In addition, where arbitration participants are located around the world, something as simple as selecting an appropriate time zone for the hearing may also be a logistical headache.[47]

44 Schmitz, *supra* note 3, at 289–90.

45 See e.g. Alison Ross, "COVID-19: participants in SIAC case share success of virtual hearing," Global Arbitration Review, April 23, 2020, 8, https://globalarbitrationreview.com/virtual-hearings/covid-19-participants-in-siac-case-share-success-of-virtual-hearing; and also J. Brian Casey and Grant Hanessian, "Ordering Virtual Hearings over the Objections of a Party," ADR Institute of Canada, 2, https://adric.ca/ordering-virtual-hearings-over-the-objections-of-a-party/.

46 DLA September 2021 Report, *supra* note 10, at 12.

47 DLA May 2020 Report, *supra* note 4, at 6; see *infra* Section 4.2.

Appropriate infrastructure is also required. One lawyer who participated in a virtual hearing before the courts of the British Virgin Islands (BVI) described the experience as a "*disaster*",[48] after the chosen platform, Skype, had to be abandoned in favour of Zoom, for technical reasons, and the BVI court, citing bandwidth issues, imposed a limit on the number of connections to Zoom.[49]

In such instances, arrangements such as that reached by ICSID, which has entered into over 23 cooperation agreements with dispute settlement institutions around the world,[50] may be invaluable. These agreements permit ICSID to connect to virtual hearings (or hold in-person hearings) from the relevant institution's facilities, allowing parties to benefit from existing infrastructure at reduced cost.[51] This may be particularly attractive to parties encountering difficulties with poor internet access/connectivity or in accessing digital platforms/software.[52]

Arbitral participants must also be comfortable with the technology required for an effective virtual hearing. As one Dubai-based practitioner noted, the reluctance of certain parties and judges to consider virtual hearings over in-person hearings likely stems from instances of lack of access to adequate facilities or technology required for virtual hearings.[53] There is potential for a vicious cycle: practitioners hesitant to try a virtual hearing are unlikely to invest in the new wave of technology and software that has been developed over recent years precisely in order to improve the quality and functionality of the virtual hearing. That being said, in the long run it seems unlikely that practitioners' fear of the unknown will prevail over, for example, client cost and sustainability concerns: arguably, the market will drive the changes it wants to see.

In practice, given the number of virtual hearings which have taken place in recent months,[54] in the face of the above possible technical challenges, plus

48 DLA May 2020 Report, *supra* note 4, at 9.

49 *Id.*

50 "Other Facilities," ICSID, accessed April 22, 2022, https://icsid.worldbank.org/services/hearing-facilities/other-facilities.

51 "In Focus: In-Person, Remote and Hybrid Hearings," ICSID, accessed April 22, 2022, https://icsid.worldbank.org/resources/content/in-focus/hearing-facilities; "A Guide to ICSID's Global Facilities," ICSID, March 10, 2020, https://icsid.worldbank.org/news-and-events/blogs/guide-icsids-global-facilities.

52 Goh, *supra* note 12, at 16.

53 DLA September 2021 Report, *supra* note 10, at 9.

54 A survey carried out by a team led by Gary Born in 2020 found, for example, "*the prevalence of fully remote hearings win the second quarter of 2020 was over ten times greater than at any time previously.*" Gary Born, Anneliese Day, and Hafez Virjee, "Chapter 7: Empirical Study of Experiences with Remote Hearings: A Survey of Users' Views," in *International Arbitration and the COVID-19 Revolution*, eds. Maxi Scherer, Niuscha Bassiri, and Mohamed S. Abdel Wahab (Kluwer Law International, 2020).

additional pandemic related restrictions, clearly such challenges are no longer insurmountable. Indeed, arguably the logistical challenges of organizing a virtual hearing are no greater or more common than those presented by an in-person hearing, and practitioners have often reported online hearing platforms working seamlessly.[55]

3.1.3 Overcoming Practical Concerns: Relevant Guidance

While many of these concerns may have presented formidable obstacles prior to the pandemic, there is now an abundance of literature, guidance, protocols and recommendations to help parties mitigate these concerns. These include, for example, the Seoul Protocol on Video Conferencing in International Arbitration[56] and the Protocol for Online Case Management in International Arbitration,[57] as well as the new rules or guidance published by a number of arbitral institutions since the pandemic began.[58]

3.2 *Confidentiality and Cybersecurity*

Clients may be concerned that unauthorized third parties might access virtual hearings, whether by hacking their way in, or by obtaining a password or recording of the hearing from an authorized participant. These concerns are unsurprising given the sensitive commercial data and trade secrets routinely referred to during arbitration hearings (which by their nature are held in private), the desire that certain disputes remain confidential for a variety of business reasons, and the potential for regulatory penalties if certain protected information is disclosed. The stakes, therefore, can be high.

In practice, however, the sharing of confidential information is a risk in connection with any hearing, virtual or not. As for hacking, this would appear to have been near non-existent in the context of virtual hearings. Even so, publicly available guides and protocols such as the IBA Presidential Task Force's Guidelines on Cyber Security[59] (released in October 2018), the ICCA-NYC Bar-CPR Protocol on Cybersecurity in International Arbitration[60] (released

---

55 DLA September 2021 Report, *supra* note 10, at 7, 12.

56 KCAB International, *supra* note 43.

57 The Working Group on LegalTech Adoption in International Arbitration, *supra* note 24.

58 Summarised in the DLA Piper September 2020 Review, *supra* note 42, at Appendix, 11, and in the Annex to this chapter.

59 "Cybersecurity Guidelines," IBA's Presidential Task Force on Cybersecurity, October 2018, https://www.ibanet.org/MediaHandler?id=2F9FA5D6-6E9D-413C-AF80-681BAFD300B0.

60 "ICCA-NYC Bar-CPR Protocol on Cybersecurity in International Arbitration (2020 Edition)," ICCA, NYC Bar, and CPR, November 21, 2019, https://www.arbitration-icca.org/cybersecurity-international-arbitration-icca-nyc-bar-cpr-working-group.

in late 2019), and the Protocol for Online Case Management in International Arbitration[61] (released in November 2020) provide helpful guidance aimed at alleviating these concerns. These guides refer to best practices such as strictly monitoring access controls, using multi-factor authentication where available,[62] locking computers when users are away from their device,[63] storing data to be shared during the hearing in a consistently used and secure repository, using a technically secure videoconference platform with access controlled by an appropriate administrator, employing virtual private networks (VPNs) and encryption, and setting parameters for processing and sharing personal data.[64] Parties can incorporate these recommendations and can adapt template provisions, for example from the Protocol for Online Case Management in International Arbitration, into their own tailored, hearing-specific protocol. Importantly, parties should select appropriate videoconferencing software from a reputable service provider. Such providers offer advice and assistance that is often essential, both at the start of and during a virtual hearing.

In light of the now near universal reliance on email and other forms of electronic communication and information sharing, confidentiality and cybersecurity concerns can arise in any arbitration proceeding regardless of the format of the hearing. Accordingly, whilst such concerns do not solely affect virtual hearings, they may require some further thought and additional, well-conceived precautions. Fortunately, there is ample guidance available. Where appropriate steps are taken, virtual hearings offer a more than adequate level of confidentiality protections as compared to in-person hearings.

3.3 *Legal Challenges*

Traditionally, virtual hearings have been viewed as somehow providing a lesser or compromised form of justice.[65] Amongst some practitioners, there is

61 The Working Group on LegalTech Adoption in International Arbitration, *supra* note 24.

62 See IBA's Presidential Task Force on Cybersecurity, *supra* note 59, at 10, 13.

63 ICCA, NYC Bar, and CPR, *supra* note 60.

64 The Working Group on LegalTech Adoption in International Arbitration, *supra* note 24, at 7.

65 See, e.g., Schmitz, *supra* note 3, at 2491 (citing "*long-held beliefs that in-person hearings are always the best method for resolution*" as a reason for avoiding virtual hearings early in the coronavirus pandemic); Andrey Panov, "Post-COVID-19 World and the Duty to Conduct Arbitrations Efficiently and Expeditiously," Thomson Reuters, August 13, 2020, http://arbitrationblog.practicallaw.com/post-covid-19-world-and-the-duty-to-conduct-arbitrations-efficiently-and-expeditiously/ (reciting common complaints about the perceived disadvantages of video hearings compared to in-person hearings).

a belief that the fundamental right to be heard is at risk. Nonetheless, since the beginning of the pandemic, with the question unsurprisingly raised more frequently, tribunals and courts have repeatedly affirmed that legal challenges to virtual hearings will generally be denied, whether based on issues of contract assent, unconscionability, or due process.[66] Challenges based solely on the fact that an award resulted from a virtual hearing—without further evidence that the circumstances of that particular hearing rendered the proceedings unfair to one party—are unlikely to succeed.[67]

In late 2020, the International Council for Commercial Arbitration ("*ICAA*") launched a research project to ascertain whether a right to an in-person hearing exists in various jurisdictions around the globe.[68] ICAA did not locate a provision granting a right to an in-person hearing in any of the seventy-seven surveyed jurisdictions examined.[69] Furthermore, the requirement for "*oral*" hearings in the UNCITRAL "*Model Law*"[70] has been interpreted by most Model

66 See, e.g., Schmitz, *supra* note 3, at 276–78; see also Yvonne Mak, "Do Virtual Hearings Without Parties' Agreement Contravene Due Process? The View from Singapore," Kluwer Arbitration Blog, 20 June 20, 2020, http://arbitrationblog.kluwerarbitration.com/2020/06/20/do-virtual-hearings-without-parties-agreement-contravene-due-process-the-view-from-singapore/?doing_wp_cron=1592903970.0123848915100097656250.

67 Cf. Grant Hanessian and J. Brian Casey, "Virtual Arbitration Hearings When a Party Objects: Are there Enforcement Rights?," *New York Dispute Resolution Lawyer* 13, no. 2 (Summer 2020): 25-29, https://nysba.org/app/uploads/2020/08/FINAL_DisputeResolutionLawyer_Summer-2020.pdf#page=18; Mak, *supra* note 66.; but see Hamish Lal, "Virtual hearings: inflammatory markers in favour of in-person hearings," Akin Gump, December 2020, https://www.akingump.com/a/web/t81viPaXGbYu3M4HTWUwJq/2egxi9/cl-dec2020-guested.pdf.

68 "Does a Right to a Physical Hearing Exist in International Arbitration?," ICCA, September 4, 2020, https://www.arbitration-icca.org/right-to-a-physical-hearing-international-arbitration.

69 "Right to a Physical Hearing Project: Newly Released Reports Confirm Core Trends and Divergences," ICCA, May 26, 2021, https://www.arbitration-icca.org/right-physical-hearing-project-newly-released-reports-confirm-core-trends-and-divergences.

70 See UNCITRAL Model Law, Article, 24(1), accessed April 22, 2022, https://uncitral.un.org/sites/uncitral.un.org/files/media-documents/uncitral/en/19-09955_e_ebook.pdf, 27 (stating that "*Subject to any contrary agreement by the parties, the arbitral tribunal shall decide whether to hold oral hearings for the presentation of evidence or for oral argument, or whether the proceedings shall be conducted on the basis of documents and other materials. However, unless the parties have agreed that no hearings shall be held, the arbitral tribunal shall hold such hearings at an appropriate stage of the proceedings, if so requested by a party*"). For an explanation of the Model Law itself, see https://uncitral.un.org/en/texts/arbitration/modellaw/commercial_arbitration.

Law jurisdictions as not specifically requiring a "*physical*" hearing.[71] Reasons include a plain reading of the term "*oral*" (*i.e.*, as distinct from written), the lack of any explicit in-person requirement otherwise,[72] and the determination under the relevant laws and regulations that the parties need only be able to produce "*oral*" (as opposed to written) evidence, such as expert/factual testimony, cross-examination, and "*oral*" argument—all of which can be done as part of a virtual hearing.[73][74]

The unlikelihood of a successful challenge to virtual hearings (without more) is also reflected in the fact that the arbitration rules of most of the major arbitration institutions either expressly provide for, or at least leave open, the possibility of dealing with matters "*remotely*" through the use of technology, including virtual hearings and telephone hearings. In 2021, for example, the ICC added a provision to its Arbitration Rules which expressly allows a tribunal to conduct a hearing remotely, regardless of any objections from either party.[75] The relevant provisions of some of the most well-known institutional rules are summarised in Annex 1.[76]

4 Virtual Hearings: Persisting Possible Disadvantages

While most objections to the use of virtual hearings have been (or should be possible of being) largely resolved, the differences between in-person hearings

71 ICCA, "Right to a Physical Hearing Project: Newly Released Reports Confirm Core Trends and Divergences," *supra* note 69.

72 Cf. Franz Schwarz and Helmut Ortner, "Austria: Does a Right to a Physical Hearing Exist in International Arbitration?," ICCA, March 15, 2021, 2-3, https://cdn.arbitration-icca.org/s3fs-public/document/media_document/Austria-Right-To-A-Physical-Hearing-Report.pdf, (examining Austria's arbitration law with respect to an "*oral hearing*" requirement).

73 Cf. Rafael Francisco Alves, "Brazil: Does a Right to a Physical Hearing Exist in International Arbitration?," ICCA, February 8, 2021, 6, https://cdn.arbitration-icca.org/s3fs-public/document/media_document/Brazil-Right-to-a-Physical-Hearing-Report.pdf, (examining Brazil's arbitration law).

74 The United Nations Commission on International Trade Law ("UNCITRAL") is the core legal body of the United Nations, whose role it is to further the harmonization of the law of international trade. A UNCITRAL Model Law jurisdiction describes those jurisdictions that have adopted legislation based on UNCITRAL's Model Law, either entirely or in part.

75 ICC Arbitration Rules, art. 26.

76 Annex 1 is included in the DLA Piper September 2020 Review, *supra* note 42, at 11.

and virtual hearings should not be ignored. Arbitration practitioners should consider how to adapt their approach depending on the hearing setting, not just in terms of the necessary practical arrangements, but also their hearing strategy and approach to advocacy. Witnesses should also not assume that remote cross-examination will necessarily be easier than an in-person interrogation. Consideration of the hearing format will be a crucial aspect of hearing preparation, for parties, their legal teams, and at least to a certain extent, their witnesses.

4.1 *Reduced Human Interaction*

One immediate disadvantage is less direct human interaction. For example, some witnesses have found isolation from their legal teams to be a dispiriting, lonely and difficult experience.[77] From the perspective of lawyers, cross-examining an opposing party's expert, for example, can prove more difficult without the client's legal team and own expert nearby helping to identify weaknesses in the testimony.[78] While multiple instant messaging options provide a quick and easy method to communicate, this may fall short of the usual hearing experience.[79] Indeed, one of the key drawbacks of virtual hearings expressed repeatedly by respondents to a survey carried out by DLA Piper in 2020 was the lack of "*feel*" for the hearing room—a loss of chemistry between counsel and the opposing side, the tribunal and the witnesses.[80]

This may also affect settlement opportunities. The constant proximity and frequent breaks during an in-person hearing provide informal opportunities for the parties to discuss issues and sometimes even to settle the dispute.[81] While true that virtual breakout rooms or intermittent discussions separate from a hearing can also be conducive to settlement, in-person interactions would seem to represent a superior alternative.[82]

4.2 *Different Time Zones*

Another practical challenge that may be faced during virtual hearings, particularly in international, cross-jurisdictional matters, is the inevitability of conflicting time zones. As one practitioner reported:

77 DLA September 2021 Report, *supra* note 10, at 12.
78 DLA Piper May 2020 Report *supra* note 4, at 12.
79 *Id.*
80 *Id.*
81 Schmitz, *supra* note 3, at 290.
82 *Id.*

> *The main downside, because this was a very international case, is the time zone differences, because most days we had to log-in at night or very early in the morning. If you are there in person then of course we do not have that problem.*[83]

In these circumstances, arguably the starting point should be for any inconvenience caused by time zone differences be distributed evenly among the parties,[84] although anecdotal evidence, including in the experience of the authors of this paper, suggests that this is not always a given. Particular thought should be given to those giving evidence: parties will of course want to ensure that their own witnesses are as fresh and alert as possible. It is likely to be unreasonable, for example, for a witness to sit through the rigour of a cross-examination very late into the evening, as drowsiness sets in.

5 The Hybrid Approach

Virtual hearings do not have to be a yes/no proposition. Rather, the opportunities and benefits that virtual hearings offer, as explored above, mean that parties are now able to choose from a range of options when it comes to hearing format. If fully in-person and virtual hearings are, respectively, at either ends of a scale, the possibilities for a hybrid approach to hearings[85] seem almost infinite.

Even before the pandemic, the choice of different formats for different types of hearings has long been a feature of international arbitration. Shorter hearings, such as those relating to case management directions and interlocutory applications, were sometimes conducted virtually or simply over the phone, but the assumption generally was that substantive and/or evidentiary hearings would take place in person. Beyond dispelling the necessity of that assumption, the pandemic has led to a greater degree of flexibility, not only in terms of alternating between in-person hearings and virtual hearings, but also within the confines of each individual hearing.

Pre-COVID, hybrid hearings sometimes involved the use of video link for one or two witnesses facing specific time, health, or other travel restrictions.[86]

---

83 DLA September 2021 Report, *supra* note 10, at 8.

84 de Luizi Correia, e Silva Abdalla, and Mateus, *supra* note 2, at 3.

85 DLA September 2021 Report, *supra* note 10, at 11.

86 See Wendy Miles, "Chapter 6: Remote Advocacy, Witness Preparation & Cross-Examination," in *International Arbitration and the COVID-19 Revolution*, eds. Maxi Scherer, Niuscha Bassiri, and Mohamed S. Abdel Wahab (Kluwer Law International, 2020), 4.

During the pandemic, however, hybrid options have more frequently and fundamentally integrated in-person and virtual components. An evidentiary hearing may now take place with the tribunal and legal teams attending in-person (particularly where they are based in the same country, for example), with some or all party representatives, witnesses or experts based abroad joining via video conference. Audio-only or a combination of video and audio can also be utilized to varying degrees.

These kinds of hearings rely on technology working as it is intended to, thus generally requiring the oversight of qualified and skilled personnel.[87] Hybrid hearings may require, for example, setting up central dashboards, providing technology facilities for participants, or providing the means to navigate between the hearing room and breakout rooms.[88] During the pandemic, significant strides in the technology necessary for fully virtual or hybrid hearings, the investment in and consequent greater availability of the accompanying necessary services and infrastructure, and the rapid increase in the legal community's familiarity with the available options now make the idea of a hybrid hearing suddenly more attractive.[89] This will particularly be the case where a hybrid hearing allows the parties to reduce the time, cost, and effort necessary for hearings, without sacrificing many of the benefits of in-person hearings.[90]

It should be emphasised that parties do not have to adopt the same cookie-cutter approach to each case. Certain countries, for example, impose restrictions on access to specific online service providers or to certain video platforms, and licensing and regulatory factors must also be considered.[91] That there is such a wide range of options means that there should be a hearing format which fits each individual case.

6 Conclusion

Parties' increasing sensitivity to legal costs means that they are looking for alternative ways to run their disputes. Virtual hearings are a potent tool, offering the possibility of cost and time savings in addition to a slew of other

87 Graham Smith-Bernal, "Virtual Hearings Point the Way Forward for International Arbitration," Legaltech news, December 17, 2020, https://www.law.com/legaltechnews/2020/12/17/virtual-and-hybrid-hearings-the-future-of-international-arbitrations/?printer-friendly.

88 *Id.*

89 *Id.*

90 *Id.*

91 DLA May 2020 Report, *supra* note 4, at 10.

benefits. Ultimately, the future of virtual hearings will depend on the experience of legal clients and the ability of tribunals to ensure that parties are given adequate opportunity to present their case. Regardless, the use of technology should drive legal practitioners to deliver services in fundamentally different and/or better ways. Radical change requires viewing the world differently, even if that means challenging entrenched practices. Arbitration hearings are no different. Among other things, virtual hearings offer a green alternative with a low carbon footprint. If they can also deliver on the promise of time and cost efficiencies, then the future of virtual hearings as a real alternative to in-person hearings will be secured.

As a result of the changes required by the challenges of the COVID-19 pandemic, virtual hearings are now seen as a real and effective option to clients and arbitration practitioners. Looking to the future of international arbitration, it seems undeniable that virtual hearings, in some form or another, are here to stay.

Acknowledgment

Ben Sanderson is Of Counsel at DLA Piper, London, Maria Scott is a Senior Associate at DLA Piper, London, and Sean Croft is an Associate at DLA Piper, New York.

Annex 1

Arbitral Institution	Provision
ICC[a]	Article 22 of the ICC Arbitration Rules 2017 ("*ICC Rules*") provides that both the parties and the tribunal are required to be proactive in making efforts to conduct arbitrations efficiently and to agree to appropriate procedural measures to further that cause wherever possible. Article 26 of the ICC Rules provides that an ICC tribunal "*may decide, after consulting the parties, and on the basis of the relevant facts and circumstances of the case*" to hold a hearing "*remotely by videoconference, telephone or other appropriate means of communication.*"
LCIA[b]	Article 19.2 of the LCIA Arbitration Rules 2020 specifically allows for any hearing to be held virtually: "*As to form, a hearing may take place in person, or virtually by conference call, video conference or using other communications technology with participants in one or more geographical places (or in a combined form)* […]".
SIAC[c]	Rule 19.3 of the SIAC Arbitration Rules 2016 allows for a SIAC tribunal to hold at least the initial preliminary hearing "*in person or by any other means*". Rule 24 of the SIAC Arbitration Rules 2016 (concerning "*Hearings*") does not directly address the issue of virtual hearings, but does not exclude them.
SCC[d]	Article 32 of the SCC Arbitration Rules 2017 (concerning "*Hearings*") does not directly address virtual hearings, but does not exclude them.
ICSID[e]	Rule 32 of the ICSID Arbitration Rules (concerning "*The Oral Procedure*") does not directly address virtual hearings, but does not exclude them.

a International Chamber of Commerce.
b London Court of International Arbitration.
c Singapore International Arbitration Centre.
d Stockholm Chamber of Commerce.
e International Centre for Settlement of Investment Disputes.

CHAPTER 7

The Question of Remote Hearings in International Commercial Arbitration

Bahar Hatami Alamdari

1 Introduction

The COVID-19 pandemic affected dispute resolution mechanisms worldwide throughout 2020. Countries around the globe had to respond to the restrictive measures taken by states to deal with the challenges created by the pandemic. Courts and arbitral institutions were forced to accommodate pandemic-related measures including social distancing and to facilitate remote hearings in order to be able to function and continue resolving disputes. In this challenging time, international commercial arbitration appeared to be more flexible than other areas of the law to accommodate remote hearings despite a number of practical challenges.[1]

Arbitration undoubtedly provides a greater amount of flexibility to parties than national courts. The conduct of arbitral proceedings, due to its consensual nature and the significant element of party autonomy, tends to foster a spirit of compromise. This may be why the use of international commercial arbitration has increased significantly over the past year.

The international commercial arbitration community was not alien to virtual and remote proceedings and, in fact, prior to the onset of the COVID-19 pandemic and travel and social restrictions, several procedural hearings had already been conducted remotely either via telephone conferencing or online platforms to accommodate arbitration participants in different countries and mitigate cost and time constraints. Substantive/evidentiary hearings previously had to be held face-to-face; therefore, it was rare to have an entire arbitration procedure conducted remotely.[2] During the pandemic, several arbitral

1 Mohamed Hafez, "Remote Hearings and the Use of Technology in Arbitration," Global Arbitration Review, May 26, 2021, https://globalarbitrationreview.com/review/the-middle-eastern-and-african-arbitration-review/2021/article/remote-hearings-and-the-use-of-technology-in-arbitration.

2 Hamish Lal, Josephine Kaiding, and Léa Defranchi, "Virtual Hearings in International Construction Arbitration: Evolution or Mitigant?," *Construction Law Journal* 37, no. 2 (April 2021): 129–141.

 | DOI:10.1163/9789004514836_009

institutions helped to facilitate virtual hearings. For instance, the International Chamber of Commerce (ICC) digitalized requests for arbitration and the London International Court of Arbitration (LCIA) set up a virtual platform to file arbitration applications with parties encouraged to file submissions electronically.

Many arbitration institutions have published guidelines on virtual hearings, facilitating virtual proceedings hearings as well as substantive hearings. After the COVID-19 outbreak, the international commercial arbitration community increased the use of remote communication among parties and arbitrators for both procedural and substantive matters. And it looks as if fully or semi-remote hearings are here to stay, even post-pandemic.[3]

The main question addressed in this chapter is whether arbitrators should have the power to order virtual hearings against the wishes of the parties. We argue that arbitrators should have such power in order to save the arbitration from frustration. In the chapter, we also explore the issue of consent to determine whether an arbitral tribunal can force the parties to consent to a virtual hearing in the event that an alternative procedural mechanism has been stipulated in the arbitration agreement. The relevance of the *lex fori* will also be examined.

The chapter will also explore the principle of 'access to justice' to determine whether an individual's right to justice can be met via online hearings in arbitration as a general theory. In the last section, some practical challenges will be discussed briefly.

2 Theoretical Challenges of Remote International Commercial Arbitration Hearings

2.1 *Autonomy of the Arbitrator in Ordering Remote Hearings*

Another crucial dilemma to address when justifying remote arbitral hearings is the extent of the power of arbitrators to hold such hearings. It can be argued that arbitration is a consensual method based on an all-party agreement. However, if one party is not willing to engage in a remote hearing, can arbitrators impose remote arbitration contrary to that party's desire, for instance, if one party argues that a face-to-face hearing is necessary in order to fully present

3 Alice Fremuth-Wolf, Ingeborg Edel, and Anna Forstel, "How the COVID-19 pandemic may shape the future of international arbitral proceedings," International Bar Association, accessed August 18, 2021, https://www.ibanet.org/article/A7F75D89-2CFD-4386-96B9-53341D0A55DA.

its case but this is not possible at the time (due to pandemic restrictions, for instance), would this result in frustration of the arbitration agreement possibly due to *force majeure*? Some scholars have debated whether arbitrators have the power to stop such frustration of arbitration agreements by ordering all parties to hold a virtual hearing.

During the Covid pandemic and even at the present time, while some pandemic restrictions are still in place, parties cannot agree as to whether hearings should be virtual, face to face or in some hybrid mode. This results in unnecessary delays in resolving disputes and administrating arbitrations. Consequently, international arbitration proceedings can become very lengthy and arguably less efficient than judicial proceedings. Ironically, one of the main reasons that commercial parties have always favored international arbitration over litigation has been efficiency, and this advantage is becoming less apparent due to the lack of parties' cooperation in determining alternative modes of procedure.

To answer this question, the legal theory of arbitration must be reviewed. More precisely, if there is a lack of consent to conduct a remote hearing from a party identified in the arbitration agreement, is there any theory justifying the arbitrator's power/autonomy to rescue the arbitration agreement from frustration and thereby force the parties involved to conduct virtual hearings? Different theories justify the judicial nature of arbitration. Various academics and legal philosophers have taken different approaches in associating arbitration with legal systems.[4] The four main theories which elaborate the notion of arbitration and its attachment to legal frameworks are jurisdictional, contractual, mixed or hybrid and autonomous theories.[5]

Jurisdictional theory is based on the idea that international commercial arbitration is governed by the supervisory power of the State which, in the majority of cases, is the State of the seat of arbitration.[6] Contractual theory argues that arbitration originates from a valid arbitration agreement conducted between parties[7] while hybrid theory suggests that it is a mixture of

4 Bahar Alamdari, "The Emerging Popularity of International Arbitration in the Banking and Financial Sector – Is this a Fashionable Trend or a Viable Replacement?," (PhD diss., University of London, School of Advanced Studies, 2016), https://sas-space.sas.ac.uk/6401/1/Hatami%20Alamdari,%20Bahar.pdf.

5 Julian David Mathew Lew, Loukas A. Mistelis, and Stefan Kröll, *Comparative International Commercial Arbitration* (Kluwer Law International, 2003).

6 F. A. Mann, "Lex Facit Arbitrum," in *International Arbitration: Liber Amicorum for Martin Domke*, ed. Pieter Sanders (The Hague: Martinus Nijhoff, 1967).

7 Hong-lin Yu, "A Theoretical overview of the Foundations of International Commercial Arbitration," *Contemporary Asian Arbitration Journal* 1, no. 2 (2008): 255, https://citeseerx.ist.psu.edu/viewdoc/download?doi=10.1.1.555.2751&rep=rep1&type=pdf.

contractual and jurisdictional theories. The most significant approach these days is the autonomous theory, which is a relatively modern approach that holds that an autonomous institution should be free from the constraints of the *lex fori*[8] and found its legitimacy in a transnational legal order.[9]

It seems that, for many years, the dominant theoretical approach in international arbitration has been contractual theory.[10] The main focus of this theory is the contractual nature of arbitration, highlighting that the main source of legitimacy of the arbitration tribunal comes from the parties' agreement to arbitrate. Contractual analysis of arbitration can seem more reasonable when one looks at the various laws and rules on arbitration worldwide. In the vast majority of national laws on arbitration or international arbitration rules, the essential and fundamental factor is an agreement between parties. The central point in this theory is based on the idea that the arbitration process is a reflection of the parties' contractual agreement to arbitrate their disputes. The arbitration award is also the outcome of this agreement, and as all the involved parties agreed to the process of arbitration, they are required to honor the award and enforce and recognize it automatically.[11]

Furthermore, the contractual theory in arbitration can rationalize the parties' duty to cooperate with the arbitration process and if a party does not comply with its contractual duties, it can be held responsible for the breach. This obligation stems from the arbitration agreement under which the contracting parties agreed to submit their disputes to arbitration. The fact that the parties decided to opt for arbitration and are compelled to do so with positive or negative duties, can also be elucidated by referring to the prior agreement between the parties in the arbitration agreement.[12] Therefore, participating in an international arbitration hearing either virtually or face-to-face is an enforceable duty on parties where there exists a freely signed arbitration agreement.[13]

On the other hand, looking at the autonomy theory, the arbitrator's power – which is independent of the agreement of the parties – is justifiable, as it does

8 The law of the seat.

9 Mohammad Bashayreh, "The Autonomy of Arbitrators: a legal analysis of the validity of arbitrator-imposed virtual hearings in response to the COVID 19 crisis," *International Arbitration Law Review* 24, no. 1 (2021): 75–91.

10 The conclusion that contract is the only source of the participation duty of parties fails to recognise the diversity of theories of arbitration. For more details, see Benedict Tompkins, "The Duty to Participate in International Commercial Arbitration," *International Arbitration Law Review* 18, no. 1 (2015): 14–26.

11 *Id.* at 4.

12 *Id.* at 14-26.

13 *Id.* at 4.

not place the arbitrator in an adversarial position vis-à-vis the parties involved and actually empowers the arbitrator to complete the mission of the arbitration entrusted and to resolve the dispute.[14]

Therefore, if the tribunal ordered a virtual hearing for both procedural and evidentiary matters, it is the parties' duty to participate and act in good faith and ultimately adhere to the tribunal's order in circumstances where there is no special procedural requirement set by the parties. Likewise, parties have a duty to comply in situations where they have agreed on the procedure to follow though the arbitrator has decided to make an adjustment and order, contrary to their wishes, as they see appropriate. As highlighted in most arbitration national laws and rules, once a tribunal has been constituted and the arbitration has started, the tribunal will have the power to fix the proceedings as it considers appropriate.[15] Tribunals often have the power to decide on procedural issues, and this is widely accepted across the international arbitration community.[16] Therefore, it can be argued that the decision to hold arbitration hearings virtually or in person, is a procedural matter. If the tribunal believes that it is in the best interests of parties to hold a virtual hearing, the parties have the duty to accept and follow the procedure put in place by the tribunal.

In one Australian case,[17] the court had to decide whether or not a virtual solution (the only option during lockdown) was feasible and appropriate and whether a virtual hearing was fair and justifiable. In this case, the Australian Federal Court decided there was no need to delay the hearing and that it could take place virtually. The applicant had raised concerns as to the stability of its internet connection and although the court recognized the issue, it did not consider this to be an 'insurmountable' obstacle. The court also pointed out that justice system institutions such as the courts must do all they can to facilitate the administration of justice. The decision reached in this case can provide some reassurance for arbitrators if they decide to hold a virtual hearing against the will of the parties involved in the dispute.[18]

---

14 Bashayreh, *supra* note 9.

15 Such as UNCITRAL Model Law Article 19 (2010) (The law of the seat should also be taken into account).

16 Lew, Mistelis, and Kröll, *supra* note 5.

17 *Capic v Ford Motor Company of Australia Limited (Adjournment)* [2020] FCA 486.

18 Kun Fan, "The Impact of COVID-19 on the Administration of Justice," Kluwer Arbitration Blog, July 10, 2020, http://arbitrationblog.kluwerarbitration.com/2020/07/10/the-impact-of-covid-19-on-the-administration-of-justice/.

The practical benefit of justifying an arbitrator's power to order virtual hearings against the will of the parties is that the award remains recognizable and enforceable, and there are no grounds for challenging it. The English Arbitration Act 1996[19] Section 33 on the general duty of a tribunal, and subsection (b) in particular, states that:

> The tribunal shall,
>
> (b) adopt procedures *suitable* to the circumstances of the particular case, avoiding unnecessary delay or expense, so as to provide a fair means for the resolution of the matters falling to be determined.

The wording of this section appears to give the ultimate power and flexibility to the tribunal to adopt the most suitable procedure to conduct the arbitral proceeding. This can apply to the context where the tribunal has decided to hold the arbitral hearing virtually as they see it as the best possible option in order to avoid unnecessary delay and expenses.

However, section 34(1) limits the power of the arbitral tribunal in handling the procedure to some extent and indicates the importance of the "parties' agreement". The section reads as follows:

> It shall be for the tribunal to decide all procedural and evidential matters, subject to the right of the parties to agree any matter.

The 'subject to parties' agreement' section signifies the fact that the parties' agreement is paramount in ordering and handling such a procedure. Therefore, the tribunal cannot order a procedure against the agreement of the parties involved.

However, it seems that if parties do not have a specific agreement on the procedure of the arbitration, it gives the tribunal the power to select and decide the procedure considered most appropriate to complete the arbitration mandate.

The requirement of following the parties' wishes has been supplemented by Section 68(2)(c) in challenging awards where the Act says:

> (c) failure by the tribunal to conduct the proceedings in accordance with the procedure agreed by the parties;

This section may provide grounds for challenging the award if the conduct of the arbitration is against the agreement of the parties, as outlined in Section 34

19 English Arbitration Act, 1996.

of the Act. It should, however, be noted that such a challenge can only be successful if the court is satisfied that this particular case has caused 'substantial injustice' within the meaning of Section 68(2) of the Act:

> Serious irregularity means an irregularity of one or more of the following kinds which the court considers has caused or will cause substantial injustice to the applicant.

The record of English case law shows that often it is rare to have a challenge and award successfully based on causing 'substantial injustice' to an applicant and that, in practice, there is a very high threshold for Section 68 challenges in order to keep the court's intervention in the arbitral process to a minimum.[20] The approach of the Commercial Court in England has been very supportive of virtual hearings except in very exceptional circumstances.

Looking at arbitration rules shows that there has been a considerable response to the pandemic from arbitral institutions, which have adopted various measures to handle the implications of the COVID-19 pandemic, and more specifically the need to cater and provide a structure for remote hearings. The COVID-19 pandemic accelerated the digitalization already ongoing within arbitral institutions worldwide and, as a result, some major institutions made changes to their rules to help with the smooth running of international arbitration procedures. In essence, most changes and amendments deal with granting wider powers to arbitrators and tribunals in terms of running procedures and deciding on the form of hearings.

Updates to the LCIA Arbitration Rules – one of the commonly used arbitration rules – took effect from October 2020. This update includes changes on different aspects of the rules, but more importantly, the use of technology in arbitral proceedings. The new rules make specific reference to virtual arbitral hearings encouraging parties and tribunals to implement technology into their procedures in order to improve the efficiency of those procedures. Article 19(2) specifically states that the tribunal may decide to hold the hearing by video or telephone conference or in person or even a combination of the three:

> The Arbitral Tribunal shall organise the conduct of any hearing in advance, in consultation with the parties. The Arbitral Tribunal shall have the fullest authority under the arbitration agreement to establish

20 For more see: *SCM Financial Overseas Ltd v Raga Establishment Ltd* [2018] EWHC 1008 (Comm). The English High Court dismissed an application under section 68(2)(a) of the English Arbitration Act, 1996.

> the conduct of a hearing, including its date, duration, form, content, procedure, time-limits and geographical place (if applicable). As to form, a hearing may take *place in person, or virtually* by conference call, videoconference or using other communications technology with participants in one or more geographical places (or in a combined form). As to content, the Arbitral Tribunal may require the parties to address specific questions or issues arising from the parties' dispute. The Arbitral Tribunal may also limit the extent to which questions or issues are to be addressed.[21]

To emphasize even further the discretion of the tribunal in terms of the conduct of such procedures, Article 14 (2) states that "the Arbitral Tribunal shall have the widest discretion to discharge these general duties, subject to the mandatory provisions of any applicable law or any rules of law the Arbitral Tribunal may decide to be applicable; and at all times the parties shall do everything necessary in good faith for the fair, efficient and expeditious conduct of the arbitration, including the Arbitral Tribunal's discharge of its general duty." Article 14(1) (ii) defines the "general duties" of the arbitrators as "adopt procedures suitable to the circumstances of the arbitration, avoiding unnecessary delay and expense, so as to provide a fair, efficient and expeditious means for the final resolution of the parties' dispute".

In April 2020, the International Chamber of Commerce (ICC) published a note concerning the impact of the COVID-19 pandemic on international arbitration titled: 'ICC Guidance Note on Possible Measures Aimed at Mitigating the Effects of the COVID 19 Pandemic'. The ICC Arbitration Rules 2021 came into force in January 2021 and the focus of this updated version of the rules is to provide for more efficient, flexible, and transparent arbitration. In the new rules, there is an entry on the digitalization of arbitration containing a provision for virtual hearings and a shift away from form-filling. Article 26 expressly gives the power to arbitral tribunals to decide on in-person hearings or remote hearings,[22] although this decision is subject to two requirements – first consulting the parties and second considering the relevant facts and circumstances of the case. Another significant point in this section is that the ICC rules not only refer to video and telephone conferencing means, but they also indicate 'other appropriate means of communication', which can be interpreted as the

21 "LCIA Arbitration Rules," LCIA, in effect as of October 1, 2020, https://www.lcia.org/Dispute_Resolution_Services/lcia-arbitration-rules-2020.aspx#Article%2019.

22 "2021 Arbitration Rules," ICC, in effect as of January 1, 2021, Article 26, https://iccwbo.org/dispute-resolution-services/arbitration/rules-of-arbitration/.

provision to make wider use of more advanced means of telecommunication or perhaps artificial intelligence in the future.

In sum, it appears that the problem of how to address a situation where one party simply insists on in-person hearings and objects to virtual hearings should be resolved by looking at the applicable law and the governing procedural rules in that particular arbitration and then deciding whether there is a legitimate exercise of power from the arbitrator to order remote hearings despite a certain party's objection.[23] More importantly, the autonomy of the arbitration to order remote hearings has to be checked with the applicable law of the arbitration and more specifically the *lex fori* of the arbitration. Once the law of the seat has been determined either by parties or arbitrators, the rules of the seat will apply to the issue of remote hearings.

2.2 *Access to Justice*

According to the United Nations (UN), access to justice is a basic principle of the rule of law.[24] Delivery of justice should be free from any discrimination and available to everyone regardless of their means or location. Courts and judicial processes must be designed in a way that makes the whole structure of the justice system accessible and available, allowing every individual to be heard and to exercise his or her rights in case of infringement of these rights. The right to a fair and effective hearing is enshrined at Article 6 of the European Convention on Human Rights (ECHR)[25], providing that every individual must have access to an independent and impartial tribunal within a reasonable timeframe and must have the opportunity to be heard on equal terms to the other party involved in a dispute.[26] The question arises as to whether online hearings are in fact a means to expand access to justice or simply to minimize it? Will online hearings create inequality amongst parties and affect the right to present a case effectively before a court?

The COVID-19 pandemic has resulted in court and tribunal closures and has threatened individual rights to access justice. This was already subject to debate, with many feeling that justice was never actually available to everyone

---

23 Mohamed Hafez, "The Challenges Raised by COVID-19, Its Impact on the Arbitral Process and the Rise of Video Conferencing," *International Business Law Journal* 1 (2021): 85–99.

24 "Access to Justice," United Nations, accessed August 18, 2021, https://www.un.org/ruleoflaw/thematic-areas/access-to-justice-and-rule-of-law-institutions/access-to-justice/.

25 Reiss Edwards, "European Convention on Human Rights (ECHR) Does it Still Apply After Brexit?," Lexology, April 13, 2021, https://www.lexology.com/library/detail.aspx?g=7e0577d5-e617-471a-8e00-5c964741965c.

26 "Handbook on European Law relating to access to justice," European Union Agency for Fundamental Rights and Council of Europe, January 2016, https://fra.europa.eu/sites/default/files/fra_uploads/fra-ecthr-2016-handbook-on-access-to-justice_en.pdf.

in society. Jurisdictions reacted differently to the challenges caused by the pandemic in terms of how they provided justice. In certain jurisdictions, there was an absolute shutdown of courts and tribunals with hearings adjourned for unknown periods.[27] These delays resulted in a substantial backlog of cases before the courts, bringing to mind the legal maxim that 'justice delayed is justice denied'. Consequently, the COVID-19 pandemic has not only had serious health implications, but it has also threatened the administration of justice.

Under these circumstances, there was an urgent need to set up a platform to address the excessive backlog of cases (there had already been a build-up of delayed court cases prior to the pandemic) and deliver justice to the public.[28] Under these circumstances, digitalization and technology came to the rescue by providing online dispute resolution systems and remote hearing solutions. Both individuals and wider societies across various jurisdictions had to embrace technology and explore various telecommunication measures in order to ensure that justice remained accessible and available during lockdown periods.

In some jurisdictions, such as England, online dispute resolution mechanisms were already in place to some extent prior to the pandemic, therefore restrictions on social gatherings only served to enhance and increase this practice. In March 2020, the Lord Chief Justice stated that it was 'of vital importance that the administration of justice does not grind to a halt'; following this statement, the judiciary started to implement changes and issue guidance on remote hearings.[29] The international arbitration community followed suit slightly later by issuing guidance and notes providing for remote arbitration proceedings.[30]

As mentioned above, the main debate here is whether the principles of access to justice can be met by providing and facilitating online judicial platforms for court hearings or arbitration hearings. Looking at the importance

27 Javier Garcia Sanz and Javier González Guimaraes-da Silva, "Video conference Hearings in Spain: new mandatory rules for court proceedings," International Bar Association, accessed August 18, 2021, https://www.ibanet.org/article/B5B479D3-228C-49B7-A170-2FD7E6F47F1D (There was a full closure in Spain for several weeks).

28 "Justice under Lockdown in Europe," Fair Trials, November 26, 2020, https://www.fairtrials.org/news/justice-under-lockdown-europe.

29 "English courts versus institutional arbitration: how do they compare in their approach to virtual hearings?," Stewarts, July 2, 2020, https://www.stewartslaw.com/news/approach-to-virtual-hearings-english-courts-versus-institutional-arbitration/.

30 More specifically LCIA and ICC changed and amended their rules to accommodate for virtual hearings.

of physical hearings, there is case law, as decided by courts, which assesses the validity and admissibility of the evidence given remotely via such unconventional means as video conferencing. The court's challenge was to decide whether the witness should in fact have given the evidence by physically attending the hearing session in order to preserve the administration of the justice and not to cause disruption in access to justice for either party.

A case[31] in the UK decided by the House of Lords in 2005 concluded that the giving of evidence by video conferencing (from applicants) fails to impact the administration of justice and is, in fact, aligned with the relevant Practice Direction[32] which provides that the use of video conferencing 'will be likely to be beneficial to the efficient, fair and economical disposal of the litigation' and therefore, the other party would not suffer injustice and prejudice since evidence is given remotely and via video conferencing.[33] It is noteworthy that this decision was reached following an examination of the circumstances of the case and the parties involved and the conclusion that giving evidence via video link would not have any significant impact on the respondent's right to access justice.

In another English case, the court decided that although it was ideal for evidence to be given physically in person, due to the special circumstances presented in this particular case and the fact that the claimant could not travel to England due to poor health, a fair trial could be achieved by taking evidence via video link from a witness in Kenya.[34] In this case, access to justice was not prevented for the party in question. This case seems to have taken into consideration the special circumstances of the witness (travel) and actually served to widen participation and access to justice. This is a very positive development. The court also highlighted that the special circumstances of the individual providing evidence should be taken into consideration when allowing for the use of video links and was of the view that video links are especially unsuitable for vulnerable witnesses who needed interpretation and may be less familiar with technology.[35] It appears from the court decision that the

31 *Polanski v Conde Nast Publications Limited* (2005) UKHL 10.

32 "Practice Direction 32 – Evidence," Justice, last modified October 1, 2020, Annex 3: Video Conferencing Guidance, https://www.justice.gov.uk/courts/procedure-rules/civil/rules/part32/pd_part32#annex3.

33 *Id.*; see also "Part 32 – Evidence," Justice, last modified April 14, 2021, Civil Procedural Rule (CPR) 32.3, https://www.justice.gov.uk/courts/procedure-rules/civil/rules/part32.

34 *Kimathi, Nyoro and others v Foreign and Commonwealth Office* [2015] EWHC 3116 (QB) and [2015] EWHC 3684 (QB).

35 *Id.*

witness needs to be of sound mind and able to demonstrate an understanding of online platforms to communicate in this way.

One should differentiate between national court hearings and international commercial arbitration hearings due to the different jurisdictional rules and legal regimes at play. Society must also importantly acknowledge that the parties involved in a court case may be prone to certain character traits or idiosyncrasies. A further point to highlight regarding international commercial arbitration is that participants are usually well-established corporations with the means (internet and technology) to use online dispute mechanisms. On the other hand, as reported in May 2020 by the Civil Justice Council of England examining the impact of COVID-19 on the Civil Justice System, lay litigants (or parties) of diverse backgrounds and demographics may not have had access to the technology and resources needed to effectively participate in remote hearings.[36]

Meanwhile, another significant finding of this report was that remote hearings can help to improve access to justice by lowering the overall cost of litigation.[37] There is no doubt that cost is a paramount factor for many individuals in terms of accessing courts and tribunals. Some argue that the broad phenomena of digitalization of justice and in particular providing online dispute resolution mechanisms, if well-designed, would widen access to justice due to the low cost, accessibility and ease of use of these mechanisms.[38] Some scholars have also argued that the problem of access to justice during the recent pandemic can be resolved by providing the possibility of holding virtual hearings especially during quarantine periods and even post-quarantine.[39] This seems to be a valid argument – especially when one considers the implications of the pandemic across the world and the fact that we are yet to emerge from it.

36 Natalie Byrom, Sarah Beardon, and Abby Kendrick, "Rapid Review: The Impact of COVID-19 on the Civil Justice System: Report and Recommendations," accessed August 18, 2021, https://www.judiciary.uk/wp-content/uploads/2020/06/FINAL-REPORT-CJC-4-June-2020.v2-accessible.pdf.

37 *Id.* at 16.

38 See generally Amy J. Schmitz and Colin Rule, *The New Handshake: Online Dispute Resolution and the Future of Consumer Protection* (American Bar Association, 2017); Amy J. Schmitz, "Building on OArb Attributes in Pursuit of Justice," in *Arbitration in the Digital Age: The Brave New World of Arbitration*, eds. Maud Piers, Christian Aschauer, and Karl-Franzens (Cambridge University Press, 2018).

39 Nelli Golubeva, Illia But, and Pavlo Prokhorov, "Access to Justice Due to the COVID-19 Pandemic," *Revista de Derecho* 9, no. 2 (2020): 47-64, http://dspace.onua.edu.ua/bitstream/handle/11300/14368/Golubeva%20N.%2C%20But%20I.%2C%20Prokhorov%20P.%20Access%20to%20Justice%20Due%20to%20the%20Covid-19%20Pandemic.pdf?sequence=1&isAllowed=y.

Virtual and remote hearings may therefore be regarded as a good practice to ensure the administration of justice.

In sum, online dispute resolution mechanisms (including virtual hearings) can make justice more accessible when properly designed.[40]

3 Practical Challenges of Remote Arbitral Hearings

There are practical challenges to virtual hearings that can burden all stakeholders in this process, including arbitrators and disputing parties. There are various debates and discussions around these practical challenges in particular relating to cybersecurity, data protection and privacy.

As discussed above, technology came to the rescue in different areas of our lives during the COVID-19 outbreak. The fact that people can access online dispute resolution mechanisms and engage in judicial proceedings from the comfort of surroundings familiar to them takes away the hostility that they may encounter in courtrooms or arbitral hearing seats, but may also raise some potential risks and concerns.

Two of the main challenges in any type of virtual communication are cybersecurity and data protection. One cannot disregard the impact of the COVID-19 pandemic on cybersecurity and the now increased possibility of cyber-attacks. As remote working has become increasingly embedded in communities, security challenges and privacy infringements have become more and more apparent.

Arbitration by nature is a private and confidential process and these two important features must be maintained during proceedings. Arbitration is a private process and is confidential to the parties involved; pleadings are not open to the public. No individuals other than parties with an interest in the case are allowed to attend the hearing. Arbitration can provide a shield for parties who, for a variety of reasons, do not wish to publicize their dispute. The issue of confidentiality and disclosure of information during proceedings is very important.[41] Using technology and conducting hearings remotely can raise privacy implications; the confidentiality of proceedings may be compromised by remote hearings as the parties involved have no control over recordings being made and over the operations of the online platforms being used.

---

40 Bridgette Toy-Cronin et al., "Testing the Promise of Access to Justice through Online Courts," *International Journal of Online Dispute Resolution* 5, no. 1–2 (2018): 39-48, https://researchcommons.waikato.ac.nz/bitstream/handle/10289/13107/IJODR_2352-5002_2018_005_102_005.pdf?sequence=18&isAllowed=y#.

41 *Id.* at 4.

In order to safeguard the virtual environment for parties and arbitrators, various guidelines have been issued dealing with different aspects of security. The Chartered Institute of Arbitration in England (CIArb) issued a guidance note called 'CIArb Guidance Note on Remote Dispute Resolution'[42] which encourages participants to exchange details in advance of the hearing, which is to some extent a form of digital handshaking.

Another important observation with respect to confidentiality and the need to secure video conferencing is that participants are encouraged to use sophisticated means of telecommunication and safe internet servers. In this regard, the Seoul Protocol on Video Conferencing in International Arbitration provides some practical steps to protect confidentiality in remote hearings.[43]

Tribunals and institutions holding remote hearings must pay careful attention to cybersecurity and data protection. The International Council for Commercial Arbitration (ICCA) and the New York City Bar Association (NYCBar) established a working group and recognized that digitalized forms of arbitration must be provided with appropriate guidance on cybersecurity. This resulting protocol – the 'ICCA-NYC Bar CPR Protocol on Cybersecurity in International Arbitration'[44] – provides advice on information security during remote hearings.

Finally, the potentially differing time zones of participants have been raised as one practical challenge facing remote arbitration hearings. Undoubtedly, in the process of international commercial arbitration, there are attendees from all around the world; when holding online tribunals, one or more of the parties will inevitably have to connect outside normal business hours or even late in the evening or early in the morning.[45] As a matter of fact, the difficulties of accommodating multiple or disparate time zones were stated as one of the top disadvantages of virtual hearings in a recent survey conducted by White and Case examining international arbitration and the way it is adapting to the changing world in 2021.[46] It seems that there is no practical solution to address

---

42 "Guidance Note on Remote Dispute Resolution," CIArb, April 8, 2020, https://www.ciarb.org/media/8967/remote-hearings-guidance-note.pdf.

43 "Seoul Protocol on Video Conferencing in International Arbitration," 33 Bedford Row, accessed April 22, 2022, https://www.33bedfordrow.co.uk/upload/files/Seoul%20Protocol%20on%20Video%20Conference%20in%20International%20Arbitration.pdf.

44 "ICCA-NYC Bar-CPR Protocol on Cybersecurity in International Arbitration (2020 Edition), ICCA, NYC Bar, and CPR, November 21, 2019, https://www.arbitration-icca.org/icca-reports-no-6-icca-nyc-bar-cpr-protocol-cybersecurity-international-arbitration.

45 Hafez, *supra* note 23.

46 "2021 International Arbitration Survey: Adapting arbitration to a changing world," White & Case LLP, May 6, 2021, https://www.whitecase.com/publications/insight/2021-international-arbitration-survey/technology-virtual-reality.

this difficulty and this might just be an inevitable cross-border element of international arbitration.

4 Conclusion

The question remains as to whether virtual hearings and online dispute resolution will expand access to justice and possibly replace conventional physical hearings. There is no simple answer and according to a recent report (July 2021) published by the Law Society of England and Wales, the use of remote hearings should be considered on a case-by-case basis; they should only happen when the court is satisfied that justice can be served via a remote hearing, weighing the importance and urgency of the hearing against factors suggesting that justice might be better served through a physical hearing.[47]

From a legal standpoint, this chapter suggests that where a face-to-face hearing is impossible and parties are strategically resisting meaningful online hearings or unwilling to take part in the process of virtual arbitration, the tribunal should be empowered to order and force parties to adhere to this form of proceeding, regardless of the apparent lack of consent from the parties. By doing so, arbitrators are avoiding frustration of the arbitration agreement in cases where parties are not acting in good faith in fulfilling their contractual obligations with respect to the arbitration agreement. The parties' failure to comply with the arbitrator's order for a virtual hearing could then amount to a breach of contract, *i.e.* a breach of the arbitration agreement.

Broadly speaking, it appears that in straightforward cases and submission-based advocacy, remote hearings such as video hearings can work well, though in contested trials this may not always be the case.[48] In a survey conducted by Baker McKenzie and KPMG in September and October 2020, participants, including arbitrators, judges, barrister and clients were asked whether virtual hearings and mediations are here to stay. The survey explored whether digital justice is an innovation that should be implemented within our judicial systems and whether or not it should outlast the pandemic.[49] One of the key findings

---

47 "Remote hearings," The Law Society, March 1, 2022, https://www.lawsociety.org.uk/campaigns/court-reform/whats-changing/remote-hearings.

48 Byrom, Beardon, and Kendrick, *supra* note 36 (This was a report published by the Civil Justice Council of England in May 2020, which examined the impact of COVID-19 on the Civil Justice System).

49 "The Future of Disputes: Are Virtual Hearings Here To Stay?," Baker McKenzie, accessed April 22, 2022, https://www.bakermckenzie.com/-/media/files/insight/publications/2021/01/future-of-disputes-campaign-brochure.pdf.

was that there is no 'one-size-fits-all' approach in virtual hearings, which supports the view of the Law Society of England and Wales. More than 75% of the respondents believed that having a full online hearing should depend on each case. If the case involves a technical matter or substantive legal issues, perhaps both procedural and substantive hearings can be held virtually. However, if the case relies on more evidentiary content or the cross-examination of witnesses, physical presence might be essential.[50]

Overall, it seems that virtual hearings are very much here to stay,[51] and one cannot underestimate the advantages offered by online hearings. There are still some key concerns in relation to the use of virtual dispute resolution mechanisms – but the rapid digitalization and use of AI in the administration of justice – particularly in relation to the use of robot arbitrators in the realm of international arbitration – is changing the industry in such a way that it may become difficult to justify in-person hearings at all.

50 *Id.*

51 Lal, Kaiding, and Defranchi, *supra* note 2.

CHAPTER 8

The Practice of Virtual Hearings during COVID-19 in Investment Arbitration Proceedings

Bjorn Arp and Edwin Nemesio

1 Introduction*

The right to be heard as a fundamental characteristic of arbitration does not include a right to an in-person hearing, not even in evidentiary hearings.[1] However, in practice, an in-person hearing is often considered a cornerstone of international arbitration proceedings, and almost tantamount to due process. The COVID-19 pandemic was a shock to this established system and the assumption of many that in-person hearings were a natural element of any arbitration proceeding. The social restrictions imposed by the pandemic, accompanied by governmental measures to restrict travel across borders, have raised with ever more strength the question whether an in-person hearing is really necessary – under the applicable arbitration rules as well as in practice. As this study will show, although the transition to virtual or remote hearings happened quickly and surprisingly smooth, some parties in investment arbitration raised their concerns about the continued use of the virtual hearing format when the health emergency subsides. It is possible that a growing number of hearings in investment cases will again take place in person.

---

* All web pages referenced in this article are updated to October 2021. The authors thank Charlene Mwaura for her editorial revision of this article.

1 Jurisdictions in many countries have recognized the right to be heard, but not gone so far to require a right to an oral (in-person) hearing. See, for instance, in Switzerland the case of *X. et consorts contre Z. GmbH*, Swiss Federal Tribunal Judgment, 4A_342/2015 of April 26 2016, BGE 142 III 360, at 4.1.1.: "Le droit d'être entendu, tel qu'il est garanti par les art. 182 al. 3 et 190 al. 2 let. d LDIP (RS 291), n'a en principe pas un contenu différent de celui consacré en droit constitutionnel (ATF 127 III 576 consid. 2c; ATF 119 II 386 consid. 1b; ATF 117 II 346 consid. 1a p. 347). Ainsi, il a été admis, dans le domaine de l'arbitrage, que chaque partie avait le droit de s'exprimer sur les faits essentiels pour le jugement, de présenter son argumentation juridique, de proposer ses moyens de preuve sur des faits pertinents et de prendre part aux séances du tribunal arbitral (ATF 127 III 576 consid. 2c; ATF 116 II 639 consid. 4c p. 643). En revanche, le droit d'être entendu n'englobe pas le droit de s'exprimer oralement (ATF 117 II 346 consid. 1b; ATF 115 II 129 consid. 6a p. 133 et les arrêts cités). [...]".

© BJORN ARP AND EDWIN NEMESIO, 2023 | DOI:10.1163/9789004514836_010

For the purpose of this analysis, and following the definitions contained in the "IBA Rules on the Taking of Evidence in International Arbitration,"[2] "evidentiary hearing" is any hearing, whether or not held on consecutive days, at which the arbitral tribunal, whether in person, by teleconference, videoconference or other method, receives oral or other evidence. The IBA Rules also define "remote hearing" as a hearing conducted, for the entire hearing or parts thereof, or only with respect to certain participants, using teleconference, videoconference, or other communication technology by which persons in more than one location simultaneously participate.[3]

This article analyzes the rules applicable to international arbitration and the practice of investment arbitration tribunals that held or will hold remote hearings during the pandemic. The goal is to determine whether the virtual format in this type of arbitration (1) has infringed upon the parties' procedural rights, (2) is a legitimate way of advancing an arbitration at times when in-person hearings may be considered too dangerous for health reasons, or impractical because of governmental limitations on travel and free movement, or (3) is a realistic option for the future, even when the pandemic is fully overcome and no restrictions to free movement exist.

2 Virtual Hearings and Arbitration Rules of International Arbitral Institutions

2.1 *ICSID and UNCITRAL Rules: Reaffirming the Powers of Arbitral Tribunals*

Reacting to the COVID-19 pandemic, arbitral institutions large and small have continued their alternative dispute resolution services through different electronic means of communication. The ICSID Secretariat, and the tribunals constituted pursuant to the ICSID rules, as well as others following ICSID Additional Facility and UNCITRAL rules, quickly adapted to the new realities and provided their services primarily through electronic means of communication.

---

2 "IBA Rules on the Taking of Evidence in International Arbitration," International Bar Association (IBA), adopted by a resolution of the IBA Council, December 17, 2020, https://www.ibanet.org/Article/NewDetail.aspx?ArticleUid=137D2AB8-DB09-42AE-A19B-FC31AED914AE.

3 "IBA Rules on the Taking of Evidence in International Arbitration," International Bar Association, December 17 2020, 8, https://www.ibanet.org/MediaHandler?id=def0807b-9fec-43ef-b624-f2cb2af7cf7b (Preamble).

In ICSID procedures, tribunals rely on Article 44 of the ICSID Convention, which states that:

> Any arbitration proceeding shall be conducted in accordance with the provisions of this Section and, except as the parties otherwise agree, in accordance with the Arbitration Rules in effect on the date on which the parties consented to arbitration. If any question of procedure arises which is not covered by this Section or the Arbitration Rules or any rules agreed by the parties, the Tribunal shall decide the question.[4]

Article 32 of the ICSID Arbitration Rules refers to the hearing, although it does not specify if the oral presentations must be done in person or by any virtual means. Consequently, the rules leave a broad margin of discretion to the arbitral tribunal to give effect to these provisions. Furthermore, Rule 26 of the Administrative and Financial Rules of ICSID provides that the Secretary General "shall make or supervise arrangements if proceedings are held elsewhere," referring to a place different than the Center.[5]

Article 17(1) of the 2013 UNCITRAL Arbitration Rules similarly provides arbitral tribunals with wide discretion to fill gaps and take procedural decisions.[6] Neither ICSID nor UNCITRAL have modified their arbitration rules to reflect any concerns about the pandemic's challenges. For the arbitrations that follow those rules, the tribunals themselves provided solutions to these challenges in exercising their powers to conduct the procedure in accordance with the chosen arbitration rules. In addition, some already existing rules became relevant, such as Article 28(4) of the 2013 UNCITRAL Arbitration Rules, which allows for the examination of witnesses and experts through means of telecommunication such as videoconferencing.[7]

---

4 Art. 44 of the Convention on the Settlement of Investment Disputes between States and Nationals of other States ("ICSID Convention"), signed at Washington, D.C. on March 18, 1965 and entered into force on October 14, 1966, 575 U.N.T.S. 159.

5 Rule 26 of the ICSID Administrative and Financial Rules.

6 Article 17(1) of the UNCITRAL Arbitration Rules, in their latest version of 2013, grants the arbitral tribunal the power to conduct the arbitration as it considers appropriate, provided that the parties are treated with equality and that each party is given a reasonable opportunity of presenting its case at an appropriate stage of the proceedings. The arbitral tribunal, in exercising its discretion, shall conduct the proceedings in such a way to avoid unnecessary delay and expense and to provide a fair and efficient process for resolving the parties' dispute. See Article 17(1) of the UNICTRAL Arbitration Rules, available online at https://uncitral.un.org/en/texts/arbitration/contractualtexts/arbitration.

7 Art. 28(4) of the UNCITRAL Arbitration Rules, as revised in 2010: "The arbitral tribunal may direct that witnesses, including expert witnesses, be examined through means of

2.2 *Rules Amendments by Arbitral Institutions*

In contrast, several privately-run arbitral institutions amended their rules with the main purpose of including the possibility for arbitral tribunals to use virtual means of communication and other technology in the administration of justice, including for conducting virtual hearings. Any such powers emerge from the tribunals' general powers – after giving the parties a reasonable opportunity to state their views – to make any procedural order they consider appropriate, with regard to the fair, efficient, and expeditious conduct of the arbitration.[8]

To further clarify the scope of the arbitral tribunals' broad powers, the ICC in early 2021 amended Article 26(1) of the ICC Rules of Arbitration to provide that the arbitral tribunal may decide, after consulting the parties, and on the basis of the relevant facts and circumstances of the case, that any hearing will be conducted in person or remotely by videoconference, telephone or other appropriate means of communication.[9] Before the addition of Article 26(1) to the ICC Rules, the ICC adopted the "ICC Guidance Note on Possible Measures Aimed at Mitigating the Effects of the COVID-19 Pandemic" on April 9, 2020, to guide parties, arbitrators, and counsel with management case techniques and the use of technological means of communication and videoconferencing to mitigate the adverse effects of the COVID-19 pandemic on arbitrations.[10] The Guidance Note develops the idea that the arbitral tribunal should strive to hold hearings virtually if it is not possible to hold a face-to-face hearing in a reasonable time, and that waiting until it becomes possible would produce unwarranted or prejudicial delay.[11]

The Guidance Note provides for the various scenarios in which either the parties or the tribunal determine that an in-person hearing is indispensable

telecommunication that do not require their physical presence at the hearing (such as videoconference)."

8 For example, Articles 22(2) of the 2021 Rules of Arbitration of the International Chamber of Commerce (ICC), 14(5) and 19(2) of the 2020 Arbitration Rules of the London Court of International Arbitration (LCIA), 22(1) of the 2021 International Arbitration Rules of the American Arbitration Association International Center for Dispute Resolution (AAA-ICDR), Rule 19(1) of the 2016 Arbitration Rules of the Singapore International Arbitration Centre (SIAC), and Article 23(1) of the Arbitration Rules of the Arbitration Institute of the Stockholm Chamber of Commerce (SCC).

9 ICC, Rules of Arbitration, 2021, Art. 26(1), second phrase.

10 "ICC Guidance Note on Possible Measures Aimed at Mitigating the Effects of the COVID-19 Pandemic," International Chamber of Commerce, April 9, 2020, https://iccwbo.org/publication/icc-guidance-note-on-possible-measures-aimed-at-mitigating-the-effects-of-the-covid-19-pandemic/.

11 *Id.* at 5, para. 25.

and possible, or instead, that a virtual hearing should be held.[12] The Guidance Note also specifies two scenarios where it may hold virtual hearings: (i) if the parties agree, or the tribunal determines to proceed with a virtual hearing, then the parties and the tribunal should take into account, openly discuss, and plan for special procedural features in that manner,[13] and (ii) if a tribunal determines to proceed with a virtual hearing without party agreement, or with party objection, it should carefully consider the relevant circumstances such as the nature and length of the conference or hearing, the complexity of the case and number of participants, whether there are particular reasons to proceed without delay, whether rescheduling the hearing would entail unwarranted or excessive delays, and as the case may be, the need for the parties to properly prepare for the hearing.[14] In addition, the tribunal should assess whether the award will be enforceable at law.[15] In both scenarios, the arbitral tribunal should provide reasons for that determination.[16]

Additionally, other institutional rules support the use of technology to increase the efficiency, economy, and expeditious conduct of the arbitration, including the hearings.[17] The Singapore International Arbitration Centre (SIAC) and the Stockholm Chamber of Commerce SCC Arbitration Rules implicitly refer to the use of technology by providing for the holding of a hearing "by any other means."[18]

In August 2020, the Secretariat of the SIAC issued a document titled "Taking Your Arbitration Remote" as a guide with considerations about the benefits and the risks of adopting remote hearings in the conduct of the arbitration proceeding, as a viable alternative to traditional in-person hearings.[19] While admitting the availability of remote hearings, the guide also recognizes that

12 *Id.* at paras. 19–20.

13 *Id.* at para. 21.

14 *Id.* at paras. 18 and 22.

15 *Id.* at para. 22. This rule is also reflected in Article 42 of the ICC Arbitration Rules, which mandates that the arbitrators should interpret and fill gaps in such a way that the procedure leads to an enforceable award.

16 *Id.* at 4, paras. 21 and 22.

17 Article 14.6 (iii) of the 2020 LCIA Arbitration Rules and Article 22(2) of the 2021 AAA-ICDR International Arbitration Rules.

18 Articles 19.3 and 19.7 of the 2016 Arbitration Rules of the Singapore International Arbitration Centre (SIAC) and 28(2) Arbitration Rules of the Arbitration Institute of the Stockholm Chamber of Commerce (SCC).

19 "Taking Your Arbitration Remote," Singapore International Arbitration Centre, August 31, 2020, https://www.siac.org.sg/69-siac-news/672-release-of-the-siac-guides-taking-your-arbitration-remote#.

they are not necessarily suitable in all types of cases.[20] The guide does not, however, clarify which cases might be suited to remote hearings. There are also three appendices with guidelines to choose the right remote hearing platform and a checklist for remote hearing procedural orders and remote hearing etiquette.

Despite this expansion of the permissive terms allowing for the use of technology to hold hearings remotely and the arbitral tribunals' discretion in the conduct of the arbitration, there is some concern that the parties may not be treated equally, that each party may not be given the right to be heard or a fair opportunity to present its case. In response to these concerns, the rules exhort the arbitrators to balance potential impacts on the right to be heard with the need to limit unnecessary delays and expense of the arbitration proceeding.[21]

2.3 *The 2020 Amendment of the IBA Rules Affecting Evidentiary Hearings*

On the other hand, regarding the taking of evidence, the International Bar Association (IBA) did not lag behind and the "IBA Rules on the Taking of Evidence in International Arbitration" were amended as a resource to parties and to arbitrators to provide an efficient, economical, and fair process for the taking of evidence in international arbitration, among other things, by including a provision on remote hearings.[22]

Article 8.2 of the IBA Rules indicates that, at the request of a party or on its own motion, the arbitral tribunal may, after consultation with the parties, order that the evidentiary hearing be conducted as a remote hearing. In this situation, the arbitral tribunal shall consult with the parties with a view to establishing a Remote Hearing Protocol to conduct the remote hearing efficiently, fairly and, to the extent possible, without unintended interruptions.[23]

---

20 *Id.*

21 Articles 22(4) of the 2021 ICC Rules of Arbitration, 14.1 of the 2020 LCIA Arbitration Rules, 22(1) of the 2021 AAA-ICDR International Arbitration Rules, Rule 41.2 of the 2016 SIAC Arbitration Rules, and Article 23(2) of the SCC Arbitration Rules.

22 "IBA Rules on the Taking of Evidence in International Arbitration," International Bar Association (IBA), adopted by a resolution of the IBA Council December 17, 2020, https://www.ibanet.org/MediaHandler?id=def0807b-9fec-43ef-b624-f2cb2af7cf7b.

23 *Id.* at 20, Article 8.2. The Rules also highlight some minimum requirements that the Remote Hearing Protocol may address the technology to be used; advance testing of the technology or training in use of the technology; the starting and ending times considering, in particular, the time zones in which participants will be located; how documents may be placed before a witness or the Arbitral Tribunal; and measures to ensure that witnesses giving oral testimony are not improperly influenced or distracted. *Id.* at 20–21.

Following this regulatory framework, as set out in institutional arbitration rules and procedural guidelines, the arbitral tribunal must decide whether to hold a virtual hearing or not. In the alternative that the rules contain a specific provision on remote hearings, the tribunal must assess whether to use its specific power that it "*may*" hold hearings remotely. In the absence of any specific provision, the tribunal will have to exercise its broad general power on the organization and conduct of the proceedings.[24]

In either case, the tribunal's power to decide on remote hearings is not without limits. Among other things, the tribunal's power is limited by the parties' agreement and the parties' right to be heard and treated equally, so as to render an enforceable award.[25]

3 Application of the Tribunals' Powers under Arbitration Rules: The Experience in Investment Arbitration

Numerous investment tribunals were surprised by the announcement of the global pandemic in March 2020 and the ensuing governmental restrictions on international travel, free movement, and professional activities. As the previous section has shown, the arbitration rules grant broad discretion to arbitrators. These rules impose upon the arbitrators an overarching mandate to conduct the proceeding in a cost-effective manner and to arrive at an enforceable outcome. The following section will review how tribunals have exercised these powers.

This analysis focuses on the discussions between the parties and tribunals about postponement or suspension of proceedings, extensions of deadlines, and other procedural exceptions, as well as the treatment of jurisdiction and merits, hearings on provisional measures, hearings in annulment proceedings, and other in-person meetings.

3.1 *Suspensions of Proceedings, Extensions of Deadlines, and Other Procedural Exceptions*

Parties ask the arbitral tribunal to suspend proceedings if the circumstances make it impossible to continue following the procedural schedule agreed upon at the outset of the proceeding.

---

24 See also Maxi Scherer, Niuscha Bassiri, and Mohamed S. Abdel Wahab, *International Arbitration and the COVID-19 Revolution* (Kluwer Law International, 2020), 76.

25 *Id.*

During the first weeks of the pandemic in March and April 2020, parties requested the suspension of proceedings or the extension of deadlines for filing of memorials in various pending cases. In principle, when both parties agree to the extension of deadlines, the tribunal will merely record the agreement between the parties. For example, in the case of *Tennant Energy, LLC v. Government of Canada*, a UNCITRAL case administered by the Permanent Court of Arbitration (PCA), the tribunal approved the parties' agreement to extend the deadlines for the claimant to file its case, and for the respondent to file an answer and a potential request for bifurcation of the proceedings.[26]

The situation is different when the parties are not in an agreement as to the extension of deadlines or suspension of proceedings. In the case of *Ayat Nizar Raja Rumrain et al. v. Kuwait*, both parties were initially in agreement as to the need to suspend the proceedings due to the pandemic and whether the first session of the tribunal should be postponed for 60 days.[27] The tribunal recorded the agreement in a letter dated April 9, 2020.[28] However, shortly afterwards, in a letter dated April 10, claimant changed its position in favor of continuing the proceedings as originally scheduled, and in particular, not to extend for 60 days the deadline to hold the first session.[29] Claimant also provided information on the urgency to rule on its request for provisional measures.[30] In this context of deciding on the request for suspension of proceedings and the claimant's request for provisional measures, the tribunal took into consideration that it has the discretion, under Article 44 of the ICSID Convention, to decide on "any question of procedure [that] arises which is not covered by this Section or the Arbitration Rules or any rules agreed by the parties."[31] The tribunal interpreted this provision by stating it has the power to suspend upon the showing of good cause.[32]

In the case of *The Estate of Julio Miguel Orlandini-Agreda and Compañía Minera Orlandini Ltda. v. Plurinational State of Bolivia*, the tribunal did not accept the state's *force majeure* argument to justify a delay of the time limit to

26 *Tennant Energy, LLC v. Government of Canada*, PCA Case No. 2018–54, José Luis Aragón Cardiel (PCA), email to the parties of July 4, 2020, re Modification of the Procedural Schedule.

27 *Ayat Nizar Raja Sumrain and others v. State of Kuwait*, ICSID Case No. ARB/19/20, Decision on Request for Suspension of Proceedings and on Request for Provisional Measures, April 23, 2020, para. 1.

28 *Id.*

29 *Id.* at para. 2.

30 *Id.* at para. 5.

31 *Id.* at para. 8.

32 *Id.*

file its statement of defense. According to the tribunal, the state had opportunity, even before the start of the pandemic, to finalize its procedural document.[33] In addition, respondent's law firm had submitted unconvincing arguments because they stated that, due to their remote work environment in their Washington, D.C. offices, they could not finish the statement of defense. At the same time, the law firm's website advertised that the firm was fully operational and could maintain fluent communication with its clients despite the COVID-19 limitations.[34] Bolivia also made requests for postponement of the time limits to file certain procedural documents, alleging *force majeure*. However, the tribunal responded that while some accommodation could be adequate, the practice from other tribunals showed that there was no reason to completely halt the procedure indefinitely:

> El Tribunal ve confirmada su postura a este respecto por la práctica en otros procedimientos, en los cuales la presentación de escritos pudo haberse retrasado, en la medida de lo razonable, y las audiencias se han reprogramado (o realizado por medios telemáticos), pero el procedimiento no se ha suspendido ni se ha determinado que fuese imposible continuar.[35]

In this context of having to choose between postponement and indefinite suspension, emerges the notion of good faith, which tribunals inevitably must balance against the real needs and constraints of the parties. For example, in this case, the tribunal mentioned the need for a good faith analysis, coming to the conclusion that the respondent state, and its lawyers, had acted in accordance with this general principle of international law:

> El Tribunal no se refiere a las citadas solicitudes con el objetivo de insinuar que el Demandado haya pretendido dilatar el procedimiento mediante la presentación de una serie de solicitudes de ampliación de plazo

33 Case of *1. The Estate of Julio Miguel Orlandini-Agreda, 2. Compañía Minera Orlandini Ltda v The Plurinational State of Bolivia*, PCA Case 2018–39, Procedural Order No 7, Respondent's Request for Suspension of the Time-limit for the Submission of its Statement of Defense, April 10, 2020, para. 41.

34 *Id.* at para. 31.

35 *Id.* at para. 38. English translation (ours): "The Court considers that the practice in other proceedings confirms its position. In those proceedings, it was possible to delay the submission of briefs, as far as reasonable, and the hearings have been rescheduled (or carried out by telematic means), but the procedure has not been suspended nor has it been determined that it was impossible to continue."

> por diversos motivos. Al Tribunal no le cabe duda de que el Demandado y sus abogados han actuado de buena fe. De hecho, el Tribunal concedió una de las solicitudes del Demandado en consideración a la situación de Bolivia en dicho momento. El Tribunal se remite a la historia procesal a fin de puntualizar que, desde su punto de vista, el Demandado ha disfrutado de un largo periodo para preparar su EDC [Escrito de Contestación] antes del surgimiento de la pandemia de COVID-19.[36]

The pandemic has also led to other procedural innovations or adaptions, such as the sole electronic filing of memorials by the parties instead of paper versions of those documents. For instance, in the case of *Gerald International Limited v. Republic of Sierra Leone*, the arbitral tribunal recognized the pandemic-related restrictions in force in various countries as sufficient justification for not having to present physical copies of the memorials.[37]

3.2 *Hearings on Jurisdiction and Merits*

In several cases, the parties consented in advance to hold the hearings on jurisdiction and merits remotely, by video conference.[38] Due to the confidentiality of some cases, pursuant to their applicable procedural provisions, it is

---

36 *Id.* at para. 35. English translation (ours): "The Tribunal does not refer to the aforementioned requests with the aim of insinuating that the Respondent has tried to delay the procedure by submitting a series of requests for an extension of the term for various reasons. The Tribunal has no doubt that the Respondent and his attorneys have acted in good faith. In fact, the Tribunal granted one of the Respondent's requests in consideration of the situation in Bolivia at that time. The Tribunal refers to the procedural history to point out that, from its point of view, the Respondent has had a long period to prepare its [Written Response] prior to the emergence of the COVID-19 pandemic."

37 *Gerald International Limited v. Republic of Sierra Leone*, ICSID Case No. ARB/19/31, Procedural Order No. 1, May 29, 2020, para. 13.4, where the tribunal justified the non-application of the physical delivery of memorials with the government-imposed restrictions: "While COVID-19 restrictive measures are in place in a country where the Tribunal, either Party or their counsel are located (§8), the requirement of physical delivery under §13.3 shall not apply, and the Parties shall file their pleadings in accordance with §13.1-13.3 via email and the file sharing platform only."

38 *Gabriel Resources Ltd. and Gabriel Resources (Jersey) v. Romania*, ICSID Case No. ARB/15/31, Procedural Order No. 33, September 18, 2020, paras. 1 and 2. In the case of *The Renco Group, Inc. v. Republic of Peru*, both parties requested in May 2020 that the hearing on jurisdiction and bifurcation be held virtually, and the tribunal accepted that request and confirmed the virtual hearing for June 12 and 13, instead of a sole day originally scheduled for an in-person hearing in Washington, D.C. on June 13. See *The Renco Group, Inc. v. Republic of Peru*, [II], PCA Case No. 2019–46, Procedural Order No. 2, June 3, 2020, paras. 1.3–1.5.

only known that the hearings were held remotely, although no details have been published regarding the decision to do so.[39] When the evidentiary hearing was conducted by videoconference, the closing arguments would usually also take place virtually.[40] When the tribunal decided for the first time on the procedural calendar during the pandemic, it often clarified that the hearing would be in-person, but that it reserved the right to switch to a virtual hearing if the circumstances so required, and after consulting with the parties.[41] For example, the standard language for this purpose was used in *Bacilio Amorrortu (USA) v. the Republic of Peru*, where the tribunal stated:

> 8.2 By agreement of the Parties, the hearing scheduled for November 15–24, 2021 as per the procedural calendar set out at Annex 1 shall be held at the facilities of the International Centre for Settlement of Investment Disputes (ICSID) at Washington, D.C., USA.

39 See, for instance, the cases of *Kimberly-Clark Dutch Holdings, B.V., Kimberly-Clark S.L.U., and Kimberly-Clark BVBA v. Bolivarian Republic of Venezuela*, ICSID Case No. ARB(AF)/18/3, where the hearing on jurisdiction was held by video conference between August 31 and September 1, 2020; see icsid website at https://icsid.worldbank.org/cases/case-database/case-detail?CaseNo=ARB(AF)/18/3; *Delta Belarus Holding BV v. Republic of Belarus*, ICSID Case No. ARB/18/9, where the tribunal held a hearing on the merits between February 1 and 9, 2021; see ICSID website at https://icsid.worldbank.org/cases/case-database/case-detail?CaseNo=ARB/18/9; and *Togo Terminal v. Republic of Togo*, ICSID Case No. ARB/18/16, where the hearing on the merits took place between October 26 and 30, 2020; see ICSID website at https://icsid.worldbank.org/cases/case-database/case-detail?CaseNo=ARB/18/16.

40 See, for instance, the case of *Telefónica, S.A. v. Republic of Colombia*, ICSID Case No. ARB/18/3. The hearing on the merits took place by video conference between April 19, and 25, 2021, and the hearing on closing arguments on July 27, 2021, also by video conference. See ICSID website at https://icsid.worldbank.org/cases/case-database/case-detail?CaseNo=ARB/18/3.

41 Among others, see *Bacilio Amorrortu v. Republic of Peru*, PCA Case No. 2020–11, Procedural Order No. 1 (Rules of Procedure), June 29, 2020, paras. 8.2 and 3; *Peteris Pildegovics and SIA North Star v. Kingdom of Norway*, ICSID Case No. ARB/20/11, Procedural Order No. 1, October 12, 2020, para. 20.2; *Patel Engineering Limited (India) v. the Republic of Mozambique*, Terms of Appointments of August 4, 2020, para. 80; as well as the Procedural Order No. 1 (Procedural Timetable and Conduct of the Arbitration), October 14, 2020, para. 19; *Carlos Sastre and others v. The United Mexican States*, ICSID Case No. UNCT/20/2, Procedural Order No. 1, May 28, 2020, para. 20.5; *Westmoreland Mining Holdings, LLC v. Government of Canada*, ICSID Case No. UNCT/20/3, Procedural Order No. 1, para. 5; *Gran Colombia Gold Corp. v. Republic of Colombia*, ICSID Case No. ARB/18/23, Procedural Order No. 7, September 21, 2020, paras. 1–4.

> 8.3 The Tribunal may order that any hearing take place by video conference in lieu of in person, if the circumstances so require, following consultation with the Parties.[42]

This language shows the agreement of the parties favoring an in-person hearing, but if the circumstances did not allow for that hearing to take place at the agreed date, a virtual hearing would suffice.[43] In the Procedural Orders, the tribunals generally did not specify the detailed criteria followed to determine whether the hearing should be virtual or in-person. In some cases, however, such as *Latam Hydro LLC and CH Mamacocha S.R.L. v. Republic of Peru*, the tribunal specified in more detail that it would consider "whether the circumstances at that time make it difficult, burdensome or dangerous to have an in-person hearing."[44] In the case of *Omega Engineerings v. Panama*, the parties disagreed on the modalities of the hearing, prompting a postponement to October 2020.[45] When it became clear that it would not be possible to hold that hearing in person, both parties consented to a virtual hearing.[46]

Both parties' consent was also required in the case of *Resolute Forest v. Canada*, where the parties initially agreed to postpone the in-person hearing from May to November 2020.[47] Thanks to the parties' agreement, the tribunal was able to schedule a virtual hearing in November 2020 instead of an in-person meeting.[48] Similarly, in *Alberto Carrizona v. Colombia*, the parties requested one postponement at the beginning of the pandemic with the aim of preserving the possibility of holding an in-person hearing.[49] However, the parties avoided a second postponement by agreeing in October 2020 to a virtual hearing to be held in December 2020.[50]

---

42 For example, *Bacilio Amorrortu (USA) v. the Republic of Peru*, Procedural Order No. 1 (Rules of Procedure), June 29, 2020, paras. 8.2 and 3.

43 Also in ICSID Additional Facility procedures can be found this approach. See, for instance, *José Alejandro Hernández Contreras v. Republic of Costa Rica*, ICSID Case No. ARB(AF)/20/2, Procedural Order No. 1 of September 28, 2021, para. 10.

44 *Latam Hydro LLC and CH Mamacocha S.R.L. v. Republic of Peru*, ICSID Case No. ARB/19/28, Procedural Order No. 2, May 13, 2020, para. 20.2.

45 *Omega Engineering LLC and Oscar Rivera v. Republic of Panama*, ICSID Case No. ARB/16/42, Procedural Order No. 4, paras. 1 and 2.

46 *Id.* at para. 5.

47 *Resolute Forest Products, Inc. v. Government of Canada*, PCA Case NO. 2016–13, Procedural Order No. 14, May 7, 2020, paras. 1.1–1.4.

48 *Id.* at para. 1.2.

49 *Alberto Carrizosa Gelzis, Enrique Carrizosa Gelzis, Felipe Carrizosa Gelzis v. Republic of Colombia*, PCA Case No. 2018–56, Procedural Order No. 11, November 11, 2020, para. 2.

50 *Id.* at para. 4.

Other tribunals made more succinct references in their procedural orders to the possibility of holding virtual hearings, especially after some time had passed since the start of the pandemic, when virtual hearings had become a more routine matter for tribunals and parties.[51]

In some cases, such as in *Gabriel Resources v. Romania*, the procedural calendar was already set up before the pandemic and included an in-person hearing.[52] When the pandemic started, the parties agreed to hold a virtual hearing during the initially set dates, and had the tribunal record a stipulation by which they consented to a virtual hearing and renounced any challenge to the virtual hearing in a potential annulment procedure:

> The Parties agree to hold the hearing virtually due to the current COVID-19 pandemic. The Parties further agree not to challenge the Tribunal's Award in any subsequent proceeding solely on the basis that the hearing was held virtually rather than in person. Such a stipulation, however, will not bar a Party from challenging an award based upon the manner in which a remote video proceeding was actually conducted.[53]

There has not yet been any annulment request against an award on grounds that the virtual hearing impaired a party's rights. Hence, it has not yet been tested if such an explicit waiver is necessary.

However, there are some cases – which are clearly outliers – in which tribunals followed a more restrictive approach. These tribunals allowed virtual hearings for most procedural issues, except for specific types of hearings. For example, in *Red Eagle Exploration Limited v. Republic of Colombia*, the tribunal expressly confirmed that the hearing on jurisdiction and the hearing on liability would have to be in-person.[54]

---

51 *ConocoPhillips Petrozuata B.V., ConocoPhillips Hamaca B.V. and ConocoPhillips Gulf of Paria B.V. Claimants / Respondents on Annulment v. Bolivarian Republic of Venezuela Respondent / Applicant*, ICSID Case No. ARB/07/30, Annulment Proceeding, Procedural Order No. 1, August 28, 2020, para. 10.1.

52 *Gabriel Resources Ltd. and Gabriel Resources (Jersey) v. Romania*, ICSID Case No. ARB/15/31, Procedural Order No. 29, April 8, 2020, paras. 6 and 7.

53 *Gabriel Resources Ltd. and Gabriel Resources (Jersey) v. Romania*, ICSID Case No. ARB/15/31, Procedural Order No. 33, September 18, 2020, para. 9.

54 *Red Eagle Exploration Limited c. República de Colombia*, Caso CIADI No. ARB/18/12, Resolución Procesal No. 1, December 12, 2019, as amended on June 2, 2020, para. 10.1.

In the case of *Rand Investments Ltd., et al. v. Republic of Serbia* both parties preferred an in-person hearing,[55] prompting the tribunal to postpone the hearing from the summer to November 2020. While this hearing in principle was set to be held in-person, the tribunal:

> [...] remained concerned about the health and safety of all hearing participants, who would be gathered in the same room for long days and would need to travel to the hearing venue, some of them on long haul flights. Further, it could not be ruled out that one or more of the participants would eventually be unable to attend the hearing due to travel restrictions or health reasons, which could jeopardize the hearing and cause a last-minute postponement or require an additional hearing, neither of which would be time nor cost efficient.[56]

However, as the date of the hearing approached, the parties again disagreed on the modalities of the hearing, and the hearing was again postponed to July 2021.[57] For February 2021, the tribunal also conveyed a hearing on provisional measures, which both parties attended without objection.[58]

In addition, at least two other tribunals did not modify the initially established in-person mode of the hearing after the pandemic broke out.[59]

Another approach to the hearing could be to only allow individual and specific witnesses to be connected remotely, in the event that health reasons prevent them from attending the in-person hearing. This possibility was expressed in *The Lopez-Goyne Family Trust v. Nicaragua*, where the tribunal stated that "[e]xceptionally, if a witness is unable to appear personally at the hearing on the merits for reasons of health or force majeure, the Tribunal may permit alternative arrangements (such as videoconference facilities), upon

---

55 *Rand Investments Ltd., William Archibald Rand, Kathleen Elizabeth Rand, Allison Ruth Rand, Robert Harry Leander Rand and Sembi Investment Limited v. Republic of Serbia*, ICSID Case No. ARB/18/8, Procedural Order No. 7, April 20, 2020, para. 2.

56 *Id.* at para. 5.

57 *Id.* at para. 9. It is not known if the hearing took place and what outcome it had.

58 *Id.* at para. 5.

59 *Ángel Samuel Seda y otros c. República de Colombia*, Caso CIADI No. ARB/19/6, Orden Procesal No. 1, April 7, 2020. This arbitration followed the 2009 Colombia-US FTA. Despite the date of the order, in April 2020, the tribunal did not mention any accommodations to the particular circumstances of the pandemic. See also the case of *Gerald International Limited v. Republic of Sierra Leone*, ICSID Case No. ARB/19/31, Procedural Order No. 1, May 29, 2020, para. 20.

consultation with the parties."[60] However, it seems contradictory that a witness may be allowed to participate remotely in a hearing, while the parties and their counsel are present at the hearing premises, because the primary reason for an in-person hearing is to allow the arbitrators to have a personal interaction with the witnesses and experts that have direct or expert knowledge of the facts or law underlying the dispute.

3.3 *Hearings on Requests for Provisional Measures*

The proceedings and the hearing in the context of requests for provisional measures are particularly time sensitive due to the urgency associated with those requests. In the case of *Ayat Nizar Raja Rumrain et al. v. Kuwait*, the claimant requested provisional measures at the start of the proceedings.[61] The tribunal confirmed that Article 44 of the ICSID Convention is applicable to a tribunal's consideration of provisional measures and articulated the criteria for its decision on whether to continue hearing that request. It stated the following:

> In deciding whether or not to exercise this discretion in the present circumstances, the Tribunal will weigh the prejudice that may be suffered by the Claimants in not having its request for provisional measures adjudicated upon immediately against the prejudice that may be suffered by the Respondent in having to defend itself under the constraints imposed by the COVID-19 pandemic. This balancing exercise essentially focuses on two issues that the Tribunal anticipated in its letter of 9 April 2020: the urgency of the Claimants' request for provisional measures against the severity of the constraints upon the Respondent resulting from governmental policies to deal with the COVID-19 pandemic.[62]

In this specific case, the tribunal considered that if the respondent provided an "undertaking" in which it would commit to not enforcing an eviction order against the claimants from the construction site that was the object of the underlying dispute, it may not be necessary for the claimants to insist on their request for provisional measures.[63] The tribunal ultimately did not adopt provisional measures.

60 *The Lopez-Goyne Family Trust and others v. Republic of Nicaragua*, ICSID Case No. ARB/17/44, Procedural Order No. 1 (Amended), February 18, 2021, para. 21.2.

61 *Ayat Nizar Raja Sumrain and others v. State of Kuwait*, ICSID Case No. ARB/19/20, Decision on Request for Suspension of Proceedings and on Request for Provisional Measures, April 23, 2020, para. 8.

62 *Id.*

63 *Id.* at paras. 20–22.

3.4 *Hearings in ICSID Annulment Proceedings*

Following the practice of the tribunal when setting up hearings in regular ICSID proceedings, as described in the previous sections, the hearing in ICSID Annulment Procedures may be held in-person or by any other means of communication as determined by the Committee after consultation with the parties.[64]

In the annulment proceeding in the case of *Cortec Mining Kenya Limited et al. v. Kenya*, the parties agreed in July 2020 to hold a virtual hearing. However, the respondent made a statement to the effect that its consent to hold the hearing virtually was not a "blanket consent" to hold such meetings virtually in the future:

> [T]he impression should not be conveyed to the Committee that the Respondent has given its unqualified consent to a virtual hearing. Rather, that the Respondent does not dispute that, in the context of the Committee's previous directions and the prevailing COVID-19 conditions, the hearing will be a virtual one, but one which will have to build into the modalities of the hearing conditions which satisfy the Respondent that the standards of the hearing equate to an in- person hearing.[65]

This statement shows that this State did not consent in general to the possibility of virtual hearings, despite the fact that today, it is technically possible. The State considered that an in-person hearing on important procedural aspects could still be necessary.

3.5 *Other Hearings and In-Person Meetings*

In the case of *InfraRed Environmental Infrastructure GP Limited et al. v. Kingdom of Spain*, the tribunal held a virtual hearing to decide on the stay

64 See, e.g., *TECO Guatemala Holdings, LLC (Claimant) v. Republic of Guatemala (Applicant)*, ICSID Case No. ARB/10/23, Third Annulment Proceeding, Procedural Order No. 1, May 17, 2021, para. 20.2; *Global Telecom Holding S.A.E. v. Canada*, ICSID Case No. ARB/16/16, Annulment Proceedings, Procedural Order No. 1, November 23, 2020, para. 18.2, and *ConocoPhillips Petrozuata B.V., ConocoPhillips Hamaca B.V. and ConocoPhillips Gulf of Paria B.V. Claimants / Respondents on Annulment v. Bolivarian Republic of Venezuela Respondent / Applicant*, ICSID Case No. ARB/07/30, Annulment Proceeding, Procedural Order No. 1, August 28, 2020, para. 10.1.

65 *Cortec Mining Kenya Limited, Cortec (Pty) Limited and Stirling Capital Limited v. Republic of Kenya*, ICSID Case No. ARB/15/29, Annulment Proceeding, Procedural Order No. 3, August 12, 2020, para. 3.

of enforcement.[66] Both parties had expressly confirmed their agreement to hold the hearings virtually through videoconferencing. On May 21, 2020, the Annulment Committee in this case decided that a hearing would be held by video conference, in addition to a pre-hearing conference.[67] On June 29 and 30, 2020, the Committee held a hearing on the stay request by video conference.[68] The parties did not object to the conduct of that hearing. As usual in in-person hearings, the virtual hearing was transcribed, and the parties were offered an opportunity to correct any material errors of the transcript.[69]

According to paragraph (4) of Rule 54 of the ICSID Arbitration Rules, a request "shall only be granted after the Tribunal or Committee has given each party an opportunity of presenting its observations."[70] In this regard, the Committee first noted that it granted the Parties two rounds of written submissions on the stay request.[71] Second, the Committee conducted a virtual hearing due to the COVID-19 pandemic and listened to the parties' oral arguments on whether or not to continue the stay of enforcement of the Award. Finally, the Committee provided the parties with several opportunities to introduce new documents to the record in support of their positions, and to comment on their own documents and on the ones submitted by the other side.[72] This case is relevant, as it puts the virtual hearing into context with other ways of allowing the parties to make their case, such as the introduction of new documents to the record, the formulation of comments on the documents from the other party, and the existence of numerous rounds of written submissions. In another case, *Westmoreland Mining Holding LLC v. Canada,* the hearing on bifurcation was set to be conducted through a video conference in September 2020.[73] Some tribunals also explicitly clarified that other procedural moments,

66 *InfraRed Environmental Infrastructure GP Limited and others v. Kingdom of Spain*, ICSID Case No. ARB/14/12, Decision on Continuation of Stay of Enforcement of the Award, October 27, 2020, para. 8.

67 On June 26, 2020, the Committee issued Procedural Order No. 2 concerning the organization of the hearing; see *id.* at para. 16.

68 *Id.* at para. 17.

69 *Id.* at para. 24.

70 Rule 54(4) of the ICSID Arbitration Rules.

71 *InfraRed Environmental Infrastructure GP Limited and others v. Kingdom of Spain*, ICSID Case No. ARB/14/12, Decision on Continuation of Stay of Enforcement of the Award, October 27, 2020, para. 119.

72 *Id.*

73 *Westmoreland Mining Holdings, LLC v. Government of Canada*, ICSID Case No. UNCT/20/3, Procedural Order No. 2, September 21, 2020, para. 1. The Order contained extensive provisions on the details that the parties should take in mind for the conduct of the hearing. A similar, virtual hearing took place on jurisdiction on July 14 and 15, 2021. See Hearing on Jurisdiction Transcript – Day 1 (July 14, 2021) and Day 2 (July 15, 2021), available on

which sometimes take place by in-person meetings, are going to be held virtually. For example, in several cases the tribunals expressly stated that they could hold the deliberation remotely, including by video or telephone conference.[74] In *Gramercy Funds Management, LLC et al. v. Republic of Peru*, the tribunal highlighted that the post-hearing oral arguments will not involve hearing witnesses, which should be considered a factor in favor of holding the hearing virtually.[75]

4 Conclusions

While in international commercial arbitration most prominent international arbitration centers have provided some type of guidance for virtual hearings and other technological innovations to address the challenges of the COVID-19 pandemic, international investment arbitration has largely been relying on the initiatives of the parties and the arbitral tribunals to deal with these issues. Quickly, a practice emerged according to which the parties either consented to the tribunals' proposal of holding virtual meetings, or to do so after one postponement, especially when the hearing was scheduled in the early weeks or months after the announcement of the pandemic. At that time, the uncertainty about the effects of the virus and the severe travel restrictions made it appropriate to postpone. Most of the hearings took place remotely. Seemingly, there has been little controversy between the parties involved as to the acceptability of the virtual format of hearings, including evidentiary hearings. In addition, this shift led to other procedural innovations or adaptions, such as the sole electronic filing of memorials by the parties instead of paper versions of those documents.

We identified only one tribunal that had explicitly included, into its procedural documents, a waiver of any means of appeal or challenge against an award that resulted from a remote hearing. In most other cases, both parties implicitly seemed to consent to a virtual hearing and renounced any challenge

---

the ICSID website: https://icsid.worldbank.org/cases/case-database/case-detail?CaseNo=UNCT/20/3.

74 *Red Eagle Exploration Limited c. República de Colombia*, Caso CIADI No. ARB/18/12, Resolución Procesal No. 1, December 12, 2019, as amended on June 2, 2020, para. 10.1; and *The Lopez-Goyne Family Trust and others v. Republic of Nicaragua*, ICSID Case No. ARB/17/44, Procedural Order No. 1 (Amended), February 18, 2021, para. 11.3.

75 *Gramercy Funds Management LLC and Gramercy Peru Holdings LLC v. Republic of Peru*, ICSID Case No. UNCT/18/2, Procedural Order No. 12, November 5, 2020, para. 1.

or potential annulment procedure. For an annulment to be successful, the arbitral tribunal must have violated additional due process guarantees besides the switch to a virtual format. It is probably too early to determine if remote hearings will contribute to more annulments than the few that so far have been recorded in ICSID proceedings. In any case, the large number of tribunals that have held hearings by video conference seems to point towards some type of general agreement between parties, arbitrators, and the ICSID Secretariat about the admissibility of this novel form of procedural interaction, especially when witness and expert testimony is being heard, or when closing arguments are made.

This survey also shows that the parties' and arbitral tribunals' acceptance to hold remote hearings was due to the severe restrictions imposed by the COVID-19 pandemic. The parties – particularly the States – made it clear on several occasions that they agreed to virtual hearings only as a response to the exceptional circumstances created by the pandemic. This exceptionalism seems to imply that in the event the world returns to normalcy, in which no health threats and no travel restrictions exist, the States will again require in-person hearings. In sum, remote hearings in investment arbitration – especially those involving witness testimony – will not fully substitute the in-person format of traditional hearings. This may seem surprising in light of the fact that parties usually consent to the virtual format and, until now, have not raised challenges against the procedure or the final award. It is also surprising because the States have traditionally criticized the high cost of investment arbitration procedures. While the virtual format saves costs, and seemingly does not impair the parties' procedural rights, these higher costs may be accepted as a worthwhile price to pay for a procedure that is perceived to be more respectful of the parties' rights.

Appendix 1
Arbitration Rules Relevant for Virtual Hearings

Arbitral Institution	Relevant Extract of Arbitration Rules	Guidelines or Protocols for Virtual Hearings/Use of Technology
International Centre for Settlement of Investment Disputes (ICSID) *ICSID Convention*	*Article 44.* Any arbitration proceeding shall be conducted in accordance with the provisions of this Section and, except as the parties otherwise agree, in accordance with the Arbitration Rules in effect on the date on which the parties consented to arbitration. If any question of procedure arises which is not covered by this Section or the Arbitration Rules or any rules agreed by the parties, the Tribunal shall decide the question.	
United Nations Commission on International Trade Law (UNCITRAL) *2013 UNCITRAL Arbitration Rules*	*Article 17(1).* Subject to these Rules, the arbitral tribunal may conduct the arbitration in such manner as it considers appropriate, provided that the parties are treated with equality and that at an appropriate stage of the proceedings each party is given a reasonable opportunity of presenting its case. The arbitral tribunal, in exercising its discretion, shall conduct the proceedings so as to avoid unnecessary delay and expense and to provide a fair and efficient process for resolving the parties' dispute.	

Arbitral Institution	Relevant Extract of Arbitration Rules	Guidelines or Protocols for Virtual Hearings/Use of Technology
International Chamber of Commerce (ICC) *2021 Arbitration Rules of the ICC*	*Article 22(1)*. The arbitral tribunal and the parties shall make every effort to conduct the arbitration in an expeditious and cost-effective manner, having regard to the complexity and value of the dispute. *Article 22(2)*. In order to ensure effective case management, after consulting the parties, the arbitral tribunal shall adopt such procedural measures as it considers appropriate, provided that they are not contrary to any agreement of the parties. Such measures may include one or more of the case management techniques described in Appendix IV. *Article 22(4)*. In all cases, the arbitral tribunal shall act fairly and impartially and ensure that each party has a reasonable opportunity to present its case. *Article 26(1)*. The arbitral tribunal may decide, after consulting the parties, and on the basis of the relevant facts and circumstances of the case, that any hearing will be conducted by physical attendance or remotely by videoconference, telephone or other appropriate means of communication.	*ICC Guidance Note on Possible Measures Aimed at Mitigating the Effects of the COVID-19 Pandemic*

Arbitral Institution	Relevant Extract of Arbitration Rules	Guidelines or Protocols for Virtual Hearings/Use of Technology
London Court of International Arbitration (LCIA) *2020 Arbitration Rules of the LCIA*	*14.1* Under the Arbitration Agreement, the Arbitral Tribunal's general duties at all times during the arbitration shall include: (*i*) a duty to act fairly and impartially as between all parties, giving each a reasonable opportunity of putting its case and dealing with that of its opponent(s); and (*ii*) a duty to adopt procedures suitable to the circumstances of the arbitration, avoiding unnecessary delay and expense, so as to provide a fair, efficient and expeditious means for the final resolution of the parties' dispute. *14.5* Without prejudice to the generality of the Arbitral Tribunal's discretion, after giving the parties a reasonable opportunity to state their views, the Arbitral Tribunal may, subject to the LCIA Rules, make any procedural order it considers appropriate with regard to the fair, efficient and expeditious conduct of the arbitration. *14.6* The Arbitral Tribunal's power under Article 14.5 includes the making of any procedural order with a view to expediting the procedure to be adopted in the arbitration by: (*iii*) employing technology to enhance the efficiency and expeditious conduct of the arbitration (including any hearing);	

Arbitral Institution	Relevant Extract of Arbitration Rules	Guidelines or Protocols for Virtual Hearings/Use of Technology
	19.2 The Arbitral Tribunal shall organise the conduct of any hearing in advance, in consultation with the parties. The Arbitral Tribunal shall have the fullest authority under the Arbitration Agreement to establish the conduct of a hearing, including its date, duration, form, content, procedure, time limits and geographical place (if applicable). As to form, a hearing may take place in person, or virtually by conference call, videoconference or using other communications technology with participants in one or more geographical places (or in a combined form). As to content, the Arbitral Tribunal may require the parties to address specific questions or issues arising from the parties' dispute. The Arbitral Tribunal may also limit the extent to which questions or issues are to be addressed.	

Arbitral Institution	Relevant Extract of Arbitration Rules	Guidelines or Protocols for Virtual Hearings/Use of Technology
American Arbitration Association – International Center for Dispute Resolution (AAA/ICDR) *2021 International Arbitration Rules*	*Article 22(1)*. Subject to these Rules, the arbitral tribunal may conduct the arbitration in whatever manner it considers appropriate, provided that the parties are treated with equality and that each party has the right to be heard and is given a fair opportunity to present its case. *Article 22(2)*. In establishing procedures for the case, the tribunal and the parties may consider how technology, including video, audio, or other electronic means, could be used to increase the efficiency and economy of the proceedings.	*Virtual Hearing Guide for Arbitrators and Parties* *Virtual Hearing Guide for Arbitrators and Parties Utilizing ZOOM* *Order and Procedures for a Virtual Hearing via Videoconference*
Singapore International Arbitration Centre (SIAC) *2016 Arbitration Rules of the SIAC*	*Rule 19.1* The Tribunal shall conduct the arbitration in such manner as it considers appropriate, after consulting with the parties, to ensure the fair, expeditious, economical, and final resolution of the dispute. *Rule 19.3* As soon as practicable after the constitution of the Tribunal, the Tribunal shall conduct a preliminary meeting with the parties, in person or by any other means, to discuss the procedures that will be most appropriate and efficient for the case.	*Taking Your Arbitration Remote*

Arbitral Institution	Relevant Extract of Arbitration Rules	Guidelines or Protocols for Virtual Hearings/Use of Technology
	Rule 19.7 The President may, at any stage of the proceedings, request the parties and the Tribunal to convene a meeting to discuss the procedures that will be most appropriate and efficient for the case. Such meeting may be conducted in person or by any other means. *Rule 41.2* In all matters not expressly provided for in these Rules, the President, the Court, the Registrar and the Tribunal shall act in the spirit of these Rules and shall make every reasonable effort to ensure the fair, expeditious and economical conclusion of the arbitration and the enforceability of any Award.	
Arbitration Institute of the Stockholm Chamber of Commerce (SCC) *2017 Arbitration Rules of the SCC*	*Article 23(1)*. The Arbitral Tribunal may conduct the arbitration in such manner as it considers appropriate, subject to these Rules and any agreement between the parties.	*SCC Platform Guidelines* *Ad Hoc Platform Guidelines* *SCC Express Guidelines*
	Article 23(2). In all cases, the Arbitral Tribunal shall conduct the arbitration in an impartial, efficient and expeditious manner, giving each party an equal and reasonable opportunity to present its case. *Article 28(2)*. The case management conference may be conducted in person or by any other means.	

CHAPTER 9

Ordering Online Arbitration in the Age of COVID-19 … and Beyond

Amy J. Schmitz

1 Introduction*

Arbitration clauses have become a norm in not only commercial business-to-business contracts, but also business-to-consumer ("B2C") and employment contracts.[1] Arbitration makes sense in commercial agreements, especially when there is need for a specialist arbitrator or protection of business secrets. This need for an expert decision-maker has been a harbinger in construction arbitration for decades, and arbitration is beneficial for international parties who seek a neutral forum and enforceable awards under the New York Convention on the Recognition and Enforcement of Foreign Arbitral Awards ("New York Convention").[2]

In the United States, courts usually enforce arbitration clauses under the Federal Arbitration Act ("FAA")[3], along with efficiency-focused arbitration and

* I thank Claire Mendes, Emily Bergman, Sarah Mader, and Ryan Thomas for their research assistance. The chapter is derived from a prior article, Amy J. Schmitz, "Arbitration in the Age of Covid: Examining Arbitration's Move Online," *Cardozo Journal of Conflict Resolution* 22 (2021): 245–92 and some parts are substantially similar to that article.

1 Of the 100 largest U.S. companies (as listed in Fortune), many have had arbitration agreements since 2010, including class arbitration waivers. Imre Stephen Szalai, "The Prevalence of Consumer Arbitration Agreements by America's Top Companies," *University of Carolina Davis Law Review. Online* 52 (2019): 234. The data shows that 81 of the 100 companies have used arbitration agreements, and 78 of those 81 companies use class waivers.

2 New York Convention on the Recognition and Enforcement of Foreign Arbitral Awards (New York Convention), 9 U.S.C. secs. 201–08; 9 U.S.C. secs. 301–07 (implementing the Inter-American Convention on International Commercial Arbitration (Panama Convention)).

3 Federal Arbitration Act ("FAA"), 9 U.S.C. secs. 1–16 (covering domestic arbitration), secs. 201–08 (implementing the Convention on the Recognition and Enforcement of Foreign Arbitral Awards ("New York Convention")), secs. 301–07 (implementing the Inter-American Convention on International Commercial Arbitration ("Panama Convention")). See also *Green Tree Fin. Corp. v. Randolph*, 531 U.S. 79 (2001) (emphasizing the "liberal federal policy favoring arbitration agreements").

contract jurisprudence.[4] This is true even if arbitration clauses are included in e-contracts per the Electronic Signature Act ("ESign").[5] At the same time, "arbitration" as it existed in 1925, when the FAA became law, has changed. Growing use and reliance on the internet has led to the emergence of online arbitration (what I have termed "OArb" in prior publications).[6] Such OArb includes using technology and digital tools to facilitate and execute processes ending in a final determination of a dispute by a neutral third party. For example, OArb may use asynchronous and/or synchronous communications. It also may involve text-only or virtual hearings, and mixtures thereof. OArb's use of technology allows parties to upload and submit supporting documentation to support their claims. Online hearings save time, cost, and stress of traveling to and attending in-person processes. Such OArb systems may even provide more accurate and complete redress for consumers than class actions – which have been criticized for providing insufficient and inequitably distributed relief in some cases.[7]

OArb is just one example of online dispute resolution ("ODR"), which generally encompasses using technology to assist in preventing and resolving disputes. Most ODR, however, is not OArb because it involves facilitation of communications to aid voluntary settlement.[8] In contrast, OArb is a distinct subset of ODR because it culminates in a final award rendered by a third-party neutral under the FAA and New York Convention.

OArb has spiked in the COVID-19 pandemic.[9] Virtual meeting technology such as Zoom, Skype, Google Meet, WebEx, and Teams has made virtual

4 See generally Jeffrey W. Stempel, "Arbitration, Unconscionability, and Equilibrium: The Return of Unconscionability Analysis as a Counterweight to Arbitration Formalism," *Ohio State Journal on Dispute Resolution* 19 (2004): 812–13 (highlighting restrained application of unconscionability in the wake of rising formalism).

5 Electronic Signatures in Global and National Commerce Act 2006, 15 U.S.C. §96 (2006), sec. 7001 (making electronic contracts enforceable to the same extent as written contracts; effective October 1, 2000).

6 Amy J. Schmitz, " 'Drive-Thru' Arbitration in the Digital Age: Empowering Consumers Through Regulated ODR," *Baylor Law Review* 62 (2010): 178–244 (proposing "OArb" as a distinct type of online dispute resolution); Amy J. Schmitz, "Arbitration in the Age of Covid: Examining Arbitration's Move Online," *Cardozo Journal of Conflict Resolution* 22 (2021): 245–92.

7 See generally Linda S. Mullenix, "Ending Class Actions as We Know Them: Rethinking the American Class Action," *Emory Law Journal* 64 (2014): 39.

8 See generally Amy J. Schmitz & Colin Rule, *The New Handshake: Online Dispute Resolution and the Future of Consumer Protection* (American Bar Association, 2017); see also Amy J. Schmitz, *Building on OArb Attributes in Pursuit of Justice, in Arbitration in the Digital Age: The Brave New World of Arbitration* (Maud Piers & Christian Aschauer, 2018), 182.

9 Melody Alger, "Conducting Arbitrations and Mediations Remotely During the Covid-19 Crisis and Beyond," 68 *Rhode Island Bar Journal* 68 (2020): 15.

hearings relatively cheap and easy. Individuals have become accustomed to online communications in the lockdown.[10] Even in large-dollar claims, such as international construction deals, COVID-19 prompted parties to arbitrate online.[11] "The increase in the use of virtual hearing rooms appears to be the result of how the practice of arbitration has adapted in response to the COVID-19 pandemic, as users have been forced to explore alternatives to in-person hearings."[12] Parties grew eager to resolve their disputes, and arbitrators began ordering virtual arbitration, even over a party's objection.[13] All have increasingly embraced virtual platforms as their best, safest, and most convenient means for moving forward.[14]

Still, some parties want traditional in-person arbitration. Respondents are particularly prone to demand in-person hearings, especially where such demands will delay hearings (and paying any awards). Furthermore, some parties may have genuine concerns for OArb: security, internet connection, comfort with technology, trust, etc.

Part II of the Chapter provides context by explaining the growth of OArb. Part III then explains how some parties may seek in-person arbitration and refuse to engage in OArb, while Part IV notes law has developed for entertaining objections to OArb.[15] Part V concludes with a call for creativity in crafting OArb that advances access to remedies and justice.

10 See "2021 International Arbitration Survey: Adapting arbitration to a changing world," White & Case LLP, accessed May 6, 2021, https://www.whitecase.com/publications/insight/2021-international-arbitration-survey/technology-virtual-reality.

11 *Id.*; Andrey Panov, "Post-COVID-19 world and the duty to conduct arbitrations efficiently and expeditiously," Thomson Reuters, accessed August 13, 2020, http://arbitrationblog.practicallaw.com/post-covid-19-world-and-the-duty-to-conduct-arbitrations-efficiently-and-expeditiously/; Mark Shope, "International Arbitral Institution Response to COVID-19 and Opportunities for Online Dispute Resolution," *Contemporary Asia Arbitration Journal* 13 (2020): 77.

12 "White & Case LLP, *supra* note 10 "When discussing virtual hearings, two key takeaways emerged from interviews. First, there appears to be a growing expectation that virtual hearings will become the default option in the future for procedural hearings and conferences." *Id.*

13 Karen Maxwell, "Could Arbitration Support Courts During the COVID-19 Crisis?," Thomson Reuters, accessed May 27, 2020, http://arbitrationblog.practicallaw.com/could-arbitration-support-courts-during-the-covid-19-crisis/.

14 Svetlana Gitman, (Esq., Vice President, Am. Arb. Ass'n/Int'l Ctr. for Disp. Resol.), in email with Amy J. Schmitz, Professor, June 30, 2020.

15 Due to space limitations, this Chapter will not go into all the guidance that has been developed around OArb, but Part IV at least gives some mention.

2 Growth of OArb in the Pandemic

The idea of OArb is not new. In fact, e-commerce providers such as eBay have been using OArb for customer claims for some time.[16] Nonetheless, there are now many OArb providers who provide text-only arbitration with no in-person hearings.[17] Moreover, traditional arbitration providers, such as the American Arbitration Association ("AAA") and others, now provide virtual hearings, especially in the wake of the pandemic. Indeed, evidence suggests OArb has expanded significantly due to COVID-19 shutdowns and health restrictions. Moreover, the trend toward OArb and virtual hearings is likely to continue post-pandemic as parties embrace the efficiencies and conveniences OArb offers.[18]

As OArb evolves, it has become among the offerings of traditional dispute resolution institutions, such as the American Arbitration Association (AAA), the Judicial Arbitration and Mediation Service (JAMS), and the International Institute for Conflict Prevention & Resolution (CPR). These organizations have long histories of offering in-person arbitration, but they are now offering virtual hearings. This institutionalization of OArb focuses mainly on virtual hearings, while other OArb providers mainly utilize text-based dispute resolution processes.

For example, the AAA offers a secure portal for parties to file claims, upload and manage their claim-related documents, and view and rank potential arbitrators for selection.[19] A similar portal is offered for arbitrators to access and manage their cases and review related files and documents.[20] In addition, the AAA offers virtual hearing capacity and guidance.[21] Accordingly, it is no

16 Schmitz, "'Drive-Thru'," *supra* note 6, at 178–244.

17 Amy J. Schmitz and Janet Martinez, "ODR Providers Operating in the U.S." in *ODR in the United States*, in *Online Dispute Resolution: Theory and Practice: A Treatise on Technology and Dispute Resolution*, eds. Mohamed S. Abdel Wahab, Ethan Katsh and Daniel Rainey, (2020), available at https://ssrn.com/abstract=3599511.

18 *See* Amy J. Schmitz, *The Arbitration Conversation*, May 31, 2021, https://arbitrate.com/the-arbitration-conversation/?_ga=2.199180335.1268613773.1622474077-605821883.1620754416 (compiling over 82 interviews with arbitrators and arbitration experts, with many noting that virtual hearings are here to stay).

19 "AAA-ICDR Technology Services," American Arbitration Association, accessed June 18, 2020, https://www.adr.org/TechnologyServices/aaa-icdr-software-and-online-tools.

20 *Id.*

21 Svetlana Gitman, "Arbitration Conversation No. 1 – Amy Chats with Svetlana Gitman," interview by Amy J. Schmitz, *Arbitrate.com*, June 30, 2020, https://arbitrate.com/arbitration-conversation-episode-1-svetlana-gitman-american-arbitration-association/; "AAA-ICDR Virtual Hearing Guide for Arbitrators and Parties," American Arbitration

surprise the AAA saw a massive increase in virtual hearings from March 2020 to date.[22]

Similarly, JAMS also offers various teleconferencing and videoconferencing options to assist in arbitration, and encourages Zoom in both arbitration and mediation.[23] At the same time, CPR offers an array of arbitration services available to clients online.[24] In the wake of the pandemic, CPR also offers online training sessions to help neutrals and advocates learn how to use Zoom to arbitrate online effectively.[25] CPR released an annotated model procedural order for video arbitration proceedings.[26] Of course, ad hoc arbitrators are also using virtual hearings – especially in the pandemic's wake.[27]

Lawyers may be resistant to change, but the popularity and efficiency of OArb will endure post-pandemic.[28] The option of having witnesses, clients, and attorneys appearing remotely reduces travel time and the likelihood of cancellations in general, which will continue to prove significant as litigants aim to save money and courts face backlogs.[29]

3 Objecting to OArb

OArb, and ODR more generally, may ease costs and stress of in-person processes. Online processes may even empower marginalized groups by easing

---

Association, accessed June, 29, 2020, https://go.adr.org/rs/294-SFS-516/images/AAA268_AAA%20Virtual%20Hearing%20Guide%20for%20Arbitrators%20and%20Parties.pdf.

22 "AAA-ICDR Virtual Hearing Case Statistics," American Arbitration Association, accessed Jun. 2, 2021, https://go.adr.org/virtual-hearing-statistics. Of 10,493 events, 5,902 cases had a virtual event (time range: March 1, 2020 – April 30, 2021).

23 "Virtual Mediation & Arbitration," JAMS, accessed June 18, 2020, https://www.jamsadr.com/online.

24 "Arbitration," International Institute for Conflict Prevention and Resolution, accessed June 6, 2020, https://www.cpradr.org/dispute-resolution-services/services-offered/arbitration.

25 "ADR in the Time of COVID-19: How Neutrals & Advocates Can Use Zoom for Mediations & Arbitrations," International Institute for Conflict Prevention and Resolution, accessed March 30, 2020, https://www.cpradr.org/news-publications/videos/zoom-for-mediations-arbitrations-covid19.

26 "NEW: CPR's Annotated Model Procedural Order for Remote Video Arbitration Proceedings," International Institute for Conflict Prevention and Resolution, accessed June 18, 2020, https://www.cpradr.org/resource-center/protocols-guidelines/model-procedure-order-remote-video-arbitration-proceedings.

27 Alger, "Conducting," *supra* note 9, at 15–16.

28 *Id.*

29 *Id.* at 17.

some of the social and power pressures of in-person communications. This is especially true using text-based processes where individuals fear stereotypes or biases based on appearance, voice, or accent.[30] Although social media is notoriously inflammatory and divisive, some individuals are less adversarial through electronic asynchronous communications because it gives them time to digest thoughts and dissipate anger before replying.[31] Furthermore, individuals may be more civil when they know the written communications will be preserved and can hurt their cases in a dispute resolution process. However, OArb is not suitable for every party and every case. A "digital divide" persists, and some may want in-person hearings for various valid reasons.

3.1 *Digital Divide*

People continue to have differential access to technology and the internet.[32] This has become glaringly apparent in the wake of the pandemic, as families without adequate access to the internet struggled to educate their children.[33] Pew Charitable Trust reported one in five U.S. parents with schoolchildren at home say it is very or somewhat likely their children will not complete their work because of lack of access to a computer or internet.[34] This alone showed how the pandemic has shined a light on technological disparity.[35]

---

30 See Avital Mentovich, J.J. Prescott, and Orna Rabinovich-Einy, "Are Litigation Outcome Disparities Inevitable? Courts, Technology, and the Future of Impartiality," *Alabama Law Review* 71, (2020): 900–4.

31 See Susan C. Herring, "Computer-Mediated Communication on the Internet," *Annual Review of Information Science and Technology* 36 (2002): 144–45 (2002); David Allen Larson and Paula Gajewski Mickelson, "Technology Mediated Dispute Resolution Can Improve the Registry of Interpreters for the Deaf Ethical Practices System: The Deaf Community Is Well Prepared and Can Lead by Example," *Cardozo Journal of Conflict Resolution* 10 (2008): 140–4 (explains evidence that less bullying occurs through online communication than F2F).

32 Thom File, "Computer and Internet Use in the United States," U.S. Census Bureau accessed May 2013, https://www.census.gov/content/dam/Census/library/publications/2013/demo/p20-569.pdf.

33 Suzanne Woolley, Nikitha Sattiraju, and Scott Moritz, "U.S. Schools Trying to Teach Online Highlight a Digital Divide," Bloomberg, March 26, 2020, https://www.bloomberg.com/news/articles/2020-03-26/covid-19-school-closures-reveal-disparity-in-access-to-internet (noting that NYC has an estimated 300,000 students without access to electronics).

34 Emily A. Vogels et al., "53% of Americans Say the Internet Has Been Essential During the COVID-19 Outbreak," Pew Research Center, Apr. 30, 2020, https://www.pewresearch.org/internet/2020/04/30/53-of-americans-say-the-internet-has-been-essential-during-the-covid-19-outbreak/.

35 Dana Goldstein, "The Class Divide: Remote Learning at 2 Schools, Private and Public," New York Times, last modified June 5, 2020, https://www.nytimes.com/2020/05/09/us/coronavirus-public-private-school.html.

The internet has become a necessity, with most of the world using the internet.[36] Asia accounts for the majority of internet usage, while Europe and North America have the largest percentage of their populations accessing the internet.[37] Furthermore, in the last twenty years, internet usage has increased 1,266% worldwide, with most traffic via mobile devices.[38]

In the U.S., Pew Research Center reported in 2021 that 93% of U.S. adults used the internet.[39] However, age creates divergence as 75% of adults over 65 vs. 96% of adults 50–64, 98% of adults 30–49, and 99% of adults 18–29 used the internet.[40] The 2019 study also showed 93% of white people used the internet, versus 91% of Black and 95% Hispanic people. Race therefore also remains a differentiating factor.[41] Income also remains an issue, as 99% of U.S. adults making over $75,000 used the internet, in contrast with 86% of adults making less than $30,000.[42]

How one accesses the internet is essential when it comes to OArb, as those with broadband access on a computer often enjoy more facility with the process because it is generally easier for them to upload documents and engage with the proceedings. This is important in light of differential access to in-home broadband. Pew reported as of February 2021, only 77% of U.S. adults used home broadband.[43] This means processes like OArb and other forms of ODR must be mobile-friendly to ensure equal access.[44] Furthermore, policy-makers and businesses must continue collaborating to expand internet access and education programs for vulnerable groups.[45]

---

36 "Key Internet Statistics to Know in 2021 (Including Mobile)," Broadband Search, accessed May 31, 2021, https://www.broadbandsearch.net/blog/internet-statistics; see also "Internet usage worldwide – Statistics & Facts," Statista, accessed May 31, 2021, https://www.statista.com/topics/1145/internet-usage-worldwide/ [hereinafter "International Fact Sheet"].

37 *Id.*

38 *Id.*

39 "Internet/Broadband Fact Sheet," Pew Research Center, April 7, 2021, https://www.pewresearch.org/internet/fact-sheet/internet-broadband/ [hereinafter "Internet/Broadband Fact Sheet"].

40 *Id.*

41 *Id.*

42 *Id.*

43 *Id.*

44 John Busby et al., *FCC Reports Broadband Unavailable to 21.3 Million Americans, BroadbandNow Study Indicates 42 Million Do Not Have Access* (BroadbandNow Research, 2020), https://broadbandnow.com/research/fcc-underestimates-unserved-by-50-percent.

45 See, e.g., Rebecca R. Ruiz, "F.C.C. Chief Seeks Broadband Plan to Aid the Poor," New York Times, May 28, 2015, https://www.nytimes.com/2015/05/28/business/fcc-chief-seeks-broadband-plan-to-aid-the-poor.html (discussing plans to expand access to the internet for the poor).

Furthermore, any use of virtual hearings should ensure parties have access to legal representation. Administrators must remain available to assist with technical issues, answer questions regarding arbitration procedures, and refer self-represented litigants to low-cost or free legal services. The best OArb practices, especially when connected with the court, must additionally include access to "kiosks" with free Wi-Fi for filing and managing OArb claims, along with human "helpers" to assist those who are not comfortable with technology.[46]

3.2 *Value of In-Person Interactions*

This Chapter has noted benefits of online communications, including cost and time savings. However, this is not to discredit or ignore the importance of face-to-face interactions.[47] Indeed, some have emphasized the importance of psychology and in-person interactions as a counterbalance to pro-ODR assumptions.[48] Even in arbitration, in-person hearings provide settlement opportunities – during hallway conversations and "breaks" in arbitration proceedings.[49] Arguably, Zoom breakout rooms and intermittent phone discussions during a proceeding may foster settlement, but in-person interactions continue to hold some importance.

Additionally, arbitrators have legitimate concerns about use of remote technology for obtaining and hearing evidence. Concerns include whether a witness has been given answers by someone else in the room or through a computer or telephone accessible, but discrete, in a remote setting.[50] Although witnesses may be clandestinely "coached" during in-person proceedings through inappropriate elevator conversations or secret notes, the online environment allows for greater leeway for inappropriate witness assistance.[51]

Still, there are some precautions arbitrators should take. For example, they should disable "chat" functions within conferencing software (such as Zoom) and warn witnesses of their duty to refrain from improper communications and to provide honest testimony based on the facts as they know them. Arbitrators may even require oaths under some arbitral rules. Furthermore, attorneys should understand they violate ethical rules if they secretly "guide"

46 Amy J. Schmitz, "Expanding Access to Remedies through E-Court Initiatives," *Buffalo Law Review* 67, (2019): 101–73 (2019).

47 Adam Samuel, "Now Plaguing Dispute Resolution Processes: Proceeding in ADR Without the Handshakes," *Alternatives to the High Cost of Litigation* 38, no. 5 (April 2020): 71.

48 *Id.*

49 *Id.*

50 *Id.*

51 *Id.*

witnesses to provide a certain response or clandestinely urge them to look at a particular document in response to a question.

Additionally, the lack of in-person proceedings may disproportionally harm those parties that are less technologically savvy. For example, individuals comfortable with and knowledgeable about using Zoom have benefitted during the pandemic by understanding the importance of lighting and placement of a camera. Furthermore, those who live in spaces with fewer distractions may have an advantage over those stuck in a crowded environment where it is difficult to focus during an online hearing. Moreover, this all becomes especially important when an arbitrator assesses the evidence presented online to reach a binding decision.

In sum, documents-only arbitration and virtual hearings have merit in many cases, especially in the pandemic.[52] Nonetheless, in-person interactions have merit, and technology has its limitations.[53] In-person arbitration should remain an option for many, and arbitrators should take special care to ensure all parties in OArb feel comfortable and have full ability to present their cases. In some cases, this may even mean the arbitrator should call for a continuance amid a virtual hearing to allow for completion through in-person hearings to be sure all parties have a full and fair opportunity to present their cases.

4 Ordering OArb Over Objection

There is no question we will see more OArb and virtual hearings even after the pandemic subsides, as many have become accustomed to the time, cost, and "stress" savings of avoiding travel and in-person meetings. At the same time, the law around the FAA continues to call for enforcement of arbitration agreements and awards, even in employment and consumer cases. Furthermore, arbitrators generally have quite a bit of discretion in determining "venue" – including an online venue – but contract and FAA limitations remain. Nonetheless, there are limitations on this discretion, and fairness must remain paramount.

---

52 See Amy J. Schmitz, "Measuring 'Access to Justice' in the Rush to Digitize," *Fordham Law Review* 88, (2020): 2381; Schmitz, "Expanding Access," *supra* note 46, at 101–160.; Amy J. Schmitz, "A Blueprint for Online Dispute Resolution System Design," *Journal of Internet Law* 21, no. 3 (2018); Schmitz & Rule, *The New Handshake*, *supra* note 8.

53 Jean R. Sternlight, "Pouring a Little Psychological Cold Water on Online Dispute Resolution," *Journal of Dispute Resolution* (Winter 2020): 1.

4.1 *Enforcement of Consensual Arbitration*

The FAA and New York Convention provide for enforcement of arbitration agreements and awards. It does not speak to virtual arbitration, as the idea would have been inconceivable at the Act's passage in 1925. Nonetheless, most have endorsed the enforcement of electronically created agreements and electronically submitted awards.[54] This is fortified by the E-Sign act, which "prohibits any interpretation of the FAA's 'written provision' requirement that would preclude giving legal effect to an agreement solely on the basis that it was in electronic form."[55]

Nonetheless, consent remains central to enforcement of arbitration agreements. The FAA only calls for enforcement of consensual and valid arbitration clauses.[56] For example, it was not enough in *Campbell v. General Dynamics Government System Corp.* that a company obscured an arbitration agreement in a mass email, where the message did not put the employees on sufficient notice they were bound by arbitration simply by receiving an email.[57] In contrast, courts have held an employer binds an employee to arbitration where there is evidence the employee logged into an online HR system with a unique login/password and pressed "accept" on the agreement.[58] These cases confirm caselaw enforcing "click-wrap" e-contracts that require one to affirmatively "click" on an "accept" button.

Nonetheless, these cases do not address enforcement of OArb per se. Does blanket assent to "arbitration" include agreement to online hearings? What if a party objects to online hearings? The National Arbitration Academy (NAA) was one of the first organizations to issue an opinion on ordering online hearings over a party's objection early in the pandemic.[59] On April 1, 2020, the NAA issued Advisory Opinion No. 26, finding the need to "provide a fair and adequate hearing" and "provide effective service to the parties" would allow an arbitrator to

54 Caleb Gerbitz, "Are Pre-Dispute Agreements to Arbitrate Online Enforceable?," *Arbitration Brief* 7, January 25, 2020, https://ssrn.com/abstract=3561674.

55 *Campbell v. Gen. Dynamics Gov't Sys. Corp.*, 407 F.3d 546 (1st Cir. 2005).

56 See *Theroff v. Dollar Tree Stores, Inc.*, 591 S.W.3d 432 (Mo. Sup. Ct. 2020) (en banc). In this case, the court held that a party did not consent to arbitration where a former Dollar Tree employee who was legally blind was never provided with a reasonable means to read and understand a form arbitration provision included in hiring paperwork. *Id.*

57 *Id.* at 559.

58 *Holmes v. Air Liquide USA LLC*, WL 267194 (S.D. Tex. 2012), *affirmed*, 498 Fed. Appx. 405 (5th Cir. 2012). See also, *In re Holl*, 925 F.3d 1076 (9th Cir. 2019) (enforcing an arbitration clause in an e-contract).

59 "Formal Advisory Opinion No. 26: Video Hearings," Committee on Professional Responsibility and Grievances, *National Academy of Arbitrators*, April 1, 2020, https://naarb.org/wp-content/uploads/2020/04/CPRG-Opinion-Summaries-4.13.2020.pdf.

issue such an order without mutual consent in certain extraordinary circumstances.[60] It may be proper for an arbitrator to order virtual hearings over a party's objection where the "hearing has been postponed previously, an opposition party is non-responsive or declines to provide a reasonable explanation, and/or the case involves continuing liability or time-sensitive matters."[61]

The NAA advisory opinion stresses before issuing online hearings, an arbitrator should be confident all involved are familiar with the video platform to be used.[62] Furthermore, the arbitrator may only order online arbitration over a party's objection where the parties will have "a fair and reasonable opportunity to present their case and will allow the hearing to move forward on the dates previously scheduled."[63] Other arbitral institutions have issued similar guidance, noting the arbitrators' discretion in ordering virtual hearings, especially where health and safety are considerations.

That said, courts are starting to face arguments that ordering online arbitration is beyond an arbitrator's authority under the FAA or similar laws. For example, a party made this claim in *Legaspy v. Fin. Indus. Reg. Auth., Inc.*[64] Legaspy asked for a temporary restraining order and injunctive relief against FINRA to stop them from holding a virtual arbitration hearing and the district court denied his motion. The parties had signed an agreement saying the hearing would be held at a time and place designated by the director of FINRA, and it would be conducted per FINRA's Code of Arbitration Procedure.[65] The arbitration was scheduled on August 17, 2020, in Florida, but because of COVID-19, FINRA told the parties on June 23, 2020, the hearing was canceled and would be either rescheduled or held electronically (through Zoom or telephone conference).[66] Legaspy argued the proceedings would be difficult and irregular, especially because the other parties needed an interpreter (they were from Argentina), and the cost would exceed his insurance coverage.[67]

60 *Id.*
61 *Id.*
62 P. Jean Baker, "Utilizing Virtual Arbitration during the Pandemic," American Bar Association, May 26, 2020, https://www.americanbar.org/groups/litigation/committees/alternative-dispute-resolution/articles/2020/spring2020-utilizing-virtual-arbitration-during-the-pandemic/.
63 *Id.*
64 *Legaspy v. Financial Industry Regulatory Authority, Incorporated*, WL 4696818 (N.D. Ill. 2020).
65 *Id.*
66 *Id.*
67 *Id.*

Nonetheless, the court found the parties agreed to abide by FINRA rules, which give the arbitrators discretion to hold virtual hearings. Accordingly, the court rejected Legaspy's arguments that "attending a hearing" meant attendance in person and found Legaspy did not provide evidence to show he could not present an effective defense over Zoom – even if Zoom may be "clunkier than in-person hearings."[68] The hearings proceeded via Zoom starting August 17, 2020, for 38 sessions through February 2021. The case regarding Legaspy settled in November 2020, and the issue regarding virtual hearings never went back to the courts.

Still, ordering online hearings or an arbitration clause calling for a virtual "location" could be unreasonable where a party lacks access to required technology.[69] In *Nagrampa v. MailCoups, Inc.*, the Ninth Circuit ruled the arbitration agreement's forum selection clause was unconscionable because it was a part of a contract of adhesion, and the place and manner were unduly oppressive.[70] In particular, the claimant would have had to travel to Boston, Massachusetts from California, which would have been unduly oppressive and harsh considering the parties' circumstances.[71] The court noted a forum is unreasonable where it would be unduly oppressive or shield the stronger party from liability.[72] Accordingly, it would be unreasonable to force a party to arbitrate online where the party lacked access to and/or comfort with the required technologies.

4.2 *Arbitrator Discretion*

As the NAA Opinion and *Legaspy* indicate, arbitrators generally have discretion to use online arbitration. The court noted in *Sullivan v. Feldman*, CV H-20-2236, 2020 WL 7129879 (S.D. Tex. Dec. 4, 2020):

> "[C]ourts have recognized that "appearing" in a particular location is easier with modern technology. For example, some courts have held that technology allows arbitration decisions to be made in a place other than where the arbitrators are physically located or the final decision is signed. *See, e.g.*, *Moyett v. Lugo-Sanchez*, 321 F. Supp. 3d 263, 267 (D.P.R. 2018) ("Despite the physical distance between the arbitrators, who may physically be in Georgia, and the FINRA litigants, who are in Puerto Rico,

68 *Id.* at 4.

69 Gerbitz, *supra* note 54, at 27.

70 *Nagrampa v. MailCoups, Incorporated*, 469 F.3d 1257 (9th Cir. 2006).

71 *Id.*

72 *Id.*

> the arbitrators 'sit' in Puerto Rico with the aid of videoconferencing technology."); *NGC Network Asia, LLC v. PAC Pac. Grp. Int'l, Inc.*, No. 09-CV-8684, 2010 WL 3701351, at *3 (S.D.N.Y. Sept. 20 2010) ("[A]n arbitration award is 'made' in the district where the hearing is held, not the place from which the award was written or mailed." (citation omitted))." *Id.* at *9.

This highlights the courts' deference to arbitrators' choice of venue, including an online forum. Accordingly, a party would have to show the arbitrator(s) exceeded the wide contours of that discretion to overturn an order for online arbitration hearings.

On a similar note, the court in *Sanduski v. Charles Schwab & Co., Inc.*, 219CV01340JADBNW, 2020 WL 4905537 (D. Nev. Aug. 20, 2020), faced an argument that a partially virtual hearing exceeded the panel's authority under FINRA rules.[73] The court deferred to the arbitrator's discretion in finding it was "not 'clear from the record that the arbitrators recognized the applicable law and then ignored it' as is required to vacate an award under §10(a)(4)."[74] The court, therefore, seemed to apply the "manifest disregard for the law" standard of review that some glean from the penumbras of FAA §10(a)(4). Easily upholding the decision under this standard, the court noted, "in fact, this panel's decision to continue with the semi-virtual hearing is not only reasonable, but it does not appear to meaningfully deviate from FINRA Rule 12401, which makes no mention of whether a panel hearing requires the arbitrators to be physically present."[75]

5 Conclusion

Technology has provided immense fuel for OArb, and its benefits became apparent in the pandemic. When properly designed, OArb may allow individuals to resolve disputes quickly and cheaply, without the cost or hassle of travel or time away from work. That is not to say OArb is perfect or suited to every case or party. A digital divide persists, and policymakers must remain vigilant in protecting access to justice.[76] Arbitration clauses calling for mandatory

---

73 *Sanduski v. Charles Schwab & Co., Inc.*, 2:19-CV-01340-JAD-BNW, 2020 WL 4905537(D. Nev. Aug. 20, 2020).

74 *Id.*

75 *Id.*

76 Rebecca L. Sandefur, "The Fulcrum Point of Equal Access to Justice: Legal and Nonlegal Institutions of Remedy," *Loyola of Los Angeles Law Review* 42 (2009): 950–54.

OArb with no meaningful opportunity for consent or participation in the process should not be enforceable.[77]

Instead, we should take the COVID-19 momentum toward OArb to advance online processes that foster access to justice. We have an opportunity to examine problems with procedures in traditional dispute resolution ecosystems, such as arbitration, and to reimagine – and not merely repeat – those procedures in an online world.

77 *Compare* Nagrampa v. MailCoups, Inc., 469 F.3d 1257, 1293 (9th Cir. 2006) (holding that the arbitration agreement's forum selection clause was unconscionable because it was a part of a contract of adhesion, and the place and manner requirements (traveling to Boston from California) were unduly oppressive and harsh considering the circumstances of the parties).

CHAPTER 10

Technology as a Vehicle to Enhance Arbitration

Aichell Alvarado

1 Introduction

There has been a sharp rise in virtual hearings or completely online proceedings in the aftermath of COVID-19. The coronavirus outbreak has accelerated the digitalization of certain disputes.[1] Despite the pragmatism of alternative dispute resolution (ADR) methods, some challenges have arisen, for instance, the management of virtual hearings or cross-examination. The former requires a different approach of advocacy than for physical hearings, and the latter is about command. Thus, online dispute resolution (ODR) can be effective, but not easy, particularly in cross-border disputes[2] where new challenges and several other factors enter the paradigm of resolving the dispute. Yet, ADR has proven to be quite resilient to such changes; hence, many arbitral institutions have started to report on the increased use of such methods in the wake of the pandemic.[3]

Challenges brought by the pandemic have raised issues that are worthy of analysis, especially because online ADR seems likely to persist through the present-day reality. This chapter provides an overall picture of the current situation with respect to virtual arbitration, *i.e.*, where the application of technology is intrinsic to the dispute process itself and where ODR is a stepping-stone to virtual dispute resolution, particularly in light of the current pandemic. The response of global arbitral institutions to the pandemic, in terms of enactment of substantive and/or adjective laws, is scrutinized; specific issues relating to the implementation and quality of ODR are also discussed; and technology, as a powerful toolbox, is examined, in particular with respect to how it can

1 Sanjna Pramod, "Covid-19 and the Rise of Online Dispute Resolution," DH Deccan Herald, July 14, 2020, https://www.deccanherald.com/opinion/panorama/covid-19-and-the-rise-of-online-dispute-resolution-861291.html.

2 Esther van den Heuvel, "Online Dispute Resolution as a Solution to Cross-Border E-Disputes," OECD, accessed April 22, 2022, https://www.oecd.org/digital/consumer/1878940.pdf.

3 "'Necessity is the Mother of Invention': COVID-19 Dramatically Accelerates Digitalisation of Arbitration Processes," Herbert Smith Freehills, July 10, 2020, https://hsfnotes.com/arbitration/2020/07/10/update-8-necessity-is-the-mother-of-invention-covid-19-dramatically-accelerates-digitalisation-of-arbitration-processes/.

enhance arbitration not only in difficult times, but also in cases where parties have agreed to its use.

2 ODR *vs* ADR

All authors would accept that alternative dispute resolution is a private procedure for settling disputes outside of the courtroom. Such procedures typically include arbitration, mediation, conciliation, or negotiation. ADR usually allows the parties to come up with more creative outcomes that a court may not be legally allowed to impose.

The term ODR is more recent; its meaning is not as uniform as ADR. For some, ODR and ADR are fundamentally the same[4], and for others, ODR is not always ADR but can be ADR.[5] Albeit confusing, there are many reasons for such opposing views.

What may differentiate ODR from ADR is the use of technology, but does ADR use technology? Certainly; however, for some, the difference is that ODR focuses exclusively on resolving the dispute(s) via the internet. Even though ODR provides new opportunities for dispute resolution, it does not create a new framework for resolving a dispute. Theoretically, ODR performs the same function as ADR, but with additional or different tools.

Mediation is considered an alternative dispute resolution method even though it is different from other ADR methods. The most notable difference between mediation and arbitration is that arbitration produces a binding and enforceable award, and the arbitrator(s) is empowered to decide. Despite this, mediation is still part of the ADR umbrella as it is a private means of resolving disputes and employs a neutral third party to resolve the dispute.

The reason why ODR is for some academics and practitioners a separate branch from ADR is because its use has increased over the years, especially during the current pandemic. Some agreements contain a so-called "multi-tier" dispute resolution mechanism, which provides for arbitration only after other contractually-prescribed procedures have been exhausted. These provisions are also referred to as "escalation clauses," "steps clauses," or "MDR clauses." These provisions can include "cooling-off" or "waiting" periods; negotiations

4 Colin Rule, "Is ODR ADR? A Response to Carrie Menkel-Meadow," *International Journal on Online Dispute Resolution* 3, no. 1 (May 2016): 8.

5 "ADR and ODR – what's the difference?" Disputes EFiling, June 11, 2019, https://news.disputesefiling.com/2019/06/11/adr-and-odr-whats-the-difference/.

between corporate representatives or officers; conciliation, mediation, or mini-trials.[6]

Mediation, conciliation and negotiation are methods that also exist in ODR but are handled differently, *i.e.*, technology is the principal means to carry out the resolution of the conflict, either through specific websites or electronic tools specifically created for this aim. Regarding ADR, technology may be essential, but it is not essential.

The above suggests that parties often agree to exhaust other means before relying on arbitration. Although ODR has deserved its spot over the years, it is not yet considered, individually, as an ADR method; both ADR and ODR are private means for resolving conflicts and exclude litigation. The ODR movement is a derivative of ADR. ODR has its own place and may be another route to reach ADR.

3 Overview of the Use of ODR during the COVID-19 Pandemic

COVID-19 has catapulted the use of ODR. During the current pandemic, arbitration hearings have been suspended. Alternatively, if it was not possible to hold an in-person hearing, videoconferencing was used. Many arbitral institutions have started to report on the increased use of such tools since the beginning of the pandemic.[7]

The emergence of the pandemic accelerated the use of electronic filing systems, document exchange and storage, and communications services. Remote or virtual models, as well as hybrid (a mixture of online and physical or in person) models were adopted in many jurisdictions to adjust to the exceptional circumstances created by the pandemic.

3.1 *Asia: The Philippines*

The courts of the South Asian archipelago of the Philippines issued some interesting decisions with respect to ODR. Concerning the courts system, the Supreme Court issued Administrative Matter No. 20-12-01-SC or the 2020 Guidelines for the Conduct of Court-Annexed Mediation (CAM) and Judicial Dispute Resolution (JDR)[8] to ensure that hearings via videoconferencing would be

6 Gary B. Born, *International Commercial Arbitration* (The Hague: Kluwer Law International, 2021), 305.

7 Herbert Smith Freehills, *supra* note 3.

8 "Re: Proposed Guidelines on the Conduct of Videoconferencing," Supreme Court of the Philippines, accessed July 14, 2021, https://sc.judiciary.gov.ph/16099/.

conducted, and outlined the Guidelines on the Conduct of Videoconferencing. The Guidelines recognize that proceedings via videoconferencing have become an alternative to in-court proceedings. In order for parties to benefit from this, they are required to file a motion.

One of the concerns about remote hearings is oral examination of witnesses. The Guidelines foresee this circumstance and state that where litigants and witnesses are testifying from remote locations, there must be technical personnel present in these remote locations to assist and address technical issues that may arise during the videoconference. Notwithstanding, the Guidelines anticipate the possibility that stakeholders may not be able to connect and immediate solutions for connectivity issues seem to be unknown, as hearings are sometimes cancelled due to poor internet connectivity.

The adjournment of hearings was a temporary solution when it was unclear when the situation would return to normal. The spread of the Covid-19 virus and the restrictive measures imposed by many governments made it impossible for many parties, counsel, witnesses and arbitrators from different parts of the world to attend in-person hearings. Thus, tribunals and parties to ongoing proceedings had the choices proposed by their governments, which typically included adjourning hearings, agreeing to "documents only" proceedings or holding entirely virtual hearings.

The Philippines certainly exploited the use of technology. Pursuant to their Guidelines, the conduct of videoconferencing shall closely resemble in-court hearings with remote locations viewed as extensions of the courtroom. The widespread misconception that human beings will soon be replaced by robot lawyer look-alikes is still far from feasible. Perhaps automatizing existing systems or procedures is the key answer for ADR.

The aim of the Guidelines was to propose a general relief to the current pandemic. The Philippines neither launched a revolutionary platform to hold online hearings nor created an innovative platform. Instead, the archipelago took advantage of the resources and enhanced existing technological tools preserving all principles of ADR. Moreover, as part of the court proceedings, parties were referred to the Philippine Mediation Center to encourage them to settle their disputes through mediation. The Guidelines will continue to be applicable even after the crisis is over.

While litigation received much of the government's attention, there were no major changes to laws regarding arbitration. Local arbitral institutions nevertheless addressed the problem. The Philippine International Center for Conflict Resolution (PICCR) offered, through its website, a set of instructions to be followed, encouraging parties to preserve, commence and/or seek resolution of their claims.[9] PICCR structured their instructions as follows:

- For *arbitration commencing proceedings* stakeholders were encouraged to communicate with PICCR Secretariat via email and submit the request for arbitration. The Respondent may file its Answer to the Request or make any appropriate requests (e.g., extension of time) within the period provided under the PICCR Rules.
- *Emergency reliefs* should be similarly filed via email.

The PICCR also issued a Guidance Note[10] intending to regulate the conduct of virtual hearings during the pandemic. Although the Guidance Note sets out useful key points for the holding of online hearings, it always allows parties to choose how to conduct proceedings. The Guidance Note states, for instance, that if a party becomes unable to participate due to technical issues, the party shall immediately notify the arbitral tribunal of the technical issue, by any means of telecommunication on which the parties have previously agreed and which is approved by the arbitral tribunal, and identify the last piece of information that was transmitted.[11]

The Philippine Dispute Resolution Center (PDRCI), the primary arbitral institution that administers arbitration proceedings in the Philippines[12] also announced measures to its users.[13] These measures focused primarily on online meetings, the conduct of virtual hearings, case management recommendations, *etc.*

3.2 *Europe: Sweden*

In Europe, Sweden's iconic arbitral institution, the Arbitration Institute of the Stockholm Chamber of Commerce (SCC) launched, in 2019, the *SCC Platform* – a secure digital platform for communication and file sharing between the SCC, the parties and the tribunal.[14] The Platform is mandatory for any communication

9 "PICCR Advisory – Our services are available online," Philippine International Center for Conflict Resolution, accessed July 14, 2021, https://piccr.com.ph/case.php.

10 "PICCR Guidance Note on Virtual Hearings," Philippine International Center for Conflict Resolution, accessed July 14, 2021, https://piccr.com.ph/media/PICCR-Virtual-Hearings.pdf.

11 *Id.*

12 Raquel Wealth A Taguian et al., "The International Arbitration Review: Philippines," The Law Reviews, July 4, 2021, https://thelawreviews.co.uk/title/the-international-arbitration-review/philippines.

13 "Guidelines on Online Meetings and Virtual Hearings," Philippines Dispute Resolution Center, Inc., August 3, 2020, https://www.pdrci.org/web/wp-content/uploads/2020/08/Guidelines-on-Online-Meetings-and-Virtual-Hearings-1.pdf.

14 "SCC Platform – Simplifying Secure Communication From Request to Award," Arbitration Institute of the Stockholm Chamber of Commerce, accessed August 10, 2021, https://sccinstitute.com/case-management/.

that involves the SCC, and it provides an archive service. Considering the SCC's dominant position for non-ad hoc Swedish seated arbitrations, this technological step made an impact on arbitration work in Sweden. This, combined with the recent amendments to the Swedish Arbitration Act[15] to modernize and improve an already established piece of legislation, is proof of Sweden's ambition as one of the top jurisdictions for international arbitration.

Case management has been digitalized since 2013, thus, the SCC body did not make paramount changes to its operations in the midst of the pandemic. Cases are initiated in the same manner as they used to be before COVID-19.[16] The Platform introduced in 2019 provides for the filing of materials for the case, procedural orders, submissions and exhibits. Only participants in the arbitration are granted access to the Platform. In parallel, the SCC launched, in May 2020, the *Ad Hoc* Platform which provides the same benefits as the principal Platform for *ad hoc* arbitration proceedings. The parties and appointed arbitrator(s) are responsible for uploading relevant material and information onto the Platform, which remains accessible for one year after the termination of the arbitration unless otherwise agreed with the SCC.

Sweden is among the well-established seats for arbitration[17] and the SCC is one of the country's premier institutions. Despite that popularity, the SCC continues to propose amendments to its rules, announcing seminars and tours in order to further the legacy. The SCC response to the pandemic was quite modest due to their robust provisions and infrastructure. It remained fully operational nonetheless, with certain team members of the Secretariat on site for necessary procedures related to arbitral proceedings.

The prominence of the SCC stems from various factors. First, the Chamber administers arbitration under both SCC rules and other rules agreed to by the parties, and secondly, it is known for keeping its rules short but comprehensive.

It should be noted that the SCC has been one of the few institutions that has issued publications, guideline, notes, and announcements to provide

15 On November 21, 2018, the Swedish legislature passed a revised Arbitration Act, intended to make the arbitration process more efficient. The revision aims at making Swedish arbitration law more easily accessible, especially for non-Swedish parties, and to ensure that Stockholm continues to be an attractive venue for international dispute resolution. The changes entered into effect on March 1, 2019.

16 "Contact Us," Arbitration Institute of the Stockholm Chamber of Commerce, accessed April 22, 2022, https://sccinstitute.com/about-the-scc/contact-us/ (Requests for arbitration shall be filed to arbitration@chamber.se).

17 White & Case, LLP, "2018 International Arbitration Survey: The Evolution of International Arbitration," Queen Mary University of London, May 9, 2018, https://arbitration.qmul.ac.uk/media/arbitration/docs/2018-International-Arbitration-Survey---The-Evolution-of-International-Arbitration-(2).PDF (stated London, Paris, Singapore, Hong Kong, Geneva, New York, and Stockholm were the top most ranked seats for arbitration).

guidance to its community about how the global pandemic may affect ongoing procedures.[18]

3.3 *United States of America*

Historically, the United States of America (US)'s major cities maintained local chambers which administered international arbitrations. Within the US, New York, Miami, and Houston have emerged as the most popular arbitral seats.[19] Among these cities, New York is considered the leading center for international arbitration. The American Arbitration Association (AAA), founded in 1926 by the merger of two New York arbitration institutions, and the International Centre for Dispute Resolution (ICDR), founded in the early 1920s,[20] are two of New York's most prominent institutions. The AAA is among the institutions that administer the highest number of arbitral disputes in the world,[21] while the ICDR, the international division of the AAA, has administrative faculty in New York and manages cases outside the US.

The AAA treated technology as an inherent factor in arbitration within their proceedings before the COVID-19 pandemic.[22] The AAA-ICDR issued the Model Order and Procedures for a Virtual Hearing via Videoconference as a model guideline to parties and arbitrators regarding different ways to address issues that may arise during a virtual hearing. The model, which is online-focused, fits

---

18 See "Checklist on Holding Hearings in Times of COVID-19," Arbitration Institute of the Stockholm Chamber of Commerce, March 16, 2020, https://sccinstitute.com/about-the-scc/news/2020/checklist-on-holding-hearings-in-times-of-covid-19/ (where guidance is located for parties, counsel and arbitrators when holding hearings in times of COVID-19 can be found); and "Stockholm Confession Camera," Arbitration Institute of the Stockholm Chamber of Commerce, September 4, 2019, video, https://vimeo.com/357744879 (for "confessions" made by SCC Secretariat when launching the SCC Platform).

19 Claudia Salomon and Irina Sivachenko, "Choosing an arbitral seat in the United States," LexisNexis, accessed April 22, 2022, https://www.lw.com/thoughtLeadership/choosing-an-arbitral-seat-in-the-us#:~:text=Within%20the%20United%20States%2C%20New,procedural%20and%20substantive%20laws%20vary.

20 Ian Macneil, *American Arbitration Law: Reformation, Nationalization, Internationalization* (Oxford University Press, 1992), 38–41.

21 "AAA-ICDR's Annual B2B Caseload Continues to Increase, Along with Level of the Diversity in Arbitrator Roster & Appointments," AAA-ICDR, February 26, 2020, https://www.adr.org/sites/default/files/document_repository/AAA_2019_Caseload_Numbers_Press_Release_02262020.pdf (The AAA administered 9,737 commercial arbitrations in 2019).

22 AAA website has services such as "Cybersecurity and Data Protection", "Technology Disputes Capabilities", and "AAA-ICDR Software & Online Tools." See "Cybersecurity & Technology," AAA-ICDR, accessed April 22, 2022, https://www.adr.org/TechnologyServices.

almost every AAA case because it has a contract form with general arbitration clauses.[23]

Despite these technological provisions, the AAA-ICDR does not have a platform to conduct hearings. Video hearings or proceedings are conducted through third-party platforms and are subject to the platform's terms and policies. As such, the AAA-ICDR equipped its users with a set of rules that may be followed on a consensual basis. During the 2020 peak of the pandemic, the AAA-ICDR registered a total of 9,538 cases,[24] in contrast with the 2019 caseload of 9,737.[25]

The AAA-ICDR provided uninterrupted services during a very unpredictable year while also issuing soft measures, such as the above model, to its arbitral community. Significantly, the dollar value of cases for 2019 totalled $18.4 billion in claims and counterclaims, while the dollar value in 2020 was $18 billion, which, given the circumstances, is remarkable. As far as new regulations, the 2021 update marks the first time the AAA-ICDR's arbitration and mediation rules have been revised since 2014.

3.4 *Latin America and Chile*

The Latin American countries have many features in common due to their Ibero-American heritage, such as their language and culture, but perhaps the most important similarity is their legal system. The Latin American region is still a developing market when it comes to arbitration, perhaps due to the long-lasting issues in many Latin countries: the corruption and lack of transparency in their court systems, not only for litigation proceedings, but also arbitration.[26]

---

23 "AAA-ICDR Model Order and Procedures for a Virtual Hearing via Videoconference," AAA-ICDR, May 9, 2020, https://go.adr.org/rs/294-SFS-516/images/AAA270_AAA-ICDR%20Model%20Order%20and%20Procedures%20for%20a%20Virtual%20Hearing%20via%20Videoconference.pdf.

24 "2020 b2b Caseload Data Shows AAA-ICDR Provided Uninterrupted ADR Services in Difficult Year," AAA-ICDR, February 11, 2021, https://adr.org/sites/default/files/document_repository/AAA-2020-B2B-Caseload-Press-Release-11Feb2021_1.pdf (2020 business to business caseload); "2020 b2b Dispute Resolution Infographic," AAA-ICDR, accessed April 22, 2022, https://www.adr.org/sites/default/files/document_repository/AAA333_2020_B2B_Infographic_0.pdf (total cases in 2020).

25 "2019 b2b Dispute Resolution Infographic," AAA-ICDR, accessed April 22, 2022, https://www.adr.org/sites/default/files/document_repository/AAA261_2019_B2B_Infographic_0.pdf (2019 business to business total cases).

26 See scandals cases that took place in the Republic of Peru as of 2019 to date, which are related to allegations of corruption brought against several Peruvian arbitrators by Odebrecht company, for example, Laura Bunt-MacRury, "Peru's House of Cards: Odebrecht scandal has engulfed the country's political class," The Conversation, June

Although Latin American countries are members of the New York Convention and have international arbitration legislation in place, Latin businesses and investors still prefer to select foreign arbitral seats.

Despite this, Chile has been able to make some substantial changes to its existing legislation. On April 2020, the Chilean National Assembly enacted Law No. 21,226, which established a legal exemption for judicial processes and hearings and also suspended evidentiary terms due to COVID-19. Law 21,226 extends to arbitration, providing that those tribunals (including arbitral tribunals) outside of the judicial scope may suspend hearings and should reschedule for the nearest possible date after the global emergency.[27] Law 21,226 also regulates technology by allowing virtual hearings. Article 6 imposes the suspension of evidentiary terms across the country, meaning a procedure can only move forward until it reaches the evidentiary phase, at which point it would have to be suspended. The scope of Article 6 has sparked a heated debate among commentators and raised questions as to whether this article is necessary or whether arbitration proceedings should be allowed to continue following an agreement of the parties. No clarification of this issue was made from the legislative branch.[28]

Law 21,226 does not expressly indicate whether it applies only to local and not international arbitration; however, given that no clear distinction is made between the two forms of arbitration, there is no reason to believe it does not apply to international arbitration, especially since the Chilean capital, Santiago, is an attached member of the International Chamber of Commerce (ICC).

Chile is also known for having the only center in Latin America with its own rules on the use of online dispute boards.[29] Since 2013, these rules have allowed online case management of proceedings and allow parties to perform activities similar to the SCC (*i.e.*, submission of documents, management of online processes, *etc.*). Chile's response to the global pandemic covered many relevant legal aspects. First, legislation was enacted to provide guidance to Chilean nationals. Second, the local and international chamber, the *Centro de*

27, 2019, https://theconversation.com/perus-house-of-cards-odebrecht-scandal-has-engulfed-the-countrys-political-class-118793.

27 Art. 2, Law 21.226.

28 Liat Tapia and Pablo Correa, "Are the Judicial Procedural Rules Issued During the Pandemic Applicable to International Arbitrations Seated in Santiago?," Kluwer Arbitration Blog, October 7, 2020, http://arbitrationblog.kluwerarbitration.com/2020/10/07/are-the-judicial-procedural-rules-issued-during-the-pandemic-applicable-to-international-arbitrations-seated-in-santiago/.

29 "Regulations on Dispute Boards," Centro de Arbitraje y Mediación, effective as of January 1, 2015, https://www.camsantiago.cl/wp-content/uploads/2020/03/reglamentos-DB.pdf.

Arbitraje y Mediación de la Cámara de Comercio, already had an online system, E-CAM, in place, which provided, *inter alia*, storage of files, electronic notification of actions and resolutions, and remote access for participants. Lastly, Chile implemented pro bono remote management of mediations for any cases not exceeding $100,000 in value.[30] This measure sought to help small businesses face the "litigious side" left by the pandemic. According to the *Centro de Arbitraje y Mediación de la Cámara de Comercio*, under these rules they will contact the parties via phone or email and schedule the date of the first online hearing. From the moment the request is received, the process will last a maximum of 30 days.

Chile's pro bono mediation proceedings for small and medium enterprises (SMEs) raises another topic: technology may be the best ally for small and medium businesses since it provides low-cost ADR procedures. The use of technology may also minimize the cost of ADR proceedings for SMEs.

For SMEs, binding online arbitration or mediation may present major advantages, especially when the parties are far apart or are relying upon a quick decision.

Arbitration has proven to be resilient during the pandemic and technology has been an important component of this durability. As a result, ODR emerged from the amalgam of ADR and technology, with a major advantage of circumventing distance-related issues. Under ODR, resolving disputes is generally more cost-effective and time-efficient (depending on the merits and value of the claim), even when compared to arbitration. ODR may also enhance inclusion. For example, the Chilean experience demonstrated that ADR can be used by small corporations to the same extent as multinational corporations and States for investment treaty claims. Small businesses do not have to be deprived of arbitration proceedings because of the cost; there are similar results with fewer resources as in a normal arbitration. For example, in small claims cases, parties can agree to use *ad hoc* arbitration and determine all aspects of the arbitration process themselves.

Ad hoc arbitration is less expensive than institutional arbitration[31] because parties only pay fees for the arbitrator(s) and lawyers; another option to reduce costs may be to select a sole arbitrator instead of a tribunal. Undoubtedly, online arbitration, which guarantees access regardless of the geographical location of participants, also reduces costs significantly.

30 "Informativo CAM Santiago," CAM Santiago de Chile, accessed August 11, 2021, https://www.camsantiago.cl/minisites/informativo-online/2020/ABR/noticia01.html.

31 Claimants have to pay an approximately of $USD2,000 to $USD5,000 just to initiate arbitration in an arbitral institution. Such amount is considered as filling fee.

Because arbitration is a consensual means of dispute resolution, substantive legislative changes were irrelevant in most countries. The flexibility of ADR makes it resistant to legislative changes, as party autonomy, including the freedom to select arbitrators, the seat of arbitration, and the applicable law, is one of the main features of international arbitration.

4 Challenges and Issues with ODR

Some users find that videoconferencing is not a perfect substitute for in-person interactions,[32] even though the use of technology is generally encouraged regardless of which alternative mechanism is implemented. Nonetheless, counsel and parties are often reluctant to use online hearings and prefer to rely on technology in other areas of the arbitration proceeding.

Technology provides many useful resources, but also many challenges. It is important to highlight that technology cannot be one hundred percent reliable. There are still many issues with technology, such as technological failure or lack of access to high-quality internet. Overall though, it improves efficiency in the arbitration process by providing useful advantages, especially for low-cost procedures or during unforeseen circumstances that preclude the possibility of physical meetings.

One concern with online arbitration involves witness examination, which play an essential role in arbitration. When examining a witness, counsel either seeks to convince the tribunal that the witness is credible or seeks to discredit the witness. Thus, declarations made by witnesses must be clear and consistent with the other evidence on record. In most cases, examinations are time-limited, and when held online, examining a witness may be challenging because every minute counts. Moreover, analyzing the demeanor of witnesses through a screen may be difficult for the arbitrator.[33]

While ODR has an advantage in overcoming geographical limitations, this advantage does not exist when enforcing the outcome of the procedure. If the outcome is a binding award, the winner will have to apply for an exequatur, possibly on the other side of the globe, as online award enforcement is still far away. If the outcome is an unperformed settlement, then the situation is more

32 Gabrielle Kaufmann-Kohler and Thomas Schultz, "The Use of Information Technology in Arbitration," Weblaw, December 5, 2005, https://jusletter.weblaw.ch/juslissues/2005/354/_4410.html__ONCE&login=false.

33 Gopika Nambiar and Kumar Karan, "Examination and cross-examination of witnesses in arbitral proceedings via video-conferencing: Challenges and the road ahead," BarandBench, October 4, 2020, https://www.barandbench.com/columns/examination-and-cross-examination-of-witnesses-in-arbitral-proceedings-via-video-conferencing.

problematic because the creditor will have to start a new court action for performance, not just enforcement proceedings.[34]

International legal instruments appear to require that awards be in writing and signed by the arbitrators. The New York Convention in its fourth article requires that the party seeking recognition or enforcement of an award must produce the duly authenticated original award. When an original is required, the production of an electronic document is sufficient if a secure electronic signature guarantees its integrity and attribution to the arbitrators. The general recognition of electronic documents and electronic signatures by many States often allows the formal requirements of local arbitration law to be respected. The difficulties that remain are often practical ones arising at the time of communication of the electronic award.[35]

5 Conclusions

The coronavirus outbreak brought an acceleration of digitalization attempts for certain disputes; however, despite how pragmatic ADR methods may be, some challenges, such as the ones explored in this paper, have arisen, *i.e.* with respect to the management of virtual hearings and cross-examination of witnesses. The management of virtual hearings requires a different approach of advocacy than the approach adopted for physical hearings. The cross-examination of witnesses is about command. Thus, ODR can be very effective, yet not an easy task particularly in cross-border disputes where new challenges and several other factors, as outlined in this chapter, enter into the paradigm of dispute resolution. Yet, ADR has been quite resilient to such changes.

Although dispute resolution procedures may use some form of ODR,[36] this research explores a more holistic application of ODR, where technology is intrinsic to the dispute process itself and where ODR is a stepping-stone to virtual dispute resolution, particularly in light of the current pandemic. Ultimately, continued learning from parties, counsel, and arbitrators will be needed to minimize the risks associated with the use of ODR.

34 Gabrielle Kaufmann-Kohler, "Online Dispute Resolution and its Significance for International Commercial Arbitration," ICC Publishing, November 2005, accessed August 7, 2021, 443, https://lk-k.com/wp-content/uploads/Online-Dispute-Resolution-and-Its-Significance-for-International-Commercial-Arbitration.pdf.

35 "Dispute Settlement: International Commercial Arbitration, 5.9 Electronic Arbitration," United Nations Conference on Trade and Development, New York and Geneva, accessed April 22, 2022, https://unctad.org/system/files/official-document/edmmisc232add20_en.pdf.

36 Videoconferencing, email and other electronic communications between the parties, hearing rooms, cloud-based storages.

CHAPTER 11

The New Landscape of Arbitration in View of Digitalization

Magdalena Łągiewska

1 Introduction

The COVID-19 pandemic recently brought various sectors of our lives to a standstill and sped up the process of digitalization. In dispute resolution, there was a shift to the electronic filing of documents and consequently limited face-to-face contact between parties. The digitalization process is inseparably linked to the future of the arbitration courts worldwide. Such digitalization (collecting e-evidence, conducting online hearings, etc.), driven by the needs created by the global pandemic, will have an impact and create a new framework for the functioning of the global arbitration system.

Digitalization is seen as a potential solution to the inefficiency of traditional courts, the weakness of judicial credibility, as well as the inconveniences to the parties.[1] The emergence of different models of online courts is worth analyzing and this chapter focuses on the so-called "smart courts" in China. The Chinese experience and accomplishments in the digitalization process offer insights that may be useful in times of crisis and thereafter.

In our view, the traditional, classic mode of functioning of courts and arbitral tribunals is becoming a thing of the past. The development of online courts will take place on many levels and involve not only the national justice systems, but also the international frameworks and alternative dispute resolution mechanisms, including arbitration. The aim of this chapter is to outline the new landscape of arbitration stemming from the digitalization process. It provides an analysis of recent changes in dispute resolution in China, presenting the overall approach to the digitalization of courts (including but not limited to arbitration courts). It touches upon the different examples of digitalization already undertaken in arbitration institutions worldwide and offers final considerations regarding the arbitration landscape after the COVID-19 pandemic.

1 Junlin Peng & Wen Xiang, "The Rise of Smart Courts in China: Opportunities and Challenges to the Judiciary in a Digital Age," *Nordic Journal of Law & Social Research* 1, no. 9 (2019): 347.

© MAGDALENA ŁĄGIEWSKA, 2023 | DOI:10.1163/9789004514836_013

In view of the examples from China, we are left with the question of whether traditional in-person arbitration proceedings will last or become outdated.

2 Chinese Smart Courts and the Establishment of Online Courts

Most models of online courts came from Common Law jurisdictions. Several factors led to their development, such as increased access to justice, reduced cost, more efficient use of litigants' time, and reduced reliance on attorneys. Some models of online courts function within the public sphere but outside the judiciary system, while others, such as "smart courts" in China, function as an integrated part of a centralized court system.[2]

In addition to the emergence of online courts, there is a new global phenomenon known as the online dispute resolution mechanism ("ODR"). This global shift towards ODR has led to developments in technology and opened new possibilities, such as Chinese "smart courts". "Smart courts" are part of a global Chinese strategy to restructure the judiciary system, and the Chinese government plays a vital role in the promotion of information and communication technologies ("ICT") that fuel the advancement of ODR.[3] These technological advances are especially significant given judicial reform conducted in China; reforms intended "to build a judicial mechanism that is open, dynamic, transparent, and convenient and improve public understanding, trust, and supervision of the judicature".[4]

In recent years in China, the process of digitalization of courts has been widely discussed not only in theory but also in practice. Digitalization of courts should be understood as all proceedings relating to litigation being conducted online, including activities such as filing cases, court trials, executions of judgement, etc. Today, with the development of new technologies, it is inevitable to use big data, cloud computing, and even artificial intelligence more frequently in online court proceedings. Digitalization seems to be a natural

---

2 Veronica Bradautanu et al., "From digitalisation to digital transformation: A case for online courts in commercial disputes?," European Bank for Reconstruction and Development, October 22, 2020, 10.

3 George G. Zheng, "China's Grand Design of People's Smart Courts," *Asian Journal of Law and Society* 7, no. 3 (2020): 561–563.

4 Mimi Zou, "'Smart courts' in China and the Future of Personal Injury Litigation," *Journal of Personal Injury Law* (forthcoming, June 2020), 1–2, https://papers.ssrn.com/sol3/papers.cfm?abstract_id=3552895; cf. "Opinion of the Supreme People's Court on Deepening Reform of the People's Courts Comprehensively: Outline of the Fourth Five-year Reform of the People's Courts (2014–2018)," China Law Translate, Febuary 26, 2015, https://www.chinalawtranslate.com/en/court-reform-plan/.

consequence of technological development resulting in improved judicial efficiency. When digitalized, the whole judicial process becomes much more convenient for people who can benefit from it, even while at home.[5]

China took the first steps towards informatization in the 1990s. Those first steps were treated as the foundation to create infrastructure for the functioning of e-government and further the emergence of e-courts. The first step was to provide courts with computers. Next, government information was digitalized. There was a need to not only design algorithms, but also to create a tool used for their collection, archival, streamlining and analysis. Based on this, it was inevitable for China to make use of the whole range of innovative technologies (including both artificial intelligence and blockchain) to create "smart courts".

This development of new technologies allowed the entire court system to become more digitalized. The Supreme People's Court in China ("SPC") plays a crucial role in this field. The SPC created large-scale databases providing information to the public about the judicial process and court management. As a result, "China Judicial Process Information Online (中国审判流程信息公开网), China Court Documents Online (中国裁判文书网), China Judgements Enforcement Information Online (中国执行信息网), China Open Trials Online (中国庭审公开网), China Justice Big Data Service Platform (中国司法大数据服务网), and Legal Information: Data Network Service Platform on Application of Chinese Law (Faxin, 法信—中国法律应用数字网络服务平台)"[6] were introduced. In addition to these national databases, each local court provides its own database. There are three principal purposes of these online platforms: first, they provide judicial transparency in China, resulting in open trials and hearings that are available for the public; second, they are seen as instruments crucial in the view of judicial management that allow the improvement of judicial efficiency; lastly, they are useful in terms of big-data analysis.[7]

It is worth adding that the term "intelligent court" was first defined by the Annual Working Report of the SPC in China. According to this report, an "intelligent court system" should aim to "make full use of technologies such as [the] Internet, cloud computing, big data, artificial intelligence and so on, to promote the modernization of [the] trial system of judgment capability, so as to achieve the highly intellectualized operation of [the] management of the people's court".[8] Considering this definition, it is possible to distinguish three key

5 Peng and Xiang, *supra* note 1, at 345.
6 Zheng, *supra* note 3, at 566.
7 *Id.* at 565–566.
8 Alison (Lu) Xu, "Chinese judicial justice on the cloud: a future call or a Pandora's box? An analysis of the 'intelligent court system' of China," *Information & Communications Technology Law* 26, no. 1 (2017): 62).

areas of the digitalization process in China: first, the process concerns intelligent case resolution; second, it refers to the intelligent office administration; and finally, it touches upon the intelligent personal evaluation.[9]

Today, the process of digitalization in Chinese courts is a "hot topic" analyzed by academics and legal practitioners. The necessity of developing this field was also highlighted by the President of the People's Republic of China, Xi Jinping, who said that "there is no modernization without digitalization".[10] A similar stance was presented by the Chief Justice and President of the Supreme People's Court, Zhou Qiang. He once stated that the entire process of judicial reform, including information construction aimed at the modernization of the judicial system, was "two wheels of cars and a pair of wings of birds".[11] Digitalization is a natural consequence of development and a prognostic of a new age, and it is challenging to modernize a country without benefiting from new technologies. To utilize digitalization, the SPC proclaimed the introduction of so-called "smart courts" in 2015–2016. The emergence of "smart courts" is widely considered to be a solution to previous challenges to the court system. "Smart courts" benefit from ICT, especially in terms of the Internet, cloud computing, big data, and artificial intelligence. These tools modernize and improve the judicial capability of the entire trial system in China. "Smart courts" are but one of the tools pertaining to the whole range of government initiatives, all of which aim to reduce the shortcomings of the judiciary system in China. These shortcomings restrain economic growth and affect public trust as well as international confidence in the appropriate functioning of Chinese courts. These initiatives together increase the professionalism and transparency of the Chinese judiciary and the accountability of both Chinese courts and judges.[12]

Notably, the Chinese people are much more aware of their rights than ever before, and although the alternative dispute resolution mechanisms are particularly popular in China, there remains a need to resolve some legal problems by using typical court litigation. However, there are not enough judges for the amount of legal cases presented, creating the need for alternate solutions, such as online courts.[13]

9 *Id.* at 63.

10 Peng and Xiang, *supra* note 1, at 346; cf. Xi Jinping, "First meeting of the central cyber security and informatization (2014)", 习近平.中央网 络安全和信息化领导小组第一次会议, 2014.

11 Peng and Xiang, supra note 1, at 346; cf. Zhou Qiang. National symposium of provosts of high courts (2014), 周强.全国高级法院院长座 谈会, 2014.

12 Zou, *supra* note 4, at 2.

13 Peng and Xiang, *supra* note 1, at 346.

By June 2019, China formed an entire "smart court" system. This system comprises the whole range of transparent and intelligent online services widely available to Chinese citizens. In addition, the internal judicial work system is directly connected to the external litigation service, which bolsters the functionality of the judiciary system within the People's Republic of China. The services are not only available on simple PCs, but also on smart mobile devices. Hence, "shared big-data platform connects government agencies, industry organizations, legal firms, and Internet companies".[14]

Due to recent achievements in the legal field, instead of a linear and isolated litigation model, China has adopted an integrated, open, and intelligent model. Thus, judicial activities do not follow a traditional pattern, but combine both online and offline integration patterns.[15]

Three online courts currently function within the territory of the People's Republic of China, located in Beijing, Hangzhou, and Guangzhou. In April 2015, the High People's Court of Zhejiang Province introduced special online e-commerce tribunals, the first online tribunals to operate in China. Those tribunals handle cases mainly relating to online monetary claims, copyright infringement, and transaction disputes. China established the Hangzhou Internet Court in August 2017 and the Beijing and Guangzhou Internet Courts in September 2018. There are currently eight specialized divisions functioning successfully within these Internet courts. Through 31 October 2019, these courts resolved 88,000 Internet-related cases out of almost 120,000 presented. Online litigation sped up the whole process significantly, with the court conducting an average of 45-minutes of online hearings and issuing a decision within an average of 38 days after the hearing. Accordingly, the Chinese judiciary saved three-fifths the time in online hearings and half the time issuing a judgment as compared to the traditional model. Online courts are remarkably effective, with the parties acknowledging first-instance judgments in most cases (up to 98% of cases handled by the online courts). There were very few appeals of judgements issued by the Chinese online courts.[16]

In sum, these three courts conduct the entire court process online, from filing a lawsuit through issuing a judgment. A special e-litigation platform has been created to provide these services to Chinese citizens, and there is also the so-called "mobile micro court" functioning as an additional tool, which is a mini-program offered on WeChat, a social media platform in China. The

14 Supreme People's Court of the People's Republic of China, *Internet Justice in Chinese Courts*, ed. Ding Lina (Beijing, 2019), 61. 中华人民共和国最高人民法院编，中国法院的互联网司法，北京 2019, 61.

15 *Id.* at 61–62.

16 *Id.* at 63–64.

"mobile micro court" aims to guarantee access to justice, even for those Chinese people who do not have access to a computer, providing broader access to e-litigation in China. This effectiveness was demonstrated during the COVID-19 pandemic, during which the Beijing Internet Court received almost the same number of filed applications as before the pandemic (Chinese citizens filed 2,681 cases during the lockdown). According to Zhang Wen, President of the Beijing Internet Court, "[t]he unprecedented public health emergency of COVID-19 has pushed courts across the country to start testing online trials. The Beijing Internet Court can share the experience from our pioneering practices and help set protocols of online litigation proceedings in cyberspace".[17] In response to COVID-19, the Beijing Internet Court prepared a special protocol which included 26 procedures that cover different aspects of online litigation, such as identity authentication of parties and dress code suitable in a video courtroom.[18]

3 Significance of Smart Courts in China during COVID-19 Pandemic

The COVID-19 pandemic influenced all aspects of our lives, most notably the judiciary system and alternative dispute resolution mechanisms, including arbitration. Chinese authorities were aware of the need to strengthen informatization and digitalization, both of which are vital in a global pandemic. Xi Jinping and Zhou Qiang highlighted the need for improving the effectiveness of "smart courts" across China, and China undertook a range of measures across their judicial system to ensure the safety of Chinese citizens and the public health as a result. Those measures included online case-handling, online payments, and electronic delivery of judgments. By implementing "smart courts", China was able to minimize the need for in-person courtroom appearances and therefore reduced the number of infected citizens. These solutions aimed to fulfil obligations related to pending cases while also limiting citizens' exposure to the virus by utilizing China's previous developments concerning "smart courts". Litigation participants registered online through available channels such as a mobile micro court, litigation service network, etc., while Chinese courts conducted sessions through remote video to prevent "close and direct contact" between participants, safeguarding the health of Chinese citizens. Chinese courts adjusted their work to the new reality by also changing offline

17 Xinhua, "Across China: Internet court handles cases despite coronavirus epidemic," Xinhuanet, March 10, 2020, http://www.xinhuanet.com/english/2020-03/10/c_138862437.htm.

18 *Id.*

litigation activities into online ones. Thus, relying on the recent developments of "smart" and Internet courts, Chinese courts carried out most litigation activities online and therefore reduced the number of required personnel.[19]

4 Different Examples of Digitalization in International Arbitration

Numerous examples already exist regarding the digitalization process in international arbitration, but in this section, some innovative solutions will be explored to introduce different approaches to digitalization in global dispute settlement.

There are many approaches to effectively use technology in arbitration. First is the idea of digital case management systems. In 2005, the International Chamber of Commerce ("ICC") introduced NetCase, a document management platform that enabled parties to monitor the online arbitration process, which is no longer used by the ICC court.

There are other similar platforms used by various arbitration institutions all over the world. For example, the American Arbitration Association ("AAA") uses AAA-ICDR service technology to ensure cybersecurity and data protection. To meet this goal, the AAA-ICDR requires that all arbitrators undergo special training on the basics of cybersecurity. Through this training, arbitrators can take necessary measures to preserve and protect the integrity and legitimacy of the arbitral proceedings.[20] Another example relates to the World Intellectual Property Organization ("WIPO"), which introduced online administrative tools. This allows the WIPO Arbitration and Mediation Center to provide time- and cost-efficient tools, such as WIPO eADR and videoconferencing facilities. With the WIPO eADR platform, the parties, as well as the arbitrators and experts, may submit all necessary documentation and communication into a special online docket. Users are notified about any system submission and can easily access and retrieve documentation from the online folder at any time. Considering cybersecurity, the WIPO eADR platform is

19 Liu Yuxi, "Demonstrating Wisdom in the Face of the Epidemic," People's Court Daily, February 10, 2020, 刘禹锡：《疫情之下彰显智慧法院担当》，"人民法院报" 2020年2月10 日，第2版: 1–2.

20 "AAA-ICDR Technology Services," American Arbitration Association, accessed August 12, 2021, https://www.adr.org/TechnologyServices/cybersecurity-and-data-protection; cf. "AAA-ICDR Best Practices Guide for Maintaining Cybersecurity and Privacy," American Arbitration Association, accessed August 12, 2021, https://www.adr.org/sites/default/files/document_repository/AAA258_Best_Practices_Cybersecurity_Privacy.

encrypted and thus ensures the appropriate level of confidentiality. If the parties are in different locations, it is possible to handle a case online by videoconference, providing a variety of solutions to ensure a timely and cost-effective arbitration process.[21] It is also worth highlighting the digitalization process of the Stockholm Chamber of Commerce ("SCC"). The SCC platform was introduced to simplify secure communications, from filing a request for arbitration through the rendering of an arbitral award. Since September 2019, new proceedings submitted to the SCC are administered on the SCC platform. It is a secure digital platform which allows parties and the court to communicate and share files, allowing participants in the arbitration proceedings to submit relevant documents, such as procedural orders, electronically. The SCC platform uses a calendar with dates and deadlines to correctly inform the parties of the practical information relating to the arbitral proceedings and also includes an archiving service after rendering an arbitral award.[22]

The International Centre for Settlement of Investment Disputes ("ICSID") decided to take more decisive action to reduce paper-filings of cases. Since 16 March 2020, applicants file cases exclusively electronically (both a request for arbitration and a post-award application, such as a request for a supplementary decision or rectification, as well as an application to the interpretation, revision, or annulment). The e-filing of documents applies as well for requests for conciliation and fact-finding proceedings. In addition, ICSID requires parties to provide all necessary documents, including witness statements and expert reports, in electronic format. The same rules apply to arbitrators, conciliators, and ad hoc committee members. This solution is designed to speed up the entire arbitral proceeding and allow the work of ICSID to be done in a more efficient and environmentally friendly way. In the view of Meg Kinnear, ICSID's Secretary-General, "[g]iven the state of information technology—and the ease with which participants in ICSID cases have adapted to online file sharing in recent years—it made sense to make electronic filing the norm" and "the result will be cost and time-savings to parties".[23] It also limits face-to-face

21 "WIPO Online Case Administration Tools," World Intellectual Property Organization, accessed August 12, 2021, https://www.wipo.int/amc/en/ecaf/introduction.jsp.

22 "SCC Platform—Simplifying Secure Communication from Request to Award," Arbitration Institute of the Stockholm Chamber of Commerce, accessed August 12, 2021, https://sccinstitute.com/case-management/.

23 "ICSID Makes Electronic Filing its Default Procedure," International Centre for Settlement of Investment Disputes, March 13, 2020, https://icsid.worldbank.org/news-and-events/news-releases/icsid-makes-electronic-filing-its-default-procedure.

contact between participants in arbitral proceedings and slows the spread of COVID-19.

Finally, the Court of Arbitration for Sport ("CAS") allows for online filing after the initiation of the arbitration proceedings. "[T]his implies the prior filing of a Request for Arbitration (Art. R38 of the CAS Code) or a Statement of Appeal (Art. R48) by email, facsimile or courier, within the deadline set out in Art. R49 of the CAS Code, as well as the allocation of a case number for the arbitration proceedings in question".[24]

Even with the recent developments and accomplishments regarding the digitalization in international arbitration, it is worth noting some challenges ahead. It is obvious that the in-person hearing differs significantly from the online hearing, and there is a need to ensure the right to be heard and the right to equal treatment. Such a goal can be achieved through "bandwidth, access-points, hardware, size and number of screens, monitoring of witnesses, 360-degree cameras; precautions against cybersecurity threats, confidentiality and data protection agreements".[25] Some arbitration institutions worldwide issued a joint statement that aimed to "assure the arbitration community that the arbitral institutions stand ready to assist users and practitioners alike, therefore supporting the use of international arbitration's potential to provide a stable and foreseeable dispute resolution mechanism in such highly unstable times". According to this joint statement, the arbitration institutions ensured that the ongoing arbitration procedures would continue and there would be no delay in pending cases.[26]

5 A Future of Worldwide Arbitration Landscape

Finding solutions to function during a global pandemic was one of the most pressing issues of 2020. The coronavirus has changed our lives and perception of reality, and some of the recently adopted solutions will likely remain with us well into the future.

Travel restrictions and social distancing requirements stemming from the COVID-19 pandemic began a new approach to global arbitration and

---

24 "E-Filing of submissions," Court of Arbitration for Sport, accessed August 13, 2021, https://www.tas-cas.org/en/e-filing/e-filing-depot-en-ligne.html.

25 Alice Fremuth-Wolf, Ingeborg Edel, and Anna Förstel, "How the COVID-19 pandemic may shape the future of international arbitral proceedings," International Bar Association, accessed August 13, 2021, https://www.ibanet.org/article/A7F75D89-2CFD-4386-96B9-53341D0A55DA.

26 *Id.*

introduced remote hearings worldwide. While some online procedural methods were used in the past, until COVID-19, most arbitral hearings were conducted in a traditional face-to-face manner.

From this perspective, the Chinese experiences and achievements regarding digitalization of courts are particularly significant during the COVID-19 pandemic, and can be widely applied in arbitral proceedings. We should draw solutions from the previous developments in terms of digitalization of the Chinese judiciary and apply them to arbitration. These experiences create new perspectives on digitalization of global arbitration systems that can be used universally, not just in crises such as a global pandemic. The process of digitalization is inseparably inscribed in the future of the arbitration courts, due in large part to the COVID-19 pandemic. Thus, digitalization driven by the realities of a global pandemic will create a new framework for the functionality of the global arbitration system. The time of arbitration in a traditional model seems to be a thing of the past, and a new era is coming, led by Internet courts. This development will take place on many levels, and will concern not only domestic but also the international judiciary and alternative dispute resolution mechanisms, including arbitration.

CHAPTER 12

COVID-19's Inhospitable? Effects on the Arbitral Community

Helena Tavares Erickson

1 Introduction

As courts and other public dispute resolution institutions ground to a halt as a result of the onset of the COVID-19 Pandemic in March 2020, Alternative Dispute Resolution ("ADR") largely marched on, providing services and assisting clients with the continued resolution of their disputes. That is not to say that there were no changes. To the contrary, COVID-19 impacted processes both for administrators and participants in proceedings, as well as, claims and settlements and may even have generated lasting trends.

The Pandemic's impact on processes was the most profound. In mid-March 2021, much of the world closed down. Offices were shuttered and individuals who worked for ADR service providers found new offices, sometimes in bedrooms and dining rooms, often sharing space with young children or dividing space with spouses. For those providers, such as the International Institute for Conflict Prevention & Resolution (CPR), whose employees were already set up with remote access to office systems and materials, the transition to these new "offices" was seamless. Others quickly sought out equipment and outfitted their staff with the requisite tools to continue to perform their administrative functions. The American Arbitration Association (AAA), for example, reported that their "Information Services (IS) team raced to set up [their] staff, hundreds of people, to work from home – though some continued in-person MBO, or "minimal business operations," to support their colleagues."[1] By the summer of 2020 while courts suspended proceedings, arbitral providers were marching forward with remote hearings.[2]

1 "2020 Annual Report & Financial Statements," AAA-ICDR, accessed June 23, 2021, 5, https://www.adr.org/sites/default/files/document_repository/AAA_2020_AnnualReport_and_Financial_Statements.pdf.

2 See, e.g. *In re: Coronavirus/COVID-19 Pandemic*, Case no. 1:20-mc-00163-CM (s.d. n.y. 2020), 9, https://nysd.uscourts.gov/sites/default/files/2020-03/20%20MISC%20154a%20(002)%20-%20In%20Re%20Coronavirus-COVID-19%20Pandemic; cf. AAA-ICDR, *supra* note 1, at 9 ("over 800 arbitration hearing days" in 2020).

For most providers who already had electronic filing and internal electronic files or platforms for storage, changes were as simple as informing claimants that paper filings would no longer be accepted, and likewise electronic payments would fully replace checks.[3] When restrictions permitted, some providers had skeletal on-site staff or made arrangements to visit existing brick and mortar offices to pick up filings and checks from claimants who either did not review website filing instructions or ignored them.[4] In contrast to the courts who could not quickly pivot in this fashion, arbitral providers were ready to serve clients.

2 Impact on Hearings

While there may have been a few weeks of pause as people around the world realized that COVID-19 was not going away soon, for parties and their counsel, arbitral and other ADR processes also marched on. Most law firms and large companies like the providers themselves were set up for remote access. Their biggest challenge was what to do about the no longer possible traditional face to face arbitral hearings or mediation sessions.

For many in the international arena, remote video proceedings were already a part of their toolbox as the unique features of international disputes sometimes dictated receiving testimony via a video platform. For others, ADR providers like CPR, AAA, JAMS and others quickly ensured that their neutrals who were not already trained in the use of such platforms had adequate access to and training in the available technologies and special issues presented by remote video proceedings.[5] Platforms like Zoom, Webex, Bluejeans, Teams, Immediation, and others rose to prominence, while entities like Arbitration Place and FTI Consulting quickly filed a niche for desired assistance for neutrals who needed technical support. Some parties postponed hearings and mediations in the hope that COVID would be mastered, but it was mediators

3 See, e.g., "File a Case," CPR, last modified March 16, 2020, https://www.cpradr.org/dispute-resolution-services/file-a-case; "Urgent COVID-19 message to drs community," ICC, March 17, 2020, https://iccwbo.org/media-wall/news-speeches/covid-19-urgent-communication-to-drs-users-arbitrators-and-other-neutrals/.

4 For information regarding various providers, see, e.g. "COVID-19's Continued Impact on ADR Providers: The Key Institutions Update Us on Plans for the Future," Securities Arbitration Alert, April 28, 2021, https://www.secarbalert.com/blog/covid-19s-continued-impact-on-adr-providers-the-key-institutions-update-us-on-plans-for-the-future/.

5 See, e.g, "Beyond the Basics: Thorny Issues in Conducting Real Arbitration Proceedings in a Virtual Hearing Room," CPR, May 4, 2020, https://www.cpradr.org/events-classes/upcoming/2020-5-4-beyond-the-basics-thorny-issues-virtual-arbitration.

and arbitrators who quickly mastered the art of creating and using on-line "break-out rooms" and "sharing screens," so proceedings went forward.

In addition to training those neutrals who needed support, arbitral providers responded quickly with model protocols and guidelines for remote video proceedings. In April 2020 just as the Pandemic was causing shutdowns around the world, CPR released its Annotated Model Procedural Order for Remote Video Arbitration Proceedings.[6] The Annotated Model Order put into one document the best practices identified by the arbitration community to navigate remote video hearings. Thanks to CPR's diversified membership, the Model Order reflects the perspectives of experienced arbitrators, in-house counsel, outside counsel and CPR staff – not only from the U.S. but also from Canada, Europe and South America. An updated Model Order was released in the summer of 2021. Similarly, the AAA-ICDR released its Virtual Hearing Guide for Arbitrators and Parties[7], JAMS released various guides and tips[8], the London Court of International Arbitration (LCIA)'s updated rules took into account the new reality of virtual hearings[9], and the Chartered Institute of Arbitrators released its Guidance Note on Remote Proceedings.[10] What all of these resources reflected was the unique ability of the arbitration community to come together at a time of crisis and deliver on the promise of alternative dispute resolution to provide a solution.

3 Impact on Claims

At the beginning of the Pandemic, it was largely anticipated that providers would be flooded with claims arising directly out of COVID-19 related issues, but while providers did see case increases, there has been a delay in the manifestation of these claims. The Pandemic has acted as both a catalyst and a

6 See "Annotated Model Procedural Order for Remote Video Arbitration Proceedings," CPR, August 26, 2021, https://www.cpradr.org/resource-center/protocols-guidelines/model-procedure-order-remote-video-arbitration-proceedings.

7 See "AAA-ICDR Virtual Hearing Guide for Arbitrators and Parties," AAA-ICDR, accessed June 28, 2021, https://go.adr.org/rs/294-SFS-516/images/AAA268_AAA%20Virtual%20Hearing%20Guide%20for%20Arbitrators%20and%20Parties.pdf.

8 See "Virtual Mediation, Arbitration, and ADR Services," JAMS, accessed June 28, 2021, https://www.jamsadr.com/online.

9 See "Updates to the LCIA Arbitration Rules and the LCIA Mediation Rules (2020)," LCIA, accessed June 28, 2021, https://lcia.org/lcia-rules-update-2020.aspx.

10 See "Remote Proceedings," CIArb, accessed June 28, 2021, https://www.ciarb.org/resources/remote-proceedings/.

brake.[11] While COVID-19 fostered claims of force majeure, business interruption, claims arising out of construction delays and numerous supply chain issues, the financial impact of the Pandemic and questions regarding the quantum of damages have slowed the pace of arbitral filings arising out of the crisis.[12] That said, some providers saw significant increases in caseloads during the Pandemic. CPR, for example, finished its fiscal year (ending June 30, 2021) with a 32% increase in caseload, and while the AAA-ICDR numbers are not yet peer-reviewed, they saw a doubling of caseload from March 2020 to December 2020.[13]

There is little to no publicly available information about actual arbitration filings, but those monitoring court filings show that the largest rise is in employment related claims arising out of COVID-19. One report notes that while employment related claims in the healthcare industry were more than double those in other sectors, the hospitality industry was also one of the areas heavily impacted.[14] Based on anecdotal evidence, commercial cases did arise in industries where contractual payments were directly related to revenue and revenue sharply declined or was even non-existent due to the forced shuttering of their businesses. Other areas seeing arbitration filings include business dissolutions, partnership disputes and insurance claims.[15]

To the extent that providers have not yet seen an onslaught of COVID related matters, it may be that arbitration cases have not materialized for providers because contracts clearly allocate responsibility for losses through carefully drafted force majeure clauses or contractual parties are settling their claims at higher rates. It has been suggested that prior pandemics such as SARS may have led to the exclusion of global pandemics and/or government orders from force majeure clauses.[16] Some companies have definitely indicated a preference for doing so. Providers have stimulated settlement by instituting COVID

11 Sarah Reynolds et al., "International Experts Discuss the Impact on the Global Economy," *Mealey's International Arbitration Report* 35, no. 11 (November 2020).

12 *Id.* at 3.

13 Jeffrey Zaino (Vice President, AAA), email exchange, June 30, 2021.

14 See Natalie M. Stevens et al., "COVID-19–Related Employment Litigation: How It Started ... How It's Going," Ogletree Deakins, February 9, 2021, https://ogletree.com/insights/covid-19-related-employment-litigation-how-it-started-how-its-going; see also Stephanie L. Adler-Paindiris and Nadine C. Abrahams, "Employment Law Developments to Monitor in 2021: COVID-19-Related Employment Litigation and Trends," JacksonLewis, January 21, 2021, https://www.litigatorsatwork.com/2021/01/employment-law-developments-to-monitor-in-2021-covid-19-related-employment-litigation-and-trends/.

15 Erin Gleason Alvarez and Peter L. Halprin (CPR Neutrals), telephone interviews, June 30, 2021. See also Reynolds, *supra* note 11, at 2.

16 Reynolds, *supra* note 11, at 1.

related mediation programs such as CPR's Integrated Resolution Program, an innovative program providing for a fixed fee mediation including a damage report and legal bench memo for the mediator.[17] The Program is designed to help small and medium-sized businesses resolve their disputes through mediation to move their business forward. Created in collaboration with Legal Innovators and FTI Consulting, the program applies to any business in the midst of a dispute between two parties concerning less than $5 million. The AAA similarly provided for fixed fee mediation for COVID related disputes.[18] Some insurance industry counsel are promoting mediation as a way to mitigate risk from the uncertainty of court rulings.[19] Court systems around the world are also incentivizing mediation by returning a portion or even all of the parties' filing fees if parties successfully mediate cases.[20] Given a global average time of 650 days to enforce a commercial contract, it is expected that resort to ADR will continue to rise as the backlogs from the Pandemic increase.[21]

In time it is expected that arbitration filings will parallel court filings. One area of expected increases is the energy sector where the industry has suffered not only from the Pandemic but also from the financial effects of low oil prices. London based providers are already seeing arbitral filings in this sector.[22] In this sector, as well as others, there will be interplay between international insolvencies and arbitral proceedings and even whether to file an arbitration may well be impacted by the possible inability to enforce an eventual arbitral award.[23] That said, those in the investment sector are warning of potential claims against governments whose decrees have impacted investment returns, signaling that there will soon be International Centre for Settlement of Investment Disputes (ICSID) arbitration claims arising out of the Pandemic.[24]

17 "Integrated Resolution Program," CPR, accessed 22 April 2022, https://www.cpradr.org/neutrals/Integrated-Resolution-Program.

18 See AAA-ICDR, *supra* note 1, at 15.

19 Peter A. Halprin, "Lessons from the Pandemic Insurance Coverage Wars Part III: Mediation as a Tool for Risk Management," SandRun Risk Blog, April 29, 2021, https://www.sandrunrisk.com/blog/lessons-from-the-pandemic-insurance-coverage-wars-part-iii-mediation-as-a-tool-for-risk-management.

20 Maksym Iavorskyi and Joseph Lemoine, "Achieving commercial justice in the new COVID-19 world," WorldBank Blogs, May 26, 2020, https://blogs.worldbank.org/developmenttalk/achieving-commercial-justice-new-covid-19-world.

21 *Id.*

22 Reynolds, *supra* note 11, at 2.

23 *Id.* at 3.

24 See, e.g., Nicolas J. Diamond and Kabir A.N. Duggal, "2020 in Review: The Pandemic, Investment Treaty Arbitration and Human Rights," Kluwer Arbitration Blog, January 23, 2021, http://arbitrationblog.kluwerarbitration.com/2021/01/23/2020-in-review-the-pandemic-investment-treaty-arbitration-and-human-rights/.

These claims will join those involving partnerships, joint-ventures, supply chains, asset purchase agreements, business interruption and event cancellation, which are already making their way through the arbitral process.[25]

4 Lasting Impacts

While for many arbitration providers the COVID-19 crisis changed the form or location of dispute resolution, it did not change the underlying substance. Dedicated neutrals continue to engage mediation parties in the centuries old form of assisted negotiation or to carefully consider evidence and render arbitral decisions or early neutral evaluations. Nevertheless, the Pandemic will have a lasting impact on the field of ADR. Many more neutrals have learned new technical skills. In some areas, neutrals with good technical skills have been able to parlay their knowledge into more work. In others, the willingness to hold in-person hearings during the Pandemic has led to increased business for others. Both, parties and neutrals, have learned efficiencies that can be gained from judicious use of on-line platforms. In an indication of the far-reaching lasting implications of the Pandemic, a private listserv has indicated that as of June 30, 2021, the United States District Court for the Northern District of California announced that until further notice the default presumption for mediations would be that they would be held via remote video conferencing. In an indication of the next likely area for debate, the Court frowned upon so- called hybrid proceedings where all parties were not either remote or present in person.

Arbitration clients have found it easier to monitor remote proceedings without having to contemplate impacts on travel budgets and notwithstanding the occasional cat or child who appears when they are not supposed to, participants have for the most part adapted to the new technologies. They, too, are likely to evaluate a default of remote proceedings at least for non-evidentiary hearings. These new forms of proceeding will no longer be the exception but will be among the options to be considered, and ADR is forever changed.

25 See *supra* notes 13 and 15.

CHAPTER 13

The Impact of COVID-19 on Arbitration

Luis M. Martinez and Michael A. Marra

1 Introduction[1]

The American Arbitration Association (AAA) was first impacted by the COVID-19 pandemic in March 2020. With lockdown orders in place throughout the United States and abroad, the AAA and its international division, the International Centre for Dispute Resolution (ICDR) were faced with a number of challenges right at the outset, including switching its work force to operate remotely to comply with the global lockdowns. The AAA-ICDR closed its 28 offices and hearing rooms and thousands of hearings were postponed and rescheduled. While expanding its telework capabilities, the top priority was ensuring that its commitment to cybersecurity, confidentiality, and data privacy were maintained.

Within days, the AAA-ICDR enabled almost its entire staff to effectively administer cases securely from their homes.

The AAA-ICDR was aided in this transition by the fact that its administrative arbitration and mediation services had been transitioned to a paperless system for some time, which was helpful during the COVID lockdowns. Moreover, the AAA-ICDR's proprietary electronic case management platforms, which were well suited for remote administration, provided another advantage. For example, the case managers use an internal administrative platform where all of the case files are available electronically and all of the administrative steps are tracked with deadlines and the requirements established by the rules for that applicable case. This platform reflects the AAA-ICDR's administrative procedures, policies, and all scheduled tasks reminding the assigned case manager of any needed next steps and serves as a repository for all of the key documents related to the specific case at hand.

In real time, users also have access to all of their AAA-ICDR case information and documents through the AAA-ICDR's WebFile® service. In addition to filing claims, parties to AAA-ICDR cases can manage all aspects of their cases

1 Parts of this chapter are based on John E. Bulman and Michael A. Marra, "Virtual Arbitration – A Passing Fancy or a Temporary Stopgap?," ABA Forum on Construction Law, *Under Construction* 22, no. 1 (Summer 2020).

 | DOI:10.1163/9789004514836_015

securely, from the filing of additional claims or counterclaims on existing cases to case-related financial functions including uploading, downloading, and viewing all case documents and creating case-specific tasks. Essentially the parties may access their cases completely remotely which had been increasingly used internationally and became universally used once the lockdowns took effect in the United States.

The third platform is the AAA-ICDR's Panelist eCenter®. This platform used by the arbitrators and mediators is directly linked to the AAA-ICDR case management system and WebFile with most of the data populated by the case managers. The arbitrators and mediators can view their cases online, access all related documents, and execute their appointment documents. The arbitrators and mediators may also complete all required training through this secure site. The result of these linked electronic platforms allowed the AAA-ICDR to be fully operational, without interruption, during COVID-19 as it quickly expanded its capabilities to work remotely.

Pragmatically speaking, logistical necessities imposed by COVID-19 have generated a lot of attention on how to conduct arbitration hearings. The advent of COVID-19 has forced parties and arbitrators to reconcile the travel and face-to-face restrictions in play with the "just, speedy and fair" requirements under nearly every set of arbitration rules. COVID-19 may well work a seed change in how arbitrations are handled.

Witness statements, audio or video conferencing of witnesses, use of arbitrator written questions, and other techniques have been used for years, particularly in international cases. With appropriate safeguards and procedures, it is not a substantial leap to conduct the entire arbitration process virtually. The question is, "Should arbitrators and parties embrace or fight virtual arbitration?" The AAA-ICDR noted during the pandemic that there was an early reluctance to holding hearings virtually. Parties were initially opting to postpone the hearings hoping to hold them in person at a later date. As the lockdowns continued much longer than expected, the parties started to accept the idea of proceeding with hearings virtually. The AAA-ICDR focused on the capabilities needed along with the resources that the parties and the arbitrators would use to assist them with virtual hearings.

The AAA-ICDR developed a page on its website that provides information on its virtual hearings services. Included are protocols for virtual hearings and model orders along with related information (https://go.adr.org/covid-19-virtual-hearings.html). Internally, staff tested various platforms for virtual hearings and participated in extensive training. There was a particular focus on the Zoom platform due largely to the preference of the parties. The "Zoom champions", as they were designated, drafted best practices and training guides for AAA-ICDR staff, arbitrators, counsel, and parties. They also suggested predetermined Zoom settings to promote privacy, security and ease of use for a virtual hearing.

Additional Resources on the site include:

- Virtual Hearing Managed Services
- Virtual Hearing Guide for Arbitrators and Parties
- Virtual Hearing Guide for Arbitrators and Parties Utilizing Zoom
- Order and Procedures for a Virtual Hearing via Videoconference

The AAA-ICDR Model Order provides a range of issues that the arbitrator and the parties should consider and discuss to set the ground rules for using a virtual hearing and incorporates sample language that can be used to memorialize the outcome of those discussions in a procedural order. It covers the logistics, technology, and the conduct for the virtual hearing.

Additional points of discussion within the Model Order include whether to proceed with the virtual hearing or not or to proceed virtually over the objection of a party. The AAA-ICDR's international arbitration rules do allow the arbitrators to proceed noting that the arbitrators have a duty to conduct the proceedings with a view to expedite the resolution of the dispute provided that the parties are treated with equality. The arbitrators may consider how technology could be used to increase the efficiency and economy of the proceedings (see Article 22 of these rules).

The Model Order highlights other aspects to consider, including the handling of the Zoom hearing invitations. The Model Order suggests that invitations are password protected and only sent to the authorized attendees. In addition, it is suggested that the parties confirm the list of attendees in advance in writing and complete advance testing of the virtual hearing to assess the video and audio quality as well as the internet links and required settings. The parties are reminded that a back-up conference call line should also be in place if the computer audio does not work properly and that the arbitrators will remind the attendees at the start of each virtual hearing that they should identify all the people in the room including if they have brought in any technicians. It also suggests that the parties also should use a single camera to show most if not all of the room and it notes that the arbitrators may ask at any time that participants take the camera and pan around to make sure that they are the only ones in the room as disclosed and to avoid possible coaching.

The Model Order also includes a section on scheduling. With international cases, arbitrators should consider the impact that time zones may have on the hearing and balance the hearing schedule accordingly so that each side has an opportunity to avail themselves of a favorable schedule at different points of the proceeding. It is also clear that virtual hearings require significant attention being paid to the participants on the screen and that has proven to be exhausting after several hours. The arbitrators have been taking note and scheduling shorter hearing days with sufficient breaks to address this fatigue factor on the parties and themselves.

2 The Arbitrator's Perspective

The applicable rules and laws make it clear that the arbitrator has the authority to order virtual hearings. AAA Construction Rule R-33(c), for example, provides that the arbitrator may allow "presentation of evidence by alternative means including video conferencing, internet communication, telephonic conferences and means other than an in-person presentation."

Having the authority and discretion to do so is one thing, ordering a shift to a virtual hearing is another. According to John Bulman, Partner at Pierce Atwood, LLC,[2] "It requires careful consideration of a number of factors. Can the supporting technology be marshalled effectively to provide a smooth hearing process? Will both parties have a full opportunity to present their cases? Will there be any impediments to conducting appropriate cross-examination? Can the confidentiality of the proceeding be maintained?" Fundamentally, due process requires that each question be fully assessed and answered "yes."

The decision is relatively easy if the parties waive oral hearings and jointly pursue a virtual hearing. When one party objects to a virtual process, the arbitrator must answer the above questions positively and evaluate additional concerns. For example, the arbitral process requires that resolution of the dispute be fair, private, prompt and economical. *See AAA Construction Rules Introduction.*

If hearings cannot be held for an inordinate (or unpredictable) period of time absent a virtual platform, this weighs in favor of opting for a virtual process. If both parties object to a virtual process, this brings into play the reality that arbitration is fundamentally the parties' agreed upon process, which may indeed be considered the process that is due. If the parties agree that they do not want to utilize the alternative virtual process, there would have to be extraordinary circumstances present for an arbitrator to overrule the parties' agreement.

---

2 John Bulman is a Partner at Pierce Atwood, LLC in Providence, RI practicing construction law and an arbitrator and mediator on the American Arbitration Association and International Centre for Dispute Resolution.

3 Dispute Resolution Rosters

In discussions with a number of arbitrators and advocates, it seems that assessing witness' credibility virtually is one of their primary concerns. Many have noted that it may be difficult to discern body language and facial expressions on a computer screen (although several arbitrators have pointed out that the virtual platform allows for uninterrupted focus on the witness, more so than in a hearing room). Credibility assessment may be a valid concern; the counter is the COVID-19 generated question as to what an in person hearing will look like in the foreseeable future as we deal with new variants. Will social distancing requirements being re-implemented include a much larger room to space participants? Will everyone be required to wear facemasks to in person hearings?

Another concern in the virtual setting is controlling the witness to make sure there is no improper communication while under examination. In some unusual instances, high tech solutions with multiple cameras scanning the room may be required but it may also be as simple as putting the witness on notice that the arbitrators may stop the hearing at any time and ask the witness to move the camera to scan around the room. Of course, it is up to the arbitrators and counsel to determine the best option for the particular case. That said, it might be that viewing someone on a screen is the better option to assess credibility and arbitrate disputes in a timely manner.

In conclusion, the AAA-ICDR has clearly seen how COVID-19 has affected the arbitration and mediation process. It remains to be seen what will be the final role for virtual hearings but all indications and the early feedback from our users is that the process is here to stay. The significant savings of time and costs where teams of attorneys, the parties and the arbitrators no longer have to travel seems to greatly outweigh the concern that the advocates may have in not being able to present their case and gauge their effectiveness by not being in the same room. Certainly, with the advances in technology the virtual hearing option continues gain in popularity. During the pandemic, the AAA-ICDR updated the cameras and the ceiling microphones for a number of its hearing facilities installing state of the art equipment in its New York and Miami offices with others to follow. The ability to preset the cameras that track the speakers and transition from different views to multiple views as smoothly as a professionally edited film increasingly provides the viewer with a greater sensation of being in the room with everyone gathered. Clearly, this advanced technology and the fact that the advocates are also increasingly becoming more proficient with their skills on these virtual platforms is an indication that virtual hearings are here to stay in one form or another. Whether we shall see hybrid applications, perhaps procedural hearings, witness testimony only, or the entire case,

COVID-19 has required an acceleration of innovation and technology for the use of virtual hearings as part of the alternative dispute resolution process.

According to John Bulman, "as counsel, arbitrators and parties become more facile in the virtual arena and the technical support becomes more standard, reliable and fluid, the economic savings of using a virtual platform may be a deciding factor."

CHAPTER 14

Impact of COVID-19 on Arbitration Centers

Elizabeth Roberts

1 Introduction[1]

This paper addresses recent innovations, trends and practical challenges to Arbitration Centers arising from COVID-19. Since March 2020 the landscape for legal services changed significantly. In particular, the emerging geographical diversification of the provision of legal services allows Arbitration Centers an unprecedented reach to customers and markets, a reach not reasonably practicable before COVID-19. Arbitration Centers benefited from the increased use of technology, and in creative and innovative ways, contribute towards access to justice. The increasing use of technology, however, has its challenges. For example, initially there were numerous instances of resistance to remote hearings by parties and counsel. This paper explores the type of objections and the manner in which courts, arbitration tribunals and Arbitration Centers have addressed them. This paper also addresses practical challenges and concerns arising from issues of privacy and cybersecurity in arbitration and offers practical and cost-effective ways to address and tackle these challenges.

2 Trends and Innovation

2.1 *Geographical Diversification of Provision of Legal Services*

On March 11, 2020, the World Health Organization ("WHO") classified COVID-19 as a pandemic.[2] The resulting health and safety measures included restrictions on movement, government issued stay at home orders, travel restrictions

1 A remote hearing is defined as one in which all participants (decision-maker, parties, legal representatives, witnesses, etc.) are not physically at the same location and usually involves attendance by video conference or teleconference. Other writings on related subjects distinguish between "remote", "virtual" and "online" to refer to hearings conducted by video or teleconference. The term remote is used for the purposes of this paper.

2 "WHO Director-General's opening remarks at the media briefing on COVID-19 – 11 March 2020," who, March 11, 2020, https://www.who.int/director-general/speeches/detail/who-director-general-s-opening-remarks-at-the-media-briefing-on-covid-19---11-march-2020.

DOI:10.1163/9789004514836_016

and physical distancing. Those measures prevented many businesses, including Arbitration Centers, from operating in-person. In this period of extreme uncertainty, Arbitration Centers were forced to re-think how to deliver products and services. Much like businesses with supply chains and production lines concentrated in one geographic region the delivery of legal services has traditionally been limited by location. Up until March 2020, the predominant practice required that parties, counsel, witnesses, experts, arbitration tribunals, court reporters and interpreters would physically attend at a hearing centre. The time of crisis brought on by COVID-19 facilitated the development of innovative and creative solutions to the sudden problem that the professional environment of individuals in the legal industry[3] was, for the most part, limited to their homes. The use of technology allowed Arbitration Centers to shift from in-person services to providing hearing and related services entirely online.

Arbitration Centers, such as Arbitration Place, adapted their onsite services to include remote formats and expanded their offerings to facilitate remote proceedings taking place anywhere in the world through the use of secure meeting platforms, case managers, document management services including electronic presentation of evidence, deployment of equipment worldwide, court reporters, translation services, tailored training and technological support services. Arbitral institutions such as the Hong Kong International Arbitration Centre ("HKIAC"), the American Arbitration Association International Centre for Dispute Resolution ("AAA-ICDR"), the International Chamber of Commerce ("ICC") and the Arbitration Institute of the Stockholm Chamber of Commerce ("SCC") have similarly adapted to keep the dispute resolution process moving forward and currently offer remote hearing services to parties.[4]

3 For the purposes of this paper, the legal services industry is defined as the practice and business of delivering professional services. This includes work done by licensed practitioners for clients as well as work carried out by organizations that provide services to individuals and corporations within the legal and alternative dispute resolution fields. This paper will focus on the impact to organizations in the latter part of this definition.

4 "Virtual Hearings," Hong Kong International Arbitration Center, accessed April 22, 2022, https://www.hkiac.org/our-services/facilities/virtual-hearings [hereinafter HKIAC]; "What We Do: Virtual Hearing Managed Services," American Arbitration Association, accessed April 22, 2022, https://www.adr.org/virtual-hearing-managed-services [hereinafter AAA]; "Hearing Centre," International Chamber of Commerce, accessed April 22, 2022, https://iccwbo.org/dispute-resolution-services/hearing-centre/ [hereinafter ICC]; "Stockholm International Hearing Centre Launches Platform for Virtual Hearings," Arbitration Institute of the Stockholm Chamber of Commerce, April 27, 2020, https://sccinstitute.com/about-the-scc/news/2020/stockholm-international-hearing-centre-launches-platform-for-virtual-hearings/ [hereinafter SCC].

In addition to the innovative delivery of services to ensure business continuity, the geographic diversification of the provision of legal services through technology allows small and medium sized businesses an unprecedented reach to customers and markets that previously did not exist. The shift to remote dispute resolution meant that Arbitration Centers were no longer limited by geographical barriers and reached a diverse range of clients. A few days after the WHO's announcement in March, Arbitration Place launched a suite of remote hearing solutions, becoming the first Arbitration Center in North America and one of the first worldwide to offer tailored services in response to limitations arising from COVID-19. Arbitration Place's suite offering generated an immediate response from the arbitration community. Seemingly overnight, Arbitration Place's client base[5] expanded from predominantly North American to international, with clients in Europe, the Middle East, Asia, South America and Australia, seeking to avoid delays and ensure the dispute resolution process continued to move forward. Prior to COVID-19, clients in Europe in Australia approached Arbitration Place principally for in-person matters. Changes to the landscape for legal services provided Arbitration Place the opportunity to work with clients all around the globe.

As time progressed and remote hearings merged into a more regularized part of the arbitration environment, Arbitration Centers continue to refine and diversify their offerings. In some parts of the world, activities have resumed (with limitations) and restrictions have eased, although, depending on the jurisdiction, restrictions have been reintroduced. These varying requirements have resulted in an increased demand for hybrid hearings that combines both in-person and online elements. One example of Arbitration Place's response to this demand involved its participation in forming the International Arbitration Centre Alliance ("IACA"), along with the International Dispute Resolution Centre and Maxwell Chambers. IACA is a global collaboration of physical, technical and professional resources aimed at eliminating challenges associated with the planning and conducting of international hearings such as distance and time zones. IACA has hearing centers in Toronto, Ottawa, Singapore and London and provides on-site and remote integrated services that enable parties to move forward with the business of dispute resolution.[6] The shifting landscape of dispute resolution in the time of COVID-19 means that Arbitration Centers will continue to adapt and respond to the needs of the arbitration community through the delivery of innovative and customized services.

5 Clients of Arbitration Place include stakeholders involved in dispute resolution such as parties, counsel, institutions, tribunals and the courts.

6 "Global Hybrid Hearings," International Arbitration Centre Alliance, accessed April 22, 2022, https://www.iacaglobal.com [hereinafter IACA].

2.2 *Technology and Access to Justice*

Prior to March 2020, technology in arbitration proceedings was used on a regular basis for certain steps such as procedural conferences, electronic document storage and some witness testimony. The usual practice for more complex procedural hearings or merits hearings, however, was for the parties, counsel and tribunal members to be physically present at the same location. COVID-19 has shifted hearings online through the use of videoconferencing platforms including Zoom, Cisco WebEx, Adobe Connect, Microsoft Teams and Skype. The shift to remote hearings propelled arbitration tribunals, counsel, parties and witnesses, all with varying degrees of comfort with technology, into an entirely digital landscape. This shift prompted a number of practical concerns relating to the potential fairness of remote hearings. The following section explores some of these challenges as well as discusses creative and innovative solutions developed by Arbitration Centers in response to these issues.

In order to proceed remotely, all participants must have access to a computer with sufficient hardware and software capabilities, a secure internet connection and a location free from interruptions.[7] From time to time, one or more participants, be it a witness, arbitrator or counsel does not have access to a computer or the computer is not sufficiently equipped for use in a remote hearing. As a result, Arbitration Centers are faced with developing solutions to the issue of uneven access to technology. Arbitration Place approached this issue through the provision of Virtual Remote Kits containing equipment with standard hardware and software requirements, customized to fit the needs of each client. The Virtual Remote Kits can be shipped worldwide and have been deployed to North America, South America, Europe and the Middle East. The Virtual Remote Kits ensure that all necessary individuals can participate in the process and that each party is afforded the opportunity to meaningfully present its case.

A second challenge is the coordination of hearing logistics including managing a large number of participants, the organization and display of a potentially voluminous documentary record and the ability to manage and resolve technical issues if and when they arise.[8] Arbitration Centers offer trained personnel to neutrally manage the technology platform and provide support to hearing participants, including troubleshooting technical issues, storing and organizing hearing documents using an online document repository and

7 *Capic v. Ford Motor Company of Australia Limited (Adjournment)* [2020] FCA 486 (Austl.).

8 Alex Lo, "Virtual Hearings and Alternative Arbitral Procedures in the COVID-19 Era: Efficiency, Due Process, and Other Considerations," *Contemporary Asia Arbitration Journal* 13 (2020): 89–93 (practical, legal and due process challenges to virtual or online hearings).

managing evidence presentation using trial presentation software. A number of Arbitration Centers offer trained service personnel including, but not limited to, Arbitration Place (Virtual Case Managers), HKIAC (Hearing Managers)[9], and AAA-ICDR (Virtual Hearing Specialists)[10], with each entity offering a customizable service tailored to the needs of the parties.

A further challenge is that not all participants have the same level of comfort with remote technology. In *Miller v. FSD Pharma, Inc.*,[11] a Canadian court case heard on April 14, 2020, at a time when Ontario was in a province-wide shutdown,[12] one party objected to a remote hearing on the basis that they would not be able to have their entire team together in one room in order to provide the support required for the hearing.[13] Two weeks later the objection to proceeding remotely on the basis that counsel would not be in the same location was raised again in *Arconti v. Smith*,[14] a separate and unrelated case. In *Arconti*, Justice Myers wrote that the only possible "unfairness" inherent in the format of a video hearing "is a lack of comfort by one counsel that he or she will be at their best in presenting evidence and making arguments using technology". Justice Myers went on to say that the need of the courts to operate during COVID-19 highlighted the availability of alternative processes, the imperative of technological competency and that "efforts can and should be made to help people who remain uncomfortable to obtain any necessary training and education".[15] The same is true in arbitration. In order to ensure that natural justice is achieved, Arbitration Centers developed and offer training to assist counsel, witnesses and members of the tribunal prepare for remote hearings and reduce the risk of technological problems through adequate preparation of the parties.[16] The training is tailored depending on the needs of the parties and is designed to ensure participants achieve familiarization and competency with the technology. Further, Arbitration Place developed and implemented procedural protocols as a response to the concern that a witness may have access to aids off screen. For example, one component is a requirement that a witness

9 HKIAC, *supra* note 4.

10 AAA, *supra* note 4.

11 *Miller v. FSD Pharma, Inc.*, 2020 ONSC 2253 (Can.).

12 Geoffrey B. Morawetz "Notice to the Profession, the Public and the Media Regarding Civil and Family Proceedings," Superior Court of Justice, March 15, 2020, https://www.ontariocourts.ca/scj/notices-and-orders-covid-19/notices-no-longer-in-effect/covid-19-suspension-fam.

13 *Miller, supra* note 11, at para. 5.

14 *Arconti v. Smith*, 2020 ONSC 2782 (Can.), paras. 32–34.

15 *See id.*

16 Arbitration Place has also delivered this training to judges and court staff in Ontario.

take a 360 degree video of the room from which they are testifying at the start of their evidence and after any breaks.

3 Practical Challenges

3.1 *Initial Objections to Remote Hearings*

The sudden shift to remote hearings as a result of COVID-19 occurred both in the practice of arbitration and the courts. A 2020 survey conducted on remote hearings in arbitration found there was a considerable amount of resistance by counsel at the outset, rather than tribunals, to schedule fully remote hearings. The study found that the average ratio of objections to fully remote hearings rose from 21% (meaning that for every 10 cases the survey respondents encountered 2.1 cases where an objection occurred) before March 15, 2020, to 46% (4.1 out of every 10 cases) after March 15, 2020.[17] In contrast, tribunals became more likely to dismiss objections to remote hearings made by one side. The survey indicated that objections were dismissed in 50% of cases heard after March 15, 2020, which is a 34% increase from cases heard prior to March 15, 2020, where objections were dismissed in 17% of the cases.[18] Notably, all of the respondents to the survey reported that no challenges were brought related to the enforcement of an arbitral award on the basis that the hearing had been held fully remotely.[19]

The confidential process of arbitration makes it so there is very little public information available where objections to remote hearings have been raised and reasons have been issued. It is instructive to look to the types of objections raised by parties in the courts and how those objections have been addressed before turning to a select number of arbitration decisions. In April 2020, the Federal Court of Australia addressed a wide variety of objections during an application for an adjournment of a trial brought by the respondent in *Capic v. Ford Motor Company of Australia Limited.*[20] The respondent argued the remote trial proposed in the circumstances of COVID-19 would adversely impact the conduct, length and expense of the trial, and categorized

---

17 Gary Born, Anneliese Day, and Hafez Virjee, "Remote Hearings (2020 Survey): A Spectrum of Preferences," *Journal of International Arbitration* 38, no. 3 (2021): 296 (survey on objections to remote hearings at the start of the pandemic in 2020).

18 *Id.*

19 *Id.* at 297.

20 *Capic, supra* note 7.

its concerns as follows: technological limitations; physical separation of legal teams; briefing and preparation of expert witnesses; lay witnesses, particularly related to cross-examination; document management; and trial length and expenses. Justice Perram considered each of the issues raised by the respondent and rejected the application, providing detailed reasons for his decision.

The court acknowledged the reality of technological limitations, such as access to hardware and software, the potential for problems with internet connections and technological glitches such as a participant dropping off or a lagging video. Justice Perram compared these potential disruptions to breaks that occur for a variety of reasons in the course of in-person hearings that necessitate the postponement of a witness' evidence or taking a witness out of order. Although a technological issue is a different type of interruption, the manner in which it is addressed, for example by pausing the hearing or shuffling the ordering of witnesses, is no different than managing breaks in an in-person hearing. Justice Perram noted that difficulties related to communication, for example counsel teams not being together in one place can be overcome through the use of instant messaging platforms such as WhatsApp[21] and the challenge of preparing and briefing witnesses and experts can be managed through videoconference technology.[22]

The court acknowledged there is a real concern for abuse of technology in the form of fraudulent witness coaching or prompting. In cases where evidence of abuse exists and is proven, it should be dealt with strongly, however, the amorphous risk of abuse is not a sufficient reason for a court to deny that a trial proceeds remotely. The respondent in *Capic* also objected to cross-examining witnesses in a remote environment, claiming that this approach is unsuitable. In addressing this issue, Justice Perram acknowledged previous decisions in Australia where the court opined on the unsuitability of cross-examination by videolink. His Honour noted the present case is distinguishable for two key reasons, the first being that previous decisions were rendered before March 2020 in a time when there were no limitations on travel and movement, and the second being that the objections were raised without the benefit of improved videoconferencing platforms such as Zoom, WebEx and Microsoft Teams, which are readily available and frequently used in dispute resolution. Next, Justice Perram addressed the respondent's submission that the large number of documents will make the hearing and document management more difficult. The court noted this issue is resolved through the use of a third-party operator and

21 WhatsApp is one example of an instant messaging platform, however, there are other suitable platforms available including Microsoft Teams, Slack and Signal, among others.

22 *Capic, supra* note 7.

related document management procedures. Finally, the court rejected the general assertion by the respondent that conducting a trial remotely will prolong the hearing and increase costs. Justice Perram noted that while this may be the case in some circumstances, there have been cases where the nature of remote proceedings has reduced overall cost and expense.[23]

As a concluding observation, Justice Perram stated that while the circumstances of a remote six-week trial for a lengthy and complex class action, with the contemplated attendance of 50 witnesses, was not ideal, it is not unjust or unfair. The climate of COVID-19 is itself not ordinary and in order to facilitate the just resolution of disputes, it is necessary to carry on using alternative processes.[24]

3.1.1 Canadian Court Cases

In March 2020, Canadian courts suspended in-person operations. Justice Morawetz, the Chief Justice of the Ontario Superior Court of Justice said at the time "right now there is no alternative but to do a virtual hearing".[25] As a result, some matters proceeded remotely without issue, while in others, objections were raised. This paper examines objections raised to remote proceedings in eight Canadian court cases. In two of the eight cases, the court initially allowed the moving party's request for an adjournment on the basis of concerns to proceeding remotely raised by that party. In *Stuart v. Doe*,[26] one party objected to holding oral discoveries remotely citing concerns about testing the credibility of witnesses, the potential for coaching of witnesses by people or aides off-screen and the unsuitability of counsel's at-home computer. The other party did not object to this position. Accordingly, the court ordered in April 2020 that oral discoveries were not required to be held "until the COVID-19 pandemic was over".[27] In *Miller v. FSD Pharma*, heard on April 14, 2020, counsel objected to the hearing of a pre-certification motion in a proposed class action on the basis that proceeding remotely would not be practical or procedurally fair in circumstances where such a voluminous documentary record existed, the matter related to complex legal issues and it was not possible for the multi-lawyer team to be together at the same location. The defendants' counsel objected and argued that the hearing should proceed remotely. The court agreed with

23 See *id.*

24 See *id.*

25 Amanda Jerome, "'Paper-based system is not going to exist anymore,' Chief Justice Morawetz says of post-COVID-19 court," The Lawyers Daily, April 15, 2020, https://www.thelawyersdaily.ca/articles/18576.

26 *Stuart v. Doe*, 2021 YKSC 11 (Can. Yuk. Sup. Ct.).

27 *Id.* at para. 13.

the plaintiff and held that it was not appropriate to compel a party to proceed under conditions where they perceive they may not be able to present the case as effectively as they would in person.[28]

However, both *Stuart* and *FSD Pharma* were later brought back to court and in both cases, the court reversed its initial decision and ordered the matter proceed remotely over the objections of one of the parties. In *Stuart*, Justice Duncan observed that practices and protections had developed since the beginning of COVID-19 to enhance the use of technology and reduce possible negative consequences. Justice Duncan noted that benefits of preventing further delay outweighed the risks of any shortcomings of the use of technology.[29] In *FSD Pharma*, Justice Morgan wrote that by the end of May 2020, counsel and courts developed the ability to conduct remote hearings in a way that minimizes problems originally foreseen with them. Justice Morgan went on to say that although there are logistical and practical challenges to remote hearings "there is nothing about remote procedure, whether large, complex, and potentially final, or small, straightforward, and interim that is inherently unfair to either side".[30]

In the other six cases examined, the court refused requests for an adjournment at first instance and ordered the matter proceed remotely.[31] Since March 2020, various judicial regions issued practice directions governing how proceedings are conducted during COVID-19. The Superior Court of Justice Practice Direction for the Toronto Region effective April 6, 2020, indicates that remote hearings are a key aspect of the court's response to maintaining the institutions essential for the continuation of the Rule of Law. Courts have recognized the processes for the continuation of court operations established under such practice directions to be a matter of scheduling that is not subject to the consent of the parties.[32]

The outcome of these cases indicate that Canadian courts characterize objections raised by parties to remote hearings as logistical and practical challenges that can be overcome through the use and availability of technological processes, rather than relating to matters of procedural fairness and prejudice.

---

28 *Miller, supra* note 11, at para. 6.

29 *Stuart, supra* note 26, at para 22.

30 *Miller v. FSD Pharma, Inc.*, 2020 ONSC 3291 (Can.), para. 10.

31 *Hubault Virgili v. Virgili*, 2021 NBCA 7 (Can.); *Guest Tek Interactive Entertainment Ltd. v. Nomadix Inc.*, 2020 FC 860 (Can. Fed. Ct.); *Aptotex Inc. v. Eli Lilly Canada Inc.*, 2020 ONSC 7460 (Can.); *Daly v. City of Mississauga*, 2020 ONSC 5097 (Can.); *Arconti v. Smith*, 2020 ONSC 2782 (Can.); *Association of Professional Engineers v. Rew*, 2020 ONSC 2589 (Can.).

32 *Association of Professional Engineers, supra* note 31, at paras. 7 and 8.

Although there will be instances where a party may be prejudiced or where the procedural fairness of a matter will be impacted, this is not the default assumption. As counsel, parties and decision makers learn new ways to do things, an element of discomfort is introduced, however, courts in Canada interpret this to be a matter of unfamiliarity rather than the result of an inferior process.

3.1.2 Objections in International Cases

Unlike the Canadian courts, a decision of the Swiss Federal Tribunal dated July 6, 2020, upheld the appeal of a party that objected to a decision of the lower court ordering a remote hearing. The implication of that decision may be narrow in application as it was made in the context of state court litigation and the court held that there was no legal basis in the Swiss Civil Procedure Code to allow for the main hearing to proceed remotely against the will of one of the parties.[33]

Shortly after the Swiss Federal Tribunal's decision, the Austrian Supreme Court dismissed the appeal of a party challenging the decision of an arbitral tribunal to hold a merits hearing remotely.[34] On July 23, 2020, the court held that the arbitration tribunal's decision to hold a remote hearing over the objection of one party does not violate the party's right to be heard and does not amount to a breach of the principle to treat both parties fairly. The court held that in circumstances of COVID-19, Article 6 of the European Convention on Human Rights supports its decision to order remote hearings by providing a means for a party to be heard. The court noted that in the current climate, the indefinite postponement of proceedings until in-person matters are permitted would lead to an adjournment of indefinite length which is not acceptable in the circumstances. The court went on to say that general allegations of unfairness are not sufficient and a party must put forward significantly persuasive factual considerations in order to succeed.[35] The United States District Court for the Northern District of Illinois Eastern Division reached a similar conclusion when it upheld an arbitration tribunal's decision to order an evidentiary hearing proceed remotely over the objection of the other party. In that case the court found that a remote hearing does not prevent a party's meaningful opportunity to be heard.[36]

33 Tribunal federale [TF] Jul. 6, 2020, DFT 146 III 194.

34 Oberster Gerichtshof [OGH] [Supreme Court] Jul. 23, 2020, 18 ONc 3/20s (Austria).

35 See *id.*

36 *Carlos Legaspy v. Financial Industry Regulatory Authority, Inc.*, No. 20-cv-4700, 2020 WL 4696818, at 8 (D. Ill. Aug. 13, 2020).

Canadian courts recognize that while there are perceived and perhaps real shortcomings with proceeding remotely rather than in-person, the benefits outweigh the risks most of the time. This perspective appears to persist internationally. The most obvious benefit to this approach is that dispute resolution will not be stopped in its tracks. A broad claim made by a party that they are concerned about "confidentiality" or "fairness" is not sufficient to justify an adjournment of a remote hearing. Tribunals and courts expect the party to specify what the particular issues are and put forward evidence that they exist. A vague statement that a party is concerned is not sufficient. The impact of COVID-19 caused Arbitration Centers to consider the meaning of due process[37] and act as a facilitator to implement solutions to concerns expressed by parties and decision-makers. These decisions indicate that the availability of alternative processes such as remote hearings and the requirement of technological competency is essential to the conduct of dispute resolution proceedings in the time of COVID-19.

3.2 *Privacy and Cybersecurity*

Technology is a useful means to support and advance dispute resolution and has been traditionally well received in arbitration. Results from the 2018 International Arbitration Survey: The Evolution of International Arbitration by White & Case denote that 61% of respondents indicated "increased efficiency, including through technology" as the factor that is most likely to have a significant impact on the future evolution of international arbitration.[38] At the same time, 78% of respondents answered that they "never" or "rarely" used remote hearings rooms.[39] Suffice it to say, times have changed since 2018. In May 2021, White & Case released the results of their survey titled "Use of technology: The virtual reality" aimed at investigating the current use of certain forms of information technology and measuring it against the results of their 2018 survey. In

37 While there is no single definition of the term "due process" in international arbitration it encompasses the principle of procedural fairness including the requirement that parties shall be treated equally and given a full opportunity to present their case.

38 White & Case, LLP, "2018 International Arbitration Survey: The Evolution of International Arbitration," Queen Mary University of London, May 9, 2018, 40, Chart 40 (Chart of survey results for factors which will have the most significant impact on the future evolution of international arbitration).

39 *Id.* at 32, Chart 35 (Chart of survey results on use of forms of information technology in an international arbitration).

significant contrast to the 2018 survey, 72% of the respondents reported using remote hearing rooms "sometimes", "frequently" or "always".[40]

The discrete and private nature of arbitration and the obligation on the part of the arbitrator and arbitration service provider to keep information confidential are well known characteristics in arbitration. While risks relating to privacy, data protection and cybersecurity are not new, COVID-19 brought about a shift where most matters continue to be heard remotely. As a result, dispute resolution moves forward on account of an almost entirely digital landscape. This presents a number of challenges including the likelihood that security incidents will cause economic loss to individuals whose commercial information or personal data is compromised and the potential for loss of integrity of data. There are other potential issues such as questions about the reliability or accuracy of data as a result of a cyber incident, the unavailability of data, networks, or platforms as a result of disruption caused by a cyber security incident and reputational damage to the system of arbitration as a whole.[41]

Before COVID-19, the arbitration community made efforts to address these issues. In late 2019, the ICCA-NYC Bar-CPR published the "Protocol on Cybersecurity in International Arbitration (2020 Edition)" (the "Cybersecurity Protocol"), which provides a recommended framework to guide tribunals, parties, institutions and service providers in their consideration of what information security measures are reasonable to apply to a particular arbitration matter. The authors recognize the close relationship between information security and data protection and emphasize the focus of the Cybersecurity Protocol to be the mitigation of information security risks. Compliance with the Cybersecurity Protocol may overlap with data protection regimes such as the European Union General Data Protection Regulation, however, it does not guarantee compliance with data protection regimes.[42]

In 2020, the International Bar Association and International Council for Commercial Arbitration released a draft ICCA-IBA Roadmap to Data Protection in International Arbitration (the "Roadmap") for public consultation, with the expectation that it will be finalized in the fall of 2021. Although in draft form,

40 White & Case LLP, "2021 International Arbitration Survey: Adaption arbitration to a changing world," Queen Mary University of London, May 6, 2021, 21, Chart 13 (Chart of survey results on the forms of information technology in an international arbitration).

41 "ICCA-NYC Bar-CPR Protocol on Cybersecurity in International Arbitration (2020 Edition)," ICCA, NYC Bar, and CPR, November 25, 2019.

42 *Id.*

the Roadmap provides guidance related to data protection and privacy obligations and addresses data protection compliance in international arbitration under general data protection principles.[43] Although both the Cybersecurity Protocol and the Roadmap were not drafted in response to COVID-19, they provide timely, useful and practical guidance to manage the issues of data protection and privacy in the current environment of remote hearings.

COVID-19 accelerated the need to address risks and gaps of confidentiality, data protection and cybersecurity as reliance on technology for the digital exchange of information and video conferencing are now essential to dispute resolution. In the second quarter of 2020, the prevalence of fully remote hearings was over ten times greater than at any time previously.[44] Arbitration Centers are uniquely positioned to address concerns related to cybersecurity and data protection by providing guidance to stakeholders involved in dispute resolution. For example, Arbitration Centers have developed protocols and procedures related to the use of technology in arbitration. Further, there are a number of practical and cost-effective measures that can be implemented in order to manage and mitigate these risks. The following constitutes a non-exhaustive list of such organizational processes:

- The use of a secure internet connection through a virtual private network as opposed to an unsecured Wi-Fi network, along with a prohibition that users may not participate in a remote proceeding through a public Wi-Fi network.
- Adequate security of software, web browsing and email addresses, ensuring that software and web browsers are up to date and that parties use paid web-based email accounts that include security features as opposed to free email accounts.
- The use of encryption for the storage of sensitive data so that only users with the encryption key can access the information and discouraging the use of removable storage devices unless encrypted.
- The use of a reputable and secure cloud computer provider that complies with all applicable data storage regulations and laws.

43 "The Draft ICCA-IBA Roadmap to Data Protection in International Arbitration," ICCA-IBA Joint Task Force, March 11, 2020 (Public consultation draft released for public comment prior to revised version to be launched late 2021).

44 Born, Day, and Virjee, *supra* note 17, at 291 (Survey on objections to remote hearings at the start of the pandemic in 2020).

- The implementation of complex username and password requirements, using a combination of uppercase, lowercase, numbers and symbols and multi-factor authentication.
- Limiting access and distribution of sensitive data and information such as personal information, client information, designs, practices, records, and other sensitive information to only necessary recipients.

The implementation of cybersecurity and data protection measures will vary depending on the circumstances of the case and on factors such as cost and proportionality. The Cybersecurity Protocol, the Roadmap and Arbitration Centers provide useful and practical guidance to stakeholders involved in dispute resolution to manage these complex issues, which will undoubtedly continue to evolve over time.

4 Conclusion

The impact of COVID-19 on Arbitration Centers is profound. Technology has markedly altered the environment of dispute resolution and paved the way for Arbitration Centers to become salient international players, advance access to justice and contribute to solutions surrounding complex issues of cybersecurity and data protection. The requirement for technological competency is essential to the conduct of dispute resolution in the time of COVID-19 and Arbitration Centers demonstrate they will continue to adapt and respond to the needs of the arbitration community through the delivery of innovative and customized services. While in-person hearings will undoubtedly return, the availability of alternative processes such as remote and hybrid hearings will have a lasting impact on dispute resolution proceedings in the future.

Acknowledgement

Many thanks go to my Colleague Christina Ma for her valuable research and assistance in reviewing this text.

CHAPTER 15

Rethinking Costs in International Arbitration

A Gift from the COVID-19 Pandemic

Bamikole Martins Aduloju

1 Introduction

The outbreak of the SARS-CoV2 (COVID-19) pandemic has, for some time now, brought the activities of many organizations in the world to a standstill, but businesses have gradually resumed in a relatively new way. With a complete end to the pandemic unforeseeable, there has been a sharp increase in the use of internet-enabled information technology to deliver arbitration services. Before the pandemic, many international arbitration centers had embraced the use of information technology but not at the speed and level experienced during the pandemic. Thus, while international arbitration centers join other world organizations to count the monumental losses they had experienced from the pandemic, the international arbitration community must not lose sight of the 'gifts' the pandemic has offered.

The most visible 'gift' to the international arbitration community has been the increase in the use of remote hearings which largely dispense with the need for the physical presence of parties, witnesses, and arbitrators. However, there is more than just the 'virtual hearing' that information technology offers the arbitration community.

This chapter identifies some of the 'innovations,' including the use of electronic filing systems, the virtual payment of filing fees and other costs, the use of virtual hearings and conferencing, the use of websites and virtual fee calculators, the use of electronic signatures and seals, and the issuing of electronic awards and procedural orders and investigates how these innovations impact costs. The rise in the use of these 'innovations' to provide arbitration services marks the beginning of a new age in the arbitration world and research demonstrates that these Covd19-induced innovations are likely to remain with the industry even after the pandemic.[1]

1 Joshua Karton, "The (Astonishingly) Rapid Turn to Remote Hearings in Commercial Arbitration," *Queen's Law Journal* 46, no. 2 (2021): 399.

DOI:10.1163/9789004514836_017

Part I and II of this chapter discuss how the adjudication of arbitration cases is being financed and its cost implication to the arbitrating parties in general and specific examples from the five leading international arbitration institutions, as identified by Gary Born.[2] Focusing on the procedural costs of arbitration, particularly the administrative and arbitrator fees, the chapter analyzes the parameters commonly used by the selected arbitration centers to charge costs (*i.e.*, *ad valorem*, hourly, or hybrid rates). In Parts III and IV, the paper explores how the pandemic has caused some adjustments in the operations of the arbitration centers, and how the adjustments are reducing the actual cost at which arbitration cases are being managed. It then argues in favor of a review of the fee scales of many international arbitration centers.

2 The Price and Cost of Arbitrating Disputes – General Setting

One of the striking differences between arbitral and judicial processes relates to finances and costs. While courts enjoy the financial support of the State, arbitration is wholly financed by the parties, either personally or through a third-party funder. Thus, whether at the making of the arbitration agreement or before a dispute is submitted to arbitration, the cost of arbitrating a case is usually of utmost interest to the parties in particular. In prosecuting their case, each party to an arbitration will expend costs at different stages of the proceedings and for many purposes. The purpose for which parties expend such costs can be grouped into two: (i) the cost of presentation/representation, and (ii) the cost of arbitration.[3] While the former covers all the monies spent by the parties to present their case before the arbitrators,[4] all other expenses are the "cost of arbitration."

In practice, therefore, when a party to an arbitration agreement feels aggrieved and decides to arbitrate its disputes, usually, its first cost consideration is the "cost of presentation/representation" which is not the focus of this chapter. Under this class of cost, the parties are concerned about the cost to present their grievance before the arbitration tribunal and put up a representation. This class of cost includes the lawyers' legal fees, monies spent to present

2 Gary B. Born, *International Commercial Arbitration*, 3rd ed. (Kluwer Law International, 2020), 174–199.

3 Stuart Dutson, Andy Moody, and Neil Newing, *International Arbitration: A Practical Guide* (London: Globe Business Publishing Ltd, 2012), 189. These authors describe them as (i) the costs of the arbitration and (ii) the costs of parties' legal representative.

4 It includes the running costs, the expenses incurred on the engagement of the services of the legal representatives (if any) as well as the factual and expert witnesses, etc.

the evidence and witnesses before the tribunal, monies spent to obtain the tribunal's assistance, and/or provisional relief (where necessary), *etc.* The focus of this chapter is the second category of cost, that is, the "costs of arbitration."

The "costs of arbitration" can simply be described as the costs of running the arbitration proceeding itself. As noted earlier, the parties are also responsible to finance these costs. An arbitration case could be likened to any project in the field of project management which requires the spending of monies and resources to exchange for the goods and services necessary to accomplish the project. Thus, the 'costs of arbitration' are incurred on either the tribunal's fees or the running of the proceedings.[5] In an *ad hoc* arbitration, for instance, the issue of the costs of arbitration often forms part of the major agenda for discussion at the preliminary meeting. However, in institutional arbitration, parties usually have a fair idea of the average costs of arbitration before the preliminary meeting. This is because most (if not all) arbitration institutions have their Schedule or Scale of Costs which itemize different purposes for which monies are needed to run an arbitration. This Schedule of Costs also sets a methodology by which an arbitration center generally calculates its "costs of arbitration."[6] The Schedule of Costs provides a rough guide to the parties because the list of costs to cover in arbitration still varies from one case to another. Nevertheless, the Schedule or Scale of Costs has proven to be a useful tool for the users of arbitration to undertake an early case assessment regarding the potential costs of arbitration.[7]

A panoramic view of the financial commitments grouped under the "costs of arbitration" in practice often starts with the payment of the 'filing' or 'registration' fee. In a matter submitted to an arbitration center, for instance, the payment of a filing fee is a condition precedent to the official submission of the Request for Arbitration. The fee varies from one center to another. For instance, the Hong Kong International Arbitration Centre (HKIAC) receives HKD 8,000 (approximately USDD1,000) as a registration fee to be paid equally among the claimants (when they are more than one);[8] at the International Chamber of Commerce (ICC), the registration fee is capped at USD5,000;[9] and,

5 Dutson, Moody, and Newing, *supra* note 3, at 189.

6 *Id.* at 190.

7 *Id.* at 79.

8 Hong Kong International Arbitration Centre, *HKIAC Schedule of Costs*, Article 4.4 Schedule 1. The currency conversion from KHD to US$ was done online by the author via https://www1.oanda.com/currency/converter/, accessed June 22, 2021.

9 International Chamber of Commerce, *Schedule of Costs to ICC Rules of Arbitration*, 2021, Article 1.1.

at the International Centre for Dispute Resolution (ICDR), the calculation of the registration/filing fees depends on the number of arbitrators adjudicating the case and whether the Schedule applicable to the case is the Standard Fee or Flexible Fee.[10]

As soon as the arbitration commences, the parties are often committed to paying a certain lump sum.[11] It is from this lump sum that the arbitral center or arbitrator literally draws monies to finance the day-to-day running of the process. The centers or arbitrators often give accounts on the spending of these monies to the parties. The lump-sum is also called by different names, such as "Advance Payment for Costs,"[12] "Provisional Deposit,"[13] "Deposit on Costs,"[14] *etc*. By this, parties simply pay monies up front to ensure a smooth running of the arbitration process. Arbitrating parties have more discretion in an *ad* hoc arbitration than in institutional arbitration to agree with the tribunal on what amount would be sufficient as the Advance Payment for Costs. For instance, the London Court of International Arbitration (LCIA) decides the lump sum and directs parties to make the payment into its account.[15] Both parties (the claimants and respondents) are to make the advance payment on costs. Nonetheless, in case the advance payment becomes insufficient, the parties would be called upon to make a "Further Advanced Payment on Costs."[16] In an *ad hoc* arbitration, parties usually agree to make such payment into an escrow account or, in some cases, into the account of any arbitral institution agreed by parties.

Meanwhile, the arbitral center or arbitrators could draw other related costs, sometimes unforeseeable, from the advanced payment on cost. For instance, upon the appointment of the tribunal's registrar in an *ad hoc* arbitration, the registrar would almost immediately need some basic things to kick-start the process. These immediate needs often include some stationery; clerical assistance; transportation; means of communication to the parties, their respective

10 International Centre for Dispute Resolution, *Schedule of Fee*, 2017.

11 Hong Kong International Arbitration Centre, *HKIAC Schedule of Costs*, Articles 10, 33.1 and 40; Hong Kong International Arbitration Centre Rules, Rule 36; International Chamber of Commerce's Rules 2021, Rule 37, Appendix III; London Court of International Arbitration's Rules, 2020, Rule 24.1.

12 London Court of International Arbitration, *LCIA Rules*, 2020, Rule 24.1.

13 Swiss Arbitration Centre, *Swiss Rules of International Arbitration*, 2021, Appendix B Paragraph 1.4.

14 Permanent Court of Arbitration, *PCA Rules*, 2012, Article 43; Swiss Arbitration Centre, *Swiss Rules of International Arbitration*, 2021, Article 41.

15 London Court of International Arbitration, *LCIA Rules*, 2020, Article 24.1.

16 International Chamber of Commerce, *Schedule of Costs to ICC Rules of Arbitration*, 2021, Article 37(5); Swiss Arbitration Centre, *Swiss Rules of International Arbitration*, 2021, Rule 34.4; HKIAC's Rules, Article 40.3.

representatives, and the arbitrators; and, other secretarial services. Hence, it is necessary to pay the "Advanced Payment on Costs" on time because it is from this lump sum that the registrar draws monies to run the administrative affairs of the arbitration.[17]

As the arbitration proceeds, parties are committed to financing some other needs that may arise. Again, as an arbitration process heads towards the hearing stage, there are more heads of cost to be financed by parties. These costs may include the payment for venue rental; the services of transcribers, translators, and experts (if any); the provision of audio systems and electricity; the provision of the necessary technological gadgets, *etc*. There could also be some other needs, though rare, such as the use of lie-detector technologies,[18] and the provision of security in a hostile venue.

The arbitrator fees are another cost in an arbitration process which the parties are committed to financing. Simply put, the arbitrator's fee is the remuneration paid by parties to the arbitrator for the skills, time, and resources expended to arbitrate the dispute.[19] The parameter used to charge an arbitrator's fee by the arbitration center depends on the policy objectives of the center's Scale or Schedule of Fees.[20] In addition, the arbitrator's 'reasonable' travel and related expenses are taken into account,[21] and in international arbitration, arbitrators often travel great distances. Besides the foregoing, the parties may also be committed to incur some other miscellaneous expenses, such as the security for costs paid by a party requesting interim measures,[22] or the cost charged for an emergency arbitration[23] or for filing a challenge application usually known as a "challenge fee."[24]

The foregoing is a general overview of how arbitration cases are financed by parties and demonstrates that the cost of arbitration could be unpredictable particularly at the commencement of the proceedings. No matter how

17 Ole Jensen, *Tribunal Secretaries in International Arbitration,* (Oxford: Oxford University Press, 2019), 312.

18 Kimberly Janiseh-Ramsey, "Polygraphs—The Search for Truth in Arbitration Proceeding," *Dispute Resolution Journal* 41, no.1 (2014): 23.

19 Nathaniel Kellerer, *Competence of Arbitral Tribunals. Are there Limits to Decide on the Arbitrators' Fees?* (GRIN Verlag, 2020), 17.

20 John Yukio Gotanda, "Setting Arbitrators' Fees: An International Survey," *Vanderbilt Journal of Transnational Law* 13, no. 4 (2000): 784.

21 Swiss Arbitration Centre, *Swiss Rules of International Arbitration,* 2021, Appendix B Paragraph 3.1.

22 Hong Kong International Arbitration Centre, *HKIAC Rules*, 2018, Article 24.

23 Hong Kong International Arbitration Centre, *HKIAC Rules*, 2018, Article 23.

24 "Fees," HKIAC, accssed November 18, 2021, https://www.hkiac.org/arbitration/fees.

methodical the parties' agreement may be, it appears that no early case assessment can predict the cost of arbitrating a dispute.[25] As observed by Stuart:

> Parties to an arbitration may even incur greater expenses than litigants, as arbitration involves the additional costs of the parties paying for the arbitrators and arbitral institution. Parties may also need to pay logistical expenses, including costs of accommodation for the hearings, the use of courtrooms in litigation is normally free of charge.[26]

Nonetheless, since many international arbitration centers do publish their schedule or scales of fees or costs (the Scale) and make the document available to the public, parties and researchers could make a rough estimate of what it may cost to arbitrate cases at each center.

3 Cost Regimes of the Five Leading International Arbitration Centers

The arbitration centers selected for the study under this section are the world's first five leading international arbitration centers, as ranked by Gary Born:[27] the ICC, the LCIA, the American Arbitration Association's ICDR, the Permanent Court of Arbitration (PCA), and the Swiss Arbitration Centre (SAC). The Scale of each arbitration center is either annexed to its rules or made a separate document, stipulating the basic heads of cost required to run the cases submitted to the center. As a result of the divergent parameters adopted by each center in designing their Scale, the cost of arbitrating a case varies from one center to another, and also from one case to another.[28]

3.1 *The ICC*

The ICC's Scale is made an Appendix to its Rules.[29] The first cost that a party is committed to paying under the Scale is the "Cost of Arbitration."[30] The Rules allow the center to spend monies deposited under this head for two

25 Dutson, Moody, and Newing, *supra* note 3, at 79.

26 *Id.* at 17.

27 Born, *supra* note 2, at 174–199.

28 Gotanda, *supra* note 20, at 783.

29 International Chamber of Commerce, *ICC International Court of Arbitration Rules*, 2021, Appendix III.

30 International Chamber of Commerce, *ICC International Court of Arbitration Rules*, 2021, Article 3.

things: the administrative expenses and the arbitrator's fees. While the former cost covers the receipted expenditures incurred by the Secretariat to run a case, the latter cost is the remuneration paid for the services rendered by the arbitrator.[31] Thus, the Scale has set some parameters to compute the cost. One of the parameters under the present framework is to charge the cost of arbitration based on the time the claimant is submitting its Request for Arbitration.[32] Generally, the center uses the Scale as the standard to determine its charges except in some exceptional circumstances.[33]

On the methodology designed to determine the cost of arbitration, the ICC's Scale uses the "*ad valorem*" system, that is, the value of the claims involved in a case forms the basis of the cost charge. Thus, the cost of arbitration is charged as a percentage of the amount in dispute.[34] For instance, under the 2017 Scale of ICC, where the amount in dispute is USD50,000 or less, parties are to pay the sum of USD5,000 as the administrative expenses (excluding value-added tax), and as the amount in dispute increases, there is a corresponding increase in the administrative expenses charged.[35] Meanwhile, in terms of the arbitrator's fees, even though the Scale does set a minimum and maximum price, the power to determine the arbitrator's fee is vested in the arbitration court, though the court is bound to consider the *ad valorem* system in arriving at its decision on the cost. Using a claim of about USD 250,000, for instance, the Scale prescribes a minimum of USD 5,756, plus approximately 1.4% of USD 250,000, which totals around USD 9,256. In sum, it implies that the minimum cost of arbitrating a USD 250,000 dispute before the ICC (that is the cost of administrative expenses and arbitrator's fees) may be placed at USD 23,256, that is, approximately 10% of the amount in dispute.[36]

---

31 Gotanda, *supra* note 20, at 783.

32 For instance, while the 2017 Scale applies to any Request received before the 1st of March 2021, every Request submitted on or after the 1st of March 2021 falls under the 2021 Scale, for cases administered by the Centre's Sao Paulo office.

33 International Chamber of Commerce, *ICC International Court of Arbitration Rules*, 2021, Article 2(1) and (2).

34 Lazlo Goerke, Frederik Horzberg, and Thorsten Upmann, "Failure of Ad Valorem and Specific Tax Equivalence under Uncertainty," *International Journal of Economic Theory* 10, no. 4 (2014): 387–402.

35 For instance, where the amount in dispute is $250,000, the Scale prescribes that the parties should pay $8,485 and 2.25% of the amount in dispute which means that the parties would be paying the total sum of approximately $14,000 as the administrative expenses.

36 The calculation made here is not an accurate representation of all cases. This calculation is based on the extant Scale and on an average assumption. However, there is a possibility that the amount arrived at in this calculation may be the minimum amount that parties can get in practical terms.

Further, under its Rules, the duty to cost and disburse monies paid to ICC by the parties is vested on the three most important 'organs' in the center. These are the office of the Secretary-General (the Secretary), the Arbitration Court (the Court), and the Tribunal (Arbitrators). These three organs have their distinctive roles in the determination of costs and the spending of monies to run the arbitration project, and they check one another. In practice, at the submission of a Request for Arbitration at the ICC, the claimant is requested to pay a non-refundable 'filing fee' of USD5,000.[37] From this point, the three 'organs' identified above activate their duty to fix and disburse the monies to run the process.

The Secretary demands that the claimant pays a 'Provisional Advance' in an amount intended to cover the costs of the arbitration. The Provisional Advance is money paid to keep the reference running until the parties get to the stage where they draw up their Terms of Reference or conclude the case management process.[38] At this stage, the Secretary calculates the Provisional Advance based solely on the claim. Current practice shows that ICC's Provisional Advance is in the range of 25–35% of the would-be Advance on Costs in a case. It is then the Court that fixes the "Advance on Cost" to be paid by both parties. It is from this pool of funds (Advance on Costs) that the administrative expenses and arbitrator's fees are disbursed or reimbursed. Notably, the Provisional Advance already paid by the Claimant is considered part of the Claimant's share in the Advance on Costs. If the Respondent submits a Counterclaim, the Court may also demand that parties pay a separate Advance on Costs for the Counterclaim. This is also applicable to Emergency Arbitration and Expedited Proceedings. However, where a party refuses to pay any of the Costs as ordered, the other party may decide to pay for the defaulting party. Meanwhile, if both parties refuse to pay or one of the parties refuses to pay for the defaulting party, the Secretary has the power to liaise with the arbitrators to suspend the proceedings.

Thus, as soon as the value of the final claim in an arbitration is ascertained, the ICC's Court would fix the final cost of arbitration following the Scale, and the cost is drawn from the Advance on Cost. However, if there is any remainder, it would be returned to the parties, and the winning party has the right to make a "costs claim" against the losing party.

37 International Chamber of Commerce, *ICC Rules*, Article 1(1) Appendix III.

38 *Id.* at Article 37(1) Appendix III.

3.2 *The LCIA*

The system of costing in the LCIA appears similar to the ICC's, save for differences in the methodology used to determine the arbitration cost, the currency base, the institutional structure, and the organs in charge of the disbursement and spending. To start with, unlike the ICC, the LCIA has four basic heads of cost for which it charges the parties. These are (i) the Administrative charges, (ii) the Fees and Expenses of Members of the LCIA Court, (iii) the Fees and Expenses of the Arbitral Tribunal, and (iv) the Fees of the Tribunal Secretary.[39] The LCIA's extant Schedule of Costs became effective in October 2020 to complement the 2020 Revised Rules.[40] Like the ICC, the LCIA also maintains an active website with an online cost calculator,[41] however, the base currency is in Pounds Sterling. It is noteworthy that, unlike the ICC, the LCIA's Schedule of Costs charges the party for the Tribunal Secretary's remuneration. This is separate from the secretariat's administrative costs, which are under the administrative charges.[42]

The LCIA Schedule adopts an "hourly rates" system to charge for costs of arbitration. Thus, the Schedule simply prescribes how much a party would pay each 'service provider' working on the case for every hour spent. These service providers include the LCIA's Secretariat, the Case Administrator, the LCIA's Court, the Arbitral Tribunal and the Tribunal's Secretary. The Schedule prescribes the costs due to each of these service providers for every hour spent on the case, regardless of the value of the claim. For instance, the extant Schedule provides that the Secretariat is to be paid £280 and £195 per hour for work done on the case by the Registrar and the Case Administrator respectively. For the Arbitral Tribunal, it prescribes £500 per hour as the maximum rate and between £75 to £175 per hour for the Tribunal's Secretary. Under the 2020 Schedule, the arbitrator's fee has been increased from £450 per hour (hitherto under the 2014 Schedule) to £500. Also, unlike under the ICC system where the parties are generally not allowed to be involved in the costing, the LCIA provides that parties' agreement should be sought, in exceptional

39 London Court of International Arbitration, *LCIA Rules*, 2020.

40 A copy of this document is downloadable from: https://www.lcia.org/Dispute_Resolution_Services/schedule-of-costs.aspx.

41 "LCIA Arbitration Costs Calculation," London Court of International Arbitration, accessed January 13, 2021, https://www.international-arbitration-attorney.com/lcia-arbitration-cost-calculator/.

42 The head of cost known as the "Tribunal's Secretary's remuneration" was introduced by the 2020 Schedule.

circumstances, before the Court can fix the arbitrator's fee at a rate higher than what the Schedule provides.

Currently, before a Request for Arbitration is accepted for filing before LCIA, the claimant is obliged to pay a non-refundable registration fee of £1,950 and to show its payment receipt.[43] Furthermore, the LCIA Rules empower the court and the arbitral tribunal to determine the cost of arbitration and coordinate how the cost deposited is being spent. Thus, one of the distinguishing features of the LCIA's cost system is that before an arbitrator is appointed, the institution's attention is drawn to what the arbitrator's fee may be under the Schedule, and his written consent is obtained before his appointment is accepted.[44] Following the Schedule, the LCIA's court then estimates how many hours the tribunal, registry, and the secretary, *etc.*, are to spend on the case. It is on this estimation that the court decides what is to be deposited to the institution as the "Advance Payment for Cost" by the parties. It is from the Advance Payment for Cost that monies are disbursed to run the arbitration.[45] Therefore, when the exact arbitration costs are finally ascertained, the tribunal would make an Order for the payment of the exact amount. If, after the arbitral reference, the Advanced Payment for Cost exceeds the total amount of the Arbitration Costs, the excess amount is to be returned to the appropriate party.[46]

3.3 *The ICDR*

The ICDR prides itself on running the most dynamic cost regime among the international arbitration centers. One of the uniqueness of its system of costing is that it uses what could be described as a three-fold parameter to charge and allocate the cost of arbitration to the parties. This means that ICDR's cost arrangement uses the combination of three methodologies: (i) *ad valorem,* (ii) hourly rates, and (iii) tiered payment systems. Thus, the cost of arbitration at the ICDR depends on the value of the claim, the number of hours of service provided, and the number of installments through which the parties will pay for costs before the rendering of an Award. This regime appears similar to both the LCIA and the ICC systems respectively in terms of the hourly rate and *ad valorem* approaches. In the "tiered payment system," while arbitration is ongoing, parties are allowed to pay the cost allocated to them in certain installments until payment is completed. However, the consequence is that

43 London Court of International Arbitration, *LCIA Rules*, 2020, Article 1.

44 *Id.* at Article 5.

45 *Id.* at Article 24 (24.1).

46 *Id.* at Article 24 (24.3).

the option selected by the parties will determine a reduction or increase in the costs to be eventually paid by the parties.

The ICDR categorizes its costs of arbitration into two major folds: (i) the Arbitrator compensation and (ii) the Administrative fees.[47] Besides these two main categories, the ICDR's Rules allow other for other expenses, such as the costs of any assistance required by the tribunal; the fees and expenses of the Administrator; the reasonable legal and other costs incurred by the parties; the costs incurred in connection with a request for interim or emergency relief; the costs associated with information exchange, *etc.*[48] Unlike the ICC and the LCIA, the ICDR does not apply the same methodologies for its Administrative fees and Arbitrator compensation. In computing the costs of the Administrative fees, the Rules use the *ad valorem* and tiered payment systems by creating two options for installments: (i) the Standard Fee Schedule and (ii) the Flexible Fee Schedule. When parties choose the former, they are allowed to pay the cost in two installments; by paying somewhat higher initial filing fees but lower overall administrative fees for cases that proceed to a hearing. The latter is a three-payment schedule that provides for a lower initial filing fee and then spreads the subsequent payments through the arbitration proceedings. Meanwhile, the administrative fees would be somewhat higher for cases that proceed to the hearing. Regardless of the option chosen by the parties, the amount to be paid is still a percentage of the amount of the claim or counterclaim which also changes depending on the value of the claim. However, for the Arbitrator's compensation (arbitrator's fees), the Rules adopt the hourly rate like the LCIA but go further to allow parties or the Administrator to decide what methodologies to use.

For instance, where a party is claiming a sum of USD 250,000 in an arbitration submitted before the ICDR, using the Standard Fee Schedule, the parties would be paying for the administrative fees, the initial filing fee around USD 3,050 and the second and last payment of USD 2,300. However, if the parties in the same arbitral reference choose to use the Flexible Fee Schedule which allows for three installments, they may be paying the sum of USD 1,900 as an initial filing fee, USD 1,950 as the second payment (Proceed Fee), and a Final Fee of USD 2,300. The Schedule also provides for the incidental costs relating to the withdrawal of cases. Under the Standard fee Schedule, while a sum of USD 600 from the initial filing fee is strictly not refundable once incurred, the other scenario depends on when the withdrawal is done and when the ICDR

47 International Centre for Dispute Resolution, *Fee Schedule on International Arbitration: Schedule of Cost*, 2017, Appendix.

48 International Centre for Dispute Resolution, *ICDR Rules*, 2017, Article 31.

receives the notice. For instance, if the case is withdrawn and the ICDR is notified within five calendar days of filing, the Initial Filing Fee (excluding the non-refundable USD 600) may be returned while only 25% of the remaining monies would be returned in case the withdrawal is done between thirty-one and sixty days after filing. In terms of the Flexible Fee Schedule, the whole of the Initial Filing Fees and Proceed Fees are non-refundable once incurred. Thus, if the case is withdrawn or settled before hearing, all Final Fees paid are refundable, though the ICDR must be notified 24 hours before a scheduled hearing date. Furthermore, under the ICDR system, where the Statement of Claim discloses 'non-monetary claims,' the *ad valorem* approach is suspended, and the Rules prescribe a fixed minimum amount to be paid in each tier of both Schedules. However, where parties seek both monetary and nonmonetary claims, parties are to pay the higher of the two filing fees.

Two organs of the ICDR are involved in the spending of the costs paid to run the arbitration. These are the ICDR's Administrator and the Tribunal. Thus, upon the filing of the Notice of Arbitration, the claimant is mandated to pay the Initial Filing Fee, which depends on the amount of claim and the Schedule.[49] Usually, before the arbitral tribunal is constituted, the Administrator conducts an administrative conference to enable parties to discuss administrative matters which may include the arbitrator's compensation.[50] Thereafter, the Administrator may request the payment of a deposit as "Advance for the Costs of Arbitration."[51] Curiously, the Rules do not prescribe what should constitute the Advance on Costs, but it may be assumed that it is within the discretion of the Administrator. Meanwhile, the Administrative fee is computed by the Arbitral Tribunal once constituted, and it takes the form of an Award against parties.[52] Nonetheless, the Arbitrator's compensation is determined by the Administrator, who must consult the parties and all arbitrators before making such a decision.[53] Thus, the Administrator is allowed to do a follow-up on the payment of both administrative fees and arbitrator's compensation and other incidental expenses such as Additional Party Fees, Deficient Filing Fees, Costs incurred for a request for interim or emergency relief, *etc.* The Administrator must also render an accounting to the parties concerning the deposits received and return to the parties any unexpended balance after the final award has been made.[54]

49 *Id.* at Article 2(4).
50 *Id.* at Article 4.
51 *Id.* at Article 39.
52 *Id.* at Article 37.
53 *Id.* at Article 38.
54 *Id.* at Article 39.

3.4 *The* PCA

The PCA runs a flexible and adaptable cost regime that is somehow similar to the ICDR's cost regime. Its cost of arbitration covers the spending of items such as "fees, reasonable travel expenses and other expenses of each arbitrator," "reasonable costs of expert advice and other assistance required by the arbitral tribunal," "processing fees," and "fees and expenses of the International Bureau," *etc.*[55] A distinctive feature of the PCA's Schedule of Fees and Costs (Schedule) is that it is largely advisory, that is, it is simply prescribed to be tailored to the needs of the parties in each case. Besides the "processing fee" which is non-refundable and a flat rate, costs on other services are charged based on hourly rates. For instance, the cost payable for the secretarial services (at its International Bureau) by its Secretary-General (SG) or the Deputy is fixed at € 275 per hour. However, the arbitrator's fees are not fixed and can be negotiated as long as the cost is 'reasonable,' considering the "the amount in dispute, the complexity of the subject matter, and the time spent by the arbitrator, *etc.*"[56]

To spend the costs on the running of the arbitration, three offices within the institution are involved. These are (i) the International Bureau or its Representatives, (ii) the SG, and (iii) the appointed Tribunal. In practice, once a Notice of Arbitration is submitted, it will be administered by the Bureau if it is accompanied by a payment of € 3,000 as a process fee which is a flat rate and non-refundable. Afterwards, the International Bureau may request the parties to equally pay an "Advance for the Costs" when the exact cost of arbitration is calculated and made known to the parties.[57] Nonetheless, non-payment of the deposit is grounds for the suspension or termination of an arbitration.[58] Unlike the LCIA, which provides an indication of the average duration of an arbitration under its rules, the PCA does not provide such an indication. Thus, the International Bureau uses its discretion to compute the most reasonable amount to cover legitimate and recoverable expenses. However, if the deposit is not sufficient to cover the cost during the arbitral proceeding, the Bureau is allowed to request more money, or "Supplementary Deposits," from the parties,[59] and it is duty-bound to give an account of the spending to the parties at the end of the case.[60]

55 Permanent Court of Arbitration, *PCA Rules*, 2021, Article 40 (2).
56 *Id.* at Article 41 (1).
57 *Id.* at Article 43 (1).
58 *Id.* at Article 43 (4).
59 *Id.* at Article 43 (2)
60 *Id.* at Article 43 (5).

The Bureau is allowed to draw monies from the "Advance on Costs" until the Tribunal is constituted, after which the Tribunal will communicate to the parties its cost in a document called "Fees and Expenses Proposal." The document contains the proposed modalities regarding how the Tribunal intends to charge its fees and compute its expenses.[61] The parties are at liberty to negotiate the rates or charges proposed. If there is no consensus, the parties have the right to refer their contention to the SG (as the appointing authority) for review and the SG has the power to make any adjustment to the 'Proposal.' Thus, at the close of the case, the Tribunal computes the overall costs incurred to run the arbitration and specifies what each party would pay.[62] The overall costs could be made part of the final award or a supplementary award.[63]

3.5 *The SAC*

In June 2021, the popular Swiss Chambers' Arbitration Institution changed its name and enacted revised Swiss Rules of International Arbitration (Swiss Rules).[64] The Swiss Rules create a robust regime on how it estimates, collects and manages costs of running the cases it administers. One of the striking features of its cost regime is that the provisions of the Swiss Rules on costs are complemented by two documents, namely the "Guidelines for Accounting of Expenses" and the "Guidelines for Advance Payments." The documents are step-by-step guides on the costs and expenses that the institution recognizes as recoverable from the parties.[65] In terms of the methodology used in calculating its fees, the institution largely uses the *ad valorem* approach. However, the Swiss Rules do not use *ad valorem* methodology to calculate the costs of arbitration, Registration Fee or Secretariat remuneration.[66] Thus, after the submission of a Notice of Arbitration or Notice of Claim, the Registration Fee is calculated using the aggregate amount of the claims made, and it increases as more claims are filed. For instance, going by the extant Schedule of Costs, while a claimant would pay CHF 4,500 as a Registration Fee for submitting a Notice

61 *Id.* at Article 41 (2).

62 *Id.* at Article 42 (2).

63 *Id.*

64 Sebastiano Nessi, "A Swiss '(R)Evolution': SCAI Becomes the Swiss Arbitration Centre and Enacts New Arbitration Rules," Kluwer Arbitration Blog, June 15, 2021, http://arbitrationblog.kluwerarbitration.com/2021/06/15/a-swiss-revolution-scai-becomes-the-swiss-arbitration-centre-and-enacts-new-arbitration-rules/.

65 A copy is downloadable from: https://www.swissarbitration.org/wp-content/uploads/2021/05/Guidelines-for-Arbitrators-EN-2020.pdf, accessed June 21, 2021.

66 Swiss International Arbitration Centre, *Swiss Rules of International Arbitration,* 2021, Paragraph 1.1 of Appendix B, Schedule of Costs.

of Arbitration with a CHF 2,000,000 claim, if the claimant decides to amend the same claim, increasing it to CHF 10,000,000, he would be paying an additional CHF 3,500 as a Registration Fee.[67] However, if the amount claimed is not quantifiable, the party will pay a flat fee of CHF 6,000 as the Registration Fee.

Thus, after the payment of the Registration Fee and exchange of documents between parties, like ICC, and using the value of the claim, the SAC's Secretary calculates the possible administrative cost and the arbitrator's fees and, therefore, estimates an appropriate "Provisional Deposit" that the claimant would pay. Then, a claimant is required to pay the "Provisional Deposit" pending the calculation of the full administrative cost. Curiously, the way the SAC determines its Provisional Deposit differs from the way this is determined by the ICC because a Provisional Deposit in the SAC is not subject to the discretion of the Secretariat; rather, it is relatively fixed in the Schedule of Cost. For instance, a sum of CHF 6,000 is the registration fee in a case with a sole arbitrator, and in a case with more than one arbitrator, CHF 6,000 is for the first arbitrator and CHF 4,000 is for each additional arbitrator.[68] Furthermore, when the Tribunal is eventually constituted, it will consult with the Court and agree on what the parties should pay as a "Deposit of Costs" to the account number provided by the Secretariat.[69] At this point, the Provisional Deposit already paid by the claimant would be considered as partial payment of its portion of the "Deposit of Costs."[70] Thus, once the monies are paid into the separate bank account managed by the Secretariat, it is only the Court that has the power to regularly release monies to the Tribunal as "an advance payment of fees, or compensation for expenses, or costs of assistance," as the arbitration progresses.[71]

As the arbitration advances to a conclusion, the Tribunal decides the full and final cost of arbitration. Although the Tribunal charges the arbitrator's fees and expenses in consultation with the Court, the Court is solely responsible for determining the administrative costs.[72] However, both offices must make the respective charges in line with the Scale provided in the Schedule

67 *Id.*

68 *Id.* at para. 1.4.

69 *Id.* at Article 41 and para. 4.1 of the Schedule of Costs.

70 *Id.* at Article 41.

71 Swiss International Arbitration Centre, *Guidelines on Account for Arbitrator's Expenses*, accessed June 21, 2021, https://www.swissarbitration.org/wp-content/uploads/2021/05/Guidelines-for-Arbitrators-EN-2020.pdf.

72 Swiss International Arbitration Centre, *Swiss Rules,* 2021, Article 38.

of Costs. Going by the extant Scale, for instance, where the aggregate claim amounts to CHF 350,000, the administrative costs would be around CHF 1,500 while the arbitrator's fees would be fixed as a minimum of CHF 19,000 for a sole arbitrator and CHF 47,500 for a three-member Arbitral Tribunal. However, if the claim increases to CHF 650,000, the administrative costs may increase to CHF 22,200 for a sole arbitrator and CHF 64,500 for a three-member Arbitral Tribunal. It is noteworthy that this calculation is made using the extant Scale which depends on the claim and other circumstances. For instance, the Rules allow the Court, in exceptional circumstances, to approve or adjust the fees of the arbitral tribunal at a figure higher or lower than the limits in the Scale.[73]

Notably, some costs are not covered under the administrative fees or arbitrator fees and expenses in the SAC's Rules. The parties would pay these separately. For instance, the administrative costs do not cover the provision of "additional support services" by the Secretariat, such as the arranging of hearing facilities, interpreters, transcribers, secretarial or logistical assistance, or the facilitating of entry visas for the arbitrators, or the production of a copy of an award, *etc.*[74] These Costs are accounted for separately from the administrative fees, and parties are duty-bound to pay either at a fixed rate or as shown by the receipt produced by the Secretariat. For instance, when the Secretariat produces an extra copy of an Award upon a party's request, there is a fixed rate of CHF 300 to be paid for each copy.[75] If a party applies to challenge the appointment of an arbitrator, he pays the sum of CHF 4,500 as a fee to determine the application. This is not the same as the fee paid for the emergency arbitration. In that case, the fee ranges from CHF 2,000 to CHF 20,000.[76] Finally, the Tribunal would consider all of these fees and expenses and compute the final

73 Swiss International Arbitration Centre, *Schedule of Costs to the Swiss Rules*, 2021, paragraph 2.6. Another variable is that where there are more than two parties involve in a case, the amount of Administrative Costs so computed should be increased by 10% for each additional party up to a maximum increase of 30%. Swiss International Arbitration Centre, *Schedule of Costs to the Swiss Rules*, 2021, paragraph 2.9.

74 Swiss International Arbitration Centre, *Schedule of Costs to the Swiss Rules*, 2021, paragraph 2.10(e).

75 *Id.* Another example is where the parties agree to stay the arbitral proceeding pending mediation, the Centre charges the sum of chf 2,000 yearly until the case resumes or terminates. *Id.*

76 Swiss International Arbitration Centre, *Schedule of Costs to the Swiss Rules*, 2021, paragraph 2.8.

figures, send a draft to the Secretariat for the approval of the Court after which it usually publishes it as part of its Final Award.[77]

4 Adjustments to the Operations of the International Arbitration Centers Post-COVID-19

Like other organizations, international arbitration centers were impacted by the COVID-19 pandemic and have since begun to manage their activities in relatively new ways. In fact, it appears that the return to business in this post-COVID-19 age has marked the beginning of a new era in the arbitration world. As observed by Karton, the COVID-19-inspired 'transformation' in the operations of arbitration institutions may remain even when the pandemic is over.[78]

Arbitration has survived many centuries and has proven itself to be a dynamic system – often quick to adapt to external factors, as demonstrated by the response of the arbitration community to the COVID-19 pandemic.[79] Wilske has reported that in the wake of the pandemic, many arbitral institutions first closed their centers completely and declined acceptance of any further hand-delivery of documents.[80] With no end to the pandemic in sight, the

77 Swiss International Arbitration Centre, *Schedule of Costs to the Swiss Rules*, 2021, Article 39 (5).

78 Karton, *supra* note 1.

79 "The Virtual Reality as International Arbitration adapts to a Changing World," White and Case LLP, May 6, 2021, https://www.whitecase.com/news/press-release/virtual-reality-international-arbitration-adapts-changing-world. See also Maxi Scherer, Niuscha Bassiri, and Mohammed Abdel Wahab, *International Arbitration and the Covid-19 Revolution*, (Kluwer Law International, 2020), 14. Stephan Wilske, "The Impact of COVID-19 on International Arbitration—Hiccup or Turning Point?," *Contemporary Asia Arbitration Journal* 13, no. 1 (2020): 7–43. "Covid-19 Coronavirus: How the APAC Courts and Arbitral Institutions Have Adapted to the Change," Allen and Overy LLP, April 3, 2020, https.//www.lexology.com/76765670.+09. "Coronavirus Increases Use of Video Evidence in International Arbitration–Will It Become the Norm," Beale and Company, March 21, 2020, https://www.lexology.com/library/detail.aspx?g=3f37fe36-3b20-4737-8e5d-392ba30b25df.

80 Wilske, *supra* note 79. Nestor Kingston Petersen, "Arbitration in the Time of COVID-19. The Romanian Perspective," Lexology, March 26, 2020, https://www.lexology.com/library/detail.aspx?g=c0b28431-4a84-45a6-ac88-9c54400015d4. Clyde & Co. LLP "Covid-19—Impact on Courts and Arbitration," Lexology, March 22, 2020, https://www.lexology.com/library/detail.aspx?g=21280ae1-a699-4a87-bbc4-f8650748faf7. Anibal Sabater, "What Covid-19 Means for Latin American Arbitration," GAR, April 29, 2020, https://globalarbitrationreview.com/article/1226 239/what-covid-19-means-for-latin-american-arbitration.

arbitration community sought a "catch-all" solution, and the deployment of internet-driven technologies was identified as the most visible alternative in this respect.[81]

The increase in acceptance and deployment of internet-driven technologies to arbitration services has been unprecedented.[82] A survey has shown that between June and July 2020, many international arbitration centers resorted to full virtual hearings three times more than before, in the second quarter of the year 2020.[83] An arbitration hearing service provider also reported that the arbitration hearings conducted in its venue moved from 95% in-person in the pre-COVID-19 era to almost 100% remote in 2021.[84]

While the arbitration system was already under pressure to embrace the use of modern technologies before the pandemic,[85] this was not without some resistance from the users of arbitration.[86] The era of technophobia within the arbitration community has now passed and as the arbitration centers continue

81 Wilske, *supra* note 79, at 12.

82 Maria Fanou and Norah Gallagher, *2021 International Arbitration Survey: Adapting Arbitration to a Changing World*, Report of White & Case LLP and the School of International Arbitration Centre for Commercial Law Studies Queen Mary University London, 2021, accessed June 21, 2021, https://www.whitecase.com/publications/ insight/ 2021-international-arbitration-survey.

83 Gary Born, Anneliese Day, and Hafez Virjee, "Empirical Study of Experiences with Remote Hearings: A Survey of Users' Views," in *International Arbitration and the COVID-19 Revolution*, eds. Maxi Scherer, Niuscha Bassiri and Mohamed Abdel Wahab (Kluwer Law International, 2020), 140–41.

84 Kimberley Stewart, "Arbitration," interview conducted on January 17, 2021, paraphrased by Karton, *supra* note 1, at 402. In the same 2021 study, White & Case and Queen Mary University conducted a comparative research which shows that, unlike 2018 when 64% of the users of arbitration revealed that they had never utilized virtual hearing rooms, in sharp contrast, 72% of the interviewees in 2021 confirmed that they have started using virtual hearing rooms at least 'sometimes' for their arbitration cases. See Fanou and Gallagher, *supra* note 82.

85 Ben Knowles, "The Future is Now: What Arbitration will look like after the Pandemic," Clyde & Co, November 16, 2020, https://www.clydeco.com/en/insights/2020/11/the-future-is-now-what-arbitration-will-look-like.

86 The recalls a personal experience with a challenge application filed to terminate the mandate of the arbitrators on grounds that they refused a physical hearing at the seat of arbitration. See *NNPC v. Total & 6 Ors.*, (Suit No. FHC/ABJ/CS/1017/2017) Unreported decision of the Federal High Court of Nigeria, Abuja Judicial Division. The arbitrators in the case resided in three different continents and had decided to conduct the interlocutory hearing through a video conference instead of being physically present in Africa. Though the challenging party appeared to have a genuine fear about the choice in favor of a virtual hearing, the objection stalled the progress of the arbitral proceedings for some years.

to use technology, some of their Rules have been amended accordingly and Guidelines have been issued to accommodate the use of technologies.[87] Although, some post-COVID-19 amended Rules and Guidelines do not adjust the cost of arbitration,[88] a study of the current operations of the arbitration centers during this post-COVID-19 era provides some insight into the impact of the recent changes on the cost of arbitration.

5 The Impact of Post-COVID-19 Changes in Arbitration on the Cost of Arbitration

5.1 *Changes in the Filing and File Management Systems of the Arbitration Centers*

The use of internet-driven technologies is impacting the filing and case file management systems of many international arbitration centers. Traditionally,

87 Some instances are the Revised Swiss Arbitration Rules which took effect on 1st June 2021, the new LCIA's Rules and Schedule of Costs released on 11th August 2020, and the 2020 ICC's Guidance Note on mitigation of the effects of Covid-19 pandemic on Arbitration Cases, etc. Swiss Rules of International Arbitration (Swiss Rules) 2021, accessed June 13, 2021, https://www.swissarbitration.org/centre/arbitration/arbitration-rules/. London Court of International Arbitration's Rules and Schedule of Costs is downloadable from https://www.lcia.org/Dispute_Resolution_Services/schedule-of-costs.aspx. International Chambers of Commerce, 'ICC Guidance Note on Possible Measures Aimed at Mitigating the Effects of the COVID-19 Pandemic,' para. 22 (2020) https://iccwbo.org/content/uploads./sites/3/2020/04/guidance-note-possible-measures-mitigating-effects-covid-19-english.pdf. In 2020, cietac issued its "Guidelines on Proceeding with Arbitration Actively and properly during the COVID-19 Pandemic," China International Economic and Trade Arbitration Commission, April 28, 2020, http://www.cietac.org/index.php?m=Article&a=show&id=16919&l=en. The ICDR also issued its "Virtual Hearing Guide for Arbitrators and Parties," AAA-ICDR, accessed April 22, 2022, https://go.adr.org/rs/294-SFS-516/images/AAA268_AAA%20Virtual%20Hearing%20Guide%20for%20Arbitrators%20and%20Parties.pdf; "Virtual Hearing Guide for Arbitrators and Parties Utilizing Zoom," AAA-ICDR, accessed April 22, 2022, https://go.adr.org/rs/294-SFS-516/images/AAA269_AAA%20Virtual%20Hearing%20Guide%20for%20Arbitrators%20and%20Parties%20Utilizing%20Zoom.pdf, and a model "Order and Procedures for a Virtual Hearing via Videoconference," AAA-ICDR, accessed April 22, 2022, https://go.adr.org/rs/294-SFS-516/images/AAA270_AAA-ICDR%20Model%20Order%20and%20Procedures%20for%20a%20Virtual%20Hearing%20via%20Videoconference.pdf.

88 For instance, one of the arbitration centres that reviewed her Schedule of Cost during the pandemic is the LCIA. However, under her newly reviewed Schedule of Cost, it increased the cost of arbitration by approximately 10%. "Ambitious New 2020 LCIA Arbitration Rules, with an Increase in Costs," Aceris Law LCC, August 22, 2020, https://www.acerislaw.com/ambitious-new-2020-lcia-arbitration-rules-with-an-increase-in-costs/.

a claimant physically visited the secretariat of an arbitration center to submit its initiating documents and pay a filing fee.[89] Upon filing, the secretariat would open a physical file for every new case, process the documents, *i.e.* sort and serialize them, reproduce and circulate them and deliver them for the use of the center, the parties and the tribunal. Although, it would be too simplistic to capture all the activities involved in the file management system of an arbitration center in just a few lines, the above description explains the basics of the conventional filing system of an arbitration center. One of the reasons why a filing fee is charged by an arbitration center is essentially to cover the cost of these secretarial services.

In the post-COVID-19 era, electronic filing systems have started to provide the desired alternative to the traditional case filing system. It appears that the ICC is leading the way in this regard, particularly considering the launch in 2005 of its 'NetCase' to provide a centralized online database of all documents submitted in an arbitration for the parties and arbitrators to access, retrieve and use.[90] Today, the system has advanced, as a Request for arbitration at the ICC may be sent by email to its Secretariat. Similarly, but more advanced, the LCIA's 2020 Rules enable a claimant or the respondent to submit a Request for Arbitration or Counterclaim electronically through the LCIA's internet-driven e-filing system.[91] This reform has been commended within and outside the arbitration community for many reasons, which include its environmental impact and its potential to reduce costs. Further, the extant SAC Rules provide that "no hard copies of the Notice of Arbitration shall be required unless the Secretariat requests otherwise."[92] That said, the e-filing path, being a relatively contemporary option, is yet not enforced or deployed on a full scale by all arbitration centers.

E-filing has always been optional under the Rules of the international arbitration centers that have deployed the technologies. With the outbreak of COVID-19, many of the centers have made it a default mode of filing. For instance, the LCIA's Rules make the electronic submission of papers a default filing method and provide that hard copies can only be filed with the prior

89 Hong Kong International Arbitration Centre, *HKIAC Rules*, Article 4.4 Schedule 1. London Court of International Arbitration, *LCIA's Schedule of Costs*, Article 1(1). International Chamber of Commerce, *ICC's Rules*, Appendix III.

90 "Information Technology in International Arbitration-Report of the ICC Commission on Arbitration and ADR," ICC (France: ICC, 2017), https://iccwbo.org/publication/information-technology-international-arbitration-report-icc-commission-arbitration-adr/.

91 London Court of International Arbitration, *LCIA Rules*, 2020, Articles 1.3 and 4.1.

92 Swiss Arbitration Centre, *Swiss Rules 2021*, Article 3.

written approval of the Registrar.[93] Also, since March 2020, the International Centre for Settlement of Investment Disputes (ICSID) requires, by default, a claimant to initiate a case by submitting its Request for Arbitration through electronic means.[94] The ICDR also offers a dedicated online e-filing platform called 'WebFile' to enable parties to file new cases electronically, view and pay all open invoices, and view all pending cases and tasks.[95] Simply put, the electronic filing system allows the users of arbitration to prepare their papers and, without the need to print, sign them electronically and simply upload them through a designated website or app to the ICDR's database. Also, when e-filing, payment of the filing fee is done electronically, and the payment invoice is what usually enables access to the designated electronic folder where the claimant's documents are uploaded. Similarly, the LCIA boasts a robust electronic file management system that manages the e-files submitted, and serializes and updates the data regularly with tracking and feedback components and protection against unauthorized access.

With the gradual reduction of physical files, not only have the logistics involved in the traditional filing system decreased, but the costs expended by arbitration centers on file management have also decreased. Cost savings can be calculated in terms of manpower needed to receive and process files, space needed to keep files secure and insured, courier delivery costs, transportation costs, stationery cost, *etc.* As more internet-driven technologies are deployed, it may even become necessary to shut down branches of some arbitration centers opened purposely for physical filing and case management. For instance, until March 2020 when filing through e-mail was introduced to the ICC, claimants had to travel to file their cases at any of the ICC's offices in Paris, Hong Kong, New York, Sao Paulo, Singapore or Abu Dhabi, and some of these branches may soon become redundant.

The increased use of e-filing may correspond to a reduction in the costs expended by arbitration centers and while the maintenance of e-filing facilities by the arbitration centers have a cost, these costs are much lower than those of a physical filing system. The e-filing system enables the arbitration centers to shift many of their tasks, under the traditional system, to the parties. This suggests a need to rethink the filing or registration fees and other administrative costs charged to the parties.

---

93 London Court of International Arbitration, *LCIA Rules*, 2020, Article 4.2.

94 "ICSID Makes Electronic Filing its Default Procedure," ICSID, March 13, 2020, https://icsid.worldbank.org/news-and-events/news-releases/icsid-makes-electronic-filing-its-default-procedure.

95 Swiss Arbitration Centre, *Swiss Arbitration Rules*, 2021, Article 2(1).

5.2 *Communications, Hearing, and Presentations*

Some of the core services offered by international arbitration centers are meant to facilitate hearings and to enable smooth communication among the providers and users of the arbitration services. Thus, the way these services are now being rendered by the arbitration centers, and perhaps the cost of such services too, are changing post-COVID-19. Traditionally, once a claimant submitted documents to the secretariat, the center would spend money making the required copies, hiring courier services for the delivery to the necessary parties and arbitrators. The documents were usually accompanied by some papers from the arbitration center such as a forwarding letter, a copy of the relevant rules, and explanatory notes on the documents forwarded, *etc.* Some international arbitration centers would scan all the documents submitted and deliver hard copies with a hard drive or USB storage device containing the scanned copies. Besides collection, duplication, scanning, dispatch, and delivery of documents submitted by the parties and arbitrators, the secretariat also accepted correspondence from parties and communicated to the arbitrators.

In some arbitral institutions, some of these roles are shared between the tribunal's secretary or registrar (if any) and the secretariat of the arbitration institution. Ultimately, the secretariat facilitates meetings and hearings when the arbitral tribunal is constituted, and proceedings commence. These meetings and hearings include preliminary meetings, emergency hearings, hearings on interlocutory applications such as interim measures, hearings of factual witnesses, challenge hearings, emergency meetings, hearings of expert witnesses, document presentations and demonstrations, skeletal hearings, final submissions, supplementary hearings for correction and additional awards, and meetings and deliberations among the arbitrators. The secretariat also communicates the final award to the parties and processes all post-award businesses and communications.

Significant logistics and project management resources are involved in facilitating arbitration hearings and meetings. A major portion of arbitration costs are spent on the booking of meeting rooms and hearing rooms; the employment of specialists such as transcribers, translators, clerks, and typists; the deployment of IT and recording gadgets; the provision of security at the venue (particularly in hostile situations); the procurement of necessary stationery, cleaning supplies and catering services, *etc.* Even well-established international arbitration institutions with purpose-built facilities outsource some of these items.

It is expected that these institutions will recoup their capital reserves for the utilization of their facilities and future expansion. Each arbitration institution gives a different name to these costs used to finance these institutional expenses. For instance, the Schedules of Costs of the SAC and the ICDR use the term "Administrative Costs" or "Fee," while the ICC uses the term "Administrative Expenses'" As discussed earlier, while some arbitration institutions charge these costs on an *ad valorem*, hourly or flat rate basis, there is usually some allowances to make a supplementary charge where the standard charges are insufficient. Also, some arbitration centers collect fees that are separate from the general fee where items are considered extraordinary costs, for example, under the SAC's Rules, the arbitration institution's request for the payment of a deposit of CHF 20,000 in respect of special proceedings for emergency relief or the payment of CHF 4,500 expected from a party invoking challenge proceedings.[96]

The recent upsurge in the use of internet-enabled information technology tools has been changing the way arbitration services are rendered. With the gradual increase in the use of electronic filing systems, the need for hard copies of documents, duplication and courier services, *etc.*, is bound to decrease. As submissions are made in digital form, the secretariat simply has to view and dispatch submissions electronically via the internet to the concerned parties and arbitrators. There is, thus, reduced use of paper and secretarial or clerical services. Under the ICC Rules and the new Guide Note on Cost, parties are encouraged to agree to the electronic signature on documents and electronic awards.[97] This is impacting the cost of arbitration and suggests that there is a need to review the scale of fees of international arbitration centers.

Likewise, the cost of facilitating meetings, hearings, and communication services have been reduced with many meetings and hearings conducted remotely via the internet. As such, money spent and the need for logistics handled by the secretariat have been reduced, yet many of the arbitral institutions still retain the old rates for administrative fees and costs.

5.3 *Human Resource Management*

While the upsurge in the use of information technologies is easing the delivery of arbitration services, the use of human personnel remains necessary. Human resources are still needed for adjudicative and administrative roles which are at the heart of arbitration center operations. While arbitrators perform the adjudicative roles, the administrative part is carried out by the personnel engaged by the arbitral center or tribunal. Their remuneration and expenses

96 Swiss Arbitration Centre, *Swiss Arbitration Rules*, 2021, Appendix B Paragraph 1.6.

97 "ICC Guidance Note on Possible Measures Aimed at Mitigating the Effects of the COVID 19 Pandemic," ICC, April 9, 2020, https://iccwbo.org/publication/icc-guidance-note-on-possible-measures-aimed-at-mitigating-the-effects-of-the-covid-19-pandemic/.

are eventually funded by the disputing parties as part of the cost of arbitration. Unsurprisingly, the use of technology is impacting and reducing the work of arbitration center personnel in the delivery of arbitral services, and is consequently impacting the cost of arbitration.

The Rules of many arbitral institutions separate arbitrator fees from expenses.[98] An arbitrator's fee is a form of remuneration for the adjudicative skills, services, and intangible resources the arbitrator has expended on the case when presiding over arbitral conferences, meetings, and hearings; inspecting documents and evidence; reading and researching; drafting and publishing procedural orders and awards, *etc.* On the other hand, an arbitrator's expenses are monies spent by the arbitrator on related utilities such as travel costs, accommodation, stationery, food, telephone and internet costs, *etc.* Arbitrator expenses are usually reimbursed when it is shown that the monies spent were recognizable and reasonable. Arbitral institutions, such as the SAC, have guidelines for the accounting of such expenses, which clearly define the expenses that are reimbursable.[99]

Since the arbitrator's expenses are not fixed charges, there may not be a need to review the cost of arbitration in respect of these expenses. On the other hand, the use of technology is impacting the arbitrator's fees, which is usually based on a Scale and fixed parameters. As explained using examples from the five leading international arbitration centers, the arbitrator's fee is generally calculated by either hourly or *ad valorem* rates. Realistically, the Scale or Schedule of Fee should set minimum, maximum, or flat rates after considering a catalogue of tasks that an average arbitrator would usually perform per hour or the complexity of a case. For instance, before the LCIA fixed the maximum rate of £450 per hour as the arbitrator's fee in its 2014 Scale, the following factors must have been taken into account: copying and reading a high volume of papers in hard copies; the risk of life from travel to and from meeting venues, conferences, and hearings; the physical examination of factual and expert witnesses; the physical inspection of documents and other evidence, *etc.*

Although the increase in the use of internet technology in the post-COVID-19 era has presented its concerns (regarding cybersecurity, confidentiality breaches, procurement of hardware and software for virtual engagements, *etc.*), one of the striking advantages of this era is that all the stresses of the non-paperless procedure have vanished. In this age, an arbitrator may stay in Europe or America and adjudicate matters in Africa or Asia from beginning to

98 Swiss Arbitration Centre, *Swiss Arbitration Rules*, 2021, Article 39.

99 "Guidelines for Arbitrators," SCAI, effective from January 1st, 2020, https://www.swissarbitration.org/wp-content/uploads/2021/05/Guidelines-for-Arbitrators-EN-2020.pdf.

the end without having to print or read through volumes of paper or travel out of his or her country. Even though these changes do not affect how the arbitrator is applying his or her skill, one could still argue, though without empirical evidence for the time being, that the removal of these stressors increases productivity and reduces certain hassles.

In the author's view, this should be reflected in the rates charged by arbitral institutions for arbitrator fees. However, it appears that many arbitration centers have yet to look in this direction. The recent experience shows that despite increased amendments to the Rules of some international arbitration institutions, the rates fixed for arbitrator fees have either remained as before the pandemic or have increased. For instance, in 2020, the LCIA increased its hourly rate for arbitrator fees from a maximum of £450 to £500. Also, there has been an increase in the rate (*ad valorem*) for calculating the arbitrator fee under the 2021 Swiss Rules as compared to the 2012 Rules.[100] Moreover, arbitration centers, such as the PCA and the ICC have not made any attempt to alter their Scales of Fees.

Like the arbitrator fees, the administrative fees or costs (as the case may be) are also due for review. Administrative fees are recovered from parties as remuneration for the services rendered by administrative personnel, including the secretary of the tribunal or secretary or registrar of the arbitral institution. The fees for personnel do not include administrative expenses. Thus, the calculation of remuneration for personnel should be like the arbitrator fee – hourly, *ad valorem,* or based on a flat rate. For instance, in an arbitration conducted under the PCA's Scale, the remuneration due to the Secretary-General is €275 per hour while the clerical staff is entitled to €60 per hour. Under the Singapore International Arbitration Centre's Scale, the administration fees are determined *ad valorem,* and charged at a minimum of SGD3,800 for all cases and capped at SGD95,000. At the HKIAC, parties are allowed to elect between the *ad valorem* or hourly rates failing which the HKIAC defaults to hourly charges, while the ICC uses *ad valorem* rates but caps the fee at USD 150,000. In all of these institutions, the increase in the use of information technology appears to have reduced the tasks of administrative staff; this may be considered a basis for review of the Scales of administrative fees or costs charged by arbitral institutions.

100 A sole arbitrator's fees under the 2012 Swiss Rules would range from a minimum of CHF 30,000 (0.38% of any amount over CHF 2,000,000) and a maximum of CHF 12,000 (+1.5% of any amount over CHF 2,000,000). Whereas, under the 2021 Swiss Rules, the same case now ranges from a minimum of CHF 32,800 (+0.32% of any amount over CHF 2,000,000) and maximum of CHF 107,200 (+1.14% of any amount over CHF 2,000,000).

6 Summary of Issues Discussed and Concluding Remarks

This chapter has examined the pre-COVID-19 cost regimes of five leading international arbitration centers. It has demonstrated how the deployment of technology to manage arbitration cases has impacted the costs of arbitration, particularly in relation to file management, communication and presentation of cases, and human resource management. It is argued that the relatively new ways of rendering arbitral services have had practical advantages and are reducing the actual costs of arbitration. As such, it is suggested that a downward review of the Scales of Fees of international arbitration centers is warranted. This review is not only important to bring the cost charged by the arbitration centers closer to the "real" cost of arbitration, but it is also important to project the true transparent nature of the arbitration system and deepen the confidence and patronage of both existing and prospective users of this method of dispute resolution.

Index

www.ingramcontent.com/pod-product-compliance
Lightning Source LLC
Chambersburg PA
CBHW071228230926
51849CB00001B/55
* 9 7 8 9 0 0 4 5 1 4 8 2 9 *